Sauer's
Herbal Cures

Sauer's Herbal Cures

America's First Book of Botanic Healing

1762-1778

Translated and Edited

by

William Woys Weaver

Routledge

New York London

Published by
Routledge
29 West 35th Street
New York, New York 10001

Published in Great Britian by
Routledge
11 New Fetter Lane
London EC4P 4EE

Printed in the United States of America on acid-free paper.
Design by Krister Swartz

Library of Congress Cataloging-In-Publication Data

Kurtzgefasstes Kräuterbuch. English.
Sauer's herbal cures : America's first book of botanic healing/
translated and edited by William Woys Weaver.
p. cm.
Includes bibliographical references and index.
ISBN 0-415-92360-3
1. Sauer, Chrisopher, 1721–1784. Kurtzgefasstes Kräuterbuch.
2. Herbs—Therapeutic use—United States—Early works to 1800.
I. Weaver, William Woys, 1947– II. Title.
RM666.H33 K8713 2000
615'.321'0973—dc21   00-056128

for
Don Yoder

Contents

Foreword

In 146 B.C. Roman general Scipio Aemilianus victoriously entered Carthage, then systematically destroyed it. Nothing was left of the great city whose constitution had been described by Aristotle as nearest to perfection. Men, women, children, monuments, steles, books—everything was eradicated. The Greek historian Polybius, a friend and adviser to Scipio who witnessed the event, recalled that the general told him of his mixed feelings about that triumph, which both delighted and worried Scipio, since he could not but wonder that the same unpredictable changes of fate might likewise fall upon Rome.

History has often been written by the winners, for every age has sustained itself upon the apologetic myths of those who in the end win political, economic, and military struggles. The rest are often consigned to oblivion. Christopher Sauer has not been forgotten, but in a sense his herbal has suffered a Carthaginian fate on three counts. First, while ingeniously published in installments (a first for American printers), the herbal was not written in the language of the ethnic majority and thus became relegated to an ever-smaller circle of German-language speakers. Second, Sauer's loyalty to the king of England put him at odds with the political currents of his own time, to the point that it cost him his fortune and livelihood. Third, and perhaps most important, Sauer's herbal espoused medical concepts that would be made obsolete in mainstream medicine within a few decades of its appearance.

The final installment of the Sauer herbal in 1777 not only appeared during the outbreak of the American Revolution but was followed, between 1780 and 1820, by a veritable revolution in medicine and the diagnosis of disease. It was soon understood that all chemical bodies were alike, whether mineral, vegetable, or animal, and that the medical signs of a particular disease were due not to the humoral condition of a specific organ—as the Sauer herbal assumed—but to specific anatomical lesions. Antoine-Laurent Lavoisier launched medicine into a better understanding of its complex chemistry, and from there the analysis of disease became more and more sophisticated through clinical examination and new devices, such as René Laënnec's invention of the stethoscope in 1816.

Since the middle of the twentieth century, a new therapeutic revolution has completely changed the prognosis of countless diseases, so obviously the change over the past century and a half is irreversible. From this point of view, it is difficult for a present-day physician to follow Sauer's classification of diseases. Indeed, no doctor would ever "treat bloody flux," "emolliate, attenuate, cleanse and open the matrix," or "strengthen and warm the nerves," and he cannot but feel dubious when he reads that clove is a good treatment "against all ailments." Does this mean that what is written in Sauer's herbal has no interest outside an anecdotal or historical one?

We must be careful not to judge this text as a whole, for it is essentially a collection of traditional empirical treatments. Some active principles may well be taken from the described remedies; but nevertheless, at the heart of this work is its knowledge of another type. It is very clear that most of the products used by Sauer are plants, the majority of which are edible and used as vegetables, herbs, or spices. Thus, we can say that what characterizes his suggested therapies is in fact a form of dietetics. It is well known that eating is the act of introducing alien elements into the body so as to destroy them and to assimilate some of their properties. That understanding is key to the appreciation of Sauer's methodology, an approach that is not on hindsight as archaic as it may seem.

Over the centuries, the understanding and interpretation of dietetic therapies have often changed, yet from the beginning of time man has wondered, Is what is good to taste good for my body? Twenty-five centuries ago, Hippocrates established the foundations of western medicine, rightly observing that cooking and medicine spring from the same roots and follow paths that sometimes meet. What we eat is a particularly important concern nowadays, obsessed as we are by carbohydrates, proteins, lipids, "good" and "bad" cholesterol, and the risks we run due to such bacteria as *Listeria monocytogenes* and *Escherichia coli*.

However, if our refinement of knowledge and treatment of pathologies due to infectious agents may be linked to our overall progress in medicine, the situation is entirely different with nutrition and dietetic therapies. Apart from some special diseases, it is in fact very difficult to know what must and what must not be eaten or what, in the long run, is good or bad for our health. Here the Sauer herbal may offer useful insights, especially regarding much-neglected vegetables like skirrets or dittander. Naturally, such investigations are by their very nature somewhat vague—how can one remember exactly what one has eaten and what the food was composed of? Moreover, the results are sometimes contradictory, so much so that nutritionists have become more cautious and hopefully wiser by advising us to eat a balanced and varied diet—man is an omnivorous creature, after all—in satisfying yet moderate quantities. This same sense of moderation prevails throughout the Sauer herbal.

Will some of the questions nutritionists are asked today find an answer among Sauer's advice? Perhaps the answer lies not so much in specific remedies, but in the therapeutic directions they suggest. Certainly the emphasis on plant-based cures and plant-based diets has returned to a more widely accepted place in Western thinking. It is to his credit that William Woys Weaver has given the English-speaking world an opportunity to read and explore this traditional book, thus saving it from oblivion, while inciting the reader to ponder its implications.

Jean-Philippe Derenne, M.D.
Hôpital Pitié-Salpêtrière,
Paris

Introduction

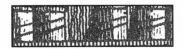

The Sauer herbal is a book of many contradictions. Assembled by Pennsylvania apothecary and printer Christopher Sauer (1721–1784), it is the first American herbal, yet it was old-fashioned and scientifically out of date even as it appeared in print between 1762 and 1778. Issued under the title *The Compendious Herbal*, it was also one of the first American books to be published in serialized form over this sixteen-year period, but few complete copies of the bound herbal now survive. As a system of botanical medicine—cures and remedies based on the use of herbs—the Sauer herbal is rooted in the medical thinking of the late Middle Ages and Renaissance, yet in its own unique way it forms a bridge between that era and eighteenth-century colonial America. It is not a product of the leading thinkers of that period but rather a barometer of the mindset of the working class. It is a people's herbal, and that is what makes it so fascinating to read over and over again.

Whatever its scientific shortcomings, this people's herbal is married to the land. Its very greenness—or better put, its pervasively green medicine—provides a link to the woods, meadows, and kitchen gardens of the past. But this greenness is no longer purely historical, for we are presently undergoing a revolution in our thinking about the way in which we as humans should relate to our earthly environment. This rediscovery of the earthly paradise, so vividly relayed to us through pictures of our planet from outer space, is slowly overthrowing the philosophical principles that have anchored religion in the past. A similar shift took place with the discovery of the New World, and this shift is nowhere more evident than in the way in which the Sauer herbal tried to accommodate New World plants such as jalap to ancient Greek theories of humoral medicine. Thus the herbal is also transitional, a tentative link between the herbals of Europe and the American herbals that appeared soon after Sauer's and which turned their focus almost exclusively to native American plants. Today, this is an herbal for lovers of plants and natural remedies. And I am very glad that I have been able to finally make it available in English for the first time.

My foremost intention in bringing Sauer's herbal before the public was to make these unique and colorful contents more widely known outside the very small circle of experts who have been privy to its existence. Aside from its interest as an historical document, for the modern reader, the herbal overflows with a peculiar mixture of quaint advice, common sense, ancient wisdom, and a practical appreciation of the botanical world that is now quite rare in mainstream medicine. There is even some humor and an unexpected touch of magic—unexpected because Christopher Sauer was extremely religious, but that in itself may offer part of the explanation. In any case, I have tried to treat all of these complex issues as evenhandedly as possible.

I must also admit that philosophically speaking I am of the old school that preaches natural remedies, but which also prescribes all remedies sparingly. I can recall my grandmother's medicine cabinet stocked with little other than *Gunn's New Family Physician* (her mother's copy) and Underwood's Salve, a camphorous, dark, sticky, honeylike patent remedy developed for infections in the hooves of horses. This salve worked doubly well on humans, like so many of the veterinary remedies in the Sauer herbal.

The small white milk-glass jar with its green paper label was an institution in my grandmother's house. It removed warts, it drew out thorns, it healed bruises and pulled infections out of the body within hours. I never quite knew why it went out of existence, and even contacted the son of the inventor to explore its revival, but to no avail. He had received some sort of ominous letter from the state medical association accusing him of practicing medicine without a license—this for a horse doctor! There was nothing really dangerous about that salve, and now that I look back on it, it seems amazing to me the range of useful knowledge that has been suppressed or lost in similar ways as the result of arrogance and fear. Christopher Sauer published many remedies like that: cheap, effective, and easy to use. His concern was for the common good, particularly for the poor who could not afford doctors—which unfortunately is most of the world.

As I came to know and understand the herbal through the meticulous labor of translation, I also came to respect it more and more. The mind of Christopher Sauer comes through. Some of his remedies for simple ills even invited trial and experimentation. On the other hand, I cannot recommend this book as a medical adviser. I am not a physician, and I am not even sure that some of the remedies can actually be measured for their effectiveness, so varied is the chemistry of each and every individual. Indeed, some of the herbs, even common coriander, may induce an allergic reaction rather than the desired cure. Such things must be taken into account. My publisher and I cannot be responsible for those who may utilize the Sauer herbal in this regard, but we can heartily recommend it as an historical document that greatly expands our understanding of herbs and their holistic applications.

William Woys Weaver
Roughwood
Devon, Pennsylvania

Part I
Christopher Sauer:
Book Printer and
Herbalist

God Save the Commonwealth!

On the twenty-first of May, 1778, the Supreme Executive Council of Pennsylvania issued an Act for the Attainder of Divers Traitors by which it seized the estates of numerous citizens. Among these was Christopher Sauer II and his son Christopher Sauer III, book printers and newspaper publishers in Philadelphia. Their properties were seized and sold at public auction for the benefit of the revolution, and as the senior Sauer later remarked, not even his reading glasses were spared. This was no ordinary auction. The senior Sauer's properties were valued at over £10,000, thus making him one of the wealthiest Germans in colonial America. With the demise of the Sauers in 1778, Benjamin Franklin eliminated his greatest business competitor, and historians have spent the subsequent centuries hashing out the pros and cons of this very ugly and tragic event. Sauer's herbal, which is the subject of this book, was conceived in happier times, but its final installment printed in the fall of 1777 appeared under those gathering clouds of controversy.

In eighteenth-century colonial America, the Sauer name was a household fixture anywhere German was spoken. Johann Christoph Sauer (1695–1758), founder of this clan, came to Philadelphia in 1724, bringing with him his family and children. Christopher Sauer II (1721–1784) had been born at Laasphe, in Westphalia, and thus grew up in America as an emigrant who always maintained a philosophical and cultural connectedness with Europe. As we shall see, this perspective shaped the framework of his herbal.

By 1738 Sauer's father had established the family at Germantown, a small German community laid out in the 1680s that over the next 200 years served as a summer retreat for wealthy Philadelphia merchants (today Germantown is part of the city of Philadelphia). There the senior Sauer established a printing business and an apothecary shop, a shrewd combination since the printing business was used to promote medicines. This marriage of interests would also eventually lead to the publication of the herbal, although the line of evolution was not altogether direct.

The senior Sauer became one of the most influential figures of his day, at least in the colonies. He began printing books for the numerous German religious congregations scattered throughout British America, including Canada and the West Indies. In 1738 he initiated a German weekly newspaper that became a mouthpiece for the

German community in North America, and in 1739, an almanac that the family continued to print up until the property seizures of 1778. It has been estimated by historians that somewhere between 10,000 to 15,000 copies of the almanac were issued annually, a huge quantity for a colonial print run, but obvious evidence of its popularity. Sauer also published the first Bible in America in a European tongue in 1743 (there were later editions in 1763 and 1776) and sold imported books dealing with a wide range of topics. Deeply religious, he published a long list of spiritual works, including a German edition of John Bunyan's *Pilgrim's Progress* and a translation of Siegvolk's *Everlasting Gospel*. This religious bent was inherited by his son Christopher Sauer II.

Christopher Sauer II is the focus of our interest, since he is the author or at least the "literary compiler" of our herbal. His father was a German Pietist who seems to have affiliated himself loosely with several sects of similar thinking. Christopher II, however, was baptized as a Dunkard (now Church of the Brethren), which placed him thoroughly in the embrace of pacifism and beliefs shared by the Quakers, Mennonites, and other plain groups. Sauer's religious fever is everywhere evident in his writings, even the herbal. In fact, in 1764—during the troubles with the French and Indians—he began issuing *Ein geistliches Magazien* (A spiritual magazine), which he distributed free to the subscribers of his newspaper. He always claimed that he was a printer and druggist in order better to serve others, and it was well known that he would not print something that he did not believe to be true—actual quotes from the period support this, even from his political enemies.

I bring this up because the herbal contains some rather fantastic material that would fly in the face of common sense unless one did actually believe in witchcraft. Yes, the herbal contains witchcraft, and I shall deal with that shortly. However, as an example of Sauer's moralizing attitudes, I need only mention his long discourse on why drinking water (as opposed to alcoholic beverages) is healthy, which appeared in his almanac for 1772.[1] In the herbal itself, his treatment of sugar, tea, chocolate, and wine is nothing short of polemical. In fact, testy and polemical would be two appropriate adjectives for many of his public pronouncements.

On this point, Sauer possessed a personality much like that of the English herbalist Nicholas Culpeper (1616–1654), sharing his views on charity toward the poor, his intense religious convictions, and his open distrust of ruling elites. Culpeper, however, died from cheap French wine and tobacco. Sauer had no such addictions, unless politics could be called his major weakness.

Sauer's politics were an unusual blend. He was openly opposed to the Stamp Act laid upon the colonies by Britain, and it is no coincidence that his tirade on tea (page 321) appeared in the installment of the herbal the same year as the Boston Tea Party. This should not be interpreted as support for the destruction of the tea, for violence of any kind was anathema to Sauer's religious beliefs; rather, Sauer took the position that tea was sinful, costly, and foolish. If people lived a straight and narrow lifestyle, there would be no tea drinking and no need to toss it off ships to protest the tax. Sauer was keenly aware that his religious freedom was his by virtue of protections guaranteed by the English crown, and he remained firm in that conviction even though it ultimately led to his financial ruin. He viewed the revolution as the machination of a small circle of rich Americans intent on preserving their financial and political positions at the cost of the poor and those who were not of English descent. To an extent, he was correct, and his disdain for rich Anglo-Americans—especially their overbearing wives—is nowhere more evident than in his treatment of sugar.

Fortunately, Sauer's pacifism made him preeminently suited to be a druggist, since this was a nonviolent way to improve the lot of his fellow man. This missionary zeal—which also happened to be quite profitable—led the Sauers early on to publish remedies and household hints in their newspapers and almanacs. Benjamin Franklin's 1749 publication of John Tennent's *Ein Jeder sein eigner Doctor* (Every man his own doctor)—a book originally written in English—was doubtless viewed by the Sauers as an attempt to break into their market, which indeed it was. This evolved into a long and sometimes bitter competition between the two businesses.

The first experiment in serializations appeared in the form of veterinary advice, which was easy to sell considering that horses were the basic mode of transportation. This material was serialized in the 1750s and eventually culminated with the publication of Johannes Deigendesch's *Nützliches und aufrichtiges Ross-Arzney Büchlein* (Handbook of practical and genuine veterinary cures) in 1770. In essence, the Sauers created a market among their readers for printed books that might otherwise have proved too expensive to publish. The same philosophy lay behind the herbal.

A Small Herbal for Little Cost

The serialization of the strictly veterinary cures stopped in 1760, although veterinary remedies were later included in the herbal. Perhaps it was coincidental, but it is worth mentioning that about this same time the Leipzig publisher Johann Friedrich Gleditschen began selling through various German booksellers in America a work called the *Vollkommenes Kräuter-Buch*, "mit Figuren der Kräuter" (Complete herbal, "with pictures of herbs"). This herbal was first published at Basel, Switzerland, in 1696 under the title *Theatrum Botanicum; das ist, Vollkommenes Kräuter-Buch*. Its author, Theodor Zwinger (1658–1724), was a distinguished Swiss physician and medical professor. His son Friedrich, also a physician, revised and corrected the herbal in 1744, and it was this edition that was sold in America and from which Christopher Sauer II drew material for his undertaking. It is very easy to see that if a serialization of veterinary remedies would prove popular with Sauer's readers, an herbal packed with home remedies for people living at a distance from doctors might be even more popular. And such was the case.

It is important to keep in mind that Zwinger's herbal is pre-Linnaean, which means that the plants are organized along archaic systems devoid of the genera and species arrangement we now use today. A case in point would be the turnip. The "hedge turnip" *(Zaunrübe)*, a poisonous herb now known as bryony, is lumped together with "yellow turnips" *(gelbe Rüben)* or carrots, "West Indian turnip" *(West-Indische Rüben)* or manioc, and true culinary turnips. None of these plants are closely related; the only features they share are a fat root and a similar name. Friedrich Zwinger apologized for his father's errors when he revised and published the 1744 edition, but he did not completely rewrite it, which would have been the only way to overhaul the plant taxonomy. Furthermore, other features that probably troubled him were embedded in the text much too thoroughly.

The elder Zwinger was conservative as a practicing physician, for he adhered to the system of humors, signatures, numerologies, and even lunar arrangements for explaining herbs and assigning their virtues. Thus a large amount of space in his book is devoted to placing herbs in their proper temperament of hot or cold, dry or moist, so that they might be paired with the right humors governing the human body. Their active qualities are defined in terms of their inherent salts, a system of evaluation that traces back to Paracelsus (1493–1541), a Swabian nobleman and physician. Proper pairing of these temperaments created a healthful balance, which was determined by the various states of the blood.

Since the liver, spleen, and kidneys regulate blood, they emerge as major considerations in almost all of the cures. This science was already obsolete when Zwinger published his herbal, so in this respect it was conservative, a good fifty years out-of-date. Yet this was precisely the kind of medicine adhered to by the common farmer. The Gleditschen publishing house was doubtless aware of the market it was targeting when it got rid of the herbal in America, for the book could not possibly appeal to serious physicians in Europe—country doctors certainly, but not the sort of physicians who waited upon kings and taught in universities.

We must view the Sauer herbal in this light, especially since Christopher Sauer carefully included the material dealing with salts and temperaments. Zwinger appealed to Sauer because this is the medical science that Sauer himself knew and which was familiar to his readers. The conservative nature of his own religious beliefs, the folk milieu in which all of the remedies are set, the sort of great-grandmother-did-it-this-way attitude, all worked together in framing the opus Sauer set about creating. The end result was an herbal that philosophically straddled two worlds: culturally it was rooted in Europe, a European thing superimposed on the New World, just like most of the herbs themselves, naturalized rather than native. This represents an interesting dimension of Sauer himself as an immigrant and loyalist, as someone who defined himself in European rather than in American terms. He was not exactly Pennsylfaanisch, as this indigenous identity later evolved. But he was German American, and so is the herbal.

Because the herbal was assembled and printed here, it is technically one of the first American herbals, if not the very first. Furthermore, realizing that a complete book would be difficult to sell without a long list of subscribers and that his audience was for the most part poor and in no position to lavish money on literary undertakings, Sauer decided to serialize his herbal by publishing it in installments in his almanac. It took sixteen years to accomplish this task, and the project actually made it to the end, in spite of the fact that for political reasons in 1776 Sauer was forbidden by the Council of Safety from publishing. Before turning over his business to his sons, Sauer hurriedly compiled the last installment—this haste being evident in the final text of the herbal itself—and created the index. This also appears to be the first book printed in America in serialized form, so it is a feat of several firsts.

It is also obvious from evidence in Sauer's text that he had an overall book in mind when he began issuing the installments; in other words, the herbal did not grow by accretion, except in a few minor ways. The initial installment was rather chaotic, and his readers later wrote to him expressing the desire to have the English and Latin names of the herbs included so that they would know what to ask for when they went into an apothecary shop where no German was spoken. Sauer published a notice to this effect in the very next installment, and thereafter included English and Latin in addition to the German. This was not too difficult to do, since Zwinger's herbal provided all the plant names in English, French, Dutch, Italian, Spanish, and Danish, with full indexes for them as well. Unfortunately, Zwinger's indexes are full of errors, and his choice of plant names is sometimes extremely odd. As a result Sauer was fooled on more than one occasion, even though he had on hand a copy of John Hill's *The Useful Family Herbal* (1755), a book that might be best described as the English equivalent of his herbal digest. The red beet/red carrot controversy on page 349 of the Sauer herbal is a good example of this confusion, and some of Hill's blunders show up in the text as well.

Yet Sauer did visualize a structure for his work, for he created a number of internal references and sometimes mentioned herbs that he planned to take up later on, and in due time he did. This means that he was working from some kind of rough text that was written out in his own hand. Proof of this emerges when we stumble on misspelled words that the typesetter obviously misread; only German script would have led to these ambiguities, some of which I mention on page 32, when I explain my method of translation. But so much for the didactic.

Right at the beginning of the project, in the heading of the very first installment, Sauer clearly stated that this was a serialized herbal; when it was completed, his readers could separate out the parts and bind them together as a book and therefore have a "small herbal for little cost." Several of these bound herbals have survived. The book, which started out without an initial title page, gradually assumed the name of the *Kurzgefasstes Kräuter-Buch* (Compendious herbal). *Kurtzgefasstes* can also be translated as "compact," in the same sense that *Reader's Digest* is, and when set against the monumentality of the truly huge Zwinger herbal with well over a thousand entries, Sauer's is indeed compact. Sauer also recognized his debt to Zwinger, for on the very last page of the Sauer herbal, beneath the index of herbs, he printed a closing statement that gave credit to Zwinger's work. Honest to the end.

In print, the herbal spans the years 1762 to 1778, but since the almanacs were actually printed in the fall of the year preceding for sale at the October market fair, the real printing dates of the herbal are 1761 to 1777. In 1778 the Sauers moved their printing press from Germantown into Philadelphia while it was under British occupation, a move that was undertaken in part due to the lawlessness then pervading the countryside around the city. However, this move was seen by the American side as outright cooperation with the British, and for this the Sauer family eventually paid a price.

The Zwinger Legacy

Zwinger's medical contributions have been studied by several European historians. Elfriede Grabner, an Austrian interested in the study of folk medicine, analyzed Zwinger in the early 1970s and attempted to place him in the context of broader folk medical themes.[2] Theodor Zwinger belonged to a group of late seventeenth-century physicians who straddled the lingering ideas of medieval medicine and the more rationalist theories then arising from academic medicine—in the herbal, the often cited Dr. Friedrich Hoffmann was one of the leading reformers of medicine at that time. Thus Zwinger's work represents an odd mixture of folk beliefs, medieval theories of sympathies and humors, and a rejection of some of the more fantastical medicines then being employed.

These would include powdered mummies, human bones and lard, moss that grew on old skulls, badger claws, and dragon's blood (a substance derived from palm trees). None of these ingredients had any measurable effect in cures, and therefore Zwinger rejected them. Nevertheless, we find such things as coral, crab's eyes, beaver cods, earthworms, pike's jaws, even powdered Dutch tobacco pipes, all employed in cures—substances incidentally that could be purchased from the Sauer apothecary shop. Zwinger's school of thinking permeates the Sauer herbal, not just because Sauer borrowed material from Zwinger's book. He himself believed in these medical practices, or he would not have printed them. Fontanels and vermifuges are two good cases in point.

Zwinger was a great believer in the value of fontanels—plugs of medical material pressed into lanced flesh so that they drain an injury and help promote its healing—and used them almost as extensively on his patients as the Chinese use acupuncture. They show up in the Sauer herbal, but only where they make surgical sense. Most common, however, are the references to worms. Worm remedies appear everywhere in the Sauer herbal, and this predilection traces directly to Zwinger.

There was a serious outbreak of bubonic plague in Basel, Switzerland, in 1667, and Zwinger attributed the root cause to parasitic worms. He came to the conclusion that worms in the human body carry disease or cause injuries that then offer contagion an opportunity to enter the body. Thus Zwinger became a great advocate of vermifuges, and for this reason a litany of remedies for killing or driving out worms appears in nearly every one of the herbal entries. Worms were a symbol of disease in German-speaking countries to begin with, so Zwinger's ideas were readily reinforced by this cultural attitude.

Doubtless this fear of worms also struck a chord with Sauer, since most of his rural readers worked in the fields without shoes, indeed rarely wearing shoes during hot weather, so they easily contracted many sorts of worms directly from the soil, not to mention coming in contact with worm eggs in the animal feces normally found around barns and barnyards. Even the eminent Dr. William Buchan of England warned that children got worms from their wet nurses (as though mothers had nothing else to fret about) and that "those who eat great quantities of unripe fruit, or who live much on raw herbs and roots, are generally subject to worms."[3] Given such attitudes, we might better understand why people wanted their food well cooked and why meals of raw fruits and vegetables were so seldom seen.

Sauer's careful sifting through material like this enables us to form a very clear picture of the illnesses and maladies that plagued colonial Germans and Americans in general. In fact, the herbal provides us with an extremely frank and unflattering picture of the state of health in colonial America, for the remedies themselves suggest the innumerable problems and sufferings that confronted everyday living in that period, from women afflicted by cracked nipples and milk fever and children with dangling rectums or runny scall on the head to stinking breath caused by rotten teeth, scurvy, or the rising up of putrid vapors from the stomach. It is all there in gruesome detail, even a cure for overdosing on Spanish fly, an aphrodisiac that no American gentleman would ever admit using.

Some of the material is so explicit that Sauer would not print the words in his herbal. Unlike Dr. Zwinger and most other physicians of his day, Sauer was totally appalled by any reference to the human genitals, to menstruation, or to conditions that might be equated with sexual excitement. Any terms connected with these things were dropped. Either the space was left blank, or the first letter of the word was left in place so that readers could fill in the rest on their own. These were words one knew but never said in public.

On the one hand, Sauer's treatment of this subject is rather prudish; he had no reservations about using the words *pissen* (to piss) or *Rotz* (snot), which evidently were common enough in barnyard conversation. On the other hand, Sauer obviously operated by a code of decorum that was quite protective of women, for a large number of the remedies in the herbal deal with maladies exclusive to the female sex. It was often necessary to consult contemporary German medical works, such as Dr. Johann Jacob Woyt's *Gazophylacium Medico-Physicum* (1784), to reconstruct Sauer's intentional omissions (Woyt at least wrote it out in meticulous Latin). Since he was writing for common people, Sauer was sensitive about offending them, and he took for granted that they would not know the Latin medical terms he had so carefully weeded out of Zwinger's text. Cryptic abbreviations therefore seemed the best way around it.

Likewise, bleeding and cupping are taken for granted. People were intentionally bled to release a surfeit of blood under certain medical conditions. The herbal contains several references to this, and its directions are quite specific. Bleeding was accomplished manually with cups and lancets, very sharp and wicked-looking to be certain, and the employment of leeches—which has incidentally undergone a rehabilitation of late, due to a better understanding of the role that the leeches play in feeding anticoagulants into the body. The obvious conclusion is that in many cases, herbs alone would not effect the cure, so bleeding and these other weapons of period medicine may be viewed as part of a continuum of upping the ante in finding quicker and more effective remedies. Over time, this occurred at the expense of the botanical cures, but now we are again looking at herbs with renewed respect.

Christopher Sauer went through the Zwinger herbal with an eye to material appropriate for America. He was most directly concerned with herbs that could be obtained in apothecary shops here, or which were already growing in American gardens. His choices are keyed especially to poor people who must find innumerable ways to treat themselves for little or no cost. This explains the frequent repetition in his text: if one herb cannot be found, then use another in a slightly different way. After all, people are different, and they react to remedies in an unequal manner.

Even the somewhat exotic-looking ingredients were in fact readily available from any number of merchants, not just from apothecaries. For example, Adam Simon Kuhn, a Lancaster, Pennsylvania, merchant, advertised the following medical supplies in the April 16, 1748, issue of the *Pennsylvanische Geschicht-Schreiber*, the newspaper published by Christopher Sauer Sr.: oils of juniper, turpentine, caraway, anise, and sweet bay; waters of lavender and hartshorn; vitriol; aqua fortis and Hungary water; coral, camphor, antimony, saltpeter, quicksilver, cream of tartar, Venice treacle, prepared aloe, myrrh, zedoary root, galingale, rhubarb, senna leaves, and licorice. Most if not all of these items appear as ingredients in Sauer's herbal.

Plan for a Physic Garden.

Sauer knew herbs firsthand because he maintained a small physic garden and had ready access to several others in and around Philadelphia, including the very extensive gardens of Dr. Christopher de Witt, established about 1720, and of Universalist preacher and physician Dr. George de Benneville of Bristol in Bucks County, Pennsylvania. (An example of such a garden from the 1623 edition of de Serrres is pictured above left.) Sauer's knowledge of plants was intimate because he could speak as a gardener—who else would concern himself about flea beetles on nasturtiums? He is extremely forthright in this regard and sometimes provides advice on how to grow herbs as well.

Yet what Sauer actually said about the herbs was a mixture of opinions; he sometimes parroted Zwinger word for word and sometimes paraphrased him; he also paraphrased other works—such as Nicholas Culpeper's *The English Physician*—and he inserted expansive passages of his own. Thus his herbal is a piece of intellectual quiltwork, just like Zwinger's and the entire herbal tradition that preceded him, one author lifting from the other. We may readily assume that no matter what the source, if it is repeated, reworded, or even scrambled through Sauer's mouth, then he considered those words his own; they formed part of his view, much as scriptural passages inform a sermon.

This is why Zwinger appealed to the ancients when attempting to establish the veracity of some medical point, or relied on a biblical quote, or cited some obscure learned work from the Middle Ages. Sauer did the same, and his herbal is loaded with extraordinary material culled from fascinating and sometimes ancient sources conflated to form a new whole. I have attempted to identify many of these sources in my footnotes to the text. The reader should be aware, for example, that the recipes dealing with apricots come not from eighteenth-century Pennsylvania, but from twelfth-century Cairo. The point is this: many of Sauer's remedies are extremely old and belong to a body of knowledge inherited and shared by many cultures, not just the Germans.

The material incorporated into the Zwinger herbal is impressive in its scholarship, with remedies taken from the great renaissance works of Joachim Camerarius the Younger (1534–1598), Charles de l'Escluse (1526–1609), Gabriel Fallopius (1523–1562), Swiss botanist and physician Conrad Gesner (1516–1565), Hieronymus of Braunschweig (d. 1534), Pier' Andrea Mattioli (1500–1577), and German physician Christopher Wirsung (1500–1571). A great portion of the Zwinger remedies published by Sauer were already over 200 years old. But Zwinger also assembled material from closer contemporaries, such as Friedrich Hoffmann (1660–1742), Louis Lemery (1677–1743), Simon Paulli (1603–1680), and Johann Schroeder (1600–1664). The culinary material, which is scattered throughout the herbal, is largely borrowed from Georg Andreas Böckler's *Der nützliche Hauss- und Feld-Schule* (The school of practical management for house and field) printed at Nuremberg in 1678, and from Johann Coler's *Economia Ruralis* (Frankfurt, 1692). Both of these encyclopedic handbooks were intended for the man of the house, since they covered a wide range of farming and household subjects. Nonetheless, Maria Sophia Schellhammer took a number of recipes from Böckler for her *Brandenburgisches Koch-Buch* (Brandenburg cookbook), first published in 1698, so the food material flowed back and forth through many different hands and many different kinds of books.

I dipped into Schellhammer's cookbook for a few illustrative recipes included in my commentaries on the herbs, for her style of cooking comes closest to what is found in the herbal and to what was more typical of an educated German woman's cooking talents in colonial America. I also assembled material from later cookery books, especially from authors who were more or less contemporaries of Christopher Sauer II, such as R. Christine Knörin (1745–1809) and Sophie Juliane Weiler (1745–1810).

This culinary aspect of the herbal is important for two reasons: food was not yet separate from medicine. The two were seen as different sides of the same path to well-being. In the eighteenth century, the French began to separate medical material from culinary so that the cookbook as a literary form evolved away from food as health to food as sensual experience. Today, there is a shift back to a more holistic view of diet and health, and for this reason, the Sauer herbal contains many nuggets of useful and indeed commonsense information. If nothing else, it makes fascinating reading for anyone who loves plants.

The other reason is that the Sauers evidently planned to publish at least two other works relative to the herbal. One was a small book on botanical medicine and midwifery written by family friend Dr. George de Benneville (1703–1793), which now resides in the manuscript stage in the collection of the Historical Society of Pennsylvania. The other was a project on cookery that now only survives in scattered fragments. Had the revolution not intervened, the Sauers probably would have gone on to publish both of these works. Sauer appreciated the importance of food and its role in dosing herbal remedies. (He might also be described as something of a dessert freak, since he exhibited definite favoritism toward sweets.) This is everywhere evident in the herbal. In fact, the procedures, the tools, the whole impression of creating food and remedies in a kitchen come through very clearly.

The Colonial German Kitchen

Sauer's culinary remedies cannot be understood unless one can also visualize the colonial German kitchen and the utter commonality of taking everyday utensils and employing them for medical ends. The Sauer herbal transports us into such a kitchen, where we are inescapably confronted by an array of objects that he takes for granted, including the soot, which is employed in remedies.

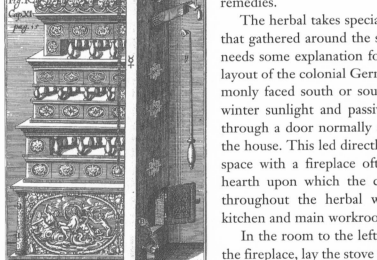

Chimney Soot (Stove).

The herbal takes special pains to mention the soot that gathered around the stove hole, and perhaps this needs some explanation for those unfamiliar with the layout of the colonial German farmhouse, which commonly faced south or southeast to take advantage of winter sunlight and passive solar heat. One entered through a door normally set toward the right side of the house. This led directly into a semipublic cooking space with a fireplace often furnished with a raised hearth upon which the cooking utensils mentioned throughout the herbal were placed. This was the kitchen and main workroom of the house.[4]

In the room to the left, behind a dividing wall and the fireplace, lay the stove room, or *Stube*, as it is called in German. Its primary feature was a cast-iron plate stove that was fed hot coals through the kitchen side of the chimney. Georg Andreas Böckler's *Furnologia* (Frankfurt, 1666) was one of the period handbooks commonly consulted for the construction of these stoves. A copper engraving of an elaborate stove from Böckler is shown (above, left). Household versions were often much plainer and not quite as tall, so that there would be a flat surface on top. Whatever its design, the stove dominated the stove room, which was the center of family activity. Meals were taken there, and it was in this smokeless space that many remedies and foods were prepared over charcoal stoves. Fumes and smoke from the stove returned to the kitchen fireplace via a hole in the wall higher up. It was the soot that collected at this opening that Sauer recommended in his remedy on page 97—

Böckler even shows a scraper for removing the soot. In short, soot was free, easy to find, and so common that even a child knew where to get it.

In many of Sauer's remedies, the reader is instructed to set a pot or some other vessel on top of a stove. It is this iron stove that is intended, and it made a very good hot plate indeed. This is also the "warm place" referred to in some of the remedies, and this is where a box of sand might be placed so that a mixture could be set into it to digest in the slow warm heat for a period of time.

In the summer, when the stove was not in use, vessels were set out in the sun, normally in that south-facing area directly outside the kitchen door known as the *Vorhof*, "front kitchen." This was a work area protected by an overhanging roof, often with a bench along the wall so that chores could be undertaken in the warm sun. This area later evolved into a porch or veranda once house design changed and kitchen doors were moved to the back of the house in the nineteenth century.

That the herbal was intended for use in this type of household is obvious from the range of utensils and objects suggested in the remedies. Directions are expressed in simple terms, and the tools employed are readily available. Doses are measured by such easily recognizable quantities as the size of a nutmeg, a handful (roughly 2 ounces), or a wineglass. Cooking times are sometimes equated with the time necessary for hard-cooking an egg—no clock required. A linen house cap is employed as a strainer, eggshells are used as containers for doses, dishes are employed to press out liquids, drinks are administered in glass tumblers or by the tablespoonful. Old pieces of linen (perhaps a corner of a discarded tablecloth) are used for swabbing injuries. Indeed the list of everyday objects employed is long and fascinating, and offers an off-hand insight into the material culture of a typical house of this period. Of course, the more affluent sorts of people employed good swanskin flannel for straining their broths and jellies, but an old clean apron would also suffice. And yes, some people had fine glass jars for storing their electuaries or wet medications, but new earthenware pots were just as acceptable—new, of course, because they would not have absorbed food from previous use.

Many of the directions concerning crockery are quite explicit, taking into account both the clay body and glaze, for some pottery could be used for acidic medicines and some could not. Indeed, most of the cooking in a colonial German kitchen was accomplished in earthenware vessels rather than metal. Because earthenware absorbs flavors, it was common practice to own several sets of pots, some used exclusively for fish, some for fowl, others for meat. Since the German kitchen was often furnished with a raised hearth, these cookpots were set on trivets at waist level and heated over coals. Otherwise, they were set down into kettles and cooked in vacuo.

Many remedies are also prepared in vacuo, that is, in tightly sealed containers so that the essential oils or volatile elements cannot escape. The properties of some herbs, such as chamomile, are destroyed by heat. Boiling them in the open air renders them worthless. These points were well understood by people in the eighteenth century and explain why certain procedures were employed and not others. Sometimes the herbal actually warns the reader in this regard.

Now that I have mentioned in vacuo, perhaps it would be useful to turn to the "digestion" of soups, since they were prepared in the kitchen and provided those caring for the ill with an array of stocks or *restaurants* for administering various herbal remedies. They may be termed sympathetic soups, since their ingredients, both liquid and herbal, were matched to the malady being treated.

The *Restaurant*, or *Iusculum Consummatum*

The *restaurant* as a type of soup is a concept much older than we generally assume, although medieval documentation is often scanty on the process of extracting the juices from a stew. This meat extraction is essentially the meaning of the word as it was used in French in the sixteenth century. The German equivalent, also dating from the same period, is *Kraftbrühe*, a "fortified" or "perfected" broth. A *Kraftsuppe* is a soup constructed from this broth and understood to contain bread, either sliced or torn into pieces. Bread shows up in nearly all of the soups that are described in any detail in Sauer's herbal. Not surprising, there is even an entry on wheat relative to bread baking and various medical uses of flour.

Two types of *Kraftsuppe* were normally equated with the *restaurant*: the restorative soup made from meat concentrates and the sympathetic soup containing ingredients for a specific cure. This distinction is somewhat artificial, since features of one might be combined with features of the other, thus creating a spectrum of possible cures, each coded by the virtues of its ingredients to a specific affliction. Dr. Johann Jacob Woyt described the *restaurant* from this medical viewpoint in 1784:

> It is now a common occurrence in medicine to convert plain soups into a vehicle for remedies, so that the medications may be taken with greater ease. *Kraftsuppen*, under the name *iuscula consummata* or restaurants, are keenly sought after, though not often in apothecary shops. They are prepared from an old hen or capon with various herbs, flowers, roots, spices and so forth according to intended purpose.[5]

As an example, he provided a soup recipe (in lugubrious pharmaceutical Latin) for a patient weakened by fever. Woyt's restaurant was made with finely chopped capon, succory root, sandalwood, borage and bugloss flowers, and cloves. These ingredients were cooked in springwater in a tightly closed pot—in vacuo—set into a kettle of boiling water. The extracted liquid was then given to the patient as a *stärkende Kraftsuppe*, a soup concentrate intended to strengthen an emaciated body. Thus the term restaurant had several meanings in Sauer's day. At one end of the spectrum, it was a form of health food or medicine; at the other end, it was an ingredient in courtly cuisine prepared in the French manner.

Johann Christian Wolf, author of the *Neues Leipziger Koch-Buch* (Frankfurt/Leipzig, 1779), epitomized the opposing Francophile tendencies in German cookery of that period, not surprisingly since the elector of Saxony (the state in which Wolf lived and cooked) was also the king of Poland and had installed French cooks in his numerous palaces. Wolf employed French names for all his recipes, and used French technical terms throughout his text. He explained how to make a *restaurant* this way:

> For a service of 12, 15, to 18 persons, take 5 pounds of veal from the shank, 2 pounds of beef, 1 pound of ham, 1 old hen, and a cock. Line the bottom of a stewpan with some thinly sliced bacon, then add the meats. On top of this, add carrots, onions, parsnips, root parsley, and celery. As soon as it has boiled up twice by a brisk fire, stir in well-made bouillon. One can also add a bundle of leeks, but do not let them cook too long. After the stew has been strained through a linen napkin folded over double, the liquid may be added to all manner of clear sauces, as well as employed in the finest glazes.[6]

I mention Wolf for an additional historical reason: his cookbook was actually used among a small circle of educated Germans in America. In fact, the copy now in my possession actually came out of a Pennsylvania attic and passed into the hands of the late Ann Hark, who consulted it when she collaborated with Preston Barba in writing *Pennsylvania Dutch Cookery* in 1950.

In any event, Wolf's liquid strained through a napkin is essentially the same kind of *kräftige Brühe* or *starke Fleischbrühe* (concentrated meat stock) that appears in many of Sauer's recipes. On the other hand, regardless of its original meaning in French, the German interpretation of *restaurant* was also sometimes rather imprecise, and another period author took this vagueness to task. He was Johann Christian Förster, who complained in his *Braunschweigisches Kochbuch* (Braunschweig, 1789) that *Kraftbrühe* was far too vague a word to use properly in high-class German cookery.[7] He published a recipe nearly identical to Wolf's, and added that in everyday situations, one cannot always choose the best cuts of meat. Therefore, he proposed to call this concentrated stock by the French term *jus*. Not all cooks might agree with him, least of all an erudite physician like Woyt.

To another similar recipe, Förster added calves' feet so that the stock was not only dense, it jelled stiff when cold. This he referred to in French as *consommé*, which is what *iusculum consummatum* literally means in Latin—a "perfected" broth. Obviously, the composition of a *Kraftbrühe* or *restaurant* was open to interpretation and nimble semantics, and many German readers of cookbooks like Wolf's and Förster's probably came away from them puzzled.

Furthermore, the rural cookery familiar to most of Sauer's readers was closer in spirit to the mid-seventeenth century than to the rococo palaces where men like Wolf and Förster cooked. Where Sauer's culinary recipes can be documented, they are almost all taken from sources dating from the 1600s. Thus, while the essential concepts were in place in his readers' kitchens, the lighter refinements of eighteenth-century cookery were not. This means that while it would probably be correct to translate Sauer's *Kraftbrühe* by any one of several contemporary terms, even double bouillon or *restaurant*, his country readers would not have used such words in daily speech. Indeed, to them a soup of concentrated broth was a *Süpplein* or *Sippli* plain and simple. Therefore I chose for my translation a more colloquial rendition, such as "strong stock" or "strong-tasting meat stock." But the real meaning was apparent to accomplished cooks here in America. They knew how to make such stocks from scratch, and among the Germans in particular, a good meat stock was considered one of the cornerstones of the cuisine.

Considering its nutritional qualities, a *restaurant* or concentrated meat stock was ideal for weak patients, just as Woyt suggested. Rural cooks did not go to the elaborate lengths of Wolf's recipe, but they did follow the general outline after their own manner, with fewer varieties of meats (or lesser cuts like beef shins), and fewer vegetables (or different ones more readily available). The ingredients could be sealed in a stoneware crock—the homey technique mentioned repeatedly by Sauer—and then set in a kettle of boiling water.

Taverns and inns operating in the larger cities and towns generally made some type of stock like this on a regular basis because it allowed the establishment to create soups and gravies quickly. Additionally, the broth could be sold to the public by the pint, quart, or gallon. Prepared soups, such as pepperpot or turtle soup, were often advertised this way. Thus people living in or near towns could easily obtain stock for a sick member of the household. Furthermore, whether stock was prepared in taverns or at home, it was common practice to take the mixture of vegetables and meat from which the stock had been extracted, dust it with flour, and then heat it up with red wine or water. This was served over bread, boiled turnips, or potatoes as a kind of thick ragout or hash. Spice powders were also added to give the mixture greater flavor. German cookery in this period, even for the sick, was anything but bland. In fact, robust flavor was an important factor, and several of the medical powders in the herbal may be employed in cookery this way.

The 1749 recipe for a dish described as "A Splendid Repast of Meat for the Sick or for Pregnant Women," which appeared under ragouts in the *Bernisches Koch-Büchlein*, should illustrate this point. It was prepared in this manner: "Mince veal, chicken or mutton as fine as when it is pounded in a mortar, then chop into it marjoram, savory, parsley, mace, and saffron. Once this is reduced to a smooth hash, place it in a small pot over the fire. Add a little wine and let it cook."[8] To fully understand the restorative nature of this spicy dish, it is necessary to consult what Sauer had to say about each of the herbal ingredients as well as the wine.

Regarding the classic method for preparing a *restaurant* by sealing it in a pot set in boiling water, Sauer often mentioned a similar use for stoneware crocks and pots. But there was actually a cast-iron implement designed specifically for making meat stocks, sometimes called a digester. Tear-shaped with a narrow neck and tight-fitting lid, it stood on three feet and was equipped with a long, looplike handle so that the pot could be hung from a hook and submerged to the neck in a kettle of water. It worked on the same principle as a glue pot, and the better grades were lined inside with tin or even porcelain.

It is well documented that the first Paris restaurateur opened his doors in 1766, even though restorative soups were sold by other establishments long before that.[9] Trendy on-premise meals in what was then callled *nouvelle cuisine* are not quite the same as selling pails of fresh stock to customers who might need it in a pinch.

Furthermore, the laws that regulated the sale of food in Paris were not in place in colonial America, where anyone could sell more or less any food they pleased—it was liquor by the drink that was subject to strict licensing. Yet it is true that the restaurant, as a place to take full meals exclusively, did not evolve full-blown in this country until the 1790s. Indeed, the French Revolution precipitated the emigration to America of numerous professional cooks, such as Jean Baptiste Julien of the Restorator in Boston, and Pierre Bossée of the Nouveau Caveau in Philadelphia. But these are developments that flow beyond the time frame of Sauer's herbal. The important point is that in Sauer's America, a *restaurant* was not a place. The meat stocks known as *restaurants* were not only made at home but available for sale in public taverns, as well as from local women (mostly widows) who supported themselves by specializing in certain cooking crafts. And on occasion, apothecaries sold them under the impressive guise of a Latin label.

The Kitchen Garden and Sympathetic Salads

In Sauer's day, medical herbs were planted in the kitchen garden. And that holistic approach, where no plant is a weed, for all are useful, should be a theme today in reconnecting us to natural things. Having said that, I should add that a lot of the plants consumed by eighteenth-century people were not from the garden at all, but gathered from the wild. They were free, and as Nicholas Culpeper pointed out in his *Pharmacopaeia Londonensis* (London, 1673), their virtues were greatest when the plants were taken from the places where they preferred to grow.

This distinction surfaces in Sauer's herbal with the use of the word *zahm*, "cultivated." There was a difference between garden-cultivated chicory and the chicory found wild in fields; their medical actions were markedly different, and the herbal points this out. This keen observation on the part of the old authors detected chemical subtleties completely lacking in much of the nutritional data we are fed today by the people who have tried to standardize everything from apples to wheat. Some of this has to do with the soil, which in the past was viewed as living nature rather than the inert dross of modern chemical farming.

The issue of worms resurfaces as we discuss greens, since some of these plants were eaten raw in salads. For certain, open-air museums do not reconstruct kitchen gardens in their full embarrassing detail because if they did, we would be forced to observe clods of "night soil" under the cabbages, and odors lingering about the parsnips that might require a handkerchief over the nose. Worms were passed in night soil, and they got back in through the kitchen, as Dr. William Buchan has already observed. Nevertheless salads were eaten and even relished, but perhaps it is significant to note that salads made of root vegetables are always precooked in some manner. This sterilizing and tenderizing may have been necessary, for teeth were not in very good shape, so anything soft was preferable.

The range of greens is striking in the Sauer herbal, for the shopping list reflects an era unprejudiced against burdock, dittander, elderberry shoots, snakeweed, sow thistle, and wood sorrel. The biodiversity of this diet is exceptional, and surely the nutritional shortcomings of some parts of the eighteenth-century menu were counterbalanced by these plants, so rich in vitamins and minerals. Cooking some of them may have destroyed part of their value, but the *erste Brühe* or cooking water (normally poured down the sink today) was viewed as food and medicine in its own right, and it is employed this way in several remedies. In any case, it was never thrown out; it was simply poured off into the stewpot always standing near the hearth and used in soups.

I have already noted the importance of the *restaurant* in serving as the basic stock for many remedial broths and foods, but we may take this a step further by adding greens. The soup then becomes sympathetic in that it agrees with the condition it is intended to cure. Borage, for example, is cooling. In a sympathetic soup it would be served at room temperature to a patient with high fever. The taste is of cucumbers, and the addition of other cooling herbs only increases its active qualities. Such light, brothy soups are not difficult to eat. Some of them are even quite savory.

Likewise, the salad could also be deemed sympathetic if the various ingredients were carefully matched to effect a cure. These ingredients can be found in the herbal and selected according to the virtues given at the beginning of each entry. The salad is an important dimension of curing because many herbs and greens completely lose their nutritional and medical properties when subjected to heat. Herbalists were aware of this, and care was taken in prescribing the raw greens best suited to this application. The delightful "sallets" of John Evelyn probably developed out of this concept, but by the time he published his book on them in 1699, the health salad had already evolved into a thing of fashion, among the gentry at least. The salad of fashion was a miniaturized garden, an edible Eden, and therefore to the status-conscious it ranked with bowls of exotic fruits and porcelain seashells filled with pickles and preserves from Italy or far-off India. The sympathetic salad was none of this.

Zuckerwaren: Medical Confections

The herbal contains numerous references to compounds made with sugar that are used as mediums for administering cures. There are five general types: the *compositum*, which Sauer rendered into German as *Latwerge* (electuary), the conserve, the preserve, the syrup, and the candy. The medical literature surrounding all of these is extremely old, and there were individuals, oftentimes women, who were true professionals in preparing them. They were also made by druggists and confectioners, as well as by gentlewomen as part of their duties in managing the estate and medicating the help who worked there. A large number of these preparations, especially the good-tasting ones, crossed over the line from medicine and appeared on the banquet and dessert tables of the well-to-do.

A number of the recipes of this sort that appear in Sauer's herbal also appear in Maria Sophia Schellhammer's *Brandenburgisches Koch-Buch*. Whether they were copied directly from her by Zwinger or Sauer, or whether both she and Zwinger dipped into an older common source, has not been determined, but Schellhammer is an excellent document for study because she represents the feminine contribution to this area of German confectionery. And since copies of her famous cookbook are known to have existed in colonial America, she is worth mentioning in connection with the Sauers. Indeed, the Sauers may have sold copies of her cookbook from their store, since they imported and sold both new and secondhand books of this type.

Schellhammer is of particular interest because the material in her book, especially the confectionery and distilling recipes, reflects her marriage to a professor of medicine. Her husband, Christian Schellhammer, practiced medicine in Jena, Helmstedt, and Kiel. Daughter of a well-known physician, Hermann Conring of Nuremberg, she published recipes for the sort of medical waters and distillations that form the substance of so many Sauer remedies, as well as culinary recipes based on some of the plants that were falling out of fashion among the middle class by Sauer's era. In reading through Schellhammer's cookbook, it is possible to get a sense of how Sauer's herbal fits together with the cookery side of the kitchen. It is almost as though Schellhammer and Zwinger should have been bound and sold together.

The *composita*, as Dr. Zwinger called them, were thick pastes of varying degrees of moisture, from stiff and rubbery to soft and jamlike. The most famous of these, and the one employed in many of Sauer's remedies, was Venice treacle, or *theriaca andromaci*, a paste consisting of over seventy ingredients. It was probably made from honey in its original form, but evidently during the late Byzantine period sugar entered the picture. It appears to have reached the Venetians through Cyprus, where they maintained sugar plantations prior to the Turkish invasion of 1571. This electuary as well as the Cure of Mithradates (a recipe for it appears under the entry for mustard) were treated in Venusinus Maranta's *Libri duo de theriaca et Mithridatio*, edited by Joachim Camerarius in 1576, which was one of the works consulted by Theodor Zwinger. Farm people did not necessarily have access to either preparation, so as a substitute they often cooked a pulped herb in apple butter and used this instead. This was a common device employed by herb grannies and powwow healers.

The conserves and preserves prepared by Sauer are rather easy to visualize. Conserves were preparations of ingredients such as violet or rose petals beaten into sugar. The texture varied from fluffy like snow to wet and sticky, depending on the amount of oils and moisture in the herb or flower being conserved. They stuck together loosely and had to be eaten with a spoon. Preserves were wet. Essentially anything boiled and impregnated with sugar, they were less stable than conserves and therefore needed better means of storage.

Syrups were made by liquefying sugar and using this as a medium for holding and stabilizing herbal virtues. Syrups were often employed for cough and chest ailments, or for internal problems. Raspberry syrup, which was actually somewhat sour due to the vinegar in it (Sauer provided a recipe), was extremely popular in the region of Pennsylvania where the Germans settled. A feature in local cookbooks down to the early 1900s, it was once used extensively as an ingredient in salad dressings, stews, and sauce preparations. It served the Pennsylvania Germans much as lemons did the Italians.

Candied medicines, such as candied lovage or angelica, were made by boiling herbs in sugar, then drying them so that they became brittle. Seeds coated with sugar were called comfits, and these too were brittle. Comfits were often colored and used as garnishes on Christmas cakes and cookies, or scattered over puddings, so their application was not simply medical. Sauer mentions comfits from time to time, but it is obvious that his enthusiasm lay with conserves in particular, and preserves second-arily. Since confectioners had the specialized equipment necessary for making com-fits and other candies, it is possible that Sauer (or his wife) did not attempt to make them in their shop. In a place like Philadelphia, it was easy enough to purchase such things wholesale, for there were numerous practicing confectioners. Furthermore, since the Sauer herbal was intended for home use, emphasis was placed on those preparations most easily accomplished in a farmhouse kitchen, and comfits were not one of them.

This emphasis on simple preparations would explain the presence of several candy recipes made by boiling sugar. They are quite easy to make in small quantities over a charcoal stove, and the directions supplied with them are for the most part quite clear and helpful, even for the clumsiest of cooks. Of all his candies, Sauer's ginger candy stands out, and something about it tells me that he actually liked to eat it when his wife was not looking. Furthermore, if butter is added, the candy can be pulled into taffy. One of the most famous of the old medical candies in the Pennsylvania German region was just such a taffy made with mint. It became a popular street food sold by vendors under the name of Mammy Bender's Belly-Guts, Mammy Bender being the old lady in Lancaster who first began selling the taffies that way.

The other sugar that appears consistently in ingredients is sugar candy or rock sugar crystals. These could be made from any grade of sugar by simple evaporation, so there was a range of colors available. The darkest crystals were the cheapest, sold to children as junk food or employed in sweetening chocolate. The clear crystals made from the highest grades of sugar were the ones called for in medical remedies. The reason for using them was the purity of the sugar itself, since white loaf sugar was often clayed or treated in some manner. Any type of adulteration would affect a remedy, particularly if the patient were sensitive to the additive; thus it was impera-tive to know that the product was safe.

Brennereien: Distillations

When I began organizing the index for the Sauer herbal, it became amply clear that there were two extremely large blocks of material embedded in the book. One was culinary recipes, and the other was herbal waters. The herbal waters are intriguing, since many of them can be traced to Hieronymus of Braunschweig's *Kleines Distillierbuch*, dating from 1500, and because they stand out so clearly in almost every page of the herbal. There had to be a reason for this.

The process for making an herbal water, an herbal salt, and then the actual spirit is outlined in Sauer's entry under lily of the valley on page 195. I will not repeat that here, but I do think it important to begin reading the herbal with the understanding that an herbal water is not necessarily alcoholic. Unless there is prefermentation, or unless the infusion is prepared like Martha Bradley's poppy water (page 149), there is nothing to rectify into spirits. It simply remains distilled water, but it contains high concentrates of all the volatile essences of the herb and anything else that goes up through the alembic. Hungary water, made from rosemary blossoms, was one of the most famous of these. Others, like elderberry blossom water, are still made today for cosmetics. Alcohol or pure spirits can be added to waters to stabilize them, but too much alcohol can also destroy the chemistry of the herbal properties, so there is a delicate balance when it comes to making good herbal waters.

In Sauer's herbal, these waters are used extensively either alone or in combination with other remedies, and for two basic reasons. First, herbal waters provided a way to supply concentrated doses of a particular herb's virtues year-round, without depending on seasonality. Second, the distilled water was chemically pure and did not contain the mineral salts found in springwater or the adulterations and pollutants that might get into rainwater.

A careful reading of the herbal makes it obvious that kidney and bladder stones were common, one of the byproducts of drinking hard water or water with high mineral content. These minerals precipitate into the kidneys and bladder. Country people who relied on drinking water from springs could satisfy themselves that their water was good, but they were also consuming minerals that in time would probably injure them—just as the present craze for bottled mineral waters may bless our bodies with similar afflictions. It makes no sense to treat sand, gravel, or kidney stones with medications served up in springwater unless the herb used is also a powerful antilithic.

For this same reason wine is employed, not because of its low mineral content but because of its acidity, which dissolves the stones. When I began separating remedies by red wine (high mineral content) or white (more acidic), I soon discovered that white wine predominated by such an overwhelming margin that wherever the type of wine is not specified, it is almost certain to be white. Sauer's attitude to wine is made clear in his little chat on this subject under wine.

The fact remains nevertheless that wine was an entry in the herbal: it was viewed as a dimension of medicine. I have explained in my introduction to its entry how wine was a part of the daily diet of the eighteenth-century Germans living in America. Indeed, this love of wine persisted, as witness continued attempts by the German element to establish viticulture in Pennsylvania and Maryland. The very first American book on viticulture is a tract (still unpublished) written by Francis Pastorius of Germantown, Pennsylvania, in 1701. The first printed book was Christian Becker's *Unterricht für amerikanische Bauern, Weinberge anzulegen und zu unterhalten* (Instruction to American farmers on the laying out and maintenance of vineyards), printed at Easton, Pennsylvania, in 1809.

The pervasive use of wine in daily life and its acceptance as a basic medium for remedies sets the Sauer herbal very much apart from similar ones written for the English. Sauer's herbal cannot be used without wine, and no matter how much he railed against abuse of the grape, Sauer recognized that most of his readers were not Dunkards like himself, and that they drank wine prodigiously. He accepted this by virtue of the fact that he did not edit out material requiring wine, although he did on occasion add a line here and there to say that cider or water might work just as well in a given circumstance. The other evidence to support Sauer's tolerance of wine drinking lies in the fact that he included recipes for hangovers—and not just one—

not to mention an excellent recipe for cherry wine that he himself had tested.

But drinking ardent spirits for pleasure was out of the question, and beverages like punch only earned his rebuke and condemnation. Considering that punch drinking was a prerogative of the rich merchant and planter class in colonial America, Sauer doubtless associated this custom with all the negative class connotations that so set him against the self-styled gentry of that period. Turn to lemons, and there is a smarting sermon on punch and the well-deserved gout it inflicts.

Brandy and rum are used almost exclusively to create essences and extracts. The process is explained several times in the herbal, but it operated this way: An herb is infused in brandy, and a clear liquid forms on the top. This is collected as an essence. If the essence is then boiled down to a thick, honeylike consistency, it becomes an extract. Sticky balls of extract could be rolled in powdered sugar to make pills. All of this is explained by Sauer in such a way that even the novice can work through it with relative ease.

Distilling of ardent spirits was quite another matter. Distilling was somewhat complicated due to the equipment, yet there was ample knowledge among the German settlers on how to make distillates. Many farmers owned stills and found the sale of these products a useful, not to mention profitable, adjunct to farming. The Mennonites in particular were excellent distillers of rye whiskey until temperance changed their attitudes about drinking. Furthermore, several distilling manuals, such as *Die wahre Brantwein Brennerey* (York, Pa., 1797), were readily available to anyone who wanted to learn the art.

Among the Schwenkfelders, a sect who resided not too many miles from Germantown, I might mention the *Neuvermehrtes Schlesisches Haus- und Wirtschafts-Buch* (Breslau, 1746). Like Böckler's housebook, this one also contains a chapter dealing entirely with distilling. There are even three folding plates showing stills and their apparatuses. Since saffron growing was one of the Schwenkfelders' cottage industries during Sauer's era, we may safely assume that saffron waters and distillates were readily available from that community.

Braucherei: Powwow Remedies and Magic

I have taken the position in this book that magic is an unnatural transfer of a force real or imagined from one object to another. The very word *unnatural* is itself loaded with numerous significations, which I shall explain shortly. However, in the Sauer herbal there are instances where an herb is laid upon an illness—Sauer's smartweed poultice, for example—and then the herb is buried in a manure pile. As the smartweed rots, the toothache goes into remission. What has taken place is a transfer; the malady has moved by some miraculous fashion into the plant, which is then destroyed. Such beliefs were so pervasive among the German element in colonial America that numerous books dealing with spells and unnatural illnesses—as Sauer himself called them—were printed and used throughout the eighteenth and nineteenth centuries. Indeed, these books are still in use among the Amish, although few Amishmen would readily admit it.

Because of Sauer's strong religious convictions, I was naturally surprised to discover evidence of such powwow remedies in the herbal, since this nonrationalist approach to medicine lay quite beyond the boundaries of mainstream medicine as it was practiced even during the eighteenth century. Yet *Braucherei* (as powwowing is called in Pennsylfaanisch) was an intrinsic part of folk belief. The term *powwowing* was adapted into English in the seventeenth century in connection with native American healers, but the concept of joining this word to European folk medicine can be traced to the period of Sauer's herbal.

The two ideas came together in a muddled sort of way in the so-called Indian doctors who claimed to have learned their expertise from native Americans. Since the Indians were believed to have been the Lost Tribes of Israel, their curative powers were sometimes given ancient biblical pretensions. I will cite one example, Peter Carlton, who advertised himself in the German-language *Philadelphische Staatsbothe* for July 28, 1775:

> Peter Carlton, doctor according to the Indian method, lives on Christopher
> Mussel's plantation, Donegal Township, Lancaster County, near John
> Bealey's Mill, on the road from Anderson's Ferry to Reading. While held
> captive by the Indians for fourteen years, he learned their medical methods,
> and he now gives treatment and also instruction.

This brand of healing became broadly popular in the nineteenth century under the guise of Indian patent remedies, or the more traditional sort of botanical medicines promoted by books like J. W. Cooper's *Experienced Botanist or Indian Physician* (Lancaster, Pa., 1840). By contrast, true powwow medicine as it was practiced among the German element was a blend of many healing techniques tracing to very old European roots. Very little of it was based on Indian remedies, regardless of claims. One consistent feature of this healing technique was the transfer of an illness into an object or the earth, as in the case of the smartweed poultice just mentioned.

Such transferral are unquestionably magic medicine, and they are endemic to most of the popular healing books written by Pennsylvania Dutch *Brauchmeischter* Johann Georg Hohman. Hohman's *Lang verborgene Freund* (Long-concealed familiar), published in 1820, is now considered a powwow classic. A *Freund* or familiar is the object through which one works spells. This term is often mistranslated as "friend," which is a more benign meaning of the word.

In the case of Sauer's wall fern, where I mention its use in protecting against hexes laid on bread, the "friend" used by the witch was normally a stick or rod run into the ground—obviously made of a very special kind of wood. The spell then traveled through the earth and came up into the neighbor's bread, thus ruining it before it baked. A leaf of wall fern was placed beneath the rising bread to prevent this force from getting through, if witchcraft was the suspected source of the baking problem. If the leaf was then tossed into the flaming oven, either the witch herself was scorched or her house was set ablaze, thus exposing her to the community. This is the unnatural transfer run full circle. Hohman's books are full of this sort of powwowing.

Witchcraft, as New Englanders of that period would have deemed it, was widespread among the Pennsylvania Germans, and it still has adherents today.

Powwowing is still so common that it does not even merit an explanation, except to outsiders whose wide-eyed reactions may or may not provoke a few words of reassurance. We are not conjuring up *Macbeth's* cauldron-stirring evil sisters or pseudo earth mothers in green linen capes, but rather a healer who intermingles herbs, magic words, charms, biblical passages, and laying on of hands to achieve cures. Rationalist physicians in colonial Pennsylvania derided this healing, but a policy of tolerance was established by William Penn himself during the only witch trial held in his colony. He said, in so many words, that if the accused could fly on a broom, let her. And that was the last we heard of witch trials in Pennsylvania.

Period references to such persons are rare and quite often euphemistic, as in the case of the notice in Sauer's newspaper for February 2, 1759: "Maria Iserloh, living with Henrich Schmitt the younger, New Goschenhoppen, urges payment by those who owe her for medicines." It was not necessary for this well-known herb granny with a fondness for youthful males to add the words "or else" to the end of her advertisement. Her notice also made it a clear public fact that she had taken up bed and board with a younger man, a proclivity that she had indulged in several times before her husband's fastidiously unmourned death in 1752. Her sexual scandals were recorded in the diary of the Lutheran minister Henry Melchior Muhlenberg. Whatever gossip they spread behind her back about her sexual prowess (a lot), the Pennsylvania Germans in her community never once doubted her curative powers.

Practitioners of powwow medicine were not only female. In fact, it was common for a male to learn the "ancient knowledge" from a female and then pass his understanding on to another female so that the line of learning alternated between sexes. Kinship was not required, although such arrangements are known to have existed in some Pennsylvania Dutch families and may trace to the Middle Ages. Several of the most popular charms date from at least the ninth century A.D. and doubtless could claim pagan roots assimilated by the early Germans. Many of the herbs discussed by Sauer had associations of this type: the daisy with Gaulish Mars, milk thistle with Brigantia, Good King Henry with her brother Lugus, and so forth. Indeed, it is difficult to escape such ancient connections when the very names of some of the herbs evoke just such a source.

A perfect example of this is goldenrod, which in Sauer's German appeared as *Heidnisch-Wundkraut,* "pagan woundwort." We might also take into account that the very word *brauchen* is not of German origin, but derived from Gaulish. Based on this, some scholars have suggested druidic origins for this type of medicine, but the truth may be much more complicated than that. In any event, it is doubtful that eighteenth-century practitioners of powwowing had any inkling of this muddled prehistory, since the evidence has only come to light more recently.

Furthermore, it is not clear from the herbal just how much Christopher Sauer himself believed in *Braucherei,* for while he was matter-of-fact about most of the remedies, when he came to the "unnatural" ones, he sometimes distanced himself from the material by noting that it came from an "old writer," or some source other than himself. Yet in many cases, the witch-stopping powers of herbs like angelica or juniper were accepted without comment, so Sauer must have been keenly aware of his audience, which might explain in part why he chose to permit such remedies in the herbal in the first place. Lest we tip the hand too much in favor of powwowing, let it be said that while such remedies may be scattered throughout the herbal, they do not play a large role in it. I have counted at most ten or eleven that would qualify.

Lastly, we must always keep in mind that Sauer's use of the term *unnatural* is not the same as the so-called Galenic division of *non-naturalia*, the loaded significations that I referred to earlier. These unnaturals were (1) air, (2) meat and drink, (3) sleep and watch, (4) exercise and rest, (5) emptiness and repletion, and lastly (6) affectations of the mind. These conditions and their various relationships to the body were much discussed by Renaissance authors on health and medicine. The *non-naturalia* were carried down into Sauer's era via such works as Louis Lemery's *Traité des aliments* (Paris, 1702). This particular book was translated into English under the title *Treatise of All Sorts of Foods* (London, 1745) and even sold in Boston, New York, and Philadelphia. For the most part, discussions of this kind were reserved for the scholarly books used as supplements to Sauer's herbal. Among these was Johann Jakob Schmidt's *Biblischer Medicus* (Biblical physician), published at Züllichau in 1743. This now brings us directly into biblical therapeutics, the antidote employed by the clergy to steer the flock clear of powwow medicines and quacks. There are several places in the Sauer herbal where Old and New Testament anecdotes overlap with Schmidt's form of therapies in perfect unison.

Biblical Therapeutics: Inward Cures for Outward Sufferings

On the title page of his herbal, Theodor Zwinger promised that his book would be useful to doctors, surgeons, apothecaries, gardeners, and men and women everywhere, but especially those living in the country at a distance from physicians. That last smattering of readers may have been the unwitting promoters behind Sauer's idea that a Zwinger digest could be sold to rural German colonists for the same reason. However, several problems emerge.

The first is literacy, which even Zwinger and Sauer knew was not universal. Secondly, even if a rich farmer could read, was the cost of owning such an expensive book counterweighed by immediate benefits? Probably not. High-sounding title pages are not a thing of the past, but the reality on the street, to put this in present-day lingo, was quite obvious. In a country setting, it was the minister and his wife who were often called upon to deal with local medical problems in neighborhoods where doctors were lacking. Taken a step further, there were ministers who actually believed that illnesses in their flock were brought on by spiritual shortcomings. Thus physical healing and spiritual healing merged into one. Sauer's herbal was cast in such a way as to prove highly useful to that sort of spiritual physician. There is ample evidence that it was used exactly in this manner.

Throughout the region settled by the Germans, whether Maryland, Pennsylvania, the Valley of Virginia, or deep into the hill country of the South, the preachers served as a focal point of the ethnic community. They were keepers of the German, for they preached in it. Like the Henkels of New Market, Virginia, they set up printing presses to further promote the word of Luther and, in some cases, their own patent remedies. Solomon Henkel's Compound Liniment of Sassafras Oil was well known in the Valley of Virginia and the Carolinas in the early 1800s. Dr. Wilhelm Stoy (1726–1801), a German Reformed minister in Lebanon, Pennsylvania, who was an actual contemporary and acquaintance of Christopher Sauer, both preached religion and practiced medicine. His cough drops and cure for mad dog bite remained popular for over a century.[10]

Furthermore, the credulity of country people in assuming special powers among the clergy has been well established on several occasions. Johann Conrad Andreae (d. 1754), a Lutheran minister in Old Goschenhoppen, gained considerable notoriety in the 1740s for his urine cures, which attracted people, flasks of urine in hand, for many counties around. The story of Lutheran minister John George Schmucker (1771–1854) of York, Pennsylvania, is similar, but for quite the opposite reason.[11] Upon inspecting a wen on the head of one of his parishioners, he happened to touch it. The man later claimed that the preacher's touch had cured him, and thus from all around the neighboring region, people began to appear at the minister's house pleading for cures. Laying on of hands is an important aspect of powwow medicine, so this association was quite natural to those who believed in it. Pastor Schmucker, however, was mortified; he eventually managed to quell the matter, but it was not easy.

On the other hand, plenty of preachers were quite willing to touch their parishioners in this manner, although Johann Jakob Schmidt's *Biblischer Medicus* was not specifically intended to be used this way. Schmidt—like Zwinger—carefully scrutinized the Bible for accounts of disease, curative herbs, and the ways in which they were used by the prophets and apostles. The Bible therefore becomes the framework for a reference book on medicine that interprets man's life and ailments in terms of moral homilies and heavenly punishments, as Sauer's discussion of tea so amply illustrates. Schmidt examined illnesses in the Bible, such as King Asa's foot problem, which he diagnosed as gout. This provided him with a discussion of gout and its treatments. Since Schmidt believed that disease arose from sin, bad air, and improper food, all three of these elements are treated extensively. There is even a section on herbs. The intent of the book was that it could be used by ministers and country doctors for curing people through a combination of medicine and prayer. The inscriptions on the blank pages of a copy that I inspected indicate that the book had been used in precisely this way by at least five generations of ministers well into the 1850s. Sauer's herbal has left a similar legacy.

The Sauer Legacy

After Christopher Sauer lost his business, his many friends and supporters came to his rescue financially. He turned to bookbinding for a living and died in 1784 after scrupulously paying back those debts. An advertisement by Lancaster,

Pennsylvania, bookseller Jacob Lahm in the December 7, 1792, *Neue Unpartheyische Lancaster Zeitung*—the local German newspaper—offered for sale "an old Swiss herbal" for 18 shillings 9 pence. There is something sad about this notice and the rather low price being quoted. I have always wondered to myself whether or not this was a copy of Zwinger, perhaps by odd chance even the one seized from Christopher Sauer and sold at auction, but of course, there is no way of knowing.

Michael Billmeyer bought Sauer's printing and publishing business and continued issuing books and almanacs for many years. Remedies from the Sauer herbal appeared over and over in Billmeyer's German-language almanacs as well as in many others throughout the early nineteenth century. In fact, in 1809 someone in Hanover, Pennsylvania, gathered parts of the herbal together in the form of a thirty-two-page book printed anonymously under the title *Ein vortreffliches Kräuter-Buch für Haus-Väter und Mütter* (An excellent herbal for husbands and housewives). That it was assembled from Sauer's herbal rather than directly from Zwinger cannot be doubted because it contains material that Sauer himself wrote—like the remark about growing anise in Pennsylvania. This is the first appearance of Sauer's herbal in true book form, albeit considerably digested.

Because of their importance to the history of book printing in colonial America, the Sauers have always remained a subject of scholarly interest. As the Church of the Brethren began to explore its own rich historical roots, the Sauers naturally surfaced as major icons in those church histories. Harry A. Brandt, one of the editors of the *Gospel Messenger*, published by the Brethren, wrote a series of articles about the Sauers that was published in book form in 1938. There was even a Sauer pageant reenacting scenes from their lives. Church historian John S. Flory recognized the value of the herbal and translated material dealing with sassafras in his 1908 history of Brethren printing.

The first serious study of the Sauer herbal, however, was undertaken by Thomas Brendle and Claude Unger in their *Folk Medicine of the Pennsylvania Germans*, issued in 1935 by the Pennsylvania German Society. This was followed in 1980 by Christa M. Wilmann's doctoral dissertation at the University of Pennsylvania, which explored the herbal as a social and cultural document. Much credit is due to Dr. Wilmann in establishing Sauer as the undisputed author of the herbal. The present book is very different from anything that has preceded. It is a complete translation that attempts to explain the herbal in terms of its botanical content.

In the past, only fragments of the herbal were studied; thus it was difficult to judge it as a unified work. What has emerged from the translation is an herbal unique for its insights and startling vignettes. I cannot forget the pointed image of a mother stroking her breasts with the hand of her dead newborn, the horse that has collapsed by the roadside, the old man whose crooked bones require him to be lifted into a tub for soaking, the willow leaves strewn upon the floor to cool the house, the scent of galingale hanging in the air. It is like peeping through the keyhole into a bedroom of the eighteenth century.

Notes

1. "Die Nutzbarkeit des Wasser-Trinkens," *Der Hoch-Deutsch Americanische Calender auf das Jahr 1772* (Philadelphia, 1771).

2. Elfriede Grabner, "Theodor Zwinger und die Heilkunde," in *Festschrift für Robert Wildhaber*, ed. Walter Escher, Theo Gantner, and Hans Trümpy (Basel: Verlag G. Krebs, 1973), 171–84.

3. William Buchan, *Domestic Medicine* (Exeter, N.H., 1843), 262.

4. Hermann Kaiser, "Kochen in Dunst und Qualm: Herdfeuer und Herdgerät im Rauchhaus," *Volkskunst* 10. (Nov. 1987): 5–10. A fuller description of the house may be found in William Woys Weaver, "The Pennsylvania German House," *Winterthur Portfolio* 21, no. 4 (winter 1986): 243–64.

5. Johann Jacob Woyt, *Gazophylacium Medico-Physicum; oder, Schatz-Kammer medicinisch- und natürlicher Dinge* (Leipzig, 1784), 1155–56.

6. Johann Christian Wolf, *Neues Leipziger Koch-Buch* (Frankfurt, 1779), 25.

7. Johann Christian Förster, *Braunschweigisches Kochbuch* (Braunschweig, 1789), 19.

8. *Bernisches Koch-Büchlein* (Bern, 1749), 4.

9. Barbara Wheaton, *Savoring the Past* (Philadelphia: University of Pennsylvania Press, 1983), 77.

10. Henry Harbaugh, *The Fathers of the German Reformed Church* (Lancaster, Pa., 1872), 2: 82.

11. William B. Sprague, *Annals of the American Lutheran Pulpit* (New York, 1869), 98.

Part II
The Compendious Herbal
(1762-1778)

Remarks about the Translation
and Use of Sauer's Measurements

My intent has been to make the translation of this herbal as useful to the reader as possible. The herbs have been rearranged in alphabetical order according to their English names. The dates provided correspond to the issue of the almanac in which the herb originally appeared. I have also added editorial head notes as well as numerous footnotes to clarify many of the issues that surface in the text of the herbal itself. Translation of the actual text, however, has necessitated a compromise almost at every turn of phrase, since Sauer's language was essentially a child of baroque German, but spoken with obvious dialect inflections. His German is also riddled with syntax and terminology borrowed from colonial English; indeed, some sentences actually appear to have been thought in English and written in German. Some sentence structure is therefore horrendous or at least tedious to follow; in places this dumpling-lumpiness was simply unavoidable. On all levels, Dr. Zwinger's herbal is much easier to read, even though it is composed in an erudite baroque German peculiar to the Swiss. But Zwinger's odd Swiss vocabulary, like *Anken* for butter (or more broadly for cooking fat), does not always appear in standard German dictionaries, not even the old and very thorough two-volume dictionary that I used while working on this project.

Sauer realized this problem, and much to his credit, he usually took Dr. Zwinger's scholarly Swiss German and retold it in his own Pennsylvanian way. But sometimes there are obvious Zwingerian passages loaded with highly specialized and clearly unavoidable medical terms, such as *zertheilen*, which means "to discuss a swelling invisibly." A discutient poultice gradually reduces swelling, thus it "discusses" it. There are probably very few doctors today who would actually say it that way, so I have translated such terms rather freely. It also becomes a toss of the coin when calling black bile "charred choler," but since Zwinger and Sauer adhered to humoral medicine, the latter term would seem both appropriate and rather more representative of the tone of the original text.

Since it was Sauer's intent to communicate with country people, he often worded things in a more colloquial manner anyway. This has created an odd mixture of expressions and a lack of consistency in describing one thing throughout the sixteen-year period that it took to issue his herbal. His *Brustgeschwüre* therefore can appear as sores of the chest, pectoral sores, or empyema. The choice is purely arbitrary. But

Sauer did weed out a lot of the learned terms, especially Latin ones. For example, *oxymel scilliticum* became sea onion honey. And where Dr. Zwinger may speak of a *compositum* (electuary), Sauer substituted *Latwerge*, a word employed by every country housewife for such things as apple butter, peach butter, or indeed, any thick jam. I have tried to preserve some of the quaint flavor of this language, but I have had to walk a middle line.

A good example of my balancing act would be the German word *Theriac*, which is used in two senses. It is either a cure-all, as employed in Sauer's discussion of an *omnimorbiam* under blue mallow, or an electuary known as Venice treacle. I refrained from translating this as Venice treacle because too many food and social historians have already misread this as a type of molasses—oddly enough, Venice treacle was sometimes employed in eighteenth-century cookery. It only looks like molasses, but it is much thicker, and quite spicy. So instead of theriac I opted for the old medical term *theriaca andromaci*; it does not appear this way in either Zwinger or Sauer, but at least it will be clear to the reader that we are dealing with a medical compound. Likewise, Sauer does not say that his "mustard compound" is mustard sauce, but that is what it is, so I have translated it that way. In cases like this, I had to reach for the sense rather than relying on a more literal rendition.

This is especially true where procedures are discussed, such as boiling, then straining, and pureeing, or where something may be prepared over smokeless heat (a charcoal brazier, for example). My own knowledge of eighteenth-century cookery and the proper deployment of hearth utensils was immensely useful in deciphering what followed what in many of the recipes. German has an interesting way of carrying implied meanings in minor twists of phrases or the addition of a simple prefix. This does not often come through in English, so I was obliged to expand verbally on some procedures, which would otherwise lose a reader completely. They are as clear as I dare make them without departing too far from Sauer's German.

In addition to this, there are numerous errors in the almanac where Sauer's apprentice typesetter obviously misread his boss's handwriting. *Yast* appeared as a mysterious new vital fluid in the body, where the ambiguous and obviously intended *Saft* would have covered a multitude of internal juices. *Mistel* (mistletoe) is very often printed as *Mispel*, the word for medlar (a pearlike fruit), thus making no sense whatsoever when employed in connection with hazelnut, linden, or oak trees. Under oak, words like *Häutlein*, "thin film," appear without explanation; it required extensive research on my part to ascertain that the white film on the outside of acorns was intended. This may seem like a curious and ephemeral ingredient for medicine, but this excretion of the tree was once considered as valuable as mistletoe and sap. One wonders, however, just how many of Sauer's readers would have worked that out on their own.

I am certain that the translation could probably be made more perfect here and there, and I may even have stumbled on a few obscure points, but for the general reader, I feel confident that this translation can be relied on. Dr. Don Yoder, professor emeritus of the University of Pennsylvania, has gone over the translation with me several times, for it took two minds to deal with the peculiarities of eighteenth-century Pennsylvania High German. There are not many people today who know how to handle that extinct hybrid language as effectively as he does.

Both of us kept in mind that the primary purpose of this book was to retrieve a long-lost classic and to unlock its fascinating secrets, and I believe our translation has kept to that goal. Medical terms are explained in a separate index at the back, and I have cross-indexed the entire herbal myself so that all of the material may be accessed more easily by subject and category.

Measurements

Sauer intended that his herbal be used in the home. Where precise quantities are called for, Sauer used standard English measures as practiced then throughout the British Empire, with two notable exceptions. I refer here to his use of the *loth* and *quint*, common household measures among emigrants from German-speaking Europe. These cannot be neatly converted into English equivalents, although very close approximations are possible.

To explain how this worked, I shall refer here to volume 3 of Johann Samuel Halle's *Magie; oder, Die Zauberkräfte der Natur* (Berlin, 1785), a book once used by Henry Augustus Muhlenberg of Pennsylvania to make just such conversions. In this volume there is a short entry called *Landapotheke* (country apothecary) which outlines the use of medical measures for the home similar to those employed in the Sauer herbal. First of all, a medical pound (dry weight) contains 12 not 16 ounces. One medical ounce equals 2 loths or 8 quints. One quint contains 3 scruples, and 1 scruple equals 20 grains.

Under liquid measures used by apothecaries, 8 drams equal 1 fluid ounce; 16 ounces equal 1 pint (also expressed by Sauer as l liquid pound); 8 pints equal 1 gallon. Other measurements include 4 gills, which equal one-half pint; 60 drops equal 1 dram. One dram is the liquid counterpart of 1 quint dry measure. Therefore, 8 quints equal 1 ounce dry measure, which equals 30 grams. One loth equals 0.5 American ounces or 15 grams. One pound (Sauer's measure) equals 24 loths or 360 grams.

All of Sauer's culinary recipes adhere to a medical pound of 360 grams, not the roughly 500 grams we now equate with an American pound. In other words, the medical pound is roughly 9 to 10 tablespoons less than a culinary one. This is enough to make a large difference in the strength of certain ingredients.

In the culinary recipes that I have added to the herbal, the quantities have been translated as given in the various texts. They are not medical measurements, but rather expressed in the highly variable measurements of the principality or dukedom in which the cookbook was printed. For example, recipes from cookbooks printed in Stuttgart adhere to Württemberg measure, recipes from cookbooks printed at Nuremberg adhere to Franconian measure, and so forth.

As a general rule of thumb, 1 loth is roughly equivalent to our modern tablespoon measure, that is, about 15 grams. Sauer used it incorrectly for both dry and liquid ingredients (a liquid loth is technically 1 dram), which means that the reader may interpret this more or less as a level tablespoon. Botanical medicines such as Sauer's allow for some leeway in measure without serious harm. Smaller and more complicated, however, is Sauer's *Quintlein*, which I have consistently transcribed as one quint because a quint is absolute measure, not something that can be made into a diminutive as his German would suggest. Technically, *Quintlein* should have been written *Quentgen* or *Quentchen*; his word seems to have been an idiomatic way of writing the medical term *Quent*. In English, *Quent* is written "drachm" or "dram."

In the cookery recipes, the absolute weights are different, for one quint is one-fifth of a loth, or in American terms, one-fifth of a tablespoon. The Germans who settled in colonial America measured things in quantities divisible by five, so they were not thinking in terms exactly like their English-speaking neighbors, not until after the revolution, when the U.S. government imposed its own set of standard measures. In any case, a quint cannot be equated with our teaspoon (which is one-third of a loth), or part of a teaspoon as we now divide it. A culinary quint is roughly 3.5 grams and should be treated as grams by anyone trying to interpret the culinary measurements.

Where Sauer used the word *tablespoon* in his text (rather than loth), he was actually suggesting that any convenient spoon will do, although this probably meant a serving spoon, which might hold as much as three tablespoons. A *Kochlöffel*, or cooking spoon, the sort generally made of wood, held about 2 loths or 2 tablespoons. But the tablespoon in Sauer does not need to be so exact; it is just something larger than a loth and smaller than an English gill (4 tablespoons).

To keep these distinctions clearly in front of the reader, I have left loths and quints in the text rather than to introduce a confusing time warp by trying to convert them into metric measure. Metric weights, as introduced by Napoleon, certainly did not exist as a form of household measure in Sauer's day. Loths and quints will also serve as a constant reminder to the reader not to regard these quantities in English colonial terms.

Finally, a valid question does arise as to why Sauer chose to mix his measures, for some are definitely English, while others are obviously German. Part of this was due to the split personality of the German community itself, which lived more isolated from mainstream English culture prior to the revolution. One might say that a "Chinatown" mentality prevailed, and as long as the German element relied on scientific, medical, and culinary books printed in Germany as a primary source of information, there was a continuing need for loths and quints. Needless to say, scientific works of the period, such as those by Johann Jacob Woyt or Johann Friedrich Zückert, whom I cite throughout the herbal, rely on measurements akin to the metric system or on standard apothecary measures that have not changed radically over time. While we cannot underestimate Sauer's ability to absorb knowledge from the books he owned, sold, or published, we must also keep in mind that he had no formal education. He presumed the same of his readers.

Agaric (White Agaric)
Polyporusofficinalis
Sauer: *Lerchenschwamm* (1778)

The Agaricaceae comprise a huge family of gilled mushrooms, some famous for their culinary merits, others infamous for their deadly poisons. The name is of ancient origin, referring to Agraria in Sarmatia, a region that supplied the fungus to Greek physcians. Linnaeus incorrectly assigned the name to a different family and genus. His error is now part of accepted nomenclature, when in fact the true agaric of the herbalists was a white corky fungus found growing on larch trees.

This fungus is native throughout Europe, Asia, and North America, but the best was thought to be the agaric from Siberia. In Sauer's day, Siberian agaric was sent to Hamburg, Germany, where it was processed for the medical trade. From there it came to colonial America, most often in powdered form.

Sauer's remarks about infusing agaric could apply either to the powder or to dry agaric of native origin. What Sauer did not mention is that agaric paralyzes the nerves of the sweat glands; thus it was considered useful in checking the loss of body liquids through copious sweating. But because it worked slowly, its power was often increased by mixing it with ground ginger or the ground seeds of wild carrot. It was also used for epilepsy (the "falling evil" mentioned below), but generally administered as an internal medicine given with syrup of vinegar.

Agaric operates through its divers earthy salts, as well as through a caustic, soft resinous component. It is thus endowed with rather bitter aftertasting compounds with the capacity to purge both by stool and urine, and to expectorate phlegm from the chest.

In particular, while it operates in expectorating phlegm, agaric also purges the veins of the heart and lungs, along with obstructed urine. But because it takes effect slowly, it is generally administered in association with other purging medications. For persons afflicted with the falling evil, an agaric decoction instead of soap should be used to scrub the head.

Agaric is employed with great favor in laxatives made with wine. But it is also possible to achieve an excellent extraction of agaric's properties by infusing it in brandy, and then boiling it to a soft extract that can then be rolled into balls and administered in the amount of twenty to twenty-four grains as laxative pills.

Agrimony
Agrimonia eupatoria
Sauer: *Odermennig* (1764)

The species name of this herb is derived from King Mithradates VI Eupator of Pontus (123–63 B.C.), who was alleged to have discovered the medical properties of this plant. He is the same king whose cure for poisoning is discussed on page 43. Sauer's agrimony

is not native to North America, although we have many related species. The
Agrimonia eupatoria hirsuta of Muhlenberg (1813), now called Agrimonia hirsuta,
is perhaps the closest American relative and was certainly widely used as a native sub-
stitute.

The agrimony of Sauer is a wild herb found growing in woodsy places or along shady
hedgerows throughout Europe. It is perennial, and its spiky yellow flowers are indeed
quite an addition to any woodland garden. The entire plant, even the roots, have a spicy
sweet scent, and for this reason agrimony was much used to flavor tea.

Agrimony is endowed with a bitter balsamic salt, and for this reason it possesses a warm, dry nature. It purges and cleanses by urine and sweat, and dries out the fluxes.

As an herb for the liver, agrimony stands foremost among other hepatic plants, for it opens severe obstructions of the liver. To achieve this, take a handful of the leaves, boil them in two quarts of water, then drink according to your wants. This decoction also loosens the spleen and drives out jaudice and dropsy, as well as fevers of long continuance brought on by obstructions of the liver and spleen. In addition, agrimony kills worms, promotes urine, and is good against cold piss.

For those with afflictions of the liver, this herb serves especially well when it is infused in white wine and then drunk on a daily basis. The dried leaves of agrimony ground to a powder and a half quint taken regularly every evening is also good for liver patients who cannot hold their water. Or, take one loth of agrimony leaves, half a loth of acorn, eighty grains of frankincense, forty grains each of coriander seeds, bole armeniac, and gum arabic; one ounce of well washed and dried chicken craw;[1] and one-fourth pound of sugar. Grind all of this to a fine powder and take a pinch of it in a glass of wine every morning and evening.

The following decoction has been found to fortify against jaundice: Take two handfuls of agrimony leaves, a handful each of succory and fumitory, two loths of celandine root, and a quint each of anise and fennel seeds. Chop it all very fine, put this in a new earthenware vessel or in a pewter jar, then pour a gallon of water over it. Cover tightly and set this in a kettle of boiling water. Let it boil for a few hours, then set aside to cool. Strain and administer a copious dose of this to the patient every morning and evening.

Agrimony ground to powder, and a half quint taken in warm wine regularly, will ward off the quartan ague. This dosage should be taken when it is thought that the fever is about to commence and it is thus necessary to lie down. One can also boil

---

1. The chicken craw is not so unusual, considering that desiccated frogs were similarly ground and administered during the Middle Ages.

three handfuls of agrimony in a gallon of water and allow the patients to drink from this according to their wants.

For scall, take the juice of freshly pressed agrimony, heat it until warm, and wash the head with it. Or, boil the leaves in wine and wash the scalp with the decoction while it is still warm.

Take one loth of dried sorrel root, two handfuls of agrimony, and one loth each of sarsaparilla and sassafras root. Boil this mixture in a gallon of water for as long as it would take to hard-cook an egg. Then strain and store away for use. This decoction strengthens a feeble stomach and liver, and cleanses the blood of mordant matter.

If agrimony leaves and elecampane root are boiled, and the feet are bathed in the liquid, this will heal cracked skin on the feet and heels caused by exposure to the cold.

The smoke of agrimony will drive away poisonous vermin.

Used as a dressing for open wounds, agrimony makes an excellent vulnerary herb for surgeons.

If one takes two handfuls of agrimony leaves and a handful each of sanicle, betony, and broad-leafed plantain, and chops it all very small, boils this in a gallon of water, then strains it, you will have a valuable vulnerary potion for healing internal injuries, provided that copious doses are taken each morning and evening. This decoction also serves as a dressing for healing fresh, external wounds.

Distilled agrimony water is quite effectual for all maladies of the liver and spleen. It opens obstructions of the same, drives out jaundice, quartan ague, and dropsy, and kills the worms, provided four or five loths of it are drunk every morning and evening. Agrimony water also serves against injuries and sores of the mouth and gums, and heals scurvy of the gums as well.

Almond
Prunus dulcis
Sauer: *Mandel* (1771)

Sauer's lengthy discourse on almonds needs little additional commentary, except for two points. The first is that both sweet and bitter almonds were mostly imported from Spain and Portugal during the eighteenth century, and for this reason they were not cheap. Sauer's parenthetical comment below that not everyone could take advantage of his advice was addressed to just those individuals for whom costly imported almonds were out of reach. We find, elsewhere in the herbal, remedies for similar conditions (such as chapped or cracked nipples) utilizing cheaper and more readily available ingredients.

The other point I should like to make is that his recipe for almond milk based on a mild lye created from calcined hartshorn is extremely old. This process dates to at least the Middle Ages and may in fact have evolved among the Greeks of antiquity. Medieval archaeological sites in many parts of Europe have yielded an abundance of evidence for workshops specializing in the processing of deer antlers for salts used in baking as well as for medical purposes. But the use of hartshorn for the production of almond milk was essentially an application affordable only by the very rich. By Sauer's era, this economic barrier, at least in colonial America, was one of the dividing lines between urban and rural standards of living.

Aside from their earthy principles, sweet almonds possess an abundance of oil tempered by salty, fluid moisture, thereby having the faculty of mollifying, of easing and soothing mordant humors, and of stilling pain. But in their shells and skins, almonds possess a raw, salty oil that burns the throat and causes hoarseness, if you indulge in them without restraint. This unhappy consequence is especially true of old almonds from which the tempering moisture has already evaporated. Shelled sweet almonds do provide the body and the blood with much nourishment, yet if eaten in the skins, they tend to constipate. On the other hand, freshly pressed oil of almonds will open such obstructions gently.

Bitter almonds possess just as much oil as the sweet ones, but the oil is mingled with certain bitter-tasting, caustic principals. For this reason, bitter almonds have the faculty of cleansing, of opening, of loosening obstructions, of promoting urine, and of allaying windiness.

Freshly shelled almonds strengthen the chest, stomach, intestines, liver, kidneys, and bladder. The freshly pressed oil of plump, sweet almonds possesses the unique faculty of easing raw, burning throats; of benefiting consumptives and hectics; of quieting the cough and burning urine; of healing disorders of the kidney and bladder; and of stilling pain in the bowels and womb. In particular, it has the reputation of easing colic and gravel, as well as the movement of stool. For these conditions, you may take three or four spoonfuls at a time.

As soon as a child is born, it can be given oil of sweet almond in order to rid it of crudities of the womb and thus prevent convulsions.

You can prepare a pleasant and nourishing panada for invalids by pounding almonds to a paste, then gently heating this over a low fire with sugar and rosewater. This food is not only healthy, invigorating, and tasty, it is also a sure remedy for diarrhea.

The oil of bitter almond is highly celebrated as a cure for deafness and disorders of the ears. Daub a piece of cotton with the oil and place this in the ear canal, but refrain from excessive application, lest the delicate parts of the ear become too flaggy.

For all fluxes of the stomach, an effective almond milk can be prepared as follows: Take one-half loth of calcined hartshorn, boil this in a quart of water, then take a quarter of a pound of sweet almonds and put them into the lye. Let them steep until the skins loosen, then plunge them into cold water so that they do not lose their properties. After shelling them, pound the almonds to a smooth paste in a wooden or marble mortar, then place this on a fine linen cloth. Set this over a bowl and pour a little of the hartshorn solution on it. Work the paste through the cloth with a wooden spoon, then add the remaining lye solution to the pressings. This almond milk can be made sweet and pleasant-tasting by adding sugar and a little rosewater. When mothers and wet nurses suffer from a deficiency of milk, give the child some of this almond milk to drink. (Not everyone enjoys the luxury of following this advice.)

To prevent cracks and ulcers on the nipples of nursing mothers, take one loth of fresh stag's tallow and let it dissolve in an earthenware vessel over a gentle fire. Add to this some unsalted butter the size of a hazelnut and a spoonful of brandy. Stir it for a short time, then take it from the fire. Continue to stir it until it thickens. One month before their confinement, pregnant women can smear this lotion on their nipples twice daily, and the nipples will never become cracked. If this preventative is neglected until the nipples are already cracked and open, then instead of brandy, add cream and a little white lead to the mixture. This will readily heal the condition.

Aloe
Aloe vera and *Aloe perryi*
Sauer: *Aloe* (1763)

Sauer made it clear in his text that he was not discussing a particular aloe species, but rather the processed juice of the aloe, which was boiled to a viscid, nearly solidified residue. This byproduct could come from any number of species. In Sauer's period, the residue was poured into old case bottles, labeled, and thus sold to apothecaries. The substance became unstable and medically worthless after a few months, so it was necessary to keep fresh supplies on hand. With these factors in mind, it is quite likely that Sauer dealt with at least two basic types of aloe, both of which were grown and processed in the West Indies.

The first of these was the so-called Barbados or hepatic aloe (Aloe vera, *sometimes called* Aloe barbadensis), *like all aloes, a plant of African origin. Several closely related species were introduced into the West Indies during the 1500s, and all of them were commonly sold under the rubric of Barbados aloe.* Aloe vera *is the best known and is a common houseplant today, for its pale gray-green leaves adorn many sunny windowsills under another popular name: burn aloe.*

The other aloe was the Zanzibar or socrotine aloe (Aloe perryi, *formerly called* Aloe zanzibarica), *which was known to the ancient Greeks and employed as a laxative. A dark green aloe with small, spiky leaves, it was considered one of the safest of all herbal purgatives. Sauer often mentioned it in this connection, especially in preparations where several laxative ingredients were combined. However, in his discussion of aloes and their uses below, Sauer did not clearly state which type he had in mind. Perhaps, for the conditions he mentioned, this distinction may not have been necessary. Lastly, aloe was also sold in dry form. This served as the basis for the powders and decoctions mentioned several times throughout the herbal.*

No part of this plant is used save the sap boiled to a thick mass, which we apothecaries then refer to as aloe. This residue possesses a dry, warm nature that is slightly astringent. It cleanses, purifies, prevents putrification, and purges gently. Aloe should be avoided by those with injuries in the privates or who are troubled by hemorrhoids, or by those who suffer from inflamed outgrowths of the fundament.

A quint of dried aloe ground fine, then mixed with half as much myrrh and strewn upon fresh bloody wounds, will glutinate the injury, heal it by encouraging the growth of new flesh, and stay all manner of putrification. For this reason, aloe is especially good when applied to old abscesses, angry fistulas, and purulent, rotten, stinking wounds. If you desire, add a little honey to the aloe to produce an ointment. This is a capital healing remedy and protects against gangrene.

Paracelsus created an excellent elixir out of aloe, myrrh, and saffron that he called *elixir proprietatis*. To make it, take one ounce each of these ingredients, grind to a fine powder, and then place the powder in a glass jar. Pour one pint of good quality brandy over the mixture, stop it up, and let this stand a few days in the hot sun or on a warm stove, shaking it frequently. This yields an excellent home remedy which can be taken in doses of twenty to forty drops each morning and evening.

Elixir proprietatis strengthens the stomach, encourages the appetite, kills worms, operates as an antidote to all manner of poisons, and serves as a prophylactic against the plague and other contagions. Some persons first place the finely ground myrrh in the above-mentioned jar with enough *oleum tarariper deliquium* to create a paste. This is allowed to stand a few days, then the other ingredients are added to it along with the brandy. This elixir is also excellent for healing new or old wounds.

Aloe will yield good results as a purgative when put into brandy bitters and taken from time to time in the morning. For those in want of such a laxative, take the equivalent of twenty to forty grains of aloe. But because this remedy is extremely bitter tasting and unpleasant, don't take it all at once, rather, mix it with comfits or with an elixir. This remedy is especially helpful to those of a phlegmatic, choleric temperament, but much less so for anyone of a hot and passionate disposition.

Horses with worms or horses that cannot urinate may be helped quite well with aloe. Take half an ounce of dried aloe, grind it to a powder, then pour hot water over this. Stir well, then administer the decoction through the horse's nostril or mouth by means of a funnel or horn. If this does not help after the first application, repeat the dosage about six to twelve hours later. For better results, a gill of olive oil can be added to the second dose.

Angelica
Angelica archangelica
Sauer: *Angelika* (1764)

By the time Sauer began publishing his herbal, angelica was already well established in colonial gardens. Its uses were many, especially in the culinary department, where the candied stems and jellies were used extensively in pastries and confections. Sauer made no mention of these culinary applications, perhaps because they were features of a refined style of cookery not commonly found on country tables. Yet J. W. Cooper's Experienced Botanist or Indian Physician *noted that even in 1840 the seeds were still commonly used to flavor homemade gin and cordials or ground and used in cookery like ground fennel. Whatever the case, Sauer was much more concerned about differentiating between the garden variety of angelica (he specifically used the word* zahm, *"culti- vated") and that which had naturalized in the wild. The reason was simple: wild angel- ica could be confused with poison hemlock (page 165), with deadly results. Furthermore, also growing in the wild was purple angelica or masterwort (page 206), a plant with distinct medical uses of its own. Purchasing angelica from an apothecary was of course the most certain recourse, especially for those in need of the dry root for carminative remedies. The best and most expensive angelica root for medical purposes was imported from Spain, but Sauer probably prepared his own as well.*

The angelica of our gardens is of a warm and dry nature, and possesses the singular faculty of repelling poisons, of fortifying the heart, of operating by sweat, and of bringing down the menses. It also kills worms, loosens obstructions, and even heals fresh wounds and old injuries. For use in medicine, the root should be gathered when the sun is in the sign of Gemini and whilst the moon is passing into Cancer.

When the winds of death are blowing, angelica makes an excellent prophylactic against dangerous contagion, provided you keep the root in your mouth and chew on it, especially if you intend to walk abroad in public places. But should anyone be attacked by pestilence, immediately administer an infusion consisting of half a quint of ground angelica root and one quint of *Theriaca Andromaci*[2] dissolved in the distilled water of holy thistle, then send the patient to bed with plenty of covers and let him sweat out the contagion.

It has been discovered through everyday use that angelica provides a particularly good remedy for injuries brought about by witchcraft. When a person is a victim of such unnatural afflictions, the following potion has proved especially effective: Take half a handful each of the leaves of angelica, devil's bit, the topmost sprigs of Saint- John's-wort, periwinkle, sanicle, Venus's goldilocks,[3] and mugwort. These herbs should be chopped fine and put into a large pewter flask with two quarts of fresh springwater and a quart of white wine. Bring this to a boil in a kettle of hot water. Once the infusion has boiled up, let it cool. When cold, open the flask, but not before, lest the properties of the herbs disperse into the air. Strain this through a cloth and administer it warm to the victim, six loths per dose, morning and evening.

For those who have drunk unclean water and are apprehensive that living vermin may have entered their persons, take every day half a quint of ground angelica root in a glass of wine.[4]

Take a loth each of angelica root, avens root, root of butter burr, holy thistle, the leaves of betony, and juniper berries, and half a loth of wormwood, and chop it all up

2. *Theriaca Andromaci*, otherwise known as Venice treacle, is an electuary consisting of some seventy ingredi- ents prepared in honey. The name derives from *theriaca*, a Roman antidote to snakebite. Sauer consistently wrote it in German as *Theriac*.

3. Venus's goldilocks or golden maidenhair is a type of moss (*Polytrichum juniperum*).

4. Dr. Sarnigshausen of Philadelphia recommended a similar infusion of ground angelica root in wine or beer as a remedy for yellow fever. See his addendum to Peter Gabriel's *Kurzer Bericht von der Pest* (Philadelphia, 1793), 63.

very fine. Put this in a large glass vessel and pour double-rectified brandy over it until it covers the mass by the breadth of a finger. Stop it up carefully and let it infuse fourteen days. Then pour off the brandy and wring out the herb mixture in a cloth to extract all the remaining juices. Keep this infusion for future use in a well-sealed glass container. Take one-half or a full teaspoonful in the morning before breakfast. This is excellent for all manner of cold disorders of the stomach, and for gripes brought on by chills. It also drives forth worms and protects against contagion and pestilential fevers.

For an excellent remedy for women suffering from hysterics, administer two doses consisting of half a quint each of ground angelica root and zedoary dissolved in water of lemon balm. Distilled angelica water and oil of angelica also possess all the above-mentioned virtues.

Anise

Pimpinella anisum
Sauer: *Anise* (1763)

Anise is an annual growing about two feet tall. The leafy part resembles coriander, although the leaves are more deeply divided and fernlike. However, unlike coriander, the flowers of anise are yellowish white and quite fragrant. The herb thrives in hot, sunny locations on rich limestone ground. Since it is native to the eastern Mediterranean and prefers hot, dry summers, anise does not always come to seed in New England. It is even less reliable in Old England. This may explain why it is so rarely discussed in old English herbals.

Anise is not missing from Gerard's herbal, for he illustrated the entire plant and even had success growing it. But Gerard devoted at best a few lines to the herb in favor of a much lengthier discussion of Chinese star anise, which by 1633 was nothing less than a luxury and most certainly a curiosity. The late British food historian Elizabeth David once observed that the English simply did not like anise and that wherever it appeared in recipes, they usually substituted caraway in its stead.

This is perfectly consistent with the cultural bias one finds in early American recipes of British origin, no better example being that of Philadelphia seed cake. This cookie was an extremely popular street food hawked during the eighteenth and nineteenth centuries under the name of Apees Cake. Those sold to English-speaking customers were flavored with caraway seed rather than anise; those sold to Germans always contained anise and were stamped with an A so that there would be no confusion. Christopher Sauer was correct in stating that anise thrives in Pennsylvania, provided it is sown early. But to sow it in March, as he suggests, is asking for trouble: March sowings are done in cold frames or under glass bells, or cloches (a popular method in that period). However, once established, anise becomes almost as invasive in our gardens as coriander and the lowly, but highly useful, chickweed (page 96).

In regions of the United States where anise may be difficult to grow, I would suggest bronze fennel. This plant is perennial and produces a seed similar in flavor to anise. It may lack some of the medical benefits of anise, but for culinary purposes it can be treated as an equivalent. In addition, the leaves of bronze fennel are extremely ornamental and provide a constant supply of salad greens from early spring until frost.

Of this herb, nothing is used save the seed. This seed contains a volatile, slightly oily salt, and thus possesses the virtues of warming, of drying out, and of opening obstructions. It fortifies the head, chest, and stomach, and purges phlegmatic humors. The seed is employed in medicine both internally and externally.

Anise operates as a galactogogue for nursing mothers, and sweetens the breath. When chewed and swallowed, it strengthens weak eyes, removes chill from the chest, staves off coughing fits, and is serviceable in cases of inveterate cough of the lungs. It warms and strengthens a cold stomach, and purges vapors. Thus, anise should be employed diligently for phlegmatic dropsy. It is also good against bellyache, colic, lumbago, and kidney pain caused by swellings or by inflammation.

When young children cry too much, add a teaspoonful of finely powdered aniseed together with an equal amount of finely powdered eggshells or crab's eyes to their breakfast and evening porridge. This quiets their colic and sour stomach, and is far safer than other much stronger remedies, or even than the highly vaunted Cure of Mithradates,[5] for this latter cure performs as good a service as Gottfried's cordial, yet proves injurious when taken too often, one dose too quick upon the other.

Aniseed placed in a bottle with rum, brandy, or wine, and a draft of it taken when needed provides adults with an excellent remedy for colic and gripes caused by obstructed vapors or chills. It fortifies the stomach and provides against divers infirmities of the chest. However, this cordial is inadvisable for children of tender years, since it is wont to enflame their delicate livers. Eight to ten drops of the oil of anise in a little sugar should prevail if taken for chest troubles; or when added to a glass of brandy, likewise prevails against colds, colic, or gripes. In fact, this latter remedy serves excellently for all the aforementioned infirmities.

Anise grows plentifully in Pennsylvania, and without much trouble, any who desire can grow enough in a small plot in his garden to fulfill the wants of his household throughout the year. The seed is sown in March.

5. The Cure of Mithradates was an electuary (pastelike marmalade) made of numerous strong-tasting ingredients, including penny cress (see page 221). A Latin recipe for it, quoted from the *Brandenburg Dispensatory*, was given in Dr. Johann Jacob Woyt's *Gazophylacium Medico-Physicum; oder, Schatz-Kammer medicinisch- und natürlicher Dinge* (Leipzig, 1784), col. 1424. The cure was considered an effective antidote to poisoning and has a long and fascinating history in medicine. It was named for King Mithradates Eupator of Pontus (123–63 B.C.), who allegedly first used it.

Apple Tree
Malus sylvestris x *Malus pumila*
Sauer: *Aepfel* (1769)

Judging by the handful of varieties now commonly seen in groceries, it is sometimes dif-
ficult to imagine the enormous selection of apples once enjoyed in early America. Joseph
Horsfield of Bethlehem, Pennsylvania, who styled himself both master gardener and a
breeder of orchard fruits, announced in 1811 that he was selling 22,000 grafted apple
trees representing over sixty varieties.[6] Writing a few years earlier in 1804, Dr. James
Mease of Philadelphia took note of this huge abundance: "Apples abound in
Pennsylvania, and in every state in the union, except in the maritime districts of the
Carolinas and Georgia, which are sandy and level and the air replete with humidity.
In Pennsylvania we have a very great variety of apples, many of which are equal in size,
beauty and flavor to any found in the world."[7] This statement was as true forty years
earlier as it was when Mease wrote it, so it is no surprise that Sauer would have found
it desirable to include home remedies based on this extremely popular fruit. While period
cookery texts focus on codlins and pippins for such things as pies and puddings, the Sauer
herbal singles out only certain types of apples for medical use. Indeed, the suggestions for
utilizing apples that have gone off or that have turned mealy for application in poul-
tices certainly exposes the native frugality so characteristic of folk remedies dating from
this period.

Apples are commonly divided into six categories, namely: watery, dry, acidulous, sweet, wine-flavored, and spicy. Watery apples are the most unwholesome, since they weigh the stomach with such a quantity of dropsical juice that the blood is rendered mordant. Apples of the dry sort, particularly the sweet ones, are difficult to digest and bring no comfort to feeble stomachs, although they are not as hurtful as the first kind. Apples that are very sour injure cold, weak stomachs, yet they are beneficial to san-guine persons of quick digestion, since they cool rather gently, keep the belly open, and thus disperse the heat.

However, wine-flavored apples that are neither sweet nor sour provide the health-iest food, on the condition that the stomach is not overloaded with them, but that they are eaten in moderation. Spicy apples, especially those with an intense, pleasant aroma, are indeed the healthiest of all. Of course, there is no lasting nourishment or fortification gained from the labors of digesting any sort of fruit, yet the spicy apples just mentioned do possess certain refreshment. They also operate well in the mitiga-tion of the sharp, acidic principal, and have been found quite efficacious in the treat-ment of scurvy. In particular, when quantities of salted meats have been consumed, these apples are quite serviceable when made use of on a regular basis, whether raw or cooked.[8]

6. "Bekantmachung," *Der Eastoner Deutsche Patriot*, October 16, 1811.
7. A. F. M. Willich, *The Domestic Encyclopaedia*, ed. James Mease (Philadelphia, 1804), 1:97.
8. This remark alludes to the fact that many poor people did not eat fresh meat regularly; apples were espe-cially important in this respect for persons who undertook long voyages, not to mention an integral part of the sailors' mess.

Cider made from ripe apples late in the fall possesses a warming, fortifying character, provided it is well aged but not yet gone sour. It is useful in treating stones and gravels when drunk in moderation. But when taken in excess, or after the cider has soured, this beverage is extremely injurious, since it induces irregular flow of the pulse and chokes the blood with mordant matter. Perhaps this fact is contributing to the reason why we are now hearing so much about new cases of flying gout and rheumatic disorders.

Half a quint of powdered frankincense put into a sweet apple that is then baked in hot ashes provides a good remedy for pectoral sores or for pleurisy, since this brings the sores to suppuration and expels their foulness. But before attempting this treatment, the patient should first be bled from the arm on the same side of the body as the pain.[9]

Sweet apples that have turned mealy, cooked to the consistency of porridge in olive or linseed oil—or better yet cooked in oil of chamomile mingled with a little saffron, and then applied as a dressing as hot as the patient can bear it—are effective against pleurisy. Heated repeatedly, this dressing diminishes the inflammation and prickling pain, or where there is no diminishment of pain, it at least brings the painful swelling to a head and bursts it open to give relief. This same remedy has also been found quite useful for backache.

A sweet apple roasted in hot coals and placed while still hot between cloths folded double may be applied to sore eyes. This remedy draws off the pain and benefits the eyes as well.

Cider pressed from very ripe sweet apples and freshly fermented may be boiled to a syrup with loaf sugar. When several spoonfuls of this are taken at a time, the syrup is quite useful against splenetic disorders, for strengthening the heart, and for dispelling faintings and palpitations, as well as melancholies caused by grief and hard times. If you infuse dried senna leaves in this syrup and then reboil it, the result is a pleasing and gentle purgative for melancholics and hypochondriacs. Besides that, it is also pleasing to the young and old, especially when a little cinnamon and cloves are added while it is being cooked.

Apples that have turned mealy, pared and with the seeds and cores removed, may be browned in fresh, drawn butter. After they are browned, lay them between a double-folded cloth and place this upon sores of the breast. This reduces the swelling or else causes the sores to head up and break. Once they have opened, daub them with a little honey, which will cleanse them and cause them to heal quickly.[10]

9. This was accomplished with blood leeches or by "cupping" with special instruments normally in the possession of individuals trained specifically in the art of bleeding.

10. A preparation called Honey Breast Balsam was advertised for sale in *Der Wöchentliche Philadelphische Staatsbothe* for December 19, 1763. The home remedy advocated by Sauer was doubtless easier to make and much cheaper.

Apricot
Armeniaca vulgaris
Sauer: *Marillen, Aprikose* (1777)

The apricot requires a Mediterranean climate to thrive to perfection. It is otherwise a troublesome delicacy since it blooms early in March and is therefore subject to frosts. And what the frosts do not finish off, curculio will sap out until the trees wither and die. Thus, in northern Europe and in colonial America, the apricot was relegated to the gardens of the wealthy who could afford the luxury of garden labor and the trouble of erecting walls and windbreaks to coddle this precious fruit to harvest. Among the English, the variety known as Moor Park was considered the best. Among the French and Germans, the yellow-fruited orange apricot was valued for its drying qualities. It was this dried, imported variety that Sauer sold in his shop, as well as the expressed oil from the kernels.

The utilization of slightly green fruit, mentioned in the last passage below, was a common feature of cookery in the mid-Atlantic region during the eighteenth and early nineteenth centuries, especially where the Germans settled. Underripe apples and peaches were similarly used in pies and preserves; numerous recipes have survived reflecting this old preference for sweet and sour.

Apricots possess most of the same virtues of peaches. But they are further endowed with a lightly effervescent juice which conceals a bitter principal that is easily corrupted. The kernels possess a sweet oil mingled with a somewhat volatile, sour liquid, whereby they operate medically by loosening and attenuating.

Apricots are better for the stomach than peaches, since they do not corrupt so quickly after they are eaten. And if they are taken at the conclusion of a meal, they block the hot vapors and thus prevent the rising of eructations. When preserved in syrup or honey, apricots make quite pleasant eating.

An oil can be pressed from apricot kernels which Mesue of old[11] wrote about as one of the foremost remedies for inflamed swellings of the arse and for hemorrhoids, since the oil cools and operates as an anodyne. Oil of apricot is also of service for a painful ear when a few drops are put into it. The head should be tilted to one side so that the oil can run in properly and then held that way for a while to ensure that the oil does its work. This oil is also good for treating cracks and warts on women's breasts, especially when it is mixed with stag's tallow and applied as a warm lotion.

When apricots are not fully ripe, they can be pared and poached in water, then put up in clean jars. Sugar boiled to a thick syrup (or honey) is then poured over the fruit and the sweetmeat thus preserved.

---

11. Mesue the Younger (d. 1015), otherwise known as Masawayk al-Maridini, was a Jacobite Christian physician at the court of the caliph of Cairo during the Middle Ages. This reference not only confirms the early medieval nature of some of the material in Sauer's herbal but is direct evidence of a Greco-Arabic influence as well.

Ash Tree (Common European)

Fraxinus excelsior
Sauer: *Eschbaum* (1776)

The ash tree belongs to the olive tribe, so it should come as no surprise that its seed, like the olive, contains a useful oil. The medical properties of the ash were well understood by the ancient Celts (it was one of their sacred plants), and it is likely that some of their herbal knowledge became embedded in many of the oldest European folk remedies dealing with this tree. For its curative powers were impressive and worked with nearly the same effectiveness as the quinine of Peruvian bark—a point noted by Sauer. In short, the ash tree served as the aspirin of eighteenth-century rural America.

*However, the ash tree of Sauer was the European species. The North American substitute was the white ash (*Fraxinus americana*), considered in most medical respects to serve as a workable equivalent. While we are more likely today to think of the ash in terms of its remarkably fine wood for cabinetry, this wood had medical uses, as Sauer pointed out below in the interesting case of the ash wood mug that was thought to imbue its contents with increased curative powers.*

Lastly, while Sauer noted the various medical applications of the ash keys or seed-pods, he failed to point out that they were also used to increase the fertility of both sexes. They therefore served several purposes in cookery, from the artistic and healthful to the pleasantly procreative. Just as olives could be pickled in brine, so too were the ash keys. They were picked while green and tender and put up for use like capers. Likewise, pickled ash keys were scattered in salads, laid over cooked fish, or mingled with the melted butter served over the asparagus that follows in the very next Sauer entry.

The leaves, bark, wood, and seeds of this tree that are used in remedies possess a somewhat resinous, penetrating oil combined with an astringent, volatile salt. These constituents not only contribute to its bitterness, but are also endowed with the faculty of loosening all thick humors of the body, of opening obstructions, and of restoring blood that has become too thick to its natural consistency. The ash also cleanses the kidneys, cleanses and heals all manner of injuries and wounds, and warms and dries gently.

Take the tender young shoots of the ash tree, chop them fine, and make a distillate from this. This water is very serviceable for restoring hearing and for dissolving fluxes stopped up in the ear. To accomplish this, warm the ash water and rinse the ears with it; also drink some of the ash water from time to time. This same distillation is also renowned for calming palsy of the hands, provided the water is warmed and the affected hands are washed in it frequently.

The inner bark of the ash tree can be used to good effect instead of lignum vitae. Indeed it operates with nearly the same results against tertian and quartan ague as Jesuit bark. For effectively treating these agues, the following bitter tonic can be administered: Take one ounce of the inner bark of the ash tree, one quint of powdered wormwood, and grind it all to a fine consistency. Put this powder into a bottle and pour two quarts of good wine over it. Shake it up, or pour it back and forth between two bottles, several times each day. Take a gill of this each morning, but before drinking it, be sure it is shaken well enough so that a proper portion of the sediment is taken in the drink. Also make certain to purge the stomach with a good emetic before taking each dose. Thus administered, ash bark promises a certain cure for the ague.

The tiny keys or seeds should be gathered in the fall when they ripen. Grind them to a powder and administer this in wine as a remedy for stones and gravel. It is also an effective remedy for jaundice and dropsy, provided it is administered frequently in half-quint doses. An oil is also distilled from ash seeds that is quite serviceable for cases of the stone or gravel. To make the remedy, take one ounce of sugar, two scruples of saltpeter, and eight drops of oil of ash seed, and grind this together so that the oil is absorbed into the powder. Give two or three pinches of this to the patient every day.

The inner bark of the ash tree can be quite serviceable as a blood purifier when used like other woody decoction for the blood.

A salt prepared from the wood and leaves of the ash tree operates with the same effectiveness in the above-mentioned conditions as the divers remedies just enumerated. If a mug is fashioned from ash wood, and the beverages for hypochondriacs are allowed to stand in it and then drunk from the same, it will agree with the patient very well.

Asparagus
Asparagus officinalis
Sauer: *Spargeln* (1770)

Sauer noted in passing, but did not enumerate, the various culinary treatments given to asparagus by his German-speaking readers. This was one of the most prized of their spring vegetables and almost a culinary rite when it came to the marriage of asparagus with shad while that fish was in season. Nicolas de Bonnefons, under the management of asparagus in his Delices de la campagne,[12] *mentioned a fricassee of asparagus cooked with a little chopped bacon and thickened with cream that certainly would have been familiar to Sauer's readers. Asparagus was also parboiled and served as a salad with oil and vinegar. And aside from simply boiling it, one of the most common methods of preparation was the* Brockle, *a type of chopped omelet. Thin stems of asparagus were cooked with bits of ham, then beaten eggs and chives were poured over them. The mixture was stirred and chopped until it cooked and set. It was served in bowls with ham stock poured over it, a perfect dish for a light supper.*

Today there is some confusion among speakers of Pennsylfaanisch over the use of the word Mickegraut, *"fly plant," for asparagus. In fact, the correct dialect word is* Schparregraas, *"sparrow grass," since true fly plant is wild indigo (Baptisia tinctoria). Both the blue and yellow wild indigos do indeed repel flies and were once used for this purpose. Asparagus does not, although the dry plant could be made into brushes to swat at flies and other pests.*

12. Nicolas de Bonnefons, *Les Delices de la campagne* (Amsterdam, 1661), 126–28.

Sauer's recommendation to use the flowering asparagus plant to enhance the flavor of wine was yet another practical application; it was intended to correct the raw quality or off-taste of the cheaper sorts of wine that were imported from Spain and Portugal at that time. A similar remedy, using oranges and cloves, is discussed under the section on wine (page 355).

Asparagus is of a middle nature, neither warming nor cooling. It is used in cookery and yields good results in medicine. For example, it operates especially by urine, and purges from the body divers watery humors by this means. However, the urine is thus rendered foul and stinking.

Cooked and eaten alone or along with other food, asparagus serves well in principal weaknesses originating from the stomach and liver, in ailments of the eyes and chest, and particularly in pulmonic consumptions. It is also beneficial to the stomach, fortifies and opens obstructions of the liver and speen, and is good against humors of the stomach, jaundice, colic, and tertian fever. In addition, asparagus is useful for easing pain in the lower back, kidneys, loins, and all infirmities of the viscera. It promotes urine and opens the kidneys, as well as the urinal ducts and bladder. It is also useful in treating those who are afflicted with gravel or with kidney stones. It helps men of a weak, phlegmatic constitution, and brings down the menses in women. Asparagus also furnishes useful nourishment for dropsical persons and the sick in general, but it is injurious to those with a damaged bladder. Furthermore, in its nourishment, asparagus also possesses an unknown property that helps to cure all ailments of the eyes.

For divers maladies of the liver, asparagus is surprisingly effective and not only loosens the obstructions but fortifies the liver as well. For jaundice, take two loths of asparagus root, half a loth of Hamburg parsley root, and a handful each of horehound, Venus's goldilocks, sorrel, devil's guts,[13] endive, and succory. Chop these herbs very fine, then put them into a jug. Pour one and half quarts of springwater on this, and stop up the jug tightly. Place the jug in a kettle of boiling water and let it stand thus for five hours over a continuous heat. Then remove the jug and let it cool. Strain the decoction and add ten loths of sugar to it. Administer one pint of the warm decoction to the patient each morning and evening.

To impart a nice aroma to wine, collect flowering asparagus and dry it in the shade. Then place it in a bag and hang this in your barrel of wine. The wine will then acquire a pleasant taste and odor.

The distilled water of asparagus should be used especially by those who are inclined toward gravel, stones, and lumbago. This purges the gravel and stones, as well as the scummy matter on which the stones form. This iscuretic possesses a first-rate capacity for opening obstructions, and provokes the urine briskly. It controls

---

13. Also called dodder of thyme (*Cuscuta epithymum*), a parasitic plant growing on thyme, milk vetch, and other small plants. Dr. John Hill noted in his *Useful Family Herbal* (London, 1755), "The common Dodder is preferable to it with us, because we can gather it fresh, the other is imported, and we only have it dry; and it looses a great deal of its Virtue in the hands of the Druggist" (124). This truism also applied to colonial America.

dripping urine and jaundice, and fortifies against the cold evil or cold piss. It also loosens up the liver and spleen, in addition to the above ailments, when taken in four- or five-loth doses each morning and evening.

For the treatment of kidney and bladder stones, Theodorus Tabernaemontanus has provided instructions on the preparation of an herbal wine that has been used with great effectiveness.[14] Proceed as follows: Take sixteen loths of asparagus root and four loths each of burdock root, the root of Hamburg parsley, burnet root, and saxifrage root. All of these ingredients should be dry and chopped up small. Put them into a three-gallon cask, which is then filled with good-quality cider. Let this ferment until still, then partake of it morning and evening.

Asparagus root is counted among the five best aperients, known in medicine as the *radices quinque aperientes*.

Balsam Apple
Momordica balsamina
Sauer: *Aepfel-Balsam* (1773)

Writing in 1837—many years after Sauer's death—Dr. William Darlington noted that balsam apples and very small balsam pears (Momordica charantia) *were still cultivated rather indiscriminately in Pennsylvania gardens, one species often used to stand in for the other.[15] This is not surprising, since the small wild form of* Momordica charantia *often shows up in European herbals under the guise of balsam apple. It was grown in Spanish America during Sauer's time and was generally known there as the* pepino. *We may presume from this that colonial druggists like Sauer obtained commercially prepared stocks from Jamaica, Cuba, or even from Mexico, where these plants still grow in great abundance even to this day.*

However, the leaf, flower, and flat black seed of the balsam apple are distinctively different from that of the pepino *or bitter melon, although the fruits of both can be used in the medical infusions noted by Sauer below. Both fruits are also rich in ascorbic acid and vitamin C, which may account in part for their effectiveness as vulneraries. And as Darlington noted, both will grow in Pennsylvania, although the balsam apple ripens much later in the season and is not as profuse as the small* pepino, *which will ramble over fences like a weedy vine. I have grown both of these side by side for many years and can vouch for these observations. For today's gardens troubled by deer, the vines are particularly valuable not only as quick ornamental screens but because deer detest the strong smell of the plants and are thus repelled from nosing deeper into the beds.*

Doubtless Sauer had access to both species, for there were individuals in colonial America who maintained momordicas in their gardens for medical or for purely ornamental purposes. But such local sources were few. We must conclude that the balsam

---

14. Jakob Theodor von Bergzaben, otherwise known as Tabernaemontanus, published an important herbal called *Neuw vollkommentlich Kreuterbuch* in 1588. Several copies of this book were brought to America during the colonial period.

15. William Darlington, *Flora Cestrica* (West Chester, Pa., 1837), 554–55.

apple (both the dried leaves and the infusion made from the fruit) was commonplace in apothecary shops. The fresh article might be seen growing in the hortus medicus *of those who practiced surgery, but it was not to be found in every farmhouse kitchen garden.*

Balsam apples, together with their leaves and flowers, possess a balsamic, oily, alkaline salt that endows them with the virtues of healing, drying, and easing pains. The fresh and dry leaves are considered a good internal and external vulnerary for all manner of injuries. The fruit or apples, put up in vinegar—or as some prefer, in strong brandy or rum—and saved for future use, can be administered to staunch the flow of blood, to consolidate fresh wounds, and to heal them over with exceptional speed.

If the wound is deep, make a pledget[16] of lint scraped from clean linen and douse it with the balsam apple infusion. Press this into the wound, and repeat the treatment daily with a fresh pledget until the wound is completely healed. For shallow wounds, simply lay a cloth over them after moistening the underside of the cloth with the infusion.

Barberry (European Barberry)
Berberis vulgaris
Sauer: *Säuerling* (1776)

Unlike Sauer's discussion of the balsam apple, which may be accepted as absolute documentation of availability in colonial America, his remarks about the barberry imply quite the opposite. His concern was for those who might seek out barberries for a special remedy, not realizing that the red currant, which was available everywhere, would do just as well. French and English barberry jam was available in some shops, but this import was expensive and not readily available to the rural public to whom Sauer addressed his herbal.

Barberries are now so common that we forget that they were introduced from Europe, and that their popularity did not increase until the nineteenth century. More important, barberries were rarely used in colonial American cookery even though they commonly appear in the English, German, and French cookbooks used by Americans of this period. American food historians have been rather careless in using period recipes verbatim without taking into account the multitudes of local alterations that Americanized the dishes. The barberry is thus a classic example; simply read red currant where it appears. For the medical applications, refer to red currants on page 257.

The barberry[17] is not nearly as common in this country as the red currant. Both yield similar results, and in all circumstances, the currant can be prepared like the barberry and applied to the same uses. Yet the barberry is somewhat more comforting in acute illnesses because it possesses a little more astringency and thus is better for quenching thirst brought on by fevers.

16. A pledget is a type of dressing for wounds; lint takes the place of cotton because cotton fibers are coarser and more likely to heal into the flesh, thus reopening the wound every time the pledget is removed.

17. Sauer also provided in his text the dialect terms *Sauerach* and *Erbselen* as synonyms for barberry.

Barley
Hordeum vulgare
Sauer: *Gerste* (1772)

The length of Sauer's discussion of barley must be taken in itself as an indication of the importance of this grain to domestic medicine. Furthermore, barley was readily available on nearly every colonial farm. This meant that even the poor could make use of it during times of illness.

Several kinds of barley were raised in colonial America during the eighteenth century, but only two were grown in the middle colonies on a commercial scale: winter barley and summer barley. In addition to these, some Germans raised bushy barley, which thrives on heavy soil. The barleys preferred for medicine were the same sorts used for making bread, beer, and whiskey. In general, the winter barleys were used for bread making while the spring planted or summer barleys were used in malting beer and by distilleries. The straw was a valuable crop for livestock. It was also common practice to roast and then grind grains of barley as a substitute for coffee.

For table consumption, barley was normally processed in two ways, one called French barley, the other pearled barley. The French barley was hulled and lightly ground so that the ends of the grain were rounded off. The pearl barley was processed further so that each grain became round, white, and polished. Pearl barley was often called for in period cookery books since it was considered more elegant, especially in soups. But the French cut barley was considered more tasty and indeed more nourishing.

The Germans who settled in colonial America were not great barley eaters, but the English, especially those in the middle colonies, were indeed quite fond of it and often used the flour in finer sorts of bread and pastry or in combination with oat flour when baking flat breads down-hearth. It is perhaps important to note this cultural difference, since Sauer attributed barley consumption to the sturdiness of warriors in ancient times and hoped that his readers would return to that simple and healthier lifestyle.

Indeed, the Germans of Sauer's era associated barley with the cookery of the Middle Ages. Such comfort dishes as barley gruel (Gersten-Mus), barley soup (Gerstensuppe), and barley flour soup (Eiergerste), might well be considered holdovers from that period. Let it be said that barley flour was often used by German immigrants in traditional Christmas breads, but that was the extent of it. In general, the German-speaking community viewed barley by itself as a poverty food or as sustenance for invalids and children. Spelt was the common grain of household consumption (a fuller discussion of spelt appears on page 345).

Barley possesses more acidulous, volatile, temperate salts and fewer oily constituents than wheat and spelt, and therefore it has been considered by writers of old to be cold and dry in nature. Barley cleanses, opens obstructions, draws out infections, operates as an emollient on lumps and growths, and eases pain. But its flour does not provide as much nourishment as that of wheat.

People in olden times preferred barley to all other grains in cookery, and it is indeed a good, healthy food for the sick and well alike. Warriors of old helped themselves plentifully to barley as a source of bodily strength, foddering on it constantly, thus earning for themselves the nickname "barley brutes." It is to be wished that people today would accustom themselves more to such a diet, and to stay with it, for doubtless they would then be freed of the numerous maladies they have brought upon themselves through gluttony and excess.

Barley can be cooked and served in divers ways. The simplest method is to boil hulled barley in water and to season it with butter and salt. Such plain fare is quite nourishing. But those who are able to boil it in freshly made meat stock will receive more nourishment, since this will strengthen the blood and thus provide food that is highly serviceable to both the sick and the healthy. The small, rolled barley called pearl barley is especially serviceable to the sick when boiled in good meat or chicken stock.

Barley cooked to porridge consistency in milk is a highly nourishing and healthy dish for all kinds of people, but particularly for children and nursing mothers. Children who eat this regularly will acquire good color and robust bodies, but the barley must be well cooked for otherwise it is too difficult to digest.

A very comforting dish for the sick can be prepared as follows: Boil hulled barley in a sufficient quantity of water until the scum rises. Skim off the scum, discard the water, and add good meat stock. Boil to the consistency of gruel, season with salt, and give this to the patient to eat, or let the patient drink some of the liquid. This gruel is most useful in all cases of acute fever, but especially in illnesses of the chest and lungs. It also increases the flow of milk in nursing mothers, and is especially useful in cases of diarrhea and other similar fluxes.

For swellings and acute inflammations of the breast, take one ounce of barley flour, half an ounce of fava bean flour, two ounces of honey, an ounce of vinegar, and half an ounce of oil of roses. Mix these ingredients and heat them over a gentle fire to form a thick mass. Spread this thickly on a cloth and lay it over the affected breast, as hot as the woman can bear it.

A barley water can be prepared as follows: Take two loths of well-rinsed barley, put this in a new earthenware pot that has been tempered in water, and add two quarts of water. Bring this to a boil over a charcoal fire until the barley begins to burst. Remove from the stove, cool, and strain off the liquid for drinking. This barley water, served plain without the addition of other ingredients, is useful in treating all serious conditions of the head, pulmonary consumption, pleurisy, jaundice, acute weaknesses of the liver, and fevers of every name.

If two ounces of sugar are added to the barley water, it will be useful in treating those who suffer from chest ailments and internal injuries because it provokes expectoration. It is also very good for those who suffer from ailments of the kidneys and bladder, since it cleanses them of foul matter and promotes healing.

To make a plaster that eases and stills the pain of bladder stones, burning urine, and the cold evil with astonishing speed, take a few handfuls of freshly parched barley flour. While still hot, stir it into good-quality olive oil or sweet butter along with an equal amount of ground hops. Brown this in a skillet, then add boiling water and cook until thick. Spread the plaster inside a double-folded linen cloth and lay it warm over the groin and lower belly.

Barley that is ground up with juniper berries, sewn into a sachet, and heated until dry can be placed on limbs pained by cold rheums. The rheums are thus drawn off and the pain allayed with great effectiveness.

Barley may be prepared like the celebrated water gruel made from oats and used to treat bilious impurities of the bodily humors. For example, take half a pound, more or less, of rinsed barley, four loths of rasped ivory, an equal amount of fresh or dried succory root, two handfuls of the purest liverwort, and a half loth each of sal prunellae and cream of tartar, and boil this in four gallons of water until it is reduced to one-fourth. Then add the rind of one orange or half a lemon. Let it cool and then strain it off into bottles. Store them in a cool place. Drink one pint of this twice a day, and if preferred, add a little sugar to sweeten it. Barley can also be cooked down to a jelly that is then dissolved in meat stock and enjoyed with useful results.

In his day, Hippocrates, the renowned physician, prescribed for most illnesses a plain drink made from barley, sometimes thicker, sometimes thinner, as the malady required.

Basil (Sweet Basil)
Ocimum basilicum
Sauer: *Basilien* (1765)

In the "Anhang von Kräutern" (Addendum on herbs) to her Oekonomisches hand-buch für Frauenzimmer, *German cookbook author Friederike Löffler discussed the role of sweet basil in middle-class cookery.*[18] *She recommended it for sauces, since it was not as strong-tasting as tarragon, and for flavoring vinegar for salad dressings. But Löffler's cookery was French-based and influenced by the food she prepared at the ducal court in Stuttgart—indeed, not too representative of the taste preferences of rural German cooks during the eighteenth century. For them, basil fell very much behind thyme, marjoram, and summer savory in popularity. But it did have its uses.*

Jacob Biernauer recommended basil for keeping away rats and mice, an old-fash-ioned application that was evidently common among the Germans in colonial America.[19] *Among the plain sects—including the Dunkards, with whom the Sauers were affili-ated—basil was called* Versammlungskraut, *"meetinghouse plant." This name derived from the fact that the herb was carried into church and nibbled on to stave off hunger during long religious services or held to the face as a nosegay against stale air. A simi-lar custom prevailed in Germany using costmary, which was pressed between the pages of prayer books and Bibles. While today we probably associate the aroma of sweet basil more with pesto or Mediterranean cookery, during Sauer's era it was one of those "churchy" odors that evoked hymns and sermons.*

18. Friederike Löffler, *Oekonomisches Handbuch für Frauenzimmer* (Stuttgart, 1795), 614.
19. Jacob Biernauer, *Das unentbehrliche Haus- und Kunst-Buch* (Reading, Pa., 1818), 22–23.

John Hill was also quick to note in his herbal that in England "basil is little used, but it deserves to be much more."[20] The situation in colonial America was similar, although it was one of the sweet herbs often placed among the "soup bunches" (bouquets of herbs and vegetables) used to flavor soup stock. For the Germans, however, its primary use appears to have been medical, as Sauer elucidates below.

Basil is warming and drying. It strengthens the head, brain, and stomach; loosens internal obstructions; and cures dizziness so long as the condition is not brought on by high blood pressure. Basil cleanses the matrix, strengthens it, and gently promotes the menses. But only the leaves and seeds are used in simples.

Due to its pleasant fragrance, this noble plant animates the mind and gladdens the heart. If its seeds are soaked until soft in water, they will discharge a white mucilage that will serve as an excellent remedy for quinsy and scurvy of the gums, provided the infusion is drawn into the mouth, held there for a time, and then churned about as a mouthwash. This mucilage also serves as a good treatment for chapped and cracked lips, for cracked nipples and chapped breasts, and for rawness in the privates, provided the affected parts are smeared with it frequently.

In the fall, the leaves of sweet basil and similar useful herbs are collected to make vermouth wines.[21] These wines strengthen the stomach, promote digestion, assuage persistent coughing, and serve as an excellent treatment for those afflicted by melancholy or sadness.

If the leaves of sweet basil are boiled in white wine and the decoction is then drunk, it will cleanse the chest and lungs of hard phlegm, as well as relieve difficult breathing and coughs of long continuance. This decoction is also useful for women suffering from chills, since it cleanses the matrix, soothes it, and frees it of the complaints that naturally attend its stoppage.

The seeds of sweet basil burned to ashes and then strewn upon warts that have been scraped hard with a sharp knife will draw out the warts right down to their roots.

If freshly pressed cider is poured over dried basil leaves and thus fermented, the resulting apple wine will not simply taste good, it will acquire the aroma of a muscatel.

The distilled water of sweet basil not only brings powerful invigoration to the head and heart, it prevents apoplexy, purifies the chest of all manner of phlegm, and dispels asthmatical pursy. Water of sweet basil is also said to be effective when a worm has crept into the body and commenced to grow there. The water will drive out the worm without injury to the person.

Water of sweet basil and borage water mixed together and a spoonful taken now and then will give very good treatment in cases of depression, enliven the heart, and ward off fits of fainting.

20. John Hill, *The Useful Family Herbal* (London, 1755), 27.

21. Although the French and Italians are known today for their vermouths, it was the Swiss who were originally famous for these wine infusions. The art of making them dates from the Middle Ages, and was probably handed down from Roman times by the monastic orders that once produced and sold them. In any case, Swiss settlers in colonial America continued this tradition.

Beet Chard (Leaf Beet)
Beta vulgaris subsp. *cicla*
Sauer: *Mangold* (1770)

The beet was one of the basic culinary vegetables of Sauer's day, and its uses were many. The chards, however, were not often discussed in English cookery books of this period, or if so, were treated as something quite unusual. In spite of this, there were many differ- ent kinds, varying in color from white to yellow to orange and bright red, and the Germans grew all of them.

Botanically speaking, chards are members of the Cicla group, which were not grown for their roots, although some sorts produced root beets that were quite tender and fla- vorful. Maria Sophia Schellhammer had this to say about Bethe *(her word for beet chards) in 1698:*

> *Large chards and Spanish chards make a dainty meal, and are quite useful in the kitchen. The leaves can be stripped off and cooked by themselves like spinach as well as in various meat broths and soups, or with red cabbage. Above all else, they benefit the health because very little fat is required in preparing them. Furthermore, they can be kept the entire winter in the cellar. The stems especially may be prepared in the following manner: Wash and poach them in cold water that is brought to a boil. Then press them out and sauté in butter. When tender, add meat stock, a little vinegar, and cream. Season and let this cook a short time, after which they may be served.[22]*

It is obvious from the herbal that Sauer was dealing with at least two kinds, red and white, for he stated as much in his original heading for this entry. Furthermore, he pre- sumed that they could be treated interchangeably, even though the white beet chard was most preferred for external medicine—the red variety being considered weaker in its medical properties.

Regarding the white chards, it is quite likely that Sauer had in mind the so-called spinach-leafed beet, which is an overwintering vegetable in Pennsylvania. Its cooked root, though woody and inedible, would produce the desired medical decoctions, and its leaves would work admirably for wounds and sores even in the dead of winter provided it was covered with straw.

Beet chards possess the capacity to emolliate, to moisten, to attenuate, to promote stool, and to cleanse and heal wounds and open sores. They are also good for draw- ing down snot and other rheums through the nose. They are also widely employed in cookery.

Because beets operate by the copious moisture they possess, salt and pepper should not be spared when cooking them. Indeed, the white beet, when boiled and eaten with raw garlic, will kill and drive forth worms.

22. Maria Sophia Schellhammer, *Das Brandenburgische Koch-Buch* (Berlin, 1732), 483–84.

The expressed juice of white beet mingled with marjoram water and rose honey, then drawn up into the nose, will cleanse the head of its surfeit of rheums. The green leaves laid as a poultice over spreading sores will heal them.

For frostbitten feet, an effective foot bath can be prepared from the decoction strained off from white beets and turnips boiled together.

Take the roots of one or more large red beets, scrub and boil them in a little water (or bake in hot ashes), and then cut them into thin, round slices. Pour some good-quality vinegar over this, then scatter shredded horseradish, coriander seeds,[23] and salt over the top. This makes a pleasing dish, especially when served with roast meat, since it encourages a hearty appetite.

The freshly pressed juice, either by itself or mingled with marjoram water, then snuffed into the nose, will loosen hard, clotted snot and phlegm, and draw them down. This will also cleanse and heal sores in the nose, restore the sense of smell, and dispel migraines and pain in the forehead.

Should a child have a badly ulcerated head, and the watery corruption will not flow off, lay the chards upon the sores and they will act powerfully in drawing out the pus. Fresh beet chards can also be put to good use on burst and runny cysts by smearing the leaves with a little unsalted butter and laying this as a poultice upon the sores. Repeated often every few days, this will keep them open and clean without pain.

Betony
Stachys officinalis
Sauer: *Betonie* (1766)

The curative powers of betony were well known to the ancient Celts. Indeed, this is one of the oldest medical plants in European folk medicine, and its virtues were further extolled during the Middle Ages. Walahfrid Strabo described the medicinal powers of betony in his ninth-century A.D. Hortulus, *claiming that it was good for every malady of the body, but especially for head wounds. Sauer's herbal echoed those sentiments. Lancaster, Pennsylvania, druggist Carl Heinrich Heinitsch promoted betony in his* Anweisung zum Gebrauch des folgenden Gekräuter *(Advice on the use of the following herbs), a little handout printed in Lancaster about 1800, which he gave to customers of his shop. In short, the printed evidence for the use of betony in early America is overwhelming. But there is some uncertainty about the exact species or subspecies utilized in the remedies.*

There are several native betonies, and those with leaves and flowers most similar to the European plant were evidently used

23. The German does not differentiate between the dry coriander seeds and the freshly picked green ones. Both were used in pickles, but the taste is distinctly different.

as substitutes. The flower of the European woodland plant—for betony is a woodland or shade-loving herb—is light purple or deep rose like its closest American cousin, but the leaf is smaller and more delicate. I have grown these herbs side by side for comparison, and note further that the European plants yield a much more intense yellow dye than the American. These subtleties may or may not have mattered in folk medicine. The American plant was easy to find in most woodlots, and Sauer's remark that the herb was cheap may also be read to mean "free for the picking." Furthermore, judging from the last line below, we may be assured that Sauer himself was a great bottler of betony syrup.

The leaves and flowers of betony, which can be gathered cheaply at the same time, possess the properties of warming and drying, of fortifying the head and nerves, and of cleansing, opening, drying, and purifying the chest, kidney, and womb.

Indeed, betony has so many virtues that when the ancients wanted to describe a man of many talents, they were accustomed to say, He has more virtues than betony. For there is no illness brought on by cold for which betony cannot be administered effectively.

Experience has demonstrated that when betony is infused in wine, and then taken as a drink, the infusion will cleanse all the phlegm from the chest and lungs, open obstructions of the spleen and liver, and drive out kidney stones. It is also serviceable in cases of dizziness, apoplexy, convulsions, trembling, numbing of the viscera, and head colds. Beyond this, betony also strengthens a feeble stomach, promotes digestion, counters jaundice and a nervous stomach, and cleanses the matrix.

The powder of dried betony flowers snuffed into the nose will clean the head of rheums brought on by a cold. The juice pressed from betony, applied to fresh wounds, will keep them clean and cause the flesh to grow together. This is particularly good for wounds of the head.

Several spoonfuls of distilled water of betony, taken often according to one's disposition, will strengthen a cold, weak, phlegmatic stomach, mollify its unwillingness to accept food, open obstructions of the liver and spleen, prevent dropsy and jaundice, and cleanse the kidneys and bladder of grit, sand, and stones. Furthermore, it will help those who are afflicted with cold piss or dripping urine, warm chills of the matrix, cleanse the chest and lungs of phlegm and pus, ease fits of coughing, and strengthen and warm a head weakened by a cold. Likewise, betony water will prevent apoplexy and falling sickness.

Fresh betony flowers ground to a conserve in sugar are a serviceable remedy for all the above-mentioned afflictions. Furthermore, they have the special virtue of operating against flutterings of the heart and pulmonary consumption. For these, administer a dose the size of a nutmeg several times a day.

The dried leaves of betony can take the place of China tea, and to better effect both medically and morally.

The essential principles of the herb may be drawn out by infusing betony in brandy, and then making an elixir from this. This can be applied very well as a remedy for all of the above maladies.

The syrup of betony prepared in apothecary shops possesses virtues of the first rank relative to all maladies of the head, as well as for healing wounds and injuries.

Birch Tree (European White Birch)
Betula alba
Sauer: Birkenbaum (1778)

> *Sauer's text is based on uses derived from the European white birch, but since the reme-dies described relied on fresh sap or leaves, it is evident that a North American equiv-alent was readily available. This would have been the paper birch* (Betula papyrifera) *or canoe birch, which is treated sometimes as the same species as the white birch and sometimes as a separate one. Whatever, it was definitely used by the Indians for herbal teas, and the colonists were quick to observe this.*
>
> *The bark of the black birch* (Betula lenta) *or cherry birch was also used in colonial America to make herbal teas, but with a distinct wintergreen taste. The sap was col-lected and boiled to make sugar. Sugar, beer, wines, and distillates had also been made from the white birch in many parts of Europe since medieval times; perhaps, in the case of the wines and beers, even earlier. The method for tapping birch sap (with spigots hammered into the bark) described by John Davies in his* Innkeeper and Butler's Guide *is identical to the manner in which we harvest maple syrup today.[24] Perhaps it is enough to note that in the 1792 Philadelphia edition of Richard Briggs's* New Art of Cookery, *there is an extensive recipe for birch wine as it was made in England.[25] In any case, Sauer's recipes lend tangible force to the argument that birch beer and birch wine have long been considered traditional beverages among the Pennsylvania Dutch as well.*

The bark and leaves of this tree contain a copious quantity of watery sap, which con-tains a rather nitrous volatile salt and a sulfurous gum. As a result, the birch tree has the capacity to emolliate, dissipate, purify the blood, promote urine, and heal wounds and injuries. Drinking a glassful of fresh sap in the morning before breakfast is con-sidered the best means of preventing stones in the kidneys and bladder. It is also very good for those old folks who are afflicted by pain when urinating, and quenches strong burning sensations in the liver.

The proper use of birch sap for the prevention of kidney and bladder stones is based on the following points:

1. Only the fresh, sweet sap should be used, and never any that has soured or begun to ferment, for this will quickly lead to gripes in the stomach or headache.
2. Do not drink more than six ounces on the first day of treatment, although after that, the dosage can be increased gradually to twelve ounces a day, as the constitution of the body permits.

24. John Davies, *The Innkeeper and Butler's Guide* (Leeds, 1806), 39–40.
25. Richard Briggs, *The New Art of Cookery, According to the Present Practice* (Philadelphia, 1792), 525.

3. After each dosage, the patient should take a little walk.

4. The dosage must be taken in the morning before breakfast, and the patient should then wait one hour before eating.

5. Should the sap fail to operate forthwith, and urination still proves difficult, the patient may make use of other diuretical medications, such as meat stock in which Hamburg parsley has been boiled, turpentine pills, or similar effective measures. Should the body become fully obstructed, an enema may be employed.

6. The use of birch sap must be continued for about three weeks.

7. The sap should be tapped early in the spring before the leaves appear on the trees, for as soon as the trees leaf out, the sap loses its effectiveness.

To make a useful birch wine, take twelve parts birch sap and one part honey, and bring to a boil in a large brass kettle. Skim off the foam, and reduce until it is thick enough to bear an egg. Then put the liquid in a wooden cask, add a little beer barm, and some cloves. Let this ferment. When fully fermented, rack it off into bottles and store away for future use. This wine is especially good in the winter, provided as much as one gill is taken in the morning before breakfast. This will purge the kidneys of thick corruptions.

Some persons are accustomed to distilling birch sap instead. This birch water has received high praise as a remedy for cases of dropsy when mixed with elderberry water and administered frequently. Used externally, birch water also removes rashes and the spots caused by measles, clears the complexion, and heals scurvy of the mouth when applied as a mouthwash.

Birch sap rubbed on the ankles and hooves of horses will strengthen them.

Poor people boil young birch branches in water, then bathe in this to cure the itch. They get good relief, especially when two parts cream of tartar and one part saltpeter are also boiled in the bathwater.

The ancients used to write on the white bark of this tree before the discovery of paper.

A fungus sometimes grows on the birch tree, which when dried and ground to a powder may be applied to bleeding hemorrhoids. This stops the discharge at once.[26]

Birthwort

Aristolochia clematitis
Sauer: *Hohlwurzel, Osterluceywurz* (1766)

Sauer recognized two types of birthwort, a longa *and a* rotunda *based on root shape. These are not separate species, yet both were of much more importance to the German-speaking population in colonial America than to the English. For example, John Hill noted in his* Useful Family Herbal *that in England birthwort could only be found in gardens of the curious, and that the root sold in apothecary shops came invariably from*

26. *Birkenschwamm* is a fungus related to agaric (page 35).

Italy or from other regions of southern Europe where it grew as a wild plant.

In Germany, birthwort is often found in very old vineyards—presumably a relic of ancient Roman occupation—but Sauer himself admitted that it was not yet cultivated in America. He failed to mention that there were many New World species closely related to it, among them Virginia snakeroot (Aristolochia serpentaria) *and the ornamental vine called Dutchman's-pipe* (Aristolochia macrophylla). *Evidently, he was very much an advocate of the Old World plant, not just for midwifery but especially as a vulnerary with miraculous powers and an antidote for venereal sores.*

In any event, the herb is bitter and so offensive tasting that it can cause some patients to vomit. Yet its primary use as a purgative for the uterus immediately after delivery should also allude to other uses less approved of, namely as an abortant or contraceptive. For this purpose it was potent and effective, and even more so when used with mugwort, as suggested in the herbal. Obviously, imported birthwort was in such demand that druggists like Sauer felt compelled to stock it. We may leave the rest to speculation, but the number of infant remains found at the bottom of privies in eighteenth-century archaeological sites in this country certainly would add evidence to a dimension of social history that has largely gone undiscussed.

To my knowledge, birthwort is not yet cultivated in this country, but I suppose it will probably be introduced as soon as possible. In the meantime, the dried root can be found in nearly every apothecary shop.

The root of birthwort is excellent and well known for its virtues of opening obstructions of the liver, spleen, and matrix; of dissolving hard phlegm in the chest, and then promoting its expectoration. Birthwort cleanses and heals wounds and sores and is very useful for sickly women who suffer from irregular menses. The root of birthwort consists of two kinds, the round and the long. The former is applied more often in internal medicine, the latter more often in external remedies.

Due to its excellent property as an antidote to poison, birthwort is also employed as an ingredient in *Theriaca Andromaci*.[27]

To bring down a dead fetus, take half a quint of birthwort root and twenty grains of myrrh and grind them to a fine powder. Administer daily with a glass of good-quality wine or with water of mugwort. This will bring down the dead fetus, force it out, purge the womb of all superfluous matter that would be otherwise evacuated naturally at birth, and restore the menses. Yet this remedy must be continued no longer than necessary, otherwise serious complications are likely to arise.

Take the leaves and root of long birthwort and boil them in a decoction of half wine and half water. Dip a piece of cloth in this and daub scabby, peeling skin with it. Also, for ringworm, vigorously wash the sores with the decoction. This will heal these conditions readily.

Birthwort possesses a considerable power in absorbing malignancies from angry flesh, and in cleansing and healing wounds and sores, provided the leaves are bruised and laid upon the injured spot. Or grind the root to a powder and gently rub this into the injury. Birthwort also draws out sharp twigs, thorns, splinters, and even arrows if

27. For *Theriaca Andromaci* or Venice treacle, see footnote on page 53.

the leaves are bruised until soft and laid over the injury. For this same reason, army surgeons use birthwort leaves in their compresses for stab wounds.

Veterinarians use birthwort for injuries to horses. If a horse is cut or hurt by the saddle, powder the injury with ground birthwort root so that it prevents infections from taking hold there. If a horse is driven too hard and collapses, take half a loth each of birthwort root, beaver's cod,[28] and sweet laurel berries. Grind this to a powder and then boil in beer or wine. Lift its head and pour this decoction down the horse's throat as warm as the animal can bear it.

Birthwort cooked in wine makes a useful vulnerary for cleansing and healing old and new wounds, running ulcers on the legs, and all manner of sores, especially in the privates, which must be washed with the decoction, then powdered with the ground, dried root.

When the freshly pressed juice of birthwort is put into old, rotten sores, it takes away all the putrid matter. For this reason, surgeons employ the juice in the salves and plasters that they administer to obstinate infections.

The distilled water of long birthwort possesses the power to cleanse the brain and chest of cold rheums, open the liver and spleen, block the onset of jaundice and dropsy, take away abdominal pains, and stay falling sickness, provided it is drunk in one-ounce doses every morning and evening. This water also serves excellently against contagion when three loths are dissolved in a quint of *Theriaca Andromaci*. Take this several times to provoke a good sweat.

When someone steps on a sharp twig, thorn, or nail, or suffers from a puncture where foreign matter becomes deeply lodged in the flesh, dip a piece of cloth in water of birthwort and lay this over the injury. It will bring the puncture to a head and draw out the splinter with the pus.

A certain royal physician at the Danish court was accustomed to boiling the powder of long birthwort in speedwell water, then dipping a piece of cloth in the decoction. He laid this warm upon old injuries that appeared to be almost incurable. They were healed so completely in such a short time that it seemed miraculous.

Blackberry (European Blackberry or Bramble)
Rubus fructicosus
Sauer: *Brombeer* (1767)

The old saying that the most neglected things have their use is certainly true in the case of the blackberry. Instead of letting them ramble over the compost pile, I grow my patch of blackberries right in the middle of my kitchen garden. The sullen heat of July is made much more bearable by this refreshing thirst-quenching fruit. In Sauer's day, few people actually cultivated blackberries, for they were mostly gathered from the wild and sold

---

28. Beaver's cod or *castoreum* was a term applied to several products used in medicine. These consisted primarily of dried beaver testicles or the dried bladders of both male and female beavers. Sometimes pig testicles were dried inside beaver bladders and sold as beaver cods. In Europe the cods of pharmaceutical quality were prepared in Lithuania. In America, the Indians sold them along with beaver furs.

in the streets by hawkers. And there were many native species of blackberry that served
as substitutes for the one described by Sauer.

Doubtless his readers were well aware of this, since the term Brombeer *was used in*
Pennsylvania High German to cover a variety of black-fruited berries of similar
appearance and taste. Sauer did not mention that blackberry jelly was commonly used
as a remedy for kidney stones—Benjamin Franklin's recipe for just such a jelly was
widely published in eighteenth-century almanacs.[29] Nor did he realize that it is one of
the best fruits for reducing free radicals in the body, a fact only recently discovered—per-
haps. For if one observes the birds and the sorts of berries they savor most, the list of
antioxidants is ready-made and hardly new.

The blackberry is endowed with the virtues of drying and of healing by gentle astringency. The unripe, red fruit, however, heals even better due to the unfermented
nature of its juices. It is also good for all manner of eruptions.

Leafy sprigs of blackberry boiled in lye will yield a black dye for the hair. The distilled water is good for sand and stones in children, provided it is administered in two-
loth doses every morning and evening. It is also usefully applied as a gargle for scurvy
of the gums.

From the unripe, red fruit, press out the juice and cook this down until thick like
honey. Dissolve some of this syrup in the distilled water to make a gargle. When gargled warm, it will heal a throat swollen from burning mucus, or tonsils and glands that
are openly abscessed.

Take the leaves of blackberries and cook them in white wine. Use this decoction
while still warm to wash sores on the shins and other places where there is little flesh
and the nerves are close to the surface. Repeat often. This will take away all the foulness and promote healing with miraculous speed. Indeed, this decoction can also be
applied to the itch and ringworm with good results, and completely heal spreading
sores on the skin.

In addition to all of this, ripe blackberries are good to eat and are certainly not
unhealthy. Oh yes, you can even prepare a splendid and very pleasing wine from the
pressed juice fermented with sugar, or a tasty syrup. Both will strengthen the stomach and cheer the heart.

Black Pepper
Piper nigrum
Sauer: *Pfeffer* (1776)

Black pepper needs little introduction, and Sauer's enumeration of its medical applica-
tions is fairly straightforward, except for one intriguing recipe: the spice powder.
Ostensibly this was intended in cookery to pique the appetite and awaken the stomach
from its lethargy. Yet a more pleasant and culinary side cannot be ignored. In fact, the

29. See, for example, the "Recipe for Making Black-berry Jelly" in *Poulson's Town and Country Almanac for
1789* (Philadelphia, 1788).

spice powder is a forgotten dimension of colonial German cookery that should reconfirm that if this cookery was plain by today's standards, it was at the least highly flavored.

Spice powders were one means of getting around culinary monotony where cookery was tied to the ebbs and flows of seasonal abundance. They were once common, and their types were many, from zesty powders for roasts and grilled meats to herbal mixtures for vegetables or fragrant saffron-ginger powders (like the one below from Sauer's herbal) for boiled chicken and poultry. There were individuals in colonial America who specialized in spice powders, and many of these powders also incorporated capsicums of various kinds, even some of the hottest ones now back in fashion.

Spice powders were even rubbed on meats prior to curing them and added to sausages, to crab boils, and to the water in which fish or shellfish were poached. They were also one of the key ingredients in the many types of pepperpot soup once sold on the streets of Philadelphia, Baltimore, and other large towns up and down the eastern seaboard.

Common black pepper is quite warming and of a hot nature. It possesses a caustic, volatile, alkaline salt and a small amount of oil. For this reason it has excellent overall properties for penetrating, opening up, dissolving thick humors, and withstanding all that is acid and sour.

Pepper will fortify a cold stomach, mollify its sharp crudities, and restore the natural yeasts of the gut to their proper effervescence and strength. It assists digestion, excites the appetite, and works as an antidote to windiness of the bowels.

An intensely flavored spice powder can be prepared in the following manner: Take two loths of pepper, one loth of ginger, half a quint of saffron, a quint each of cloves and galingale, and grind all of this together until it forms a fine powder. Use this as a seasoning on food.

Many people have discovered that the following remedy is of great usefulness against the ague, namely: Pepper, calamus, zedoary, ginger, and gentian infused in brandy or rum. Take a sip of this before each onset of a chill. Some infuse pepper in wine and drink this as a remedy for fits of shivering brought on by ague.

Professor Joels[30] has written thus: For all kinds of ague, nine peppercorns should be taken every morning and continued for a time. This cure has already proved helpful to those suffering from tertian and quartan fevers.

An oil may also be distilled from pepper, which in its efficacy and virtues resembles the oil of cloves. Three to four drops of this oil combined with gentian-root extract or wormwood water, and taken before the onset of a fever, will dispel the tert-

---

30. Professor Joels has not been identified.

ian and quartan fevers, especially if the stomach has been thoroughly purged beforehand. On the other hand, pepper can be highly dangerous in all illnesses that overheat the body, since its use will increase rather than decrease the heat, thirst,
inflammations, pains, and other contingent symptoms. Such caution should also be
exercised in the case of other strong spices.

Blueberry (European Blueberry)
Vaccinium myrtillus
Sauer: *Heidelbeere* (1771)

*The fruit under discussion is known in Europe by a variety of terms: whortleberry,
bilberry, and common blueberry, to name a few. In the Palatinate, where many
Pennsylvania Germans originated, the blueberry is called* Weele, *a dialect word not
easy to translate. However, Sauer's more standard German name means "heath berry,"
for it was upon heath lands or in open patches in the forest that this fruit was commonly
found.*

Under the name of Heidelbeere, *German settlers in America gathered three basic
species: the highbush blueberry* (Vaccinium corymbosum), *the lowbush blueberry*
(Vaccinium angustifolium, *formerly called* V. pennsylvanicum), *and the New Jersey
blueberry* (Vaccinium caesariense). *We may also include huckleberries* (Gaylussacia
baccata) *under this general rubric, since country people were not exacting when it came
to scientific nomenclature. Indeed, we may safely presume that all of these various
berries were used interchangeably in folk medicine. They were also used extensively in
cookery.*

Heidelbeere-Brockle *was a popular summer dish made by placing the berries in a
bowl of milk, then sprinkling this with sugar and broken pieces of bread, resulting in a
type of mush.[31] The berries were also dried or even smoked for use during the winter,
the smoked ones normally added to sausages. And of course, there was blueberry wine,
which resembles a robust merlot when well aged and remained a popular health drink
well into the late 1800s.[32]*

Blueberries are endowed with a delicate juice. They act upon injuries by glutination,
and they lower blood pressure by slowing the flow of overheated blood.

Fresh and dried blueberries are employed to treat bloody flux and other forms of
diarrhea; the fresh berries are excellent for quenching thirst caused by fevers. When
dried, ground to a powder, and administered as an infusion in the water of blue mallow, blueberries not only allay the symptoms of bloody flux and operate against diarrhea but are also good for stones, gravel, sand, and foul matter afflicting the kidneys.
Blueberry juice can be boiled down into an electuary that is even more efficacious for
all of the above conditions.

Press the juice of fresh blueberries and boil this down to a syrup with sugar. This

31. Jean Maust Monn, "Berries for Sale," *Casselman Chronicle* 1, no. 3 (autumn 1961): 5–6.
32. See for example the recipe for blueberry wine in *Der Farmer Kalender für das Jahr 1881* (Philadelphia, 1880).

will produce a pleasant remedy that is useful in reducing high blood pressure. It is also effective for treating blood-spitting, burning fevers, and similar afflictions arising from high temperature and thirst.

Some people also put blueberries into olive oil and then boil them—blueberry leaves can also be added. Once the oil has absorbed the juices of the fruit, strain it through a jelly bag or fine cloth. If the head is rubbed with this ointment from time to time, it will prevent the loss of hair. The oil can also be strengthened further with the oils of nutmeg and mastic and repeatedly rubbed warm over the belly of persons afflicted by fluxes of the stomach or with vomiting.

Blue Mallow
Malva sylvestris
Sauer: *Pappel, Käsepappel* (1770)

There are several varieties of mallow that belong to this species. Some are short, others are tall, and considerable tinkering has occurred to improve the ornamental character of the flowers. Nothing yet is quite as appealing as the old blue mallow of this herbal. It is tall, rangy like a hollyhock, and invariably requires staking. But it cuts such a handsome show in the herb garden that it should not be overlooked by anyone who enjoys flowers. In any case, it is also a great bee plant, and butterflies adore it. Yet the flowers are not really blue, rather an intense royal purple. They turn blue when dried, and the tea made from them is quite refreshing—a point not mentioned in the herbal.

Sauer also noted, but without further comment, that blue mallow was served as a table vegetable. In this respect it was once an important feature of medieval cookery, but gradually declined in popularity, especially during the eighteenth century, when it was replaced in cookbook literature by spinach. However, country people continued to cook with it, boiling the leaves and young shoots as greens. The greens were also chopped and added to egg Brockle *or* Dummes, *a type of chopped omelet discussed under asparagus on page 48. In fact,* Pappel-Dummes *was considered quite healthy as a spring dish.*

The green seedpods, called "cheeses," were likewise gathered as food and cooked much like green peas—they are used medicinally in one of the remedies below. The cheeses can also be brined after the manner of capers and thus applied as attractive garnishing for winter fare, or simply eaten by themselves as a pickle.

Blue mallow is moderate in its nature, lying halfway between hot and cold. It softens hardness and swellings and suppurates by means of its mucusy juices and gentle-acting salts. Pagan priests of old inscribed their secrets on mallow leaves, for which reason Pythagoras thought them sacred. The herb is also very useful for all manner of internal and external afflictions, for it is known as the ancient omnimorbiam, that is, a panacea for all illnesses. Likewise, it has also served as food.

For blockages of the urine, put some mallow leaves and a little garlic into white wine. Cook this down until reduced to one-third, then drink this regularly until the condition is cured.

As an antiscorbutic for putrification of the gums and scurvy, take two loths of refined honey and a quint each of ground mallow and powdered saltpeter, and mix together thoroughly. Rub this on the gums until they are healed.

When the root of blue mallow is dug up in April under the light of a full moon and then hung on the nape of the neck, it makes a capital remedy for the eyes. For it will act as an antidote to both inflammation and rheums running from the lids.

Mallow cheeses boiled with peas in strong lye, or boiled in the patient's own fresh urine, will cure scall provided the scalp is washed with this decoction on a daily basis. The decoction should be applied warm. A piece of cloth dipped in this and laid over the condition will also heal it.

For those afflicted with gravel and kidney or bladder stones, the following loin bath will prove useful, since it softens and opens constrictions in the urinary ducts. Take four handfuls of blue mallow, two handfuls each of marshmallow, chervil, and ground ivy, and a handful each of chamomile blossoms and flaxseed. Boil this in a large kettle of water. Let the decoction cool, then pour it into a tub. Set the patient in the tub to soak.

A useful clyster can also be made from blue mallow that is quite effective in keeping the body open in cases of colic or hysterics. To make it, take a handful each of blue mallow, marshmallow, veronica, and violet leaves, and a loth each of flaxseed and anise. Boil these ingredients in water, then strain. Take a pint of the decoction and add to it a few spoonfuls of molasses and just as much olive oil. Fill a bladder and apply as a clyster as warm as the eye of the fundament can bear it.

Distilled water of blue mallow is quite serviceable for body sores, eases bloody flux, and heals injuries to the womb, kidneys, and bladder. It also opens up the urinary ducts so that stone, sand, and foul matter may be more easily discharged.

What has just been ascribed to mallows is likewise valid for hollyhocks. This is true because they work in quite a similar manner, and all of their natural endowments may be treated and applied interchangeably.

Borage
Borago officinalis
Sauer: *Burretsch* (1767)

Under borage, Sauer introduces the restorative soup of the sort that became fashionable in the seventeenth century and then took over soup cookery entirely by the end of the eighteenth. Initially, these were sympathetic soups designed to match the medical properties of the ingredients with specific cures and afflictions. In her Augsburgisches Koch-Buch *(Augsburg, 1788), Sophie Juliane Weiler published a century-old recipe for calf lung soup fortified with herbs for curing coughs and weaknesses of the chest.[33] Her herb soup in the same cookbook was intended as a specific for cooling the body and purifying the blood. However old-fashioned they may have seemed in the 1760s and 1770s, we may safely presume that for Sauer's readers, health soups were still a com-*

33. Sophie Juliane Weiler, *Augsburgisches Koch-Buch* (Augsburg, 1788), p. 652.

mon feature of home cookery and that borage soup was certainly one of them.

A model for the borage soup alluded to in the herbal, the one complained of that uniformed doctors were recommending, can be found in the Vollständiges Nürnbergisches Koch-Buch *of 1691. It is a simple preparation made with meat stock, borage leaves, and young shoots chopped small, and then cooked gently for as long as it takes to hard-cook an egg. (Good cooks even then did not boil their food to shreds.) The soup was then seasoned with nutmeg and cardamom and served over a slice of bread with a little grated cheese sprinkled over the top. This is certainly not a difficult soup to make, but Sauer was indeed right in pointing out that cooking borage destroys its medical properties.*

For medical purposes, borage is gathered when the sun moves into the sign of Gemini or into the sign of Cancer. The root, leaves, and little flowers are the parts used, and they have the property of warming gently, of defending the heart, of refreshing the spirit, of opening obstructions of the spleen, and of encouraging a glad disposition.

The distilled water of borage delights and enlivens the heart, guards against fainting spells and tremblings of the heart, cleanses the blood, and banishes melancholy and tormented dreams, provided six to eight loths of the cordial are drunk regularly according to one's preference.

Conserve of borage is prepared like rose conserve, namely: Take two parts of loaf sugar and one part flowers, and grind this in a marble or wooden mortar until reduced to a fine powder.[34] Then set aside and store for later use. This sugar strengthens the heart and spirit and serves as an antidote to all manner of poison, but it is especially effective for cases of depression, provided it is administered often in doses the size of a nutmeg.

For melancholy, many doctors advise lifting the spirits by cooking borage in broth. But by boiling the soup, the subtle, volatile salt is lost from which the herb derives its foremost action. It is better, therefore, when borage is prepared as a restorative in combination with scorzonera root, lemon balm, burnet, chervil, and viper's bugloss (or as many of these ingredients as one has on hand). Put them in a well-covered pot to cook with the broth. In this manner, the effectiveness of the broth will be strengthened, and it may be consumed every morning and evening over a long period.

A cordial can be prepared by infusing the flowers in brandy. Thirty or more drops of this taken often will strengthen the heart and bring cheer. It is made better and even more effective when tincture of antimony[35] and calendula water are mixed with it.

34. *The Queens Delight* (London, 1671) identified this conserve and the method of making it as Italian. In fact, the Venetians and Genovese acquired this technology on Cyprus. The flowers of both the common blue borage and the much rarer white borage were utilized in conserves.

35. Antimony is a metal regarded as a poison, but since it induces vomiting, its emetic properties were recognized in medicine. The tincture or "wine" of antimony was less violent and used as a diaphoretic; that is, to induce perspiration. However, when combined with the substances suggested here, it undergoes a chemical transformation and becomes a strong narcotic. Dr. William Buchan complained in his *Domestic Medicine* (Exeter, N.H., 1843) that the quality of the tincture was so variable that its use should be considered dangerous, a fair warning to anyone who may want to experiment with this substance.

Today it is customary to distill water of cinnamon together with the juice pressed from borage so that the water is rendered all the more effective and fortifying to the heart.

Bracken (Fern Brake)
Pteris aquilina
Sauer: *Farhrenkraut* (1763)

This handsome fern is also native to North America, where it grows in open woods, often attaining the height of three or four feet. The uncoiled fronds have been cooked and eaten as spring greens for centuries, and they can even be fermented to make beer. But since the plant grows on barren ground, it is also associated with barrenness in women, and the leaves as well as the cooked shoots will cause abortion. This is the reason for Sauer's warning to pregnant women—advice that should be carefully heeded by women today, since fern greens are now back in style at high-end restaurants.

Bracken is of a warm and dry nature and possesses the capacity to open, to cleanse, to purify, and to heal. It abates all that is bitter and acidic, and is especially serviceable for various ailments of the spleen. However, it is highly injurious to pregnant women.

Should a horse fall to the ground and no one knows what ails it, lay a piece of bracken root under its tongue. It will then begin to urinate and stand up again—so writes Mattheolus.[36]

For those who have been burned by fire, by scalding water, or by boiling oil, take the root of bracken and press out the juice. If the root is too dry, first moisten it with rosewater or springwater. This expressed juice is deemed one of the best remedies for burns.

Take a handful of bracken leaves and root chopped up fine and heat this in one quart of wine. Cook until reduced to one pint, and use this vulnerary to wash out wounds. The dried root of bracken ground to a fine powder and strewn into the freshly washed wound will hasten its healing excellently.

The dried root of bracken ground to a fine powder and administered in doses of one-half to one full quint will make a powerful vermifuge. The patient should take it in the morning prior to eating, and if possible, during the waning of the moon.

Broad Bean (Fava Bean)
Vicia faba
Sauer: *Bohnen* (1776)

One of the lingering European features of colonial American cookery was its continued dependence on broad beans. They were widely consumed by both the English and

---

36. Pier' Andrea Mattioli (1500–1577) was a famous Italian commentator on the writings of Dioscorides. He also wrote an *Historia Plantarum* (1561) and the posthumous *Hortus Medicus Philosophicus* (1588). This latter work is the source of his medical advice.

German settlers, and the varieties were many. Philadelphia seedsman Bernard M'Mahon offered fourteen varieties for sale in 1803, and those were just the ones popular at the time in England. We have very little information about the kinds of broad beans cultivated by the German community, but doubtless they were more like the old seventeenth-century small, flat, or round-seeded types popular in northern Europe. They were normally dried and eaten during the winter in soups and porridges. And as the herbal points out, they were also ground into flour, which had many uses. Sauer enumerated the medical applications, but the flour was also combined with rye or spelt flour for baking flat breads. Additionally, the ash of the broad bean plant makes a rich fertilizer that was used to increase the productivity of colonial German kitchen gardens.

The juice in broad beans holds a middle position between cold and warmth. The beans themselves possess a rather large quantity of volatile, gentle salts, along with sundry balsamic oils, and therefore provide good nourishment, cleanse the body, and operate by urine.

In medicine, broad beans are used externally more than internally, for they tend to bloat the belly by creating quantities of vapor, and give rise to dross thickish blood. They are difficult to digest, and charge the mind with fantastical dreams. However, when they are properly cooked, broad beans provide ample and healthy nourishment.

A good cure for loss of hearing: Boil broad beans in water until they are well cooked. Pour off the cooking water and place the beans in a shallow bowl. Set a funnel over the hot beans and let the steam rise through the funnel into the affected ear. Repeat this several days in succession, and this will improve the hearing. Others recommend scattering broad bean flour over hot coals and letting the smoke rise through a funnel into the ear. For some, this has promptly restored their hearing.

Broad bean flour is good for all manner of swellings on the bosoms and in the privates when cooked in milk until thick and then made into a plaster. This is laid warm over the affected place. When boiled in equal parts water and vinegar, and laid warm over inflamed swellings of the privates, it will disperse them quickly.

Broad bean flour cooked with milk to a pap is good for all kinds of stomach fluxes and for diarrhea. The flour can also be cooked and used to great advantage as an emollient plaster.

When the member swells so that one cannot urinate, as can easily happen to those afflicted by the stone when the stone settles in the duct, then cook some broad beans in milk to a porridge consistency. Apply this thick and warm around the member.[37] This treatment has already helped many who were thus afflicted.

Several loths of water of broad bean flowers drunk in the morning before breakfast will promote urine and drive out gravel.[38] Yet this remedy is even more efficacious if one-half quint of broad bean salts from the apothecary are added to each dose.

The straw of broad beans burned to ash and made into a lye with water will powerfully dispel through the urine the fluxes of dropsical persons.[39] Drink the lye-water

37. The "member" in this case is male.
38. The spirit or water of broad bean flowers is also sweetly fragrant.
39. By straw, it is understood to mean the dead plants, which were indeed used as straw and fodder since ancient times, though they turn an unappetizing black.

often in doses of up to five or six loths. Or, make use of the salts made from the straw and dissolved in a serviceable spirit or julep. Take a dose of up to one-half quint every six to eight hours.

If the ashes of broad bean straw are mixed with garden soil, and then parsley seeds are planted in this, the seeds will germinate quickly.

Brooklime
Veronica beccabunga
Sauer: *Bachbunge, Wasserbunge* (1765)

> *Brooklime, also known as water pimpernel, is a perennial wild salad plant found along streams and ponds, or growing on wet, marshy ground. The large, smooth, fleshy leaves are generally used in spring salads much like watercress. The flowers are blue. The plant is not native to North America and therefore should not be confused with American water pimpernel* (Samolus floribundus) *or with American brooklime* (Veronica americana), *neither of which were recognized in pharmacopoeias of the period. European brooklime was raised artificially in physic gardens in this country and sold as a botanical medicine. The Shakers promoted it as late as the 1850s and 1860s. The plant has now naturalized as an escape in several places on the East Coast.*

The virtues of brooklime are such that it warms and humidifies, purges the blood of foul humors, drives out crudities by provoking urine—and operates through other passages as well—eases obstructions of the viscera, dissolves hard phlegm, relieves breathing, cleanses scorbutic melancolic blood, opposes all manner of astringency, and cleans and heals inner as well as external wounds. In most cases, it shares the same virtues as watercress, although it is somewhat milder in its operation.

Brooklime leaves should be gathered when the sun is in the sign of Gemini. For those who suffer from scurvy or from kidney stones, the leafy part is quite effective during early spring when eaten in salads made without a vinegar dressing. Brooklime is also a valuable vulnerary. Whoever has suffered an injury, take a leaf of this herb, put a little salt and a cobweb on it, then tie it tight over the wound with a cloth. If one boils brooklime in beer and lays it on the shins, it will heal open sores resulting from scurvy. For anyone who suffers from swollen feet, take brooklime, sprinkle it with salt, and bind this around them.

For those who drink four loths of the freshly pressed and strained juice, or eight to ten loths of the liquid distilled from it, every morning and evening for one month, brooklime will cleanse thick, foul, scorbutic blood, heal blocked fluxes and dropsy, and expel tertian and quartan ague. One can also distill watercress, plantain, and scurvy grass the same way,[40] or press them together to mingle their juices, and use thus.

Above all else, brooklime shares in common every virtue of watercress and the broad leafed plantain. When brooklime is boiled in water for use as a plaster and laid

---

40. A recipe for this compound under the name Antiscorbutic Water appeared in Michael Krafft's *American Distiller* (Philadelphia, 1804), 199.

on warm, it checks the pain of hemorrhoids.

The distilled water of brooklime is celebrated for provoking urine and for breaking up kidney stones, for killing worms in the gut, and in particular for staying disorders of the spleen, provided one drinks a gill of it regularly in the morning and evening.

Bryony (White Bryony)
Bryonia dioica
Sauer: *Stickwurz, Zaunrüben* (1772)

The Sauer herbal is not altogether explicit about the species of bryony intended. But since Sauer gives one of the German names as Zaunrüben, *"hedge turnip," and this is always equated with the French* navet du diable, *we may conclude that our subject is the red-berried* Bryonia dioica. *It was much more commonly used by old herbalists than European white bryony, and in fact the two operate rather differently on the body. In any case, Sauer's choice of the term* Stickwurz *was patently incorrect because this is a common name for wood sorrel (page 359), a totally different plant. It is possible that his typesetter misread* Gichtwurz, *which is indeed one of the common dialect names for bryony.*

Perhaps it is also worth noting that Sauer placed bryony (as hedge turnip) beside true turnip in his original German, as though the two were somehow related botanically, which they are not. White bryony is a member of the cucumber tribe that develops a large, fleshy perennial root. The plant is poisonous, but it is this poison that was used in small quantities for medical purposes. Furthermore, white bryony is not native to North America.

Material on bryony is not common in early American medical literature, although Sauer's competitor, Heinrich Miller, discussed bryony in his Der Neuerste, Verbesserte und Zuverlässige Americanische Calender *(Newest, most improved and reliable American almanac) in 1770. However, no mention of bryony appears in American adaptations of such mainstream works as William Buchan's* Every Man His Own Doctor *(New Haven, Conn., 1816), yet its use among the Pennsylvania Germans is certainly confirmed by Miller, Sauer, and others. Their advocacy of this potent botanical curative was somewhat ahead of their times, inasmuch as bryony later became one of the chief herbs advocated by Samuel Hahnemann, founder of homeopathic medicine. Or at least, bryony fit the philosophical framework of homeopathy, which naturally drew on much older themes.*

In spite of this popularity, the plant is certainly not naturalized in the middle states, and because of its rampant habit it is not easy to bring under domestication. In the wild, its tangled vines engulf entire shrubs and small trees. Yet because it was used fresh in Sauer's remedies, we must presume that bryony was indeed readily available and that Sauer could rely upon this source as required. This availability is further substantiated by the presence of a recipe for Compound Bryony Water in Michael Krafft's American Distiller *(Philadelphia, 1804). Otherwise, foreign bryony root, collected in the autumn after a hard frost, must have been imported and stored much like barreled potatoes.*

Bryony possesses an acidic, caustic salt in its juice, from which it draws its capacity to purge, to open, and especially to operate in the expulsion of superfluous water from the stomach by means of urine and stool.

The juice from fresh bryony root taken in doses of one or one and a half loths will draw off these waters via the stool and urine, while at the same time curing the onset of dropsy. Additionally, it opens blockages of the liver and spleen, and operates against both common yellow jaundice and obstructive jaundice. It also purges the stomach not only of worms but even snakes, toads, and similar creatures, as the renowned Bartholinus has demonstrated by remarkable example.[41]

The roots of bryony pared of their outer skin, pounded fine, and boiled with sugar to the consistency of an electuary, will on occasion fully dispel the falling evil and mother fits. Administer it in doses the size of a nutmeg twice a day.

Fresh bryony root ground and mixed with linseed oil, heated until very warm, then applied warm to the hips, will take away the pain of sciatica. Indeed, this lotion will also cure pleurisy and take away bruises or livid marks on the skin.

Bryony water distilled from the fresh roots has proven helpful to asthmatic persons, and will cleanse the kidneys, expel gravel, open obstructions of the liver, spleen, and matrix, and cleanse and purify inveterate wounds and unhealed sores, provided these conditions are washed with warm bryony water regularly.

Buckshorn Plantain
Plantago cornopus
Sauer: *Krähenfuss* (1774)

Sauer's choice of plant names has sometimes led to unintended confusion, and in this case, the wrong plant could be deadly. Krähenfuss, *the German name supplied by Sauer, is much more commonly attributed to a European species of wild geranium called bloody crowsfoot, or to a species of buttercup. One helpful clue lies in Sauer's Latin:* cornopus, *which is more correctly rendered in German as* Krähenfusswegerich *(crowsfoot plantain). True crowsfoot (the buttercup) is not used internally since it is poisonous, a "ferocious biting herb" to quote Nicholas Culpeper, hot and dry by virtue and under the dominion of Mars. Thus the second clue is in Sauer's remedies, for they are not only internal and cooling, the plant discussed is even eaten in salads.*

Buckshorn plantain is a small European plant with handsome antlerlike leaves that have been in use both as a food and as a medical herb since ancient times. It grows wild along the coast of northwestern Europe and will even take root between pebbles and stones near the beach. Like scurvy grass (page 280), it is biennial, remains green during the winter, and thus is an excellent source of cold weather salading. It will only naturalize in regions of this country with mild winters, but does quite well in cold frames

41. There were two Danish physicians by this name: Kasper Bartholin (1585–1629) and Thomas Bartholin (1616–1680). The latter Bartholin wrote a well-known book on anatomy that was translated into English in 1663. He is the assumed originator of the remarkable cure. The affliction, however, was thought to have been the work of witchcraft. A popular woodcut showing the patient puking snakes, toads, and other vermin was still in circulation during Sauer's lifetime.

*in my southeastern Pennsylvania garden. It normally runs
to seed in June. But if planted in the spring, it will produce
seed in the fall, so the plant can be grown as an annual. This
is doubtless how it was treated since its introduction into our
kitchen gardens in the 1600s.*

Buckshorn plantain is cold and dry, and possesses a mild,
saltpeter-like salt, together with a gentle, mucusy sap.
These give it the strength to contain all febrile humors
of the blood, and to work gently in this constricting
action. The plant is eaten in many places as a salad, or
cooked and eaten together with other greens. It is useful
against dropsy, gravel of the loins, kidney stones, fluxes of
the belly and matrix, and blood-spitting, and for prevention
of contagion.

For all of the afflictions just mentioned, drink anywhere
from one-half to a full gill of the distilled water of buckshorn
plantain. The fresh juice of the plant is administered in doses
of half this amount.

Burdock (Great Burdock)

Arctium lappa
Sauer: *Kletten* (1763)

*Sauer differentiated between two similar species, the great burdock (Arctium lappa)
and the lesser burdock (Arctium minus). He made it abundantly clear from his
German (grosse Kletten) that it was the former that interested him. This is a plant
that is now naturalized in most parts of North America. It was an important vegetable
during the Middle Ages, and even in Sauer's day it was cultivated in kitchen gardens
for its greens and roots. Indeed, Johann Friedrich Zückert noted in his* Materia
Alimentaria *(Berlin, 1769) that the young leaves were cooked as greens and the stems
prepared like asparagus, although, due to their rustic nature, recipes for these preparations did not commonly appear in genteel cook books.*

*In a fit of macrobiotic enthusiasm, I introduced burdock into my own kitchen gar-
den, only to have it invade every corner of the property and thoroughly cover the compost bins with its verdure. It repays neglect and abuse with abundance, which is why the
poor in colonial America valued it so highly, not to mention its many valuable uses for
curing both the human and animal inhabitants of the farm. As one final note, I should
also point out that burdock never dropped out of the rural diet of the Pennsylvania
Germans. Articles extolling its uses appeared in German-American almanacs throughout the nineteenth century, and as late as 1950, local recipes for cooking it could be found
in such regional newspapers as the* Allentown Morning Call.

The great burdock possesses a warm and dry nature. It has the capacity to open, to attenuate, to dissipate, to facilitate breathing, and to operate by urine and sweat. It also cleanses and heals wounds and sores. The seed, taken in one-quint doses every two weeks, will prevent stones in the kidneys and bladder.

The root of the great burdock, chopped into small bits and then given to sheep afflicted with coughing and disease, will bring relief to them with particularly good effect.[42]

When a horse is moon-eyed,[43] or has other infirmities of the eyes, it should be fed burdock leaves, the leaves of wild marjoram, valerian, and gentian mixed with its fodder.

The leaves of burdock bruised until limp and laid over old wounds, sores, and dislocated joints that have been reset will heal them quickly and completely.

The root can be preserved in sugar as with calamus. This is excellent for those who are afflicted with sand, gravel, and foul matter in the kidneys, as well as for those who are short of breath or plagued by severe coughing. As a remedy, take several pieces of the candied root in the morning prior to breakfast, and continue until the condition is abated.

Cook the root of great burdock in wine. Strain and drink a full tumbler of the liquid frequently for a complete cure of quartan ague.

The fresh leaves and root of burdock chopped and cooked in butter will yield a splendid salve for all manner of burn injuries. It will draw out the pain and infection caused by the burn and heal the flesh.

Burnet (Lesser Burnet)
Pimpinella saxifraga
Sauer: *Bibernelle* (1765)

True Bibernelle *is* Sanguisorba officinalis *or great burnet, as it is often called in English. But since Sauer used the German term* kleine Bibernelle *in his text, and the various virtues and uses agree with what is said in other herbals, there is not much doubt about the genus and species intended here. This herb is also called burnet saxifrage in English; indeed, it goes by a long list of common names, including salad burnet.*

This is the garden herb of old that was raised as a spring green, for its young leaves are quite refreshing in salads and taste like cucumber. They were also infused in wine or beer for cool tankards and other spring drinks. As Sauer's herbal points out, it was the root that was most highly valued in medicine, and this was harvested in the spring just before the appearance of the leaves—in Sauer's garden, this would have been early March. The greens, which develop quickly after spring thaw, were greatly relished by the Germans in colonial America. Friederike Löffler published a typical spring salad recipe in her Ökonomisches Handbuch für Frauenzimmer *(Stuttgart, 1795), 431. Note that burnet is first on her list; all the rest may be found elsewhere in Sauer's*

42. The point is that sheep are liable to catch cold after spring shearing; the problem can spread quickly in a herd if it is not attended to promptly.

43. This term is commonly used for horses that are blind, but it is also a symptom of the onset of distemper. It is easy to spot because the eyes of the horse will be enlarged and weeping profusely.

herbal: "For this herbal salad, take burnet, chervil, sorrel, succory, young nettles, gar-
den chicory, liverwort, dittander, the tender leaves of young daisies, rampion, and tar-
ragon. Chop all of these ingredients together and season well with salt, pepper, chives,
vinegar, and olive oil" (431).

Burnet possesses the properties of warming, drying, emolliating, dissipating, and
repelling poison by operating through the urine and sweat. It defends mankind
against all types of poison, and is useful to every part of the belly, since it warms and
strengthens the stomach, liver, kidneys, and bladder. The root should be administered
diligently during the outbreak of contagious diseases. Additionally, the leaves make a
capital vulnerary, and not simply for fresh wounds, but for healing old injuries as well;
thus the leaves may be employed in preparing the potion.

It is the current opinion in France that if people make diligent use of burnet, they
will not be harmed by the bite of a mad dog. For burnet has the special power to repel
hydrophobia caused by such an animal bite.

Burnet possesses a marvelous way of increasing milk if wet nurses simply wear it
as a posy between their bosoms. This promotes a strong flow of milk within a few
hours.

The distilled water of burnet taken in doses of four or five loths each morning
purges gravel, sand, and stones; promotes urine; cleanses the kidneys, urinary ducts,
and bladder of foul matter; repels poison; cleanses the blood of impurities; and protects against contagion.

Burnet root can be preserved in sugar like succory root. If a small piece of this is
eaten in the morning and evening, it will improve a cold stomach, strengthen digestion, stay the colic, bring warmth to the matrix, protect against contagion, and cleanse
the kidneys and bladder of sand, stones, and foul matter.

If burnet flowers are put up in sugar conserve like rose and betony conserves, and
administered from time to time in doses the size of a nutmeg, it will dispel melancholy notions and fantastical caprices of the mind. It will also strengthen the head and
bring down cold rheums, as well as alleviate dizziness and ague. Burnet conserve is
likewise good for fevers arising from the stomach; it stays colic and headache, protects against contagion, strengthens the heart and memory, and is good for treating
the stone, coughs, and obstruction of the liver.

Butterbur
Petasites vulgaris
Sauer: *Pestilenzwurz* (1778)

Butterbur is related to coltsfoot in that both were preferred for homeopathic remedies.
But in Sauer's time, the plant was mostly employed as a cardiac tonic or as a heart stim-
ulant among the English. The English name is derived from the fact that the large
leaves were used for wrapping butter when it was sent to market, the idea being that
the leaves were antiseptic and would therefore protect the butter from impurities. The

German name, which means "pestilence root," alludes to the fact that butterbur was used as protection against the plague. By extension, it was seen as an effective alexipharmic against all sorts of poisons and contagious diseases.

John Hill advocated butterbur as an antipestilential in his Virtues of British Herbs *(1770); indeed, he considered it more powerful than any other. The timeliness of Sauer's treatment of butterbur should not be overlooked, since a "putrid fever" had broken out in Europe and caused many deaths. While patients in England died in droves from being bled, the Germans managed to escape the worst on account of butterbur. This greatly enhanced the reputation of the herb in the eyes of many period physicians. Furthermore, the medicine was cheap.*

In Europe, butterbur grows wild in wetlands and bogs. It is considered one of the most pernicious of all weeds to eradicate, and for this reason it is rarely introduced into gardens. Since the plants reach anywhere from six to fifteen feet in height and have large leaves, they more or less choke out any other plants growing nearby. The fact that butterbur is naturalized only in southeastern Pennsylvania would seem to underscore its intentional introduction by the Germans or by dairy farmers, since this region was at one time a great center of butter and cheese production.

Butterbur possesses a warm and dry nature and operates by means of a volatile, aromatic, bitter salt. Thus it has the properties of attenuating, opening, repelling all manner of poison, easing the breathing, killing worms, promoting urination and other things therein related, as well as operating by sweat. The roots must be dug up early in March and then dried for later use.

Long experience has proved that this root can be used quite advantageously against infection, hence it is called "pestilence root."

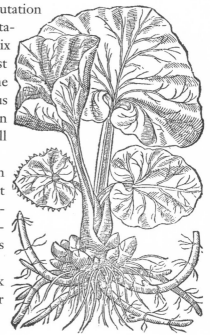

The distilled water of butterbur root has a similar reputation for preventing infection. If someone is infected with contagion during an epidemic, immediately give the person six loths of butterbur water in which a quint of the best *Theriaca Andromaci* has been dissolved. Then send the patient to bed beneath many covers so that vigorous sweating can commence. Butterbur water administered in tablespoon doses to women will still mother fits and kill worms.

The essence extracted from the root by infusing it in brandy, given in frequent doses of fifteen or more drops at a time, produces a splendid prophylactic against pestilential fevers and other like contagions. It also opens obstructions of the lungs, liver, spleen, and matrix, and dispels jaundice and dropsy.

If this essence is reduced by cooking until it is thick like honey, it may be employed profitably in pill form for all of the above-mentioned afflictions.

Butterbur root can also be candied like calamus and eaten as a sweetmeat for preventing these same diseases.

Cabbage and Collards
Brassica oleracea
Sauer: *Kappes, Kohl* (1767)

Most of what Sauer reports on the uses of cabbage agrees with attributes enumerated by Nicholas Culpeper. However, the Sauer herbal makes certain distinctions between cabbages for medical use and those for general consumption. For example when Sauer uses Kohl *and* Kappes *side by side, the implication is that the first is collards (young cabbage), while the latter is a fully formed head as shown in the woodcut. In either case, the preferred types for medicine were the red varieties or very dark purple-gray kales. It is difficult to be more specific than that, since our knowledge of the cabbage varieties grown by the German community in colonial America is quite incomplete. Roter Trummel (red drumhead) would probably answer for the required red variety. Chou quintal de Strasbourg or quintal d'Alsace are improved varieties (still extant) of a type of winter cabbage grown in southwest Germany at least since the 1600s. These are almost exclusively sauerkraut cabbages and would thus meet the requirements of the sauerkraut remedies mentioned in Sauer.*

It is apparent that seed was imported from Germany on a regular basis during the eighteenth century and that the German farmers here depended on imported cabbage seed more than seed for other vegetables. The reason was this: to maintain the purity of the variety, at least sixty-four cabbage plants must be overwintered for seed stock the following year. Very few cabbages overwinter unprotected, so they must be dug up with their roots and stored. In short, this commits a large portion of food stock for seed purposes, so very few farmers went to this trouble. But cabbage was stored in pits for winter use, so the remedies mentioned by Sauer could be made almost any time during the year—an extremely important point. Sauerkraut, however, was only made during cold weather, thus a summer hangover would require a different remedy.

Lastly, Sauer included a remedy using kohlrabi seeds. Kohlrabi is indeed a cabbage, so it is in its correct place in the herbal. Kohlrabi is also one of the oldest documented types of cabbage grown in the Rhineland and could correctly be described as ancient. By noting that the Germans of antiquity used cabbage as medicine, the herbal has anointed these plants with a certain mythical incontrovertibility. Cabbage and ethnic identity therefore become inseparable.

The leaves of cabbage possess the properties of attenuating, of driving out foul matter through the urine, and of healing wounds. Red cabbage is especially good for all maladies of the chest, provided it is prepared as a syrup and taken in daily doses. Poor people who suffer from consumption can boil the leaves of red cabbage or of blue kales and make for themselves a broth sweetened with a little sugar. They should drink one or two pints of this every day continuously until recovered. This remedy has already saved many resigned to death by their doctors. In general, collards and full-grown cabbages make for very healthy food, except for those plagued by vapors, since cabbages of all kinds will not agree with that condition at all.

An ancient author reported that the German tribes gave their sick cabbage leaves as medicine for every kind of ailment many centuries before they had doctors.

A quint of kohlrabi seeds ground to powder, cooked in meat stock, and administered warm as soup will prove quite useful in treating colic.

Cabbage is by virtue the antithesis of wine and wine grapes, hence some people eat it while at table in order to ward off drunkenness. Others eat a few chopped leaves with salt and vinegar, thinking that by this means they will be protected, and that the wine will not affect them. Anyone who has made himself miserably drunk on wine, and then eats a meal of sauerkraut, will soon become sober and bright.

Cabbage leaves laid upon severe injuries and wounds will take away burning and alleviate the pain. They are also very healing to the gouging pain of infected sores.

The urine of a boy who has eaten cabbage for several days in succession is said to be excellent for healing all kinds of old sores, fistulas, cancers, skin abrasions, and ringworm.

To treat hoarseness and to expectorate hard mucus from the chest, take freshly pressed cabbage juice and dissolve crystal sugar and honey in it so that it becomes quite sweet. Drink some of this syrup warm several times a day. This is good not only for hoarseness and raw throat but also for coughs and all manner of chest ailments.

Fresh cabbage leaves are highly praised for their ability to keep broken blisters flowing and clean.[44] But care should be exercised in this treatment that fresh leaves be applied at the most every two hours, and indeed heated as hot as the patient can bear them. Therein lies the secret and advantage of this cure.

The liquid from preserved cabbage or sauerkraut is extremely useful for extinguishing any kind of burn one might suffer from. For this treatment, dampen cloths in the liquid and lay them over the affected spot. Repeat this often until the burn is drawn out. This also promotes quick healing.

Calamus (Sweet Flag)
Acorus calamus
Sauer: *Kalmus* (1763)

Renaissance botanist Charles de l'Escuse noted in the 1570s that calamus was a useful antiseptic in medicine.[45] *He also accepted the explanation that calamus was introduced*

---

44. The herbal is not specific. *Blasen* can be blisters, pimples, or cysts.
45. Ernst Roze, *Charles de l'Escuse d'Arras* (Paris, 1899), 75.

into Europe by the Tartars (a fact still under dispute). This was echoed by Polish botanist Szymon Syrénski (1541–1611), who also presumed in his Zielnik Herbarzem *(Kraów, 1613) that calamus entered Europe during the Tartar incursions into the Polish kingdom during the 1200s. In late medieval fish cookery, calamus leaves were often used as a flavor substitute for bay leaves in places where bay leaves were not available—as well as a garnish. Therefore, what we know for certain is that calamus was firmly in place in Europe by the 1300s and that, as a plant originating from the area of the Black Sea, it was not indigenous to northern or western Europe. Furthermore, in cold-climate regions where it was eventually planted, calamus became infertile. It could not be reproduced by seed, but rather by root division.*

It is more likely that dried and candied calamus was traded by Byzantine and Armenian merchants long before calamus was finally planted in medieval herb gardens. Once the Turks came to power in Constantinople, they assumed a monopolistic control over the sale of this herb—all the more reason for Europeans to plant it. But the real motivation behind the medieval demand for calamus was its perceived antiseptic strength in warding off the black plague. By extension, calamus was used against all types of contagious disease, a general application tracing back to Byzantine medicine.

Indeed, calamus was the foremost ingredient in a popular colonial American medicine called Fever Bitters. The recipe, which was said to prevent fever and ague, was published in the August 6, 1787, Pennsylvania Gazette *in response to an outbreak of disease in several coastal towns at that time:*

> *Take of common meadow calamus, cut into small pieces; of rue, wormwood, and chamomile or centaury or horehound, of each two ounces; add to them a quart of spring-water, and take a wine glass full of it every morning fasting. This cheap and excellent infusion is far more effectual then raw spirits, or the strongest bitters made with spirits, in preventing fevers and never subjects the persons who use it to an offensive breath, or to the danger of contracting a love of spirituous liquors.*

This last remark is somewhat prophetic in that the American love affair with patent medicines in the nineteenth century became little more than a socially acceptable way to get a buzz without imbibing Demon Rum.

Calamus possesses many volatile, sharp, oily, aromatic principles well mixed in its salts, and thus has the virtues of warming, of opening, of strengthening the brain, stomach, and matrix; of attenuating tenacious humors, and emolliating and opening obstructions of the spleen, liver, kidneys, and matrix resulting from them. According to ancient wisdom, calamus is of a warm, dry nature.

One loth of calamus boiled in wine and then drunk will heal the weakness and vapors springing from cold phlegm, whether due to wind colic, pain in the side, asthmatic coughing, cramps, or obstruction of the liver and spleen. It also helps those who, due to a fall or to being struck hard by an object, suffer from internal bleeding and painful urination. In addition, this decoction is useful against the bite of snakes and other poisonous beasts, and is therefore generally classified under antidotes to poisoning. Anyone with digestive troubles should take powdered calamus and cinnamon in a wineglass of vermouth.

Calamus root can be preserved in the following manner so that it is pleasant to eat—each morning, one or more little pieces of this preserve should be eaten before going out into thick miasmas or foggy air. Take calamus root and peel off the outer skin. Cut it lengthwise into thin slices. Boil them in water until tender, then let them dry for a length of time in an airy place. Reduce some sugar, the finer the quality the better, over a gentle heat until it becomes thick like honey. Add the slices of calamus root and cook together for a short time. Pour the preserve into an earthenware vessel and let it stand for a few days. If the syrup should become runny due to moisture from the calamus, pour it off and reboil until thick. Pour it again over the calamus, then store away for future use.

Or, take calamus root as aforementioned, peel it and cut into thin slices lengthwise. Then boil in water as above. Take loaf sugar and pound it to a powder as fine as flour. Put the sugar on cooking parchment. Take the calamus slices, as wet as they come from the cookpot, and roll them one at a time in the sugar so that the sugar clings to them. Lay the slices in an airy place so that they may dry out. You can keep calamus this way from year to year (provided you don't keep eating it!).[46]

This candy is a very good remedy for old feeble persons of weak digestion, for it warms the stomach and all other internal organs, and when put up as a preserve in syrup, it agrees with the chest especially well.

Camphor
Cinnamonum camphora
Sauer: *Campher* (1764)

Camphor was of course an import from the Asian tropics. The best sort was said to come from Borneo, and according to Pomet, it was refined for the medical market in Holland.[47] Dutch camphor was the standard product found in colonial apothecaries, and it played a rather curious role in folk medicine. Nowhere is this more evident than in Sauer's herbal.

First of all, it was erroneously thought to prevent contagion, which is why it figured so importantly in such popular protective remedies as Thieves Vinegar, or Räuber-Essig, as it was called in German. This was a solar distillation that was daubed on handkerchiefs held over the nose and mouth as one walked about in neighborhoods afflicted by contagious disease.

46. This is Sauer's remark, from which we may presume that he may have had a fondness for this candy— and a sense of humor as well.

47. Pierre Pomet, *A Complete History of Drugs*, 2 vols. (London, 1712), 1:181.

Camphor is acrid smelling, but because it will keep moths out of clothing, it does not follow that it will do the same with bacteria and other agents of disease. In fact camphor is poisonous, and enough of it will cause convulsions and severe damage to the brain. Yet Sauer was a great believer in camphor, if we are to judge by the amount of space he devoted to it. For the most part, however, his uses are external, or when taken internally, they represent very small doses in the form of camphor brandy (Sauer's own recipe is supplied). His point about pregnant women avoiding the use of camphor should be taken seriously; if camphor suppresses sexual passion and drives out worms from children, a large dose will also expel a fetus. Thus camphor (especially camphor brandy) also served as a clandestine abortant.

Camphor is an oily, volatile salt, and therefore it possesses the virtue and capacity to withstand all corruptions of the blood, of containing and sweetening the mordant matter of poisonous humors, of promoting sweat, of dissolving and dispersing all obdurate crudities of the blood, of calming a raging and unruly spirit, of thinning sluggish blood around the heart and restoring it to its natural flow and motion. It can also hold fits in check.

Camphor also protects the body from corruption, and thus can be added to those medicines that are prepared to protect against pestilence, poison, and the bite or sting of venomous beasts. A dose of camphor equivalent to the weight of a few grains of barley dissolved in a small glass of scabious or sorrel water is good against a contagious ardent fever. Dissolved in a small glass of purslane water and given to children, camphor will dispel their worms.

For anyone attacked by falling sickness or fits, administer three drops of distilled oil of camphor in a tablespoonful of linden blossom water.

Cotton, moistened with a few drops of distilled oil of camphor and then laid upon an aching tooth, will stop the pain. The same preparation inserted into the ears will strengthen weak hearing and halt buzzing and ringing in the same.

According to the old proverb, camphor dispels the desire for wanton pleasures:

Für der Geilheit wildes Rasen,
Halte Campfer an die Nasen.

For stallion-lusting after wild grass,
Hold camphor to the nostrils.[48]

To this end, now and then take a dose of a few grains weight of camphor pills with spirit of water lily.

For burning and inflamed eyes, take one quint of prepared cadmia,[49] two grains of

48. This is not a horse remedy. *Geilheit* is something that affects young men. It was called "running of the reins" in Sauer's era; today we call it excessive horniness. The clue is really in the spirit of water lily that follows the saying, since this was a common remedy for extinguishing venereous actions, "passing seed when one is asleep"—in short, settling the brain of "frantic persons," to quote Nicholas Culpeper.

49. Cadmia is an old term for calamine, a mineral used in medicine. The German word is *Tutia*, from *tutia alexandrina*. The best calamine sold in colonial America was imported from Orleans, France.

camphor, and two loths each of plantain, fennel, and rosewater. Mix these ingredients together, and from time to time put a few drops into the corner of the affected eye.

The following excellent poultice for treating gangrene can be made from camphor. Take two loths of avens root, one loth of angelica root, two handfuls of water germander, and a handful each of rue, holy thistle, and wormwood. Chop this up and cook in equal portions of water and white wine. Strain off two quarts and add half a loth each of aloe, myrrh, and camphor that have first been dissolved in brandy. Mix together well. When required for use, warm it up and moisten clean cloths with the liquid. Lay them hot over the place that is putrid with gangrene.

Pregnant women should avoid using camphor on all accounts.

A person who suffers from frequent vomiting should take camphor brandy. Dissolve in it good-quality *Theriaca Andromaci*, then spread this thick on a cloth. Lay the cloth over the pit of the stomach, and it will not only halt the vomiting, it will also strengthen the heart.

Camphor combined with ground rue and juniper berries and bound with cloths over the wrists and ankles, and anywhere else one can take a pulse, as well as hung around the neck in a sachet so that it lies against the heart, will draw out feverish infections with powerful action.

Camphor makes a splendid remedy for cases of hearing loss, not just in persons for whom the condition was brought on by high fever but also in those who had no fever at all. This is because it calms feverish delirium and induces a gentle sleep. For example, take a tablespoonful of juniper berries, a handful of rue, half a quint of opium, four grains of musk, and pound this altogether. Put it into a little rag sachet and dip it into camphor brandy. Hold this under the nose frequently, and rub it on the forehead, temples, and anywhere one can take a pulse.

Camphor brandy is good for all manner of swellings freshly raised from a fall or from being fallen upon, or from being struck or crushed. Such injuries should be washed immediately and often with warm camphor brandy, or a cloth may be dampened with it and applied slightly warm as a dressing. Also, for sundry bone dislocations and sprains, and for broken arms and legs, camphor brandy will ease the swelling until the bone is reset. Even after the bone is set, the injury should be dressed diligently or gently rubbed with the brandy frequently.

In cases of catarrhous disorders, apoplexy, or sudden uneasiness in the heart and a furious rushing of the blood, it is very helpful to take immediately one-half or a full tablespoon of camphor brandy. If necessary, repeat this dosage in thirty minutes or within an hour.

When a person becomes overheated in the harvest field, or elsewhere has inadvertently taken too cold a drink, and feels or anticipates that this will come to no good consequence, drink forthwith one tablespoon of camphor brandy. This will dissipate the shock suffered by the system and no further harm will ensue, provided the individual does not wait too long to take the remedy.

To make good camphor brandy, take the best West Indian rum (or spirits), or double distilled brandy, and dissolve into it as much camphor as the rum or brandy can absorb. At all times, keep the glass vessel in which it is stored well stopped, and continue to keep it stopped after every use.[50] It is to be hoped that all heads of the family would keep this remedy on hand in their houses.

Caraway
Carum carvi
Sauer: *Kümmel* (1767)

Caraway is one of the most commonly used of all the herbs in colonial German-American cookery. It appeared in kitchen gardens with the very first wave of settlers and remained popular well into the nineteenth century. It was used in baking (in cookies, cakes, and all sorts of breads), as well as in cookery, from salads and soups to vegetable and meat dishes. It was also distilled to make Kümmelwasser, or caraway schnapps, a drink that is still regarded as a home remedy.

The Sauer herbal mentioned the culinary usefulness of this herb but did not expand on it. Yet German cookery books commonly employ caraway in medicoculinary recipes designed to mitigate some of the side effects of overconsumption, in particular flatulence. The following example is typical. Understood is the fact that the caraway (no amounts are given) is first ground to powder, or at least coarsely broken in a mortar:

> *Put caraway and a piece of rye or toasted wheat bread in water, or if you will, in half water and half meat stock. Season and let this cook until thick. Add drawn butter, ginger, pepper, grated nutmeg, and saffron. Let it boil up again, then serve over sliced rye bread.[51]*

The medical dimensions of this soup are better understood when the virtues of the various ingredients are taken into account. The value of rye bread in this case is fully explained under Sauer's discussion of rye on page 268.

Caraway possesses a mild, oily volatile salt from which it has the capacity to warm, to dissipate, to open, to dry, and to repel. It is warm and dry by nature. These days it is not only used in medicine but also employed in the kitchen in the preparation of food.

Caraway is good for windiness and swellings of the stomach, and eases gripes in the gut. It should not be used every day, otherwise it will cause paleness of the complexion.

Should a horse have a pain in the stomach, take a half loth each of caraway, rue, and fennel seeds. Grind to a powder, mix with wine, and pour it warm into the horse's mouth.

To ease ear aches, take caraway, fennel, and juniper berries and grind them to a powder. Put this in a sachet, heat it,[52] and lay it over the ears as hot as the person can bear it.

Caraway seeds can be eaten frequently in doses of up to one quint for treating windiness.

---

50. This is to prevent evaporation. Exposure to air weakens the camphor.
51. *Vollständiges Nürnbergisches Koch-Buch* (Nuremberg, 1691), 38.

A few drops of caraway oil taken in a tablespoon of wine is a first-rate cure for the gripes and for bellyache caused by cold and vapors.

A handful of caraway boiled in a pint of water and given to a woman in labor to drink warm will dispel the fierce pains and promote delivery.

Cardamom

Elettaria cardamomum

Sauer: *Cardamömlein* (1776)

Sauer introduced a common confusion into the herbal when he equated cardamom with grains of paradise in his heading to this herb. In Ceylon, Elettaria cardamomum major *is sometimes called grains of paradise, but Sauer made it clear in his German that he was discussing only one plant, the "lesser" cardamom, which is a different variety from the Ceylonese herb. True grains of paradise is* Afromomum melegueta, *or melegueta pepper, which comes from West Africa. It was used extensively in medieval cookery and served as an ingredient in a drink called hypocras. Herbal literature of this period was muddled even further because Chinese star anise was often called Siberian cardamom. Probably, in the common parlance of country people who were not aware of scientific distinctions, cardamom also went by the name of grains of paradise. But for our purposes, let us stick to the right plant.*

Sauer does not mention it, but cardamom seed was used extensively in Christmas cookery among the Germans in colonial America. It was an ingredient in gingerbread and various types of cookies and cakes. It was also made into comfits so that it could be eaten as a breath freshener after a meal, or chewed, as Sauer noted, to take advantage of its many medical virtues. It was also converted into a once-popular form of schnapps. A recipe for it, under the name of Cardamom Aquavitae, appeared in the Die wahre Brantwein Brennerey *(York, Pennsylvania, 1797).*

Cardamom is somewhat warm and dry in nature. It possesses a right temperate, moderately sharp, volatile oily salt, and therefore has the capacity to warm the stomach thoroughly, to strengthen it, to disperse all manner of vapors, to operate by urine, and to cleanse and strengthen the matrix.

Cardamom is of great service to all internal maladies that arise from cold or chills. It disperses the noxious vapors, promotes digestion, awakens the appetite, and strengthens the head, heart, stomach, and matrix. It is particularly good for those who are afflicted with trembling of the heart, fits of swooning, and dizziness.

To make an excellent stomach powder, take one quint each of cinnamon, ginger, and calamus; half a quint each of cardamom and anise; twenty grains each of pepper, mace, and cubeb; and six loths of sugar, and grind it all together to form a fine powder. Half a tablespoon of this powder taken in wine will strengthen and warm a cold stomach, increase digestion, and dispel the vapors.

A few seeds of cardamom ground to powder, mixed with sugar, and then added to

52 In private homes, this was generally done on the plate stove. Refer to the editor's discussion of stoves on page 12. Also refer to soot on page 97.

children's porridge will stay their colic and prevent fits.

If anyone were to describe the excellent virtues of this priceless spice according to all its special applications, the task would be formidable. Cardamom is endowed with a warmth pleasing to the nature of man, which causes no harm to the viscera and bodily parts, thus it can be chewed alone in the mouth and enjoyed without the accompaniment of other food. This is not possible with pepper, ginger, cloves, and similar warming spices.

Cardamom promotes urine, produces a pleasant-smelling breath, and is above all else serviceable for obstructions of the liver, spleen, and veins of the heart and lungs.

Carline Thistle
Carlina vulgaris
Sauer: *Weisse Eberwurtz* (1764)

This is a biennial thistle that grows flat against the ground with a yellow flower that emerges from the center of the plant. The German name means "boar's root," and historically the plant was associated with magic. The only part used in medicine was the root, which was often assigned more curative powers than it deserved, among them a certain remedy for the plague. The dried roots were the material of medical commerce, and in this form the herb was sold by Sauer. Furthermore, it is an Old World plant, so the thistle had to be imported. It has not naturalized in this country, thus there is little likelihood that it was cultivated here. Also, Sauer recognized two distinct varieties, the "white" carline thistle used internally and the "black" carline used externally.

Carline thistle is of a warm and dry nature. It withstands poison, sweetens sharp, salty blood. It opens obstructions of the liver, proud flesh, the spleen, veins of the heart and lungs, and the lungs themselves. It also promotes urine and dispels sand, gravel, and stones.

Dried carline thistle ground to a powder and taken in a half-quint dose kills tapeworms, opens obstructions of the liver, matrix, and spleen, and dispels jaundice and dropsy. It promotes urination and withstands all contagion, particularly the plague. Similar benefits may be obtained from the water distilled from the leaves and roots at the end of August.

The black carline thistle is not easily employed as an internal medicine, but if boiled in wine and used to wash out wounds, it will cleanse and heal them completely.

Cassia
Cinnamomum aromaticum
Sauer: *Cassia* (1777)

Cassia was preferred over cinnamon by the German chocolate makers in colonial America. It was also added to coffee, and by 1800 it had became one of the defining spices in the regional cookery around Philadelphia. However, Sauer complained of its scarcity, so we may judge from this that the supply was not only better but also much more abundant following the Revolution.

The dried bark was cut into strips and sold in bundles, which resembled reeds due to their shape and color. Indeed, they were called reeds (Röhren) by the German merchants who sold them, and their quality was highly variable. The seeds, which resemble cloves, were used in cookery and are still a popular condiment in Pennsylvania German pickles.

Cassia is an excellent laxative that operates by driving all sorts of unwholesomeness from the blood and the body. Only the pithy inner rind of the bark is used in medicine. Taken in one-ounce doses, it drives out heat and gall from the belly, and is always safe for old and young, as well as for pregnant or nursing mothers. It is serviceable to those who are afflicted with sand and stones, especially when mixed with a little turpentine and gum of benzoin.

It is quite a shame that this noble and so delightful-tasting plant cannot grow in this country, and as a result cannot be had anywhere except in apothecary shops. Yes, even then it is often too old and completely dried out. As a consequence it is never so pleasant tasting and good as in the lands where it grows.

Castor Bean (Castor Oil Plant)
Ricinus communis
Sauer: *Wunderbaum* (1778)

Although the tree originated in tropical India, it is now widely dispersed through cultivation. In temperate regions, where it is often grown purely as an ornamental, the plant rarely grows beyond ten or fifteen feet tall. In the tropics it will attain three times that height. Several varieties of castor bean were grown as ornamentals in colonial Pennsylvania (including red-flowering varieties similar to the present-day cultivar 'Carmencita'). The German name for the castor bean (Wunderbaum, or "tree of miracles") might explain the high opinion country people once had of its medical actions. Its other common name, Palma Christi, also suggests a plant that is blessed. Sauer, however, did not hold it in high regard.

His commentary on the castor bean assumed the form of a firm warning. Proof of his low esteem is obvious: he did not include any recipes for its use. His hesitation was due in part to the violence of its purging powers, but we may also wonder whether he did not see firsthand the frightening results of people (or overly curious children) who managed to eat the seeds or to overdose on the oil extracted from them. The seeds resemble large ugly ticks, which should be warning enough, and they must be picked out of spiny hulls. Whatever the case, Sauer recognized that the beans were grown in many parts of colonial America, but wanted to discourage their use in favor of other, safer medications.

In its seeds, the castor bean possesses a powerfully caustic salt and poison. Consequently, it not only operates on the stomach as an overly violent emetic, but also often causes dangerous irritations and burning. Thus it should never be used internally, except by those who are definitely known to possess extraordinarily strong constitutions, and even then it should be administered with the utmost precaution.

Catnip
Nepeta cataria
Sauer: *Katzenminze* (1773)

> *The ancient city of Nepete is said to have lent its name to this herb, which was sacred to cats. The leaves and the flower heads are rich in vitamin C, which is doubtless one reason why the plant figured in old cold remedies. But in general, this was an herb dedicated to female medicine, and much more widely used among the English-speaking community in colonial America than among the Germans. It was also an herb used by midwives to promote evacuations after delivery.*

Catnip is of a warm and dry nature and possesses virtues similar to lemon balm and other herbs for hysterical complaints. Hence the infusion is useful for warming the womb, cleansing it, and allaying fits. But on account of its disagreeable odor and bad taste, catnip is not much used.

Celandine (Greater)
Chelidonium majus
Sauer: *Schellkraut* (1767)

> *An advertisement in the* Germantauner Zeitung *for April 18, 1786, announced that one Casper Kirling of Hamburg, Windsor Township, Berks County, Pennsylvania, could cure cancer and fistula. He was what rural people at that time commonly referred to as a "Schellkraut doctor" because his medicines were based in large part on this efficacious herb—most likely celandine water. Certainly Sauer's remedies described below provide a glimpse into the complexities of this branch of healing.*
>
> *Sauer's vernacular name for celandine is actually a corruption of* Schwalbenkraut, *"swallows' herb." This name is derived from ancient Greek and is evident in the Latin name. In spite of its lowly status today, celandine was once held in very high esteem by medieval alchemists. They believed that gold could be extracted from the yellowish juice exuded by the stems and roots. It was this same yellow juice that the ancient Greeks claimed swallows used to open the eyes of their newly hatched chicks. In materia medica, the sap is known to remove warts if it is applied to the warts on a regular basis. Recent chemical analysis of the plant has revealed the presence of very strong alkaloids related to those found in opium poppies, so the herb should be treated with respect. In fact, the Pennsylvania Dutch use it to treat poison ivy.*
>
> *Celandine is not native to North America. It was introduced from England in the seventeenth century, although the Pennsylvania Germans were by far its greatest users*

in the eighteenth and nineteenth centuries. The plant has naturalized in many parts of the eastern United States.

Celandine is warm and dry in nature. The plant possesses many volatile, caustic, alkaline salts in addition to numerous balsamic, astringent particles in its sap. Consequently, its virtues are those of loosening hard phlegm, eliminating internal obstructions, promoting urine, purifying the blood, and cleansing all manner of external wounds and abscesses.

If a horse should develop cataracts, take celandine, including the root, wash it thoroughly, and pound it to a pulp in a mortar. Squeeze the juice through a cloth, then take three loths of this liquid, add two loths of good vinegar, one-half loth of salt, a quint of finely powdered ginger, and one loth of good, fresh honey. Mix this well and spray it into the horse's eyes three times a day. This helps dissolve the cataracts and has been pronounced effective many times.

Celandine can be rubbed on the skin to prevent hair from growing in that place.[53]

Juice of celandine, mixed with equal parts of wine and vinegar, heals eczema of the scalp on certain people, provided they rub the scalp with it every so often. Open sores can be irrigated twice a day with fresh celandine juice. The juice applied to warts and corns several times a day will make them soon disappear.

Celandine pounded to a pulp with rue, vinegar, and salt and smeared on the soles of the feet provides a good remedy against jaundice. Or, place fresh celandine leaves inside the shoes and let the patient walk in them without stockings, making certain to refresh the leaves every day.

The distilled water of celandine is a valuable remedy for healing cancer and open sores. Every morning and evening drink four or five loths of it and wash the affected parts with the water. It is also useful against obstructions of the liver and spleen, and in jaundice and fevers brought on by liver complaints. For jaundice, take three loths of plantain and as much celandine water every morning. Celandine is an excellent eye medication for clearing the vision, for driving away dancing spots before the eyes, for curing eyes that weep and water, and for curing sores in the corners of the eyes. Celandine will strengthen the eyesight if the eyes are daubed with celandine water, or if a few drops are put into the eyes. Otherwise, wash the infected parts with it.

For intermittent fevers, take a tablespoon of celandine juice with as much whiskey or rum. Take this regularly one hour before the onset of chills. The same can be done for jaundice if celandine juice is taken twice a day and continued for a period of time.

53. The reason for this may seem obscure. It was a technique used primarily by women to remove unwanted facial hair.

Centaury
Centarium Erythraea
Sauer: *Tausenguldenkraut* (1768)

Of all the German names in Sauer's herbal, this one is among my favorites: "thousand gulden plant." A thousand pieces of gold may seem like exaggeration, but the fact is, for medical purposes, centaury was mostly gathered from the wild in Europe. Its well-known action as a stomachic and tonic, its usefulness for dyspepsia and heartburn, and its preeminence as an antiseptic laid a tempting bounty on all stands of the wild herb.

Centaury is an Old World gentian. It became naturalized in French Canada and New England by the early eighteenth century, and this doubtless provided the American market with a supply of the plant. But it was also introduced into physic gardens in many of the English colonies, with the Moravians taking a lead in its cultivation in German-speaking settlements. Since there were physic gardens in Germantown, where Sauer lived, it is quite possible that the fresh herb was only a few doorsteps away.

To some extent this was confirmed by the widespread use of centaury tea during the most desperate days of the yellow fever epidemic that struck Philadelphia in 1793. Sauer's tea (mentioned below) was prescribed by Dr. Sarnigshausen in his addendum to Peter Gabriel's Kurzer Bericht von der Pest *(Philadelphia, 1793), for use in the German neighborhoods of the city. However, Sauer's enthusiasm for certain shop preparations made from centaury may be viewed as self-promotional, since he manufactured and sold these products on a regular basis.*

Centaury is of a warm, dry nature and contains coarse, astringent, oily particles of salt. Therefore centaury possesses the virtue of attenuating, of opening, of promoting urine and sweat, of killing worms, and of awakening the appetite.

A handful of centaury leaves, together with the flowers, boiled in two quarts of water and drunk frequently, is a good tea for tertian fever, asthmatic gasping, and coughs of long continuance. It will open congested livers and spleens, as well as drive out jaundice and dropsy. Boiled in wine and drunk thus, centaury will still colic and kill worms.

For cases of dropsy, it is quite serviceable after the third day to administer one quint of centaury powder, together with a little powdered anise and caraway in a glass of wine.

Of all the herbal bitters, centaury justly deserves the highest approval.

The distilled water of centaury is very powerful in dissipating all putrid fevers of the stomach, and brings good comfort to pale, sickly women. It kills worms, dispels jaundice and dropsy, warms and strengthens a cold stomach, and stills colic. Likewise, when a person begins to bloat after a fever, then centaury water is very powerful in dissipating the swelling. It will open obstructed livers and spleens when half a gill is taken in the morning before eating.

Externally, centaury water can be used to advantage in drying out weeping wounds, in cleansing all fistulous sores of pus, and in promoting their healing. After rinsing the affected place, strew the finely powdered leaves of dried centaury in it, or prepare a thin ointment with the powdered leaves, fresh sap, and honey. Put the ointment on a lint pledget and lay this in the wound or sore. Or, irrigate open fistulas with centaury water or sap by means of a small syringe.

Young children who are plagued by worms should be given a tablespoon of centaury water now and then before eating.

A useful extract is made from centaury leaves in apothecary shops, which is particularly good for the liver and for persons suffering of jaundice. From a quint of this extract, make fifty-four pills and take nine each day. In addition to this, druggists also prepare a salt from centaury, which should be taken in doses of half a quint in six loths of centaury water when one is taken down by quartan ague. It is also serviceable given in similar doses for jaundice and dropsy. A tincture can also be prepared from centaury flowers, and given in one-tablespoon doses for all the above-mentioned afflictions.

Chamomile (Common and German)
Chamaemelum mobile and *Matricaria recutita*
Sauer: *Camillen* (1762)

> *Of all the numerous applications to which chamomile is put in old herbals, Sauer concentrated on the maladies most familiar to his colonial readers: recurring fevers and agues, particularly those afflicting children. Dr. Sarnigshausen devoted considerable space to the uses of chamomile teas for yellow fever in 1793, even to the extent of adding several drops of elixir of vitriol to "acidulate" the doses. But plant historians will be happy enough to note that Sauer mentioned two sorts of chamomile of very different genus and species: the "Roman" chamomile (Matricaria recutita), which we call German chamomile in America, and the common perennial or sweet-scented variety (Chamaemelum mobile). Both of these plants have naturalized in this country, and were growing in many rural gardens by 1762, but it was the sweet-scented that was considered official for use in medicine.*

The noble Roman chamomile and the common sweet-scented chamomile are warm and dry in nature. They have fine virtues for staying all manner of pains, for emolliating, for healing, for opening, and for dispelling windiness and vapors.

For quartan ague, take one quart of good wine and put it in a new earthenware vessel that can be well sealed. Stand this for one hour over glowing coals, then add half a handful of chamomile flowers. Seal it tightly, but do not let it boil.[54] Afterward, pour it out and take one gill of the liquid. Add one-half quint of cream of tartar salts,

---

54. The reason for this is that the oils in chamomile are highly volatile and evaporate quickly when heated. Even the tea should be made by infusing it in cold water for ten minutes; otherwise it loses its effectiveness upon exposure to boiling water.

and give this to the patient, even if the fever is just beginning, and let him sweat it out. At the onset of the second attack, repeat as before, except that the dose of cream of tartar salts is increased by the amount of five peppercorns more in weight, and increased in this amount each time the fever returns. Thus the fever will soon decline, particularly if the patient purges the stomach with a good emetic prior to each dose.

A fine oil of chamomile can be prepared when one takes olive oil and adds chamomile flowers; the more flowers, the stronger it becomes. After it has stood four to six weeks in the sun, strain it through a clean cloth, press it well, and store away in a well-sealed glass vessel. With this oil one can heal ague of the head in children without injury.

For colic in young children, this oil is quite excellent when their stomachs are smeared with it frequently while it is warm. When the lower abdomen is smeared with it, it will break blocked urination. When used in a clyster, it eases all manner of pains in the bowels. In particular, such a clyster is of incomparably good use for diarrhea and painful fluxes of the gut.

Chamomile boiled in wine, and laid upon the belly as warm as the person can bear it, stills colic and mother fits.

Cherries (Sweet and Sour)
Prunus avium and *Prunus cerasus*
Sauer: *Kirchen* (1771)

Cherries were indeed the "national" fruit of the German settlers in America, and they planted the trees wherever they could. It was common to see them in avenues along country roads and lining private lanes to farms. Cherries, fresh or dried, figured largely in the cookery, and it should come as no surprise that Sauer included a large amount of material on this fruit. His recipe for cherry wine is particularly engaging, along with his testimonial regarding its keeping qualities.

Sauer not only discusses sweet and sour cherries (two separate species), but the use of cherry heartwood as well. In particular, two types of cherries are mentioned: morellos or Milan morellos (a late-fruiting variety) and the sour agriot, which is perhaps better known by its French designation griotte *(the German name is* Weichselkirschen, *or* Vistula cherry). *There was a common* griotte *and a* griotte d'Allemagne, *to name only two, just as there were numerous subvarieties of morello. Without having precise lists of the various sorts of cherries sold among the Germans in Sauer's day, we can only surmise that the plantings were a mixture of imported Dutch, English, and German trees. Country people did not overlook wild cherries either, for it is well documented that they also made wine and various distilled beverages from them. However, one of the most delightful recipes in the herbal is the one for cherry butter made with white wine. Sauer used it as an electuary for the sick, but it was just as popular in cookery. It was spread on bread, on cake, and even used as a topping for cheesecake and as a filling in pies.*

Concealed in the juice of sweet cherries is a sulfurous or oily spirit from which they derive their capacity to enliven the spirits, and to revive the head and nerves. However, they should not be eaten too copiously, because they can easily ferment in the stomach and bring on diarrhea.

On the other hand, sour cherries, by virtue of their acidic semivolatile or spirituous juice, temper and quench internal hotness and coursing of the blood; cool sharp, inflamed bile; and in general are good for a bilious stomach. Cherries that are quite sour also possess the ability to glutinate and to block, especially those that are dried.

A spirit or spirituous water is distilled from black cherries, which, taken in tablespoon doses, is a fine choice remedy for lameness of the limbs, apoplexy, fits, loss of speech, and so forth.[55] Those who are apprehensive about the threat of apoplexy or who are inclined to fits should take a tablespoon of black cherry water frequently.

This water contains a sulfurous, burning spirit, and is distilled as follows: Take sweet black cherries according to want, mash them to break the pits, and put them in a sound cask until they have fermented and become like wine. Thereupon, distill the juice as with other fruit, until a spirituous water develops. A similar water can be distilled from sour cherries, which is serviceable for hot, feverish maladies and pestilential fevers, for it cools all internal organs, arouses the appetite, quenches thirst, operates by urine, and cleanses the kidneys and bladder.

The kernels of cherry pits drive out mucus and sand from the kidneys. They can be taken either dried and ground to powder, or mashed fresh with the juice or distilled water of parsley, and drunk thus. The freshly pressed oil from these kernels is good for lumbago, when applied externally as an ointment.

The sap of cherry wood, which possesses a capacity to dissipate and to attenuate, is good for loosening phlegm in the chest and for quieting coughs of long continuance. Grate a half quint into wine and drink this infusion frequently.

If black cherries are mashed and distilled without first turning to wine, a spirit or cherry schnapps will not result, as it generally does with the fermented juice in the manner described above and known as cherry brandy. Rather, only a strong cordial water results, which is used, and not without justification, together with all sorts of strengthening potions, or just taken alone as a tonic.

To make an electuary of morello or agriot cherries: Take the aforementioned cherries picked of their stems, as many as are wanted, and cook them in an earthenware pot with a little white wine until they loosen from the pits. Then work them through a hair-sieve with a wooden spoon. Take one pound of this puree together with half a pound of powdered sugar. Reheat this in a new, glazed stoneware pot over a gentle charcoal heat. Stir constantly so that it does not burn and stick to the bottom, and continue stirring until it attains the thickness of a fruit butter once it cools. This electuary is quite effective in quenching thirst and refreshing the sick. It is very comforting to overheated stomachs, and is useful in all ardent fevers and illnesses. It also operates by urine and promotes the appetite.

To make a pleasant cherry wine: Take black or red sour cherries, as many as are wanted, crush them only enough so that the pits remain whole. Then put them in a tub with a bunghole on the side close to the bottom and lay a wisp of straw on top.

55. This was used with powdered mistletoe as a remedy for epilepsy. Refer to mistletoe on page 214.

Let the juice run off, then take as much water as there is juice, and pour the water over the cherries. Let this stand on the fruit for a few hours. Then let it run off into the cherry juice.

Put this in a clean cask, and to each gallon of liquid, add two pounds of brown sugar. Stir until all the sugar is dissolved and no more lies on the bottom. Then cork the cask tight and drill a tiny hole as thick as a straw beside the bung hole so that it can get a little air. The cask should be left to lie on the floor of a cool cellar or spring house until the wine is completely fermented.

Then tap it off from the must, thoroughly scrub out the cask, and add to each gallon of wine one-half pound of sugar, or if it is preferred very sweet, a full pound. When the sugar is completely dissolved, return the wine to the cask and bung it up. After several months, this will become a very pleasant wine, which may be enjoyed with or without water.[56] It quenches thirst, cools when it is excessively hot, and strengthens the heart. But just remember not to take too long in making the wine, lest the juice begins to ferment before it goes into the cask, otherwise it will become slightly acid or completely sour. I have kept such wine over ten years, and it is still as good or even better than it was in the first year.

Chervil

Anthriscus cerefolium
Sauer: *Kärfel* (1769)

> *One of the most popular of the old garden herbs, chervil is now widely naturalized in many areas where Germans settled. It is especially useful since it seeds in the summer and reappears in the fall so that there are plants throughout the winter from which to pick fresh greens. Wild chervil or "turnip" chervil was also planted here and is now more commonly known as earth chestnut* (Buniam bulbocastanum). *It too is evergreen and can be cooked in soups, although the taste of the greens is strong and more like parsley than chervil.*

Chervil is not only useful in the kitchen, it possesses excellent virtues as medicine. It is middling warm, and has numerous nitrous, mild, and well-mingled oily components. Thus it possesses the capacity to attenuate, to operate by urine and sweat, and to provide the blood with good balsamic nourishment.

The leaves of chervil used in cookery are healthy for the stomach and head. They purify the blood and excite the appetite. Thus chervil is particularly healthy when used regularly in foods given to those who suffer from the following illnesses: weakness of the head, dizziness, maladies of the chest and lungs, body sores, abscesses, sciatica and back pain, blockage of the urine, kidney and bladder ailments, gravel and stones.

For blood congealed within the body, the following potion is extremely beneficial: Take two handfuls of chervil leaves, a handful each of sanicle and wintergreen, and

56. Germans in the eighteenth century often mixed water with strong or heavy wines, a common practice among women and also for the wine given to children.

chop them fine. Put this in a pewter jug and add two quarts of wine. Stop up the jug and set it in a kettle of boiling water. Let it stand and simmer over a constant heat for four hours, then strain off the liquid and administer it lukewarm to the patient in doses of one gill every morning and evening. Besides treating blood clots, it will also heal all internal wounds and injuries. Under such circumstances, it is extremely useful to the patients if they take chervil in all of their soups and other foods.

A salad made from young, tender chervil dressed with vinegar, olive oil, and salt will restore a lost appetite.

Chervil greens boiled in lye and used for washing the scalp will get rid of dandruff, scurf, and mites in the hair.

Chervil leaves, mashed to a cataplasm and mixed with honey for use as a plaster, are useful in treating cancerous sores.

Chervil leaves, fomented in fresh butter and worked into a salve, are a proven remedy for colic when applied thick and warm on the abdomen.

Chervil leaves mashed to a cataplasm and fomented in a pan with a little wine and butter will ease stressful urination. The cataplasm is spread between two cloths and laid as a plaster over the abdomen as warm as the patient can bear it.

A few loths of chervil juice taken in warm soup or chicken broth are a soothing remedy for colic, especially if some leaves are also fomented in butter and then applied to the navel as warm as the patient can bear it. Furthermore, this fomentation is quite useful when children have eaten too much and their stomachs commence to bloat. Likewise, when applied frequently and warm to the lower belly, it is an excellent remedy for those who cannot pass their water.

The distilled water of chervil, taken every morning and evening in doses of four or five tablespoons, is very good for dissipating blood congealed in the body resulting from apoplexy, hard falls, or severe blows.[57] It will also heal internal injuries. Additionally, it forces out urine and gravel, breaks up kidney stones, and is good for lumbago and pleurisy.

Chickpea
Cicer arietinum
Sauer: *Ziser Erbse* (1776)

We know that the Germans in colonial America planted garbanzos or chickpeas, but very little has been recorded about the types and uses given this important plant. There are occasional references in the Pennsylvania German newspapers to chickpeas imported from Europe, so the demand must have outstripped local production. Linguistic evidence also supports the former popularity of chickpeas, because Kicher *or* Kicherli, *the Pennsylfaanisch dialect words for chickpea, were remembered and used in speech into the late nineteenth century.[58] However, the chickpea was gradually replaced by beans and is*

57. Nicholas Culpeper attributed this statement to Hieronymus Tragus, otherwise known as Hieronymus Bock (1498–1554), German herbalist and physician.

58. Historical evidence is muddled, however, by the fact that *Kicherli* or *Kicherling* is also a term for chickling vetch *(Lathyrus sativus)*, a near-relative of the garden pea introduced from Silesia in the 1730s. It was a poverty food grown mostly for its spring greens.

now thought of as something almost exclusively Mediterranean.

The Sauer herbal throws revealing light on the colonial situation by mentioning a number of medical uses and at least two distinct varieties, a red and a white. The red chickpea was probably a small-seeded variety similar to the desi *types of India. It is evident from Sauer's herbal that it was also used much differently from the white-seeded kinds. From either type, the green or unripe seeds could be harvested like shelling peas. However, chickpeas were more commonly eaten in the winter, either boiled to a hummus-like porridge (eaten like bean dip) or converted into soup, as mentioned in the herbal.*

Chickpeas are warm and dry by nature and possess an alkaline, volatile salt, together with a few inherent oily particles. Thus they have the capacity to penetrate gently, to open blockages of the liver, kidneys, and matrix, and to promote urine. When they are used in cookery, they must be well cooked, lest they give cause to numerous vapors. They provide decent nourishment, and give increase to milk in nursing women.

Drink the broth from boiled chickpeas as an antidote to gravel in the loins. The broth will promote urine and the menses and open obstructions of the liver, spleen, and kidneys, and serves well against jaundice and the onset of dropsy.

For burning, dripping urine, take half a pound of red chickpeas and ten pounds of pure springwater, and boil until reduced by one-third. Then add one loth of licorice; a small handful each of the tender leaves of blue mallow, marshmallow, and agrimony; and two loths of the shelled seeds of watermelon or pumpkin. Continue to boil until the mixture is reduced by another third, then strain it. Now you have a valuable remedy that can be taken as a potion every morning before breakfast for ten days in succession. But before using the remedy, clean out the body with a serviceable laxative. However, chickpeas are not useful in cases of injured kidneys or bladder, since they work them too much.

For nursing mothers, a soup made with chickpeas is quite beneficial, particularly when parsley is cooked with it.[59]

A good plaster for tumors and abscesses, be they inflamed or hard, can be prepared in the following manner: Take white chickpeas and boil them in water until soft. Then pound them in a mortar. Cook the mash with honey until thick. Spread this warm on a cloth or piece of leather, then lay it over the tumor or abscess. If this cannot reduce the tumor more, it will at least ripen it for opening.

Chickweed
Stellaria media
Sauer: *Hünerdarm* (1767)

Chickweed had many uses in colonial America, especially among the poor. The whole plant was sometimes chopped and boiled in lard until it became crisp and the lard turned

---

59. It is understood here that the chickpeas are cooked in meat stock and then pureed with the broth. Many recipes for this type of soup are extant. It was normally served over a piece of bread.

green. This was strained and used as a cooling ointment for piles and sores. The plant was also used fresh in poultices. And because the juice was effective against scurvy, the greens were eaten boiled or in salads and pies for their health-giving virtues. Sauer mentions water of chickweed, but did not explain that it was also taken as a cure for obesity—perhaps he did not believe that. But his discussion of chickweed's usefulness in driving out milk is unique and draws upon an old Pennsylvania German midwife tradition. However, the instructions dealing with the hand of a dead baby are witchcraft of the most authentic kind, since their effectiveness depends upon a transfer between the dead hand and the woman's breast. The profound psychological effect on the mother cannot be discounted. It conjures a scene of extreme sadness and torment, one of the most haunting images in Sauer's herbal.

Chickweed is cold and moist in nature. It operates by a mildly nitrous, volatile salt, from which it possesses the capacity to open, to cool, and to resist poison.

A water is distilled from chickweed that is good for those with fever and consumption, if they drink a dose of four or five loths, as they see fit. It is also serviceable for children who are overtaken by oppressive heat, as well as for those who suffer from fits. Administer a tablespoon dose from time to time.

The juice pressed from the fresh plant is very serviceable to children for colic in the stomach, if they are given a dose of one-half to a full tablespoon.

The fresh plant, laid often upon the bosoms, flushes out the milk of new mothers. This is very useful in cases when the mother has weaned the child, or when the newborn has died, and the milk is causing her pain. Indeed, in the latter instance, there is an approved remedy for dislodging the milk: take the hand of the dead baby and stroke the bosoms downward with it. They will lose their milk quickly.

Chimney Soot
Nonbotanical
Sauer: *Schornstein-Russ* (1777)

This is undoubtedly one of the most unusual medications in Sauer's herbal, yet it is no more fantastic than tar water or some of the other substances then employed in remedies. However, this should be set in context, since soot was commonly associated with a disease called chimney sweeper's cancer, a horrible and fatal skin affliction prevalent among the young boys who worked as chimney sweeps. Want of cleanliness was generally given as the root cause, not the soot itself, but the association was clear.

Be that as it may, Sauer was a great believer in soot, and even differentiated between the several types and the various byproducts derived from them. He was also well aware that the average person would not possess the type of equipment necessary for making these byproducts, and for this reason assumed a first-person role in advising alternative applications. Using soot for ague may seem a far stretch, but for someone living deep in the countryside, this may have been the only alternative available.

Chimney soot has many excellent properties when it is well processed and its oil, spirit, and salt are separated from one another and individually prepared. But because this is such a difficult task, the average person cannot undertake it. Thus, I will only advise a few things that may be accomplished on one's own, namely: For ague, take half a handful of vitreous soot, such as that which collects over stove holes, grind it very fine, and put it into a pint of milk. Drink half of this one hour before the onset of chills is expected, and the other half the next day about the same time. Such a remedy, albeit unorthodox medicine, has given good service quickly and often to those afflicted with this tormenting malady.

Grind sparkling chimney soot to a fine powder, and take a quint dose of this in meat stock or with distilled water. This will dissolve clots of blood in those who have taken a severe fall, repel pleurisy, and operate by sweat.

Those who can obtain the volatile spirits of soot as prepared in some apothecaries will experience good effects when it is taken in doses of thirty to forty drops. This distillate operates powerfully by sweat, gives vent to air upon the chest and about the heart, alleviates internal inflammations brought on by pleurisy, and stills the pain. It also dispels a trembling and troubled heart during bilious fevers, stays palpitations, and is quite serviceable for the falling evil.

Chives
Allium schoenoprasum
Sauer: Schnittlauch (1772)

Regardless of the herbal's cautionary stance on chives, it was the culinary herb par excellence among the rural Germans of Pennsylvania, Maryland, and Virginia. The Mennonites are said to have brought pots of it to America when they came here in the early 1700s, and the herb was used extensively to flavor Schmierkees (cottage cheese) *and soups. From a health standpoint, the main danger from chives appears to have been from eating them raw, as for example, chopped into a salad. It was raw chives that were thought to give rise to the various unhealthful conditions and injuries noted below—all of the medical applications require that the herb be cooked or heated up.*

The warning material was placed first doubtless because many of Sauer's country readers made common use of an even stronger relative of the garden variety. This was Akerlauch (field garlic) *or wild chives, which was already well naturalized by Sauer's generation. The American Philosophical Society ran a public notice in the* Pennsylvania Gazette *of September 15, 1768, stating that it was seeking "any Method that has been found effectual for destroying Garlic, which is become so prejudicial, especially in old Fields." Dr. William Darlington noted many years later that this species* (Allium vineale) *was introduced from Wales in the late 1600s in order to flavor spring milk for cheese making. But tastes changed by the middle of the eighteenth century, and its use was deemed uncouth and countrified.[60] It also tainted butter, and thus became a nuisance once butter production evolved into an established industry. Nevertheless, rural people continued to use wild chives as a condiment, especially for green goose, and its medical applications were the same as true culinary chives.[61] Its flavor, however, is quite strong, and even when cooked it must be eaten with discretion.[62]*

When chives are used in cookery, they induce vapors, and fill the blood with sharp corruptions and the brain with troublesome dreams. They operate by urine and sweat and are very harmful to the eyes as well as to anyone who may suffer from injuries to the kidneys or bladder.

When boiled with barley and thus eaten as porridge, chives disperse phlegm in the chest and help with its expectoration. They also promote a clear, steady voice.

Take chives and pound them to a cataplasm. Foment this quickly in a skillet, then smear it as a warm poultice over the soreness caused by pleurisy.[63] This often allays the pain very quickly and hinders further difficulty in that place. Some also extol this remedy for snakebite and burns. However, in general, chives are used more in cookery than in medicine.

Chocolate
Theobroma cacao
Sauer: *Cocus* (1777)

Chocolate meringue, chocolate cream, chocolate ice cream, chocolate soup, chocolate cake, chocolate cookies. All of these are treated by Friederike Löffler in her popular 1790s cookbook. By Sauer's era, chocolate was indeed well integrated into middle-class diets both in Germany and in colonial America, the one difference being that chocolate was cheaper here than in Europe. But behind chocolate lurks the subject of vanilla, which the Germans closely associated with chocolate in cookery and medicine.

Thomas Jefferson made an exasperated comment in 1791 about the lack of vanilla in Philadelphia and then sent off to Paris for pods, this when ships were coming in

60. William Darlington, *Flora Cestrica* (West Chester, Pa., 1837), 215. This type of cheese has been reinvented in the form of a Welsh farmhouse cheese called Tintern. Rather than using flavored milk, it actually contains bits of chives and onion. Its rind is green.

61. The use of *Allium vineale* as a condiment on goose probably traces to the Middle Ages. This use is well documented by the sixteenth century, especially in northern Europe. See, for example, C. Anne Wilson, *Food and Drink in Great Britain* (New York: Barnes and Noble, 1974), 122.

62. For this reason, onions took precedence in genteel and courtly cookery. William Byrd of Virginia, for example, dined on boiled goose with onion sauce at Governor Spottswood's in December 1710; see William Byrd, *The Secret Diary of William Byrd of Westover, 1709–1712*, 2 vols., ed. Louis B. Wright and Marion Tinling (Richmond, Va.: Dietz Press, 1941), 1:265. When wild chives were in season, it was common to hash them and cook them with the onions to make the sauce green. Sorrel was also sometimes added. This played against the gamy taste of wild fowl.

63. Foment *(bähen)* is Sauer's term. It means to bathe or poach the chives in just enough warm water to create a soft mash. This was done very quickly, in one or two minutes.

almost daily from the Caribbean laden with produce from Spanish America. His remark, which has created a mythology of its own among food historians, was perpetuated by Marie Kimball's Thomas Jefferson's Cook Book, *a collection of recipes most of which postdate the life of Jefferson considerably.[64] Vanilla came from Santo Domingo (where it was introduced) and from Guatemala (where it was native) during the eighteenth century. The Guatemalan vanilla was commonly shipped from Mexico along with jalap (page 181). Its uses were several.*

John Hill described vanilla in considerable detail in his Useful Family Herbal *(which means that his old associate Hannah Glasse must certainly have known about it too), writing, "The Pod is the part used; it is a Cordial and Restorative, it opens Obstructions, and promotes the Menses, it operates by Urine, and by Sweat, but is not much used. Some put it into Chocolate, to give it a Flavor, and to make it more cordial and restorative, this is done in the grinding up the Nuts to the Cake, and we buy it by the Name of Vanilla Chocolate."[65] If Jefferson had sent his man to a Philadelphia chocolate maker, or to the right ethnic apothecary, he probably would have gotten what he wanted.*

The Germans used vanilla to sweeten pipe tobacco, to make vanilla creme (a type of custard prepared in a double boiler), and as an additive to chocolate. Johann Jacob Woyt published a Spanish recipe for making bars of chocolate consisting of ground cocoa, sugar, pepper, cloves, vanilla, anise, and achiote.[66] Philadelphia chocolate makers preferred cassia to cloves, but this was the basic composition of so-called vanilla chocolate. Johann Friedrich Zückert acknowledged in 1769 that vanilla was considered a comestible, but noted that it was mostly consumed in combination with chocolate in Spanish-speaking countries.

The reasons why Sauer did not include vanilla and why Hill said that it was little used in England stemmed from one economic consideration: vanilla was extraordinarily expensive. At that time, vanilla pods were gathered from wild plants, which was both labor-intensive and unpredictable as a crop. It was therefore a luxury and out of place in an herbal for working-class people. Chocolate, however, was readily available in colonial America, and country taverns served it regularly. We now know that chocolate contains catechin, a flavonoid that is a strong antioxidant. In short, it has very healthful properties. Let us now look at the ways Sauer used it.

Nothing is eaten from the cocoa tree except the kernel of the nut, which contains considerable oil and some rawish salts. From these derive its pleasantly bitter taste. Cocoa has a temperate faculty for easing sharp humors, for sweetening a sour stomach, for attenuating thick, mucusy fluxes, for refreshing the spirit, and for quieting diarrhea. But when too much chocolate is eaten, it can cause constipation.

Cocoa nuts provide much nourishment, but they should not be consumed daily, lest they thicken the blood. Known everywhere are the chocolate cakes made from

64. Marie Kimball, *Thomas Jefferson's Cook Book* (1938; reprint, Charlottesville: Univeristy Press of Virginia, 1976), 10.

65. Thomas Hill, *The Useful Family Herbal* (London, 1755), 377–78.

66. Johann Jacob Woyt, *Gazophylacium Medico-Physicum; oder, Schatz-Kammer medicinisch- und natürlicher Dinge* (Leipzig, 1784), 497 and 2370–71.

these nuts and the drink called chocolate.[67]

The drink is temperate, but rather more cooling than heating. If it is to be drunk daily, it should not be taken very strong, but generously mixed with milk. Otherwise, it will cause thick blood. It is most agreeable to those who sit a great deal or who are inactive. It is quite serviceable for the ill, since it supplies good nourishment and is easily digested. It is also useful for persons suffering from coughs, because it loosens phlegm and promotes expectoration. Furthermore, it invigorates and fortifies the spirit, strengthens the heart, heals injured lungs, eases difficult breathing, and revives limbs wearied from hard labor. It also stays hefty stools and diarrhea, especially when a little nutmeg is grated into it. Chocolate is prescribed for the thirst brought on by bloody flux, diarrhea, and tenesmus.[68] Due to its own fattiness, chocolate counters and nullifies acids that eat into the gut, restores mucus to the lining of the intestines, and binds them gently without causing further injury.

Anyone who has grown accustomed to drinking chocolate every day has very fine nourishment indeed, but the medical effectiveness is lost that otherwise would have resulted if the drink had been taken only on occasion. Sad, melancholic persons should refrain as much as possible from drinking chocolate, since it thickens the blood and as a consequence leads to even greater melancholy.

Cinnamon
Cinnamomum zeylanicum
Sauer: *Zimmet* (1771)

The bark of cinnamon is endowed with an earthy substance possessed of an aromatic oil united with a volatile salt. From this derive its fine properties for thinning the blood, for strengthening the heart and nerves, for awakening the appetite, and for stilling colic. The ancients esteemed it for its warm, dry nature.

A fine stomach powder that can be enjoyed with food can be prepared from cinnamon. It consists of the following ingredients: one ounce of cinnamon, a half ounce each of ginger and sugar, a quint of saffron, and fifteen grains each of cloves, mace, galingale, and nutmeg. Grind it all very fine and mix together thoroughly. Take a few pinches of this daily, and it will warm and strengthen a cold feeble stomach.

When half a quint of ground cinnamon is drunk in warm wine in the morning before breakfast, it will dispel the vapors, promote urine and the like, help a cold stomach and head, strengthen the eyesight and heart, and open blockages due to jaundice and the commencement of dropsy.

Water of cinnamon distilled with wine and taken in tablespoonful doses will give people the strength to overcome all illnesses arising from cold. It will warm and strengthen the limbs, take off phlegm and windiness, settle a stomach that cannot hold food as well as gripes of the belly, protect against fainting, and drive out urine.

---

67. Chocolate was sold in hard cakes like modern baker's chocolate. Wood engravings depicting these cakes appeared in sales announcements in many Philadelphia newspapers during the eighteenth century.

68. This is a medical term for the sensation of urgent bowel movement or urination when in fact nothing happens. The condition is sometimes extremely painful.

It will also sweeten the breath and help against shortness of breath, cramps, and apoplexy. It is particularly well known as a remedy for maladies arising from a cold matrix.

Finely ground cinnamon sprinkled on a toasted dinner roll or on a slice of white bread, which is then dipped in wine and eaten while still warm and fresh, is very strengthening nourishment for the heart and stomach and a cordial to the spirit of those weakened by illness in cases where no fever is present.

Cinquefoil (Five-Leaf Grass)
Potentilla reptans
Sauer: *Fünffingerkraut* (1762)

Cinquefoil is strongly antiscorbutic and served as an ingredient in many medieval spells and remedies. Its uses among the Germans varied considerably from the applications advocated by English herbalists; a comparison with John Gerard or Nicholas Culpeper makes this clearly evident. Of interest here is its preparation as a mouthwash and tooth remedy, not to mention the image they create of the general condition of colonial mouths among the rural poor. Sauer's electuary or jam given to consumptives resembled butterscotch and was sometimes eaten simply as a confection. Where the Old World herb was unavailable, it was generally substituted with the native Potentilla canadensis, *which is endowed with similar virtues.*

Cinquefoil and its root have the capacity to dry, to glutinate, to withstand acidulous corruptions, to nullify bitter poisons, and to cleanse and heal wounds. It is best when gathered at the beginning of May and dried in the shade.

One loth of cinquefoil root boiled for a short time in half a gallon of water, and the decoction drunk repeatedly, will strengthen a weak head and dry the fluxes in it. It is also serviceable for bloody flux and all manner of fluxes of the belly, also in cases of quartan ague.

The root of cinquefoil chewed daily will preserve the teeth from decay and prevent toothaches. Likewise, when the root is boiled in wine and the mouth is rinsed with the decoction every morning, this will heal all sores in the mouth.

For consumption, take the freshly pressed juice of cinquefoil, strained honey from the comb, and fresh May butter, all of equal weight. Cook this until it thickens to an electuary. Then store in a glazed or plain redware pot. Consumptives should take a tablespoon of this every morning and let it dissolve slowly in the mouth, then swallow it.

To heal scurvy, scurvy of the gums, and sores in the throat, the following mouth-wash is very useful. Take one handful of cinquefoil with its roots, half a handful each of scabious, plantain, and rose petals, and boil this in two quarts of springwater until reduced by one-half. Then strain it through a cloth and dissolve into it a quarter of a pound of rose honey and half a loth of alum. Wash the mouth and gums with this often, and also gargle with it in the back of the throat.

Boil the leaves and roots of cinquefoil together. Wash the mouth with this decoction often, holding it in the mouth for a long period. This will get rid of evil smells arising from the teeth and bad taste in the mouth.

Citron
Citrus medica
Sauer: *Citrone* (1774)

Citron was one of the earliest imported products mentioned in colonial Philadelphia sources, and most of it came fresh or in preparations from the West Indies. It was raised in the English colonies of Barbados and Jamaica for export to England, where citron water had become fashionable by the late 1600s. Citron water was a social beverage of considerable cost, and as an ingredient in juleps, it was a great favorite of Pennsylvania's first governor, William Penn. His physicians advised against it since it was contributing to his gout, but he ignored them.

Sauer veered away from citron water altogether—it was no longer fashionable in his day—but he enthusiastically recommended citron in various forms to those who could afford it. There is perhaps no more telling comment in the herbal about the great differences that divided the colonial rich from the poor than the one here dealing with citron. Indeed, it was still a luxury, whether for medicine or cookery. That Sauer was honest enough to remark that cream of tartar would work quite as well, might be taken as a jab against those who equated cost and pleasant taste with medical effectiveness. That theme surfaces in his discussion of sugar (page 313) and ought to be kept in mind while reading through the preparations that follow. Lastly, while citron remained a luxury (it is still expensive today), the West Indian lime rose to take its place. By Sauer's day, limes were plentiful and cheap, and they were doubtless used as less expensive substitutes in many of the citron remedies mentioned in the herbal. This point is reinforced by the fact that in the original 1774 installment of the herbal, lemons, limes, and oranges followed immediately after the citron entry.

For medicine, it is mostly the fruit of the citron tree that is made use of. The outer yellow rind contains oily, volatile, spirituous juices from which it derives its capacity to warm, to open, and to penetrate. It stills windiness and vapors, furthers insensible transpiration of the humors of the blood,[69] withstands poison, maintains and

69. According to the system of humors, this takes place after the fourth concoction of the blood. It is a type of evaporation or invisible perspiration of waste products that occurs after the blood is transformed into tissue and bodily organs. It is not the same as perspiration or sweat.

increases a lively spirit, disperses rheums of the head, and strengthens the heart and stomach.

The sour juice is composed of divers salty and somewhat volatile ingredients by which it cools, thickens, draws together, and thus dispels the overplus of ardent humors, coursing of the blood, and thirst. It will also dispel pestilential fevers arising from caustic, alkaline poisons. It will operate by sweat and urine as well, and cheer the heart and excite the appetite, indeed, it is quite useful as a remedy for fevers in general. The seed is opening, thinning, and cleansing to the kidneys, as well as promoting sweat. The flowers are enlivening and strengthening. They refresh the spirit and thin the blood.

A syrup is prepared from citron juice or lemon juice in the following manner: Take one pint of the juice pressed from the rinds, which have first been rasped on a grater, and a fourth of a pound of the grated yellow zest. Put them together in a glass jar and let this stand three days in a warm place well stopped. Then completely press out the liquid. Add one and a fourth pounds of white loaf sugar and let this dissolve over a gentle charcoal heat. This will develop into a delightful syrup that can be made into a julep with water. The julep is very beneficial when drunk for the heat of fevers and coursing of the blood. This same syrup withstands poison, strengthens the heart, and is very serviceable in cases of ardent pernicious fever.

A valuable essential salt can be made from citron juice in the following manner: Take freshly pressed citron juice, as much as you want, and boil it in a clean stoneware pot until reduced to one-half. Then set this in the cellar so that a fine salt crystallizes. This is useful for dispelling bilious humors of the stomach, for keeping the body open, for awakening the appetite, and for cooling hotness. But this is only available to the rich. The poor must serve themselves with meaner remedies. For them prepared cream of tartar will have nearly the same effectiveness, only it does not taste as pleasant.

Citrons preserved in sugar are very serviceable to pregnant women who are plagued by uncommon desires. They drive out melancholy, are useful in reviving an enfeebled body, strengthen the heart, withstand poison, and are thus quite effective during times of pestilence or other contagious illnesses.

The preserved rinds of citron strengthen a cold stomach, promote digestion, dispel reeking breath, and provide against tremblings and weakness of the heart. The entire citron, with rind and fruit, is effective against severe scurvy.

Clary Sage
Salvia sclarea
Sauer: *Scharlachkraut* (1772)

The German name for this herb means "scarlet wort," in reference to its old use in curing scarlet fever (which Sauer does not mention among his cures, oddly enough). One of its other common names in English is eyebright, and for the treatment of the eyes, this herb was one of the most important. It was native to Switzerland, so it was well known to Zwinger, and doubtless the Germans made more varied use of it than the English. It was not introduced into England until 1562; thus it came rather late into the reper-toire of English folk remedies.

There are several varieties of clary, as Sauer implies, but the one deemed most use-ful to medicine is a biennial that prefers well-drained, indeed, very dry soil. It grows quite tall and is strongly aromatic, although the odor reminds most people of an unpleas-ant cat scent. The whitish flowers can be fermented with sugar to make an herb wine that resembles French Frontiniac. It is this pleasant taste to which Sauer refers. The Germans in America evidently used clary sage to doctor off-tasting wines. The trick was well known, since German wine merchants were the first to use clary as a wine adul-terant, mixing it with elder flowers, thus converting a raw, cheap Rhine wine into a fake muscatel. The same could be done with the raw Portuguese wines once so common before the revolution.

Clary sage, particularly the fragrant variety planted in gardens, operates through its flowers and leaves, which possess a volatile, mildly balsamic salt mixed with earthy components. From these, clary derives its capacity to warm, to dry, to open, to dissolve. It strengthens the head, nerves, stomach, heart, and matrix; sweetens and improves salty, sour blood; and cleanses and heals wounds and injuries.

The dried leaves, ground to a powder and snuffed into the nose, will draw down snot, cleanse the brain of rheums, and also cause a little sneezing.

It is customary to take the fresh green leaves, mix them with eggs, and then fry this in butter. This results in a pleasant omelet that strengthens the stomach and cleanses the kidneys.[70]

The mucilaginous juices drawn out of the seeds when soaked in rosewater, then mixed with the water of fennel, will take away inflammation, redness, and pains in the eyes. Dip a small piece of cloth in the mixture and lay it warm over the eyes.

If the leaves are boiled in water and then used warm as a douche, it will strengthen and cleanse the matrix of all cold phlegm, bring down the menses, and cleanse the kidneys.

It is possible to draw out an essence from the leaves of clary sage when infused in brandy. It is good for all of the above enumerated maladies when taken in doses of one-half to one full tablespoon.

If this herb is put in wine, it will give it a delightful flavor and strengthen the stom-ach and a cold head as well.

If it is prepared and drunk like tea, it is good for colic and mother fits.

When the kernel of the seed of clary is placed in the eye, dust and other corrup-tions will adhere to it, just as it customarily does when crabs' eyes are used.[71]

70. Sauer does not actually say "omelet," but rather *Küchlein*, which can be interpreted as the same thing, since it is flat. Actually, the range of preparations made like this was rather broad, from small pancakes to some-thing akin to a thick crepe. If the egg preparation was chopped as it was cooked (a common technique, since this was easier to eat), it became a *Brockle*. For more on the *Brockle*, refer to page 48.

71. Crab's eyes are employed in a number of places in the herbal. These are indeed the eyes of the animal, and they were commonly used in medicine due to their chalky consistency when ground. For removing parti-cles from the eyes, they are perfect, since they absorb water and thus draw out the irritating substance.

Cloves

Syzygium aromaticum
Sauer: *Krämernelken, Nägelger* (1770)

> *The Sauer herbal refers many times to stomach powders, or "stomachic" powders, as they were then called. Under cloves, we are given two recipes. These powders were quite important in the eighteenth century, and since they also strengthened the stomach, they were considered cordials, which meant that many people simply took them on a regular basis to feel better. On close analysis, the cordial powders also look like lists of ingredients for gingerbread. Gingerbread was dipped in wine and eaten for the same medical reasons as the sliced bread mentioned by the herbal.*

Cloves possess considerable quantities of pungent oil mixed with volatile salts. For this reason cloves have all of the properties ascribed to cinnamon, but operate to a higher degree.

Cloves are used to great advantage in both cookery and medicine. They provide against all ailments of the head that originate from cold, as for example, apoplexy, convulsions, trembling, and numbness of the limbs.

For those afflicted by a cold, feeble stomach that cannot properly digest and is given to casting, make the following stomach powder: Take a half loth each of calamus and galangale, a quint each of cinnamon, ginger, and cloves; a half quint each of mace and black pepper; and twenty loths of sugar. Grind all of this to a fine powder, and take half a tablespoon sprinkled on a slice of bread soaked in good wine.

Cloves are also good for vapors of the stomach and gripes brought on by cold, for which one can make the following stomach powder: Take one quint of cinnamon, a half quint each of cloves, mace, anise, fennel, ginger, and galangale; and eight loths of sugar. Grind this to a fine powder and take in the doses given in the preceding remedy.

For choking, casting of the stomach, and diarrhea brought on by cold, take a slice of toasted bread, dip it in wine, and sprinkle powdered cloves on it.

Cloves are also quite useful for faintness of the heart, provided one distills a spirit from them, and then drinks a tablespoon of this water from time to time. Chewed in the mouth, cloves will also defend against dizziness and alleviate faintness of the heart.

If powdered cloves are sprinkled on the crown of the head, this will take off cold fluxes. But first, the crown must be dampened with strong brandy so that the powder sticks to the head.

Oil of cloves will invigorate all parts of the body, cleanse melancholic blood, strengthen the head and heart, and is particularly good against fainting. For these conditions, take two drops of clove oil in one tablespoon of wine each morning. This will also allay the gripes and warm the body. If a few drops of this oil are put on cotton and applied to aching teeth, it frequently allays the pain.

Clove Gillyflower (Clove Pink)
Dianthus cf. *caryophyllus* x *Dianthus plumarius*
Sauer: *Garten Nägelger* (1776)

*There is now a society devoted to the collection and preservation of this charming gar-
den perennial. For those who are not enthusiasts, it is almost impossible to understand
why this flower held such sway over eighteenth-century gardeners until it is met with
in the wild. By chance, I happened to be walking through the ruins of ancient Kourion
in Cyprus just as the wild pinks were coming into full bloom. The air was filled with
their sweet clovy scent, and walking on them, crushing them underfoot like a carpet of
weeds, only made the air that much headier. Indeed, it was a spiritual tonic, and when
I smell the pinks in full bloom in my own garden each June, the haunting potency of
those unforgettable wild Cypriot flowers returns.*

*I suppose all the cultivated sorts that we now enjoy trace their ancestry to hybridized
relatives of those wild plants with tiny pink flowers. However, the cultivated plants are
no longer pure species, since hybridization has made their genetic makeup very complicated. By Sauer's era, there were several species and many varieties crossed and re-
crossed with one another, and German gardeners doted on all of them. The red one that
Sauer mentioned was indeed the variety preferred by apothecaries. It appears to be similar to an extant dianthus called 'Sops in Wine.' Sauer's clove pink was a deep, rusty
oxblood red, double, rather frilled and full headed, resembling a miniaturized carna-
tion, but of a shade rarely seen today.*

*M. Daniel Pfisterer, a preacher at Köngen in Württemberg, compiled a hand-illus-
trated book in 1716 showing, among other things, all the clove gillyflowers in his garden, including the red one of medical reputation. Lest there be any doubt that this was
the sort used by German druggists, Pfisterer added beneath the picture a little couplet
in forced verse: "The clove gillyflower anguishes as much as the apothecary grumbles."[72]
This we must take as an allusion to the tedious job of plucking the petals for the conserves, syrups, and vinegars that Sauer discusses below.*

The blossoms of the clove gillyflower are warm and dry in middling strength, and
possess a mild volatile salt with thin balsamic oils. Therefore, they have the particular virtues of strengthening the head, heart, and liver, and of enlivening the spirit.

A sugar or conserve can be made from the garden variety in the following manner: Take eight loths of petals from the full-blown flowers. Chop or grind them with
sixteen loths of finely powdered sugar in a marble or wooden mortar until fully pulverized, then put up in an earthenware vessel for later use. If the conserve becomes
too dry, moisten it with a little rosewater or wine. It can be taken in doses the size of
a nutmeg according to need for strengthening a cold rheumy head, feeble eyesight,
or a weak heart and matrix. It is a valuable medicine for dizziness, apoplexy, and palsy,
and prevents fits in children. It is also good for the stomach, promotes digestion, stills
casting of the stomach, stops diarrhea and mother fits, and even kills worms.

72. M. Daniel Pfisterer, *Barockes Welttheater: Ein Buch von Menscher, Tieren, Blumen, Gewächsen und Allerley
Einfallen*, 2 vols. (1716; facsimile reprint, Stuttgart: Quell Verlag, 1996), 1:66.

A very useful and cordial syrup can be made from clove gillyflowers in the following manner: Take one pound of the plucked petals of full-blown rust red gillyflowers and put them in a new, well-glazed earthenware pot. Pour two quarts of boiling water over them, cover tightly, and let this stand overnight. Then strain and reserve the infusion. Take another equal quantity of fresh petals, and put them in the pot. Bring the reserved infusion to a full boil and pour it over the petals. Repeat this three or four times, the more often it is done, the stronger the syrup. Then strain the infusion through a cloth into the above-mentioned new pot. Let this stand eight days well covered until thoroughly settled and clarified. Gently pour off the clear part from the sediment, and add to each pint or pound of this liquid one-half pound of white sugar. Let them cook together over a gentle heat on a charcoal stove until the mixture attains a honey consistency. Then store away for later use in a well-stopped bottle. A tablespoon dose of this syrup, taken once or several times a day, will strengthen the head, heart, stomach, liver, and matrix. In children, it is good for warding off convulsions, and particularly serviceable for killing their worms, or for administering together with bad-tasting medicines or laxatives, since the syrup has such a pleasant flavor.

An excellent vinegar can be prepared from clove gillyflowers in the following manner: Pluck the petals from the caps, then dry them in the shade. Put them in a bottle with good vinegar (wine vinegar is best), and let this stand in the sun eight days well stopped. Otherwise, the bottle can be placed in a stoneware crock with cold water. Stand the crock on a trivet over a fire until the water comes to a rolling boil, then the vinegar is ready. It is good for fits of fainting when daubed on the nose, temples, and pulse. Or mist the face with it for protection during times of pestilence or other contagion. Under those circumstances, the hands and face should also be washed with it regularly.

Coffee
Coffea arabica
Sauer: *Caffee* (1771)

Sauer's discussion of coffee does not begin with the usual litany of comments concerning the plant's place in the universe of hot and cold humors. Rather, he talks about boiling it. What is not obvious to those of us who read his words today is that some of his rural readers may not have known the important medical difference between roasted and unroasted coffee. The beans were sold "green," although ripe beans are red, and once fermented in the sun, they turn brown. They were either roasted to order at the place of purchase, or brought home and roasted there. For the purposes of medicine, it was imperative to emphasize that the "green" seeds were essentially worthless, although it was common knowledge that if women chewed them, they could induce abortion (Sauer did not touch that subject).

But the reader does not get off so easily, for obviously Dr. Zwinger and others had made an elaborate analysis of coffee and tried to match up its virtues with the various humors characterizing human types as they were then understood. The Beauties of Creation *(Philadelphia, 1796) listed these medical benefits derived from coffee: "The coffee berries are generally ripe in April: they are esteemed as being of an excellent drying quality, comforting the brain, easing pains in the head, suppressing vapors, drying up crudities, preventing drowsiness, and reviving the spirits." The Sauer herbal is in general agreement with these remarks.*

Where the discussion of coffee becomes more complicated is in the last section devoted to the blood, and I have added a brief footnote explaining how that worked in sympathetic medicine. Blood was said to pass through several stages of combustion. Sauer's descriptive term for one of the final conditions of blood was verbrannt, *burned up or consumed. English sympathetic physicians would have used the words* cooked *or* charred *in reference to the thick, darkly colored, residue-laden blood that was considered so deleterious to the body. Coffee could make this condition worse in certain people, which is why Sauer included it.*

Sauer also mentions milk coffee, which should not be confused with café au lait; milk coffee is made with milk alone, no water added. In essence, it is brewed in much the same way that we make instant cocoa. This was a health drink, but it was also commonly given to children and invalids. Barley coffee and rye coffee, which are also mentioned, were likewise considered health drinks, but among the rural poor, it was this kind of grain coffee that was consumed on a daily basis rather than the imported article.

When the unroasted beans are boiled in water, the water derives few of the medical virtues of the plant. But if the beans are first roasted, then ground to a powder and thus boiled, the volatile, oily, alkaline salts will be drawn off into the water. Its virtue and action is such that coffee awakens and increases the bodily energies, loosens internal blockages, and dissipates fluxes and the crudities that accumulate from time to time. It also promotes the circulation of the blood, frees the chest of fluxes, opens the kidney passages, and in short, revives the entire body and clears the mind promptly.

Coffee can be drunk at any time of the day, but for those who have feeble stomachs, it will bring more benefit when taken before or after a meal. Then it will help to promote digestion, hinder windiness and vapors, and even protect against humors rising from the belly. Those who want to use it for green sickness and the onset of dropsy, as well as for coughs and tightness of the chest, and so forth, may take it in the morning before breakfast, as well as just before or right after eating.

Although many despise it, this beverage possesses excellent therapeutic powers for dealing with many of life's sundry conditions and afflictions. Firstly, those who are plagued by rheums of the head, weak memory, headache, dizziness, and frequent drowsiness will discover good results for all of these maladies if they drink coffee every morning one hour before breakfast or also right after eating it, or right after supper, and continue this habit for a considerable time.

Coffee is also good for drunkenness, which it quickly dispels, provided the person is not too greatly sotted—this can be determined though daily trial. For this purpose, however, the coffee must be weak lest it overheat the blood. This effect on drunkenness is the reason the public coffeehouses in England were forbidden for a time, on account of the people who gathered there for sober drinking, and who contrived intrigues and hatched plots. On the contrary, everyone was allowed to visit the wine shops because with that beverage, clear thinking does not hang together as well, and thus many secret designs may fall to the wayside.

When they must read, write, and study at night, scholars and students can drink coffee with excellent results right after supper, or without supper, for sleepiness is thereby hindered, the mind awakened, and the digestion well stimulated.

If the eyes are held over a vessel in which there is hot coffee, and the warm steam allowed to rise into the eyes frequently, it will make them bright and clear, and take away swelling, inflammation, and pain, as well as sties that form between the eyelashes.

To treat a burning throat, coughs, and shortness of breath that arise from cold fluxes and hard mucusy phlegm, coffee can be partaken of just as well before breakfast as after it.

Those who are inclined to consumption, or who have already been attacked by it, can benefit from milk coffee, which can be prepared in the following manner: Take fresh cow's milk and bring it to a boil. Then add one-half or three-fourths of a loth of ground coffee and sweeten to taste with sugar. Let this boil a little more, then strain well and give it warm to the patient in the morning and evening, provided there is no high temperature. By using milk coffee, many people have been quickly cured during the commencement of consumption, or have had their symptoms lessened, if they would simply persevere with the treatment for a considerable period of time.

As a beverage, coffee serves those well who suffer from palpitations and who are in danger of developing dropsy of the chest. It opens blockages of the glands and veins of the chest, and draws down phlegm through the urine. But it is particularly healthful for the stomach when it is drunk after meals or even prior to eating, since it promotes digestion, lowers blood pressure, sweetens and transforms sour vapors brought on by heartburn, colic, green sickness, iliac passion, and sand or mucus in the kidneys. It awakens the appetite, strengthens the nerves, checks rising humors, and disperses the vapors and windiness.

When coffee is made weak, it possesses an excellent ability to quench thirst and to cool overheated coursings of the blood.

In protracted illnesses that originate from a bad stomach, this healing beverage will bring the patient quickly back to his feet.

For blockages of the liver and glands in the stomach, and the dropsy that generally arises quickly from this condition, and which also often results in puffing of the skin over the entire body, coffee is a tested remedy. Such afflictions have already been entirely dispelled from some people, because coffee frees the blood of its excessively watery components through its diuretic power. Those who are inclined to dropsy can thus keep themselves free of the malady if they drink strong coffee regularly.

Kidneys bloated with mucusy matter, sand, and stones can be well cleansed by this diuretic beverage. Therefore, all persons inclined to kidney and bladder stones or blockages of the urine should drink coffee diligently, since by this means they will be protected on occasion from these painful ailments, or at least live in greater relief. This is because coffee dispels coarse, salty particles from the blood. For this last reason coffee is highly praised among the Swedes, Danes, and Hollanders as a remedy for flying gout.

Thin persons who possess a choleric, melancholic temperament, and along with it equally astringent and blackened blood and a restless, sanguine, overly watchful spirit, must refrain from drinking coffee. For by its use, they may easily induce their blood to course excessively and drive out the vital spirits so that the entire body may sink into inertia or exhaustion. But if this leanness is not caused by sharp, charred cholers but rather arises from a feeble stomach, then may they drink coffee to good effect.

Thin persons whose condition is caused by the first-mentioned temperament would fare better with rye or barley coffee, particularly roasted barley coffee. When it is prepared like coffee, it is completely beneficial and healing, particularly since real coffee would be too warming and too drying in nature for them. Coffee made from rye lies between these two extremes, and in particular operates by virtue of its somewhat nourishing and strengthening principals. For most people, it is the healthiest of all everyday beverages. In conclusion, those of cold, watery natures may drink real coffee, the stronger the better. Those of ardent, dry natures should drink barley coffee. And those who are between these two types should drink rye coffee, so that each will have a beverage that is natural to his humor.

Colocynth Melon
Cucumis colocythis
Sauer: *Coloquinten* (1767)

This is an annual plant resembling a watermelon, except that the leaves are extremely curled and the plant is covered with many hairs. It grows in sandy wastes in areas of the eastern Mediterranean and was an important medical product even in ancient times. It was normally sold dried, either as a dried mass of the pulp or as dried whole melons, which were called "apples" in the apothecary trade. Sauer evidently was able to offer both fresh and dried colocynth. Since colocynth is easy to grow on hot, sandy ground, doubtless there were places in or near Philadelphia where this was accomplished. There was a definite medical market for such melons, but they are also violently poisonous—one and a half teaspoons of the powder is normally fatal. This is why the herbal urged precaution in their use, and why Sauer's readers were warned not to be taken in by door-to-door quacks.

The primary application of colocynth was for the "French disease" or syphilis. Externally, it was used against body lice. It was one of the medicines commonly resorted to by military physicians because of the prevalence of these maladies among soldiers.

Both the fruit and the seeds of the colocynth possess a highly volatile, raw, irritant, bitter salt combined with oily, resinous substances. Therefore, colocynth not only purges the blood much too drastically but also, when taken even on occasion, its caustic poisons eat into the stomach and bowels, causing severe inflammation. Indeed, colocynth can easily induce gangrene in those parts, hence it is inadvisable to make use of it. Many people have been sent to their graves by accepting such medicine from country peddlers.

Notwithstanding, colocynth has been used to good effect by some physicians for the French disease. According to the condition of the patient, take half of a fresh colocynth melon, more or less. Put it in a glass vessel and pour good white wine over it. Let this stand well covered overnight. The next morning, gently pour off the clearest part of the wine without pressing the fruit. Give this wine warm to the patient to drink. The patient should continue this five or six times, and when doing so, should avoid cold air. In this manner, he should be freed of this nasty affliction sooner than by any other method. Also, one hour each time after taking the wine, the patient must drink a cooling herbal soup prepared from lettuce, endive, purslane, strawberry leaves, plantain, and the like. This wine infusion is also considered serviceable in cases of sciatica. Some people are of the opinion that by merely scooping up the flesh of the melon and smelling it, the nauseous bitter odor can indeed cause the stomach to purge itself.

Take anywhere from fifteen to twenty or thirty grains weight of the spongy flesh of one colocynth. Tie this in a bag and boil it for making a clyster. Administer the liquid to those who are afflicted by somnolence or apoplexy.

Wormwood and colocynth boiled in equal parts water and wine, and used for washing the head, will kill lice. Rubbed warm over the belly, it will expel all worms.

When dried colocynth is infused for a time in water, softened, and then distilled, it will yield an oil. If two or more drops of this oil are rubbed on the navel, it will cause a purging of the gut and bowels.

Columbine (European Columbine)
Aquilegia vulgaris
Sauer: *Agley, Glockenblume* (1766 and 1773)

Sauer published material on the columbine twice in the herbal, once in 1766 and again in 1773. This in itself should underline his conviction about its medical importance, especially for childhood diseases. In 1773 Sauer dropped the last two paragraphs dealing with the rarity of the plant and added more material relating to medical uses. These have been conflated into the 1766 text so that all of the pertinent information reads like one entry.

The comments about the scarceness of columbine, however, ought to be of great inter-est to horticultural historians, since they place the introduction of the herb in a very clear time frame. Sauer acknowledged that the plant could be found in some gardens (he had it in his), and indeed it is well documented in several physic gardens planted by the Moravians during the 1760s. But the Moravian seed came from Germany, and this would seem to imply that columbine was not at all common. By deleting these remarks eight years later, did Sauer mean to suggest that the plant had become more readily available? It is difficult to say because space constraints seem to have dictated content of the herbal more than anything else. Two things are certain: the native wild columbine was not viewed as a workable substitute; and the Dutch considered the Old World columbine among the most important herbs in their repertoire of remedies. We might logically conclude from this that they were also among the earliest of the Europeans to plant it in North America. If so, their settlements were few and scattered, which might in part explain the scarcity.

Columbine or "bell flower" is of a warm, dry nature.[73] It possesses the capacity to open, to heal, and to cleanse the blood.

To open blockages of the liver and spleen, take a few handfuls of columbine leaves and boil them in one-half gallon of white wine. Strain and drink a half gill every morning and evening. This also takes away jaundice through the urine and the beginning symptoms of dropsy, stays colic and mother fits, and strengthens the urinary vessels.

To make a valuable powder for jaundice: Take a quint each of columbine seeds, shaved ivory, and saffron. Grind these to a fine powder, then divide into six equal por-tions. Take one dose each morning, six mornings in succession, thoroughly dissolved in water of succory.

Powdered columbine seeds taken in a half-quint dose in plantain water in the morning before breakfast and two hours before supper will dispel jaundice through the urine in a very short time.

Another remedy for jaundice: Take one loth of the minced root of columbine, one-half loth of shaved ivory, a quint of ground columbine seeds, and half a quint of saffron. Put this in a half gallon of white wine and drink a small tumblerful in the morning before breakfast and again in the evening.

A quint of ground columbine seeds taken in a glass of wine is very helpful to women who are experiencing a painful birth. If it does not help after the first dose, repeat it again so that its properties may be proven.

The powdered seeds of columbine are as good for young and old as the distilled water of columbine or the juice pressed from the leaves, when they have gotten the purples or the red measles.[74] Neither will they break out further, nor will they recur, provided the dosage is taken with a small glass of wine. This remedy is heavily used

73. Bell flower is one of the common German names for columbine. In German, it is *Glockenblumen*. In English, this name is used for a different flower altogether.

74. The purples or rush is a condition given as *purpurea hemorrhagica* in period medical books. Called *Friesel* in German, it is characterized by bloody spots and bubbles in the skin. There is both a red and a white variety.

in the Netherlands when given in doses of one-half to a full quint, and as a result has saved many children from death.

If the root of columbine is chewed in the morning before breakfast, it will take off the early symptoms of stones and of gravel in the loins, and fully stop their development.

If three or four loths of water of columbine are drunk in the morning before breakfast, they will make a valuable remedy for opening blockages of the liver and spleen, and for getting rid of colic and jaundice. This will also heal sores in the mouth when used as a mouthwash.

When a small child has scurvy of the gums, wrap a little piece of rag around your finger and dip it in water of columbine. Then wash the child's mouth and tongue with it.

A half quint of powdered columbine seeds taken often in a small drink of linden blossom water will dispel dizziness and fits.

Because water of columbine is not to be had in this country, people here must use the freshly pressed juice instead, or else dry the herb in the shade. Then brew and drink it like tea. Prepared thus, the leaves of columbine are also an excellent remedy for colic and various mother fits.

Because this excellent herb is so rare in many parts of this country, people would do well if they would plant this flower in their gardens. It would then not only be very useful for medicine, as is to be seen from the description above, but it also would ornament the garden in a choice manner with a pleasing flower.

Comfrey
Symphytum officinale
Sauer: *Schwartzwurtz, Wallwurtz* (1768)

It is a pity that the herbal was not more expansive about the many uses of comfrey, for this is one very showy herb that should be found in every garden. Not only do the flowers attract bees and butterflies, the chopped leaves are a wonderful remedy for reviving sick and weakly plants. Just mulch the chopped leaves around the base of the plant-patient, and within a week it will begin to take on new vigor and color.

This is because comfrey contains many rare but important trace minerals that are important to the function of all living things. Herbal physicians long ago discovered this, and wisely understood that the most critical components were concentrated in the roots. Therefore, the roots must be harvested before the plant begins to send up shoots, which is the reason the herbal states that March and April are the preferred months for digging it.

The young shoots were often covered with straw and blanched so that they could be cooked much like cardoons. The young leaves were also eaten as cooked greens, but when the plant becomes too large, the leaves toughen and become prickly. Indeed, comfrey was once a common kitchen garden herb, and it is evident from Sauer's herbal that it was already well established in colonial America by the 1760s.

Comfrey operates by a mild salt, together with mucilaginous balsamic principals. Thus it possesses the capacity to cool, to emolliate, to glutinate, to mitigate the sharpness of bodily humors, and to settle and heal the blood. It is the root of comfrey that is mostly used in medicine. It should be dug up in March or April during a full moon.

Toward the end of May, a distillate can be prepared in water from the leaves and root. An essence and extract of the root is commonly made this way: Take as much comfrey as you want, and boil it in water until it becomes thick and mucusy. Pour over this just enough brandy to cover it, then let it stand for a few days in warm sand.[75] Carefully pour off the essence that has formed on the top, and store away for future use. This essence is good for all manner of hemorrhages, fluxes, bloody flux, ruptures of the groin, and wounds. The dose should be twenty to forty drops at a time, taken frequently. If the brandy is allowed to evaporate so that the decoction achieves the thickness of honey, there will be more than enough extract for pills. For the same illnesses just mentioned, the extract should be given in doses of fifteen to thirty grains.

Surgeons ought to hold comfrey in high regard, because it is quite useful in treating all sorts of wounds, ruptures, and injuries. They can make a fine astrictive with it by taking powdered comfrey root and spreading it on hemp that has been moistened in warm water. This is then laid over the wound. It will quickly cleave to it, harden, and bind it together.

Prepare a decoction of one loth of dried comfrey root boiled in two quarts of water and drink it. This will serve well against bloody flux, severe overflow of the menses, ruptures, sores of the lungs and kidneys, blood spitting, and pissing blood.

The root of comfrey, chopped and pounded, then vigorously pressed, will yield an oil or fatty matter that, if distilled in the sun for a time, is good for open injuries, wens, and the itch, as well as for syphilitic and leprous sores.

The distilled water of comfrey root is good for healing all internal and external injuries, ruptures, and sprains. It also checks blood-spitting, consumption, all manner of fluxes of the belly, pissing blood, and bloody flux. The dosage for these conditions is one-half gill taken frequently. If a cloth is moistened with this water and laid over the affected place, it will heal wounds, abscesses, chapped lips, cracked nipples, and cracked skin on the hands and feet.

Comfrey root preserved in sugar is useful in treating bloody flux and other fluxes of the stomach. It stops blood-pissing, cleanses the chest and lungs of pus and hard phlegm, and defends against blood-spitting and consumption, provided a small piece of it is eaten often according to need.

---

75. The herbal simply states "over warmth," but the understood technique was to place the bottle or alembic in a kettle full of sand, which was then set over a charcoal stove or on top of a plate stove. This yielded a constant, even, low heat that was necessary for separating and clarifying the lighter components from the sediments. The only other way to accomplish it was by solar distillation, which is highly dependent upon the vagaries of the weather and far more time-consuming.

Coriander

Coriandrum sativum
Sauer: *Coriander* (1764)

On the subject of coriander, the herbal makes some interesting observations as well as a few telling omissions. First, the widespread belief among German country people that coriander was mildly poisonous led to its neglect as a culinary herb in the fresh state. This may be accounted for by the fact that there are many people who have an allergy to the plant, and their reactions were viewed as a sign of danger. Treating the seed with vinegar (a strong acid) altered the chemistry of the seeds, a practice that was not only common but preferred by Sauer. In spite of this, some people did put the green (unripe) seeds into pickles and herbal vinegars because the flavor at that stage of ripeness is sweeter and because the pickling vinegar was thought to counteract the lurking poisons.

Candied coriander seeds, or coriander comfits, were popular in the Middle Ages and remained so into Sauer's era. Doubtless, he sold them from his shop. They may be considered both medicine and dessert food, since they were commonly served at the end of eighteenth-century meals of even the most modest pretensions.

Not mentioned, however, was coriander water, a fashionable cordial. The rise of its popularity may be traced to the seventeenth century. In Le Confiturier françois (Paris, 1667), a section is devoted to les eaux d'italie *(Italian waters), and among them we find coriander water. It stands alongside anise water, orange water, and citron water, "Italian" waters that are mentioned elsewhere in Sauer's herbal.*

Coriander is of a warm and dry nature. It strengthens the stomach, promotes digestion, and dissipates windiness. Some people are of the opinion that the seed of coriander operates by a rather poisonous principle, and thus advise that vinegar be poured over the seeds and that they be allowed to soak in it for twenty-four hours. The vinegar is then poured off, and the seeds dried and put up for later use. Yet others write that there is no poison in the seeds at all, although they allow that it may be good to prepare coriander seeds in the above-mentioned manner. However, if the seeds are over a year old, the vinegar treatment is not necessary.

Coriander seeds prepared as above and used alone dispel a putrid stomach and the vapors arising from it, and provide for a sweet-smelling breath.

When the seeds are coated with sugar, they are quite delightful to eat, and greatly strengthen the head and stomach. They provide against dizziness and stinking breath, protect against apoplexy, and flush the mouth and stomach of crudities after eating, provided a few of the comfits are taken regularly.

A cordial and strengthening potion for the sick can be prepared in the following manner: Take three loths of licorice, a quint each of anise and coriander seeds, and two tablespoons of whole-grain barley, and cook this in a gallon of water until somewhat reduced. Then add two gallons of fresh water, strain, and give to the patient to drink.

Corn Poppy (Red Poppy or Corn Rose)

Papaver rhoeas
Sauer: *Kornrose* (1774)

This is the poppy that invades wheat fields in England, and which can be found under cultivation in Germany even today. The Germans raise it primarily for its seeds, which, like those of the garden poppy, yield an oil similar to olive oil. In the Middle Ages this oil was widely used in Central Europe as an inexpensive grade of cooking oil during Lent and on fast days. The leaves were cooked as a green vegetable, and the syrup mentioned by Sauer was also used in cookery to flavor soups and pottages.

The Germans brought this plant to America and considered it an important addition to their kitchen gardens, but it never naturalized here to any extent and remains only an occasional escape. It is a pity, because large amounts of petals are needed to make most of the remedies mentioned, especially the syrup. The somewhat strange remedy for pleurisy, which calls for crab's eyes, boar's tusk, and the jaw of a pike, traces directly to Zwinger and his school of medicine. These ingredients are better understood when viewed as a source of high-grade calcium. They were readily available in apothecary shops.

Corn poppies are cold in nature and possess a sharpish, bitter, volatile salt with balsamic, oily components. From these it derives its capacity to ease, to open, to stop pain, to dissipate coughing, and to bring sleep.

It is a proven remedy for pleurisy: Take one quint each of corn poppy flowers, crab's eyes, boar's tusk, pike's jaw, peach pit, and holy thistle seeds. Grind it all to a fine powder, then administer half a quint frequently to those who are afflicted with pleurisy, after first bleeding the vein on the arm of the affected side.

The distilled water of corn poppy is serviceable in ardent fevers, for pleurisy, quinsy, and overflowing of the terms, provided a few tablespoons of it are taken frequently. When it is mixed with water as a gargle, it will check all inflammations of the throat, quinsy, and scurvy of the gums. Water of corn poppy is also a valuable remedy for Saint Anthony's fire,[76] and injury or corruption of the privates by an infected swelling, when a small piece of cloth is moistened with it and then laid over the affected place. It also removes red spots on the face, when washed with it twice a day.

A conserve or sugar may be prepared from corn poppy petals, which is also very useful for coughs, pleurisy, ardent fevers, dry throat, and related illnesses of the chest.

A syrup prepared from corn poppies halts severe inflammations during ardent fevers, checks quinsy, and is particularly good for pleurisy and all manner of coughs when a tablespoon dose is sucked into the mouth slowly according to the patient's liking.

---

76. Sauer used two words, *Rotlauf* and *Wildfeuer*, both of which are normally translated as Saint Anthony's fire. What he intended were two separate conditions that went by the same general name: ergotism *(Rotlauf)* and erysipelas. Ergotism was caused by a fungus on grains, primarily rye (see page 268).

Cottonweed (Cudweed, Golden Mothwort)
Graphalium uliginosum
Sauer: *Rheinblumen* (1770)

Sauer took the English name for this herb from John Gerard's herbal, and if one reviews Gerard's comments and illustrations (there are several plants bearing this name), it becomes obvious that a number of very different species have been lumped together. This made identification of Sauer's Rheinblumen *somewhat complicated, since the Latin was given as* Stachys citrina, *which is the golden stoechas of other herbals, and an entirely different plant. The problem is that cottonweed is an old synonym of cudweed, which is indeed the plant depicted in Zwinger's herbal as well as Gerard's. But as Gerard pointed out, it also had yet another name: golden mothwort. It was a pungent-smelling herb that came from Italy and the Mediterranean and which was imported and sold dry in the eighteenth century.*

Cottonweed is of a warm and dry nature and possesses numerous oily, volatile bitter salts. It opens, dries, disperses, cleanses, heals, and operates by urine.

Boil a handful of cottonweed in two quarts of water and drink this decoction. It will kill worms and will also be useful against obstructions of the liver and jaundice. It will operate by urine and dissolve the mucus and sand in the kidneys.

Boil cottonweed in lye and wash the head with it. This will get rid of mites and lice on the scalp.

If cottonweed is laid among the clothes, it will keep away moths and beetles.

Cottonweed smoked like tobacco is good for toothaches and draws down rheums from the head.

Cranesbill
Geranium pratense, Geranium cicularium
Sauer: *Storkschnabel* (1778)

The wild geranium (Geranium maculatum) of North America is often erroneously equated with this in remedies, but it is the European plant that Sauer is discussing. Its applications were quite different from those of our native plant, and its importance to doctors and especially surgeons cannot be underestimated. Since it is especially useful when fresh, doubtless it was grown in shady corners of many colonial gardens. The pink flowers are quite decorative in the late spring, and the plant is relatively resistant to drought. The drier the location where it grows, the more pungent the leaves, and the more pungent the leaves, the stronger their action in remedies.

Cranesbill possesses a middling warm and dry nature, and the virtues of opening, dissolving, dissipating, cleansing, and healing.

When the plant is picked fresh, wilted on a hot hearth, and then laid fresh every day on legs swollen up with dropsical, phlegmy fluids, it will dispel the swelling in due course.

For those suffering from cancerous injuries to the chest and other parts of the body, this herb is of service internally as a vulnerary potion. Externally, it is used in salves and vulnerary plasters.

If cranesbill is laid upon the inflamed breasts of nursing mothers, it will dispel the swelling and stop the pain.

This herb is excellent for ardent fevers, provided it is pulped with vinegar and a little salt so that the cataplasm can be bound to the soles of the feet. It will draw out the fever immediately. If the leaves are mashed and stuck into the nostrils, it will stop bleeding of the same.

The distilled water of cranesbill, taken in three- or four-loth doses before break-fast, will dissolve clotted blood in the body, promote urine, and operate against sand in the bladder, as well as sand and stones in the kidneys. It is a certain remedy for scurvy and great heat in the mouth during fevers. If the tongue becomes extended and fully split due to heat, soften a few quince seeds in cranesbill water so that it creates a thin mucusy liquid. Take a small feather and brush this in the cracks and on the tongue. It will both cool and heal it. For scurvy of the mouth, this water is also good when the mouth is washed with it often.

Crowsfoot (Upright Meadow Crowsfoot, Buttercup)
Ranunculus acris
Sauer: *Hahnenfuss* (1767)

A common meadow herb in Europe, crowsfoot is easily recognized from other buttercups due to its tall stem and smooth flower stalks. The plant is perennial, although it dies back in the winter. The leaves will generally cause skin irritation even if handled for a short time, and many a picnic has been ruined by people sitting among the cheerful yellow flowers. John Hill remarked, "Some are so rash as to mix a few Leaves of this among Sallet, but it is very wrong; the Plant is caustic and poisonous." He added further that it was an excellent plant for external applications in raising blisters, but then reconsidered his advice: "It is a Wonder they are not more used for this Purpose, but we are at present so fond of foreign Medicines, that these Things are not minded."[77] Quite the reverse in colonial America, where this was indeed a foreign medicine until it quickly naturalized in our meadows.

There are some fifteen kinds of crowsfoot, but all of them possess just about the same element, a volatile, caustic salt, and for this reason they are hot, dry, and sharp. If they are laid green upon the unprotected skin, they will cause burning and raise blisters. For this reason they should never ever be used in internal remedies.

For hip gout, take the leaves, pulp them, lay them as poultice over the hurtful place, and let them remain there until they raise a blister. In this way, they will draw up into the skin such angry, painful humors as are there. Then lance the blister with

77. John Hill, *The Useful Family Herbal* (London, 1755), 106–7.

scissors so that the malignant humors flow out, and rub the cut with fresh, unsalted butter. Or take a fresh cabbage leaf and warm it, smear it with the butter, and lay it over the spot. This will ease the pain caused by the burning and heal it in a few days, although the stomach should be purged before applying the poultice.

Crowsfoot is also laid upon plague boils that refuse to come to a head.

For divers rheums of the eyes, chop a handful of fresh crowsfoot leaves together with the flowers and spread this for several hours over the head, which has previously been shaved clean of all hair. This will draw out the rheums from reddened eyes.

The dried powdered root of crowsfoot put into the holes in aching teeth will make them fall out at once without pain.

For numbness in the limbs, the following ointment is effective: Fill a clean glass bottle with the freshly fomented leaves, flowers, and root of crowsfoot. Pour linseed oil over this until the bottle is full. Close it up tight, and let it stand in the sun for four weeks during the dog days of summer. Then rub the numbed limbs with this in the morning and evening.

Daisy
Bellis perennis
Sauer: *Masslieben, Gänseblümlein* (1766)

Some people are in the habit of calling these English daisies, for they are still quite popular as a spring ornamental flower. Our hot summers often kill them off, which is perhaps why they have not naturalized as prolifically as crowsfoot or some of the other herbs mentioned in this herbal. I find them rather delicate and much more successfully grown in partial shade, especially where it is moist. Nevertheless, they are an excellent border herb due to their smallness, and if the dead flowers are kept picked throughout the season, the plants will continue to bloom for a long time. Sauer's hesitancy in recommending a native substitute is understandable because there is nothing to recommend. Of the two species that are known to grow here, only the western daisy (Bellis integrifolia) is native, and it cannot be employed in the remedies below.

The leaves as well as the flowers of the common daisy possess an excellent faculty for thinning; for cleansing and healing internal and external wounds, abscesses, injuries, and fistulas; for dissolving all manner of clotted and stagnating blood, as well as thick phlegmy humors and fluxes. For the latter, the daisy makes them more fluid and thus dispels them through expectoration, sweat, or urine. The daisy is especially serviceable for blockages of the lungs, liver, spleen, kidneys, and mesenteric vein.

Daisies, with or without the leaves, heated in water and the resulting decoction drunk warm often, will be of particular service to those who have injured themselves by taking too cold a drink during excessive heat. For those suffering from coughs of long continuance and consumption, this will also check their condition. Indeed, this potion will also heal these afflictions completely. It dissipates all stagnating and clotted blood; in some cases it dissolves retained phlegm, purifies scorbutic salty, bitter blood; and cleanses the kidneys from all sand and foul matter. It also promotes the healing of all injuries and wounds.

For children plagued with coughing, it is customary to boil the flowers—fresh or dry—in milk. This is then strained, and their porridge prepared with it.

Or, take the fresh leaves, pulp them, press out the juice, and make it very sweet with rock candy. Give the child one-half to one full tablespoon of this sweetened juice. A fully grown person may take two tablespoonfuls or still more if desired. This remedy has caused injury to no one.

Take one handful of daisy leaves and flowers together with half a loth of snake-root[78] and boil them in one quart of wine mixed with one quart of water. Or, with the addition of a half loth of wormwood salts, boil it all in half a gallon of water. Taken in six to ten loths per dose, this will heal jaundice and dropsy.

A conserve or sugar can be made from the leaves and flowers in the same manner as mentioned under marjoram. This is of excellent service in divers cases of chest and liver complaints, particularly for coughs, consumption, and blood-spitting. Administer a nutmeg-size dose once a day for some days running.

A syrup of daisies can be prepared thus: Take one and a half pounds of daisy flowers and bruise them a little. Pour over them two pounds of fresh springwater. Let this infuse twenty-four hours well covered in a warm place. Then press out the liquid through a cloth so that it is clear. To this add one and a half pounds of loaf sugar and then boil it in a new earthenware pot over a gentle fire until it becomes as thick as honey. This syrup is of excellent service for coughs, abscessed lungs, and wounds to the chest and other parts, as well for blockages of the liver and spleen, and for the dissolving of clotted blood. Take one tablespoonful of this each morning and evening.

The dried flowers, leaves, and root can be ground to a fine powder, rock candy added, and from this mixture doses of a few pinches three times a day may be administered. If kept up faithfully for a period of time, this will prove serviceable for consumption and dropsy as well as diarrhea, particularly if at the same time the leaves and roots—fresh or dried—are boiled in water, and the decoction drunk daily with the powder.

Daisies are employed in particular for vulnerary potions and for those afflicted by maladies of the lungs.

Small daisies, when they are still quite young, may be eaten as salad with salt, vinegar, and olive oil. This will promote stool. The leaves can also be poached in meat

78. This is not Virginia snakeroot, rather the European plant *Actaea racemosa*.

stock and thus drunk for the same results. For this reason, mothers are accustomed to boiling the leaves and flowers in water to give to young children, so that they may keep their bowels open.

The distilled water of daisies heals sores in the lungs, all internal wounds, and injuries of the gut, provided it is administered in the morning before breakfast and in the evening two hours before meals in five- or six-loth doses.

It would be hoped that all good wives would cultivate this herb in their gardens, because experience has shown that it is an excellent remedy for both the common and the whooping cough in young and old. But it is by far a better remedy for children in divers situations. The daisy grows exceedingly well in this country, but it must of course be cultivated. I know nothing about those that grow wild here, though they be similar to those that are cultivated in Germany.

Dame's Rocket
Hesperis matronalis
Sauer: *Abendviole* (1775)

Dame's rocket is now so widely naturalized in this country that many people think of it as a native plant. The wild ones display a mix of off shades ranging from pinkish white to vibrant purple. Under cultivation good colors can be selected out, but the one the Germans liked most was a pure white double sort. Indeed, in the 1716 manuscript picture book of Württemberg minister M. Daniel Pfisterer, the double white dame's rocket is held up as a symbol of moral perfection, while the other colors were seen as degenerate.[79] While the modern attitude toward dame's rocket is mostly as an ornamental, Sauer's discussion is enlightening in the varieties of ways the plant was once employed. The suggestion about using the flowers on salads is quite winning, given their pleasant fragrance.

According to old thinking, dame's rocket was warming and drying, particularly the seeds. They possess divers spirituous elements mixed with volatile oily salts. From this derives its virtue and faculty to loosen, to open, to dissolve thick phlegm, to expel through the urine and sweat, and to ease difficult breathing.

The juice expressed from the leaves taken in doses of three to four loths in the morning and evening will purify scorbutic bitter residues of the blood through sweat and urine. It will loosen humors of the chest, produce free and easy breathing, and open all internal blockages. It will also expel thick matter and sand from the kidneys and excite the appetite. Similar results may be had by drinking six to eight loths of the distilled water of dame's rocket.

If the fresh leaves are chopped and mixed with warm white wine, and wounds or injuries are rinsed with the infusion while the leaves are laid on the hurt, this will cleanse, purify, and prevent putrification of the flesh, as well as promote immediate healing. The expressed juice from the leaves possesses the same virtues.

79. M. Daniel Pfisterer, *Barockes Welttheater*, 1:158.

If this juice is mixed with honey water and drunk, it will purify and quickly free the chest of phlegm, and in due time ease and dispel coughing.

If a half quint of the seeds is administered now and then, this will prevent the growth of stones in the kidneys and bladder. It will operate on sand and mucusy matter by means of the urine, and kill worms as well.

The distilled water of dame's rocket taken for fourteen days in six- to eight-loth doses every morning and evening will heal the itch and scabbiness.

The fresh flowers may be scattered on salads for the ornamental appearance as well as health. On the other hand, the dried flowers, together with winter roses, self-heal, and crabs crushed while alive, all fomented in water, then strained and mixed with a little rose honey or mulberry juice, will yield a fine gargle. Administered warm, it will get rid of inflammations of the throat and swelling of the tonsils and glottis.

Deadly Nightshade (Belladonna)
Atropa belladona
Sauer: *Nachtschatten* (1770)

The medical virtues of this highly dangerous plant have been known and well under-stood for many centuries, although its uses have changed greatly over time. The poison-ous alkaloid atropine is just one of several chemical constituents that give belladonna its potent effect on humans—many other mammals are not poisoned by it and eat it freely. In any case, the root is the most poisonous part yet the least likely to be eaten by accident. The berries, which often attract the attention of children, can prove fatal to them, but adults often recover. The action of the poison also depends on the soil where the plant grows, dry, loose soils making it more potent than heavy clays. The same holds true for the poisonous constituents in rhubarb (page 260). Also note in the remedies that the leaves and juice of belladonna are never heated to a high temperature, since heat breaks down many of the chemical constituents and thus neutralizes them, a medical point well understood by the old herbalists.

Otherwise, Sauer's discussion of belladonna is rather brief, but he repeated the often-held idea that it was a certain cure for cancer, a theory that gradually declined in pop-ularity during the eighteenth century. Of greatest interest is Sauer's use of belladonna as a remedy for poison ivy, perhaps one of the earliest recipes of its kind to respond to this all-too-common American malady.

Nightshade is cold in nature and operates by a fetid-smelling oil together with sharp, poisonous salts, for which reason it is not used internally in medicine.

Anyone who eats the berries of belladonna will become mad and unintelligible, as though possessed by the devil. Indeed, the herbalists of old maintain that some have died from eating it.

The fresh, green leaves wilted on a hot hearthstone and applied frequently to breasts infected with hard tumors or cancerous swellings will soften them and dissolve them in a marvelous manner. The juice expressed from the leaves can also be used without hesitation on similar cancerous growths.[80]

Should anyone be poisoned by the vine that grows on trees, and has young shoots not unlike grapes, they should take deadly nightshade leaves and mash them.[81] Press out the juice, and wash the poisoned parts with it several times a day, as well as laying the cataplasm over the infected areas. Thus will the patient experience good benefit from it.

Devil's Bit
Scabiosa succisa
Sauer: *Abbiss* (1763)

> *The name devil's bit refers to a legend concerning the irregular shape of the root. It is alleged that the devil bit off a piece, and thereafter the plant retained a crook in its root. This is also alluded to in the German name, which literally means "bitten off" or "bitten away." The Pennsylfaanisch name is* Deifelbiss, *a literal translation of the English. The name devil's bit is also applied to a number of native plants that are unrelated to the Old World herb.*
>
> *Furthermore, is important to keep in mind that devil's bit should not be confused with scabious (Knautia arvensis), an herb that was once assigned to the same genus under the old designation* Scabiosa arvensis. *Like most herbalists of his day, Sauer treated the two plants as interchangeable in terms of medical effectiveness. This was a useful point to know, since scabious had naturalized in most of New England and the middle colonies by the 1760s; devil's bit had not. Devil's bit was planted here, but for some reason it did not move into the wild. This point is pertinent because devil's bit was among the most popular of all the herbs in Pennsylvania German botanical medicine. Indeed, even within the last twenty years or so, it was possible to find devil's bit in many rural pharmacies in that part of the country. It has been speculated that one of the reasons the Pennsylvania Germans had such a low rate of heart attack years ago was their frequent use of devil's bit in herbal teas, as devil's bit is extremely active in dissolving clots in the blood. The plant is collected and dried in September.*

Devil's bit is warm and dry in nature, like true scabious, and in an emergency, one can be used for the other. It has the capacity to purify the blood, to resist poison, to promote perspiration, to cleanse, and to heal, and is particularly good for the liver and spleen.

The leaves of devil's bit are highly renowned as a remedy against the falling evil, plague, and mother fits, and also for dissolving blood that has clotted within the body. Take two handfuls of the leaves and one handful of the roots, and boil this in one gal-

---

80. Winter aconite, dog's bane, and water hyssop were similarly applied, especially where the tumors were open or weeping, for otherwise this would allow belladonna to enter the body.

81. The vine here described is thought to be poison ivy or perhaps poison oak. Sauer actually calls it *Nebengiftkraut,* which can either mean a closely related plant, or a plant that is just as poisonous.

lon of water for as long as it takes to hard-cook an egg. Then let the patient drink this decoction frequently.

The leaves together with the root of this herb are highly praised for healing all injuries caused by stabs, slashings, or bullets. For this reason, surgeons apply them quite successfully in vulnerary potions for their wounded patients. The following potion is very useful for all of the above-mentioned conditions: take two loths of devil's bit root, a handful each of devil's bit leaves, whitlow grass, goldenrod, sanicle, and wintergreen. Chop all of these ingredients very fine. Boil them in one gallon of fresh water until reduced to one quart. Strain, and let the patient drink half a pint every morning and evening.

If a horse should have dull eyes or the worm, chop the root and leaves of devil's bit very fine and give it to him mixed with his fodder.

Two ounces of devil's bit root boiled in one gallon of white wine for as long as it takes to hard-cook an egg, and the resulting decoction drunk frequently, will dissolve blood congealed internally as a result of a severe fall. It relieves pressure on the heart and mother fits, withstands all manner of poison, and is good during times of pestilence.

The following potion can be prepared for contagious diseases, especially the plague: Take the entire plant of devil's bit, along with its well-washed root, and chop it fine. Take two handfuls of scabious leaves and a handful each of the leaves and root of tormentil and the leaves of holy thistle, all previously dried in the shade and ground to a fine powder. Also add a handful of juniper berries coarsely ground. If masterwort is on hand, add one ounce of that. Put all of this in a glass vessel and pour enough wine or brandy over it so that it fully covers the herbs. Let this stand a few days well stopped over warm sand or in the sun. A tablespoonful of the extract is quite excellent if taken every morning while contagious diseases are spreading.[82]

If someone is bitten by a snake or any other venomous creature, or even by a mad dog, a small tumblerful of this essence should be taken with one loth *Theriaca Andromaci* dissolved in it. This will work against the poison powerfully and bring on a copious sweat. If the bitten member of the body is immediately bound tightly above the wound, and the wound is well bled by cupping, it will heal without further injury.

If a person has taken cold, they should likewise take the extraction dissolved in *Theriaca Andromaci* and sweat well several mornings in succession. Or, if a cold drink has been taken during the heat of summer, and it is noticed that evil consequences may be developing, take one tablespoon of this extraction at once and repeat the dose every morning a few days in succession. In this manner, a serious illness can be avoided at little cost.

The distilled water of devil's bit is very useful against the falling evil. It withstands contagion, cleanses the chest of phlegm, dispels pursiness and coughing, and disperses pleurisy and blood congealed in the body. Drink four to five loth of it morning and evenings.

---

82. The extract in this case is the clear, highly concentrated liquid that forms on the top. This is the part collected and used.

The juice expressed from fresh devil's bit leaves mixed with vitriol will heal ringworm and bad cases of purulent scurf when they are rubbed with it.

If someone has a swelling or an old abscess in the throat or mouth, there is nothing better than when devil's bit is boiled in water, strained, gargled, and rolled in the mouth thoroughly, then spit out. It will also dissolve hard phlegm and ease the swelling.

Dill
Anethum graveolens
Sauer: *Dillkraut* (1766)

Historically, the Germans recognized many sorts of dill, Bärendill, "bear's dill," Kühdill, "cow's dill," Himmeldill, "heavenly dill," and many others, although not all of these herbs were botanically related. Culinary dill, however, was a cultivated herb, although it will sometimes naturalize on warm, sandy ground. It must have been introduced here very early, since it was considered a necessary plant for pickling and brining. This application is clearly preserved in yet another old German name for dill: Kümmerlingskraut, "cucumber plant."

In cookery, dill was employed almost as generously as parsley by the colonial Germans, and doubtless it stood out as one of the defining flavors of that old cuisine. However, Sauer did not pay much attention to the culinary side, which certainly needed no explanation, but instead has provided us with a very long list of interesting medical uses. The foot bath is especially worthy of note, because it really does relax the feet and softens the skin without leaving an overpowering dill odor.

The leaves of dill, and especially the seeds, possess a volatile, oily, bitter, sharp salt from which the plant derives the same virtues as fennel seed, namely, to thin, to dissipate, to bring swellings to a head, to increase milk, to disperse vapors, to bring gentle sleep, to strengthen the stomach and matrix, and to still pain. The leaves, flowers, and seeds are employed.

If dill leaves, together with their stems, are burnt to ashes and then strewn on old wounds, particularly in the privates, it will heal them entirely. Some mingle the ashes with honey to make a salve and then spread this on linen lint and put it into the holes of old wounds. This cleanses them, dissolves the putrid flesh, and heals them fully. The ashes of dill leaves take away not only putrid flesh, but also the proud flesh left on fresh wounds that prevents them from healing together. On this subject, an ancient poet once said:

Sie, die alles wilde Fleisch aus den bösen Wunden frisst,
Ruhret nicht, bis dass man rein und durchaus getheilet ist.

Thou dill, who consumeth all the untamed flesh of angry wounds,
Never resteth till thy work be neatly accomplished.

The distilled water of dill weed, taken in two- or three-loth doses in the morning and evening, will bring an increase in milk to nursing mothers, disperse windiness in the lower parts, protect against hiccups, and force down urine. If it is held warm in the mouth, it will get rid of toothache, for it draws out the painful fluxes.

If dill seed is ground fine, olive oil poured over it, placed in a glass bottle over a hot stove or in the hot sun for eight to fourteen days, then pressed out and smeared warm as a lotion on the stomach, it will get rid of colic, stomach pain, and sundry other internal and external pains. This will also disperse boils, swellings, and hard lumps. It will immediately help young children who have the hiccups when rubbed warm on their belly.

The root and sprigs of dill, heated in water and then drunk in glassful doses, will cleanse the kidneys, and force down urine, foul matter, and sand.

An oil may be distilled from dill seeds just like the oil from anise. If four to five drops of it are taken in a tablespoon of almond oil, this will get rid of hiccups immediately.

This herb is also useful for boiling in foot baths for people who have trouble sleeping.

If the fresh leaves are wilted on a hot hearth and laid upon the head, it will get rid of headache.

Dittander
Lepidium latifolium
Sauer: *Pfefferkraut* (1777)

This large herb has become well established in my garden, and I can only suggest as a warning to others that it is quite invasive. It spreads underground by means of long, ropy roots that can be used like horseradish in cookery. However, its benefits to the eighteenth-century farm table were many, for its huge productivity and freedom from pests were probably two very high points long ago. The plant is best grown in a long row like sorrel (which it vaguely resembles) so that it can be harvested as needed and trenched on both sides to keep it within bounds.

During hot weather, the leaves turn tough and strong-tasting, thus its appeal is more as a cool-weather potherb and one that can be improved by a touch of light frost as well. Like horseradish, cooking dittander greatly reduces its pungency, but this also decreases its medical virtues. While dittander has not been recorded officially as naturalized, I have seen it in many places throughout the region settled by the Germans, particularly in isolated spots east of the Susquehanna River near old Mennonite settlements.

Above all else, dittander is warm and dry, thus it will make the skin raw and raise blisters when bare skin is rubbed with it. For it is endowed with divers volatile, alkaline, sharp salts, and possesses throughout the same virtues as horseradish. It is useful to note here that when this herb is boiled any length of time, the volatile salts and their properties are fully lost.

In England, midwives cultivate dittander with great diligence, so that they may put the root in drinks for women in labor that they may deliver more quickly.

If dittander is wilted on a hot hearth, then pulped and laid as a poultice upon the hips, it will dissipate the pain or hip gout readily.

The leaves are prepared hot with vinegar and sugar, but the root is cooked in milk. They are served as condiments with roasted meats. In Switzerland, it is customary to eat the leaves raw with meat. Some chop the leaves, then add black pepper, sugar, and vinegar and eat this as a salad with meat dishes. Made thus, it strengthens the stomach, awakens the appetite, and encourages digestion.

When dittander is laid in wine and the infusion drunk regularly, it will open blockages of the spleen, drive away scurvy, and purify the blood of hypochondriacs.

Dittany (White Dittany or Burning Bush)
Dictamnus albus
Sauer: *Dictam* (1769)

This unusual Old World herb is still cultivated for its striking flowers and fragrant, lemon-scented leaves. The plant exudes a vapor that is highly flammable and can be lit with a match, hence its name "burning bush." Dittany was extremely popular as an ingredient in various compound medicines during Sauer's era, and the dried leaves could be used as a substitute for tea. However, Sauer only refers to the dried root of commerce, so it is quite likely that the plant itself was not under cultivation in the colonies to any large degree. Furthermore, being a native of southern Europe, it is not known to have naturalized in Pennsylvania, which would also suggest that the medicine was imported rather than domestic. However, a New World plant did supply country people with a workable equivalent. This was Cunila origanoides, *variously known as stone mint or American dittany. It can be found in dry woods and thickets throughout the middle states.*

Common dittany is of a warm, dry nature and operates by its acrid, bitter, somewhat oily salty components. Thus it possesses the uncommon power to penetrate, to open, to promote urine and the menses, and to assist birth. It can also kill worms and withstand all manner of poison.

One-half quint of the finely ground root of common dittany taken in pennyroyal water will promote difficult urination and menses. It will bring down a dead fetus, kill worms, and alleviate cold mother fits. The ground root is also used to good effect in antidotes to poison.

Dwarf Elder
Sambucus ebulus
Sauer: *Attig, Niederholder* (1765)

> *Since this plant is not native to North America, in all probability the American or sweet elder* (Sambucus canadensis) *was used in its stead. The fruits of the black haw* (Viburnum prunifolium) *were sometimes employed as American substitutes, but Sauer is correct in pointing out that only the imported electuary was available in shops.*

Dwarf elder possesses quite the same faculty as black elder; however, its roots and berries are much stronger in operating by urine. For this reason it is recorded that it is warm and dry by nature.

Dwarf elder, like black elder, is employed for dropsy.

If the young shoots are poached in wine and eaten as salad, they will loosen the bowels.

When dwarf elder seeds are ground to powder and a half quint is taken in white wine every morning, this will prove good against dropsy. Similar results may be had by infusing the inner bark in wine and drinking this daily.

The distilled water of dwarf elder flowers and the electuary made from dwarf elderberries possess the same virtues as elder flower water and elder jam, and are prepared in the very same manner. Those who are suffering from dropsy should be given one to two small dabs of the electuary to eat. This will weaken and drive out the watery fluxes after a time.

All parts of the dwarf elder plant can be employed very effectively, from the root right up to the top shoots. For the most part, however, only the electuary is found in apothecary shops.

Elderberry (Black Elder)
Sambucus nigra
Sauer: *Holder, Holunder* (1771)

> *Here, the native American sweet elder* (Sambucus canadensis) *could be used as an acceptable equivalent to the European black elder, which is the plant treated in the herbal. The 1802 edition of the midwife's manual,* Kurtzgefasstes Weiber-Büchlein *(Harrisburg, 1799), advocated the use of elderberry bark in a remedy for burns: "A salve for burns, which is well known among us and esteemed by persons of quality, is made as follows: Take fresh sheep's manure and the inner green bark of young elderberry branches. Chop the bark fine and heat it with the manure in fresh, unsalted butter that has not been washed in water. Strain this through a cloth. Thus you will have a salve for burns of more value than one would pay for all my books" (50–51). We certainly hope so.*
>
> *Nowhere are the folk remedies more fascinating than when we turn to the elderberry. Sauer's discussion contains a number of unusual points worthy of note. The tech-*

nique for making elderberry wine with dried balls of mashed fruit is ingenious and works infallibly. The idea of using young sprouts as a purgative salad is not unique, but it does open a whole unexplored area of salad making in the seventeenth and eighteenth centuries, focusing attention on the underlying medical reasons for eating salads in the first place.

This is better understood when we consider that the medieval idea that raw foods were injurious persisted among rural populations well into the eighteenth century. Once salads became fashionable, this attitude changed. But to further elaborate upon Sauer, there were sympathetic salads just as there were sympathetic soups. These were not always pleasant but, like the purging sprouts of elderberry, were employed to deal with a specific medical condition.

On this point, a wide variety of uses were derived from the elderberry blossoms. We may better comprehend why elderberry blossom fritters were so popular among the German element: this was a tasty way to administer spring tonic. But the medical value did not stop there. Sauer goes on to discuss its virtues in dealing with Saint Anthony's fire (ergotism), which is further discussed under rye (page 268). In short, the old German saying that the elderberry bush was the poor man's medicine cabinet is certainly verified by the array of cures discussed below.

The blossoms of the elderberry possess a somewhat volatile, spirituous salty principle combined with a trace of sulfur. From this derives its faculty for acting internally by forcing sweat and urine, and by dissolving phlegm; and for acting externally by dissipating and staying pain. The berries possess a similar sudoforic juice, from which a fine electuary is prepared. The young shoots are endowed with a sharp, caustic salt in their sap, from which they derive their faculty for purging both the stomach and the bowels vigorously. Those of a strong constitution can easily eat a dozen such shoots in purgative salads. The inner bark possesses similar virtues, although not with as strong an effect internally, but applied externally it acts powerfully. The leaves and stems have a milder effect.

A half dozen young shoots of elderberry taken alone, or cooked with spinach, and eaten as salad, will immediately purge choler, water, and phlegm with both emetic and laxative action.

Elderberry vinegar is good for the stomach, excites the appetite, and disperses thick, tough phlegm.

If the fresh leaves of the elder bush are worked to a cataplasm and laid upon finger worms, they will heal the problem quickly.

If two or three tablespoons of the distilled water of elderberry blossoms are drunk in the morning and evening, they will be beneficial for opening the chest, for curing dropsy, for opening blockages of the liver, spleen, and kidneys, and for promoting sweat during fevers.

The electuary made from elderberries is useful against all poison, swellings, and dropsies, because it expels the injurious humors through sweat, provided a copious tablespoonful is administered.

Mash ripe elderberries in a marble or wooden mortar, then mold this into balls the size of a pigeon egg. Let them dry a little in the bake oven, then put ten or twelve balls in a large bottle or small keg. Pour over this a good white wine, and let it infuse for a while. This will yield an excellent elderberry wine, which if drunk from time to time, will cleanse the blood, clear mucusy matter and sand from the kidneys, protect against the onset of dropsy, ease breathing, and cleanse watery humors from the blood.

If elderberry blossoms are boiled in milk with a little saffron, and laid as a warm plaster over the joints, this will be of great benefit to those afflicted by gout or pain in the joints. If elderberry blossoms are boiled in water and then some camphor brandy is added, this will dissipate and stop pains. If they are laid over the sores, the blossoms will get rid of Saint Anthony's fire. For those who are concerned by weeping of the sores, take elderberry blossoms and rub them to crumbs. Combine this with a like quantity of rye flour, and heat the mixture in a skillet. Lay this warm over the sores, and as soon as it becomes cold, heat it again. Continue thus until the Saint Anthony's fire is gone. This is a known and tested remedy, and it would be beneficial if everyone kept it on hand, and planted elderberries on their property.

Elderberry blossoms drunk as tea will encourage sweating, dissolve clotted blood, and get rid of Saint Anthony's fire. If they are boiled in sweet milk, and the decoction drunk diligently, this will purify the blood and dispel scurvy, for it operates powerfully not only by dispelling corruptions through the sweat, but also through the urine and stool. If nursing women boil the dried blossoms in fresh milk, moisten a cloth with this, and then lay it warm upon the breasts, this will greatly increase their milk. If it is laid warm upon the head, it often stops headache and induces sleep.

Juice pressed from the inner bark and taken in two- to three-tablespoon doses will operate against tough phlegm in those afflicted with dropsy. It is also common practice to boil this bark in water or milk, and give it as an everyday drink to dropsical persons. It will carry off dropsical waters powerfully both by the stool and the urine.

Fresh ivy leaves chopped together with the inner bark of elderberry, fomented in butter and then pressed through a cloth, will yield a valuable salve for burns. If the injured members are rubbed with this salve diligently, it will quickly reduce the burning and heal the wound.

If the pith from the small stems of elderberry is chopped and half a quint taken internally from time to time, this will make an excellent remedy for those afflicted by sandy mucus retained in the kidneys. It will force it out, promote urine, and heal pains in the loins.

Put the electuary of elderberry in a bottle and pour brandy over it so that it covers it by the thickness of a few fingers. Then stop it well and set it in sand or ashes on a warm stove, and let it stand in the warmth for a few days, shake it up every day. Then strain it off. This will yield a reddish essence, which, if taken in half-tablespoon doses, will promote sweating quite nicely, and cleanse the blood and kidneys of watery humors.

Another very powerful essence can be made in the following manner from elderberries: Grind a goodly portion of the dried ripe berries and pour brandy over this.

Let it stand eight days in warm sand, then strain off the red extract and put it up in a well-stopped glass vessel. This essence is particularly renowned for treating swellings of the matrix and cramps. One or two tablespoons are taken at a time. This is done every morning before breakfast continuously until the condition abates.

Elecampane
Inula helenium
Sauer: *Aland* (1762)

Elecampane was another herb of great importance to the Pennsylvania Germans. Indeed, it was the very first herb published in Sauer's herbal. The flowers were used to make wine, and the roots were put up in preserves both as a culinary confection and as medicine, especially for consumptives. Since Sauer mentioned elecampane preserve but did not provide a recipe, the following is taken from the Vollständiges Nürnberg-isches Koch-Buch *(Nuremberg, 1691):*

Pare and cut the elecampane roots into thin slices. Let these stand overnight in conduit water.[83] *Put a kettle of water over a fire and when it boils, add the sliced elecampane. Let them boil together for as long as it takes to hard-cook some eggs, then pour off the water. Place the elecampane in a sieve so that it may drain. After that, dissolve sugar over a fire and add the poached roots. Let them boil hard until one believes the sugar may be thick enough. Then add half an achtel of rosewater and let it boil up again. Let it cool a little, then put the preserve in a pot tightly covered and set away in a cool place. If the syrup becomes thin, it can be strained off, strengthened with sugar, and further boiled to the correct thickness.(786)*

During the yellow fever epidemic of 1793, Dr. Sarnigshausen of Philadelphia recommended infusing elecampane root in wine or beer, or chewing it instead of tobacco as a means of protecting oneself from con-tagion. During the nineteenth century, elecampane remained an important herb in Pennsylvania German botanical medi-cines, both domestic and veterinary. J. W. Cooper's Experienced Botanist or Indian Physician *(Lancaster, Pennsylvania, 1840) continued to promote it as a purgative and stimulant, and some eighty years after the appearance of the herbal, L. W. Weber's* Der kluge Land-Medicus und Haus-Apotheke *(Chambersburg, Pennsylvania, 1846) actually repeated material lifted directly from Sauer.*

83. *Röhrwasser* or conduit water is brought into a city via an aqueduct or wooden pipes (usually elm wood). It could be obtained at public fountains. The intention of the recipe was to ensure that the water was pure and clean, not taken from an open spring or river. In short, it meant water of certifiable drinking quality.

Elecampane is warm and dry in nature. It possesses numerous balsamic components from which it draws its capacity to open, to dissolve, to ease difficult breathing, to stop coughing, to withstand poison, and to strengthen the stomach.

The root of elecampane preserved in sugar is a choice remedy against pursiness and shortness of breath. It promotes expectoration, cleanses the chest, and is helpful to consumptives and to those afflicted with gravel.

A fine electuary can be prepared in the following manner: Take one-half pound of good-quality honey, let it come to a boil, then scum it off well. Add to it three loths of dried, powdered elecampane root. Stir well until it thickens to a proper consistence. This is good for coughs and asthma, for cleansing the chest of phlegm, and for promoting its expectoration, when a few dabs of it are taken three or four times during the course of the day.[84]

Elecampane root boiled in water, and the decoction drunk with twelve or more drops of spirit of tartar in the morning and evening, is effective against colic, coughing, asthma, apoplexy, paralysis of the limbs, and so forth.

Elm Tree (Common Elm)
Ulmus campestris
Sauer: *Rusten, Ulmenbaum* (1776)

The remedies discussed in the Sauer herbal are more or less specific to the common European elm. This seems to indicate that the dried byproducts of this tree were imported and readily available in apothecaries, as well as the eau d'orme, *the sweet, sticky water gathered from leaf galls. This liquid was once a great cosmetic commodity.*

When American colonists needed fresh substitutes, they turned to the native American elm (Ulmus americana) *for bark and sap, and to the slippery elm* (Ulmus fulva) *for its mucilaginous inner bark. Between these two elms, all of the remedies and applications discussed by Sauer could be prepared. Slippery elm was especially preferred for vulnerary cures and became a standard feature of American botanical medicine by the nineteenth century.*

The bark, branches, and leaves of this tree possess numerous uneffervescent, earthy components by which they glutinate and astringe. Due to their mucilaginous alkaline moisture, they heal wounds and injuries. The green seed envelopes, however, contain an abundance of mucusy alkaline volatile liquid, which is a good discutient, and dispels inflammations of the eyes.

Elm cleanses, draws together, and heals wounds.

The ground bark, taken in a quint dose with wine, will act as a laxative and drive out the phlegm in the lower parts, and particularly watery humors. This is a remedy among farmers.

The water found in the wrinkled galls on the leaves, and gathered when fresh in

---

84. Sauer actually wrote *Messerspitz,* "tip of a knife blade," for the dosage. This is a general term in German for a pinch or a dab. He did not intend that the medicine be administered from the blade of a knife.

July, will make the complexion fair and the skin smooth when the face is washed with it. Fallopius used and recommended it for healing wounds.[85] The oil distilled from it is even more powerful in its medical action. For those who have a child afflicted by a bubonocele, take a small piece of cloth and dip it in this water, then lay it over the injury. Keep the child in a sturdy bandage.[86]

If an elm tree is split, a liquid will flow out of the heartwood. When the head is moistened with this, it will cause hair to grow and prevent hair loss. The same results are also accomplished when the inner bark is boiled for a long time in water, and the fatty scum that rises to the top skimmed off. Smear this fat on the bald spot.

Endive
Chicorium endivia
Sauer: *Endivie, Andivien* (1764)

Few readers of this herbal would suspect that endive played an important role in colonial German diet, but the fact is, it was just as important as cabbage. Judging from the rather extensive (and laudatory) comments Sauer devoted to the subject, it is easy to see that endive fell into the category of a cure-all. But the medical virtues were not all imaginary, for endive shares many of the known and highly beneficial constituents of dandelion and wild chicory or succory.

Evidently, several varieties of endive were cultivated in colonial kitchen gardens. The known German varieties were rote selbst schliessende *(red self-folding),* breite Winterendivien *(broad-leafed winter endive),* krause Winterendivien *(curly winter endive), and brown, yellow, and green summer endives.[87] The summer endives were characterized by leaf color: bronze, yellow-green, and dark green respectively. Furthermore, the seed was always sold under saladings; thus we have a picture of remarkable variety in both color and texture whether raw or cooked.*

Endive is of a cold and dry nature and possesses the ability to draw up or glutinate. These days, endive is commonly used in the kitchen, and great pains are taken to keep it green over the winter for salads and for boiling. This herb is eaten copiously in cooked preparations, whether boiled with meat, or in soups, or cooked to a puree. It is of great service in the treatment of the following afflictions: It can cool a bilious stomach in good order and restore its ability to digest. It can help all bilious disorders of the head, stomach, liver, and all other internal parts and bodily members, as well as cases of madness, furious nosebleeds, obstruction of the liver and spleen, passionate lusting for unchaste things, great thirst, jaundice, and tertian and quartan agues; and it is particularly beneficial when contagion is raging across the land. For endive

85. Gabriel Fallopius (1523–1562) wrote several medical works, including *Observationes Anatomicae* (1562), *De Simplicibus Medicamentis Purgantibus* (1565), and a book on the preparation of pills, oils, ointments, unguents, and syrups.
86. A bubonocele is an inguinal hernia, usually an incomplete type that forms a swelling in the groin resembling a bubo. The condition is as awful as it sounds.
87. *Dillenburgische Intelligenz-Nachrichten* (Dillenburg, Germany, 1791), 107.

cools and mollifies inflamed blood, restores the stomach enfeebled by fever to its proper order, and is serviceable in cases of blood-spitting and fluxes of the stomach, as well as acute gout. But endive is particularly good as healing nourishment and medicine for pregnant women who experience strange cravings for preposterous foods. Lastly, endive is an antidote to heartburn and acid stomach.

To treat obstruction of the liver and all other afflictions of the liver caused by fever, take a handful each of endive leaves, strawberry leaves, true liverwort, and succory. Chop them very fine, and pour a gallon of fresh springwater over them. Let this boil for as long as it takes to hard-cook an egg, then strain it through a cloth. Give half a pint of this decoction to the patient every morning and evening. Or, the herbs can be boiled in milk or meat stock, and a pint administered every morning before breakfast. Before and after this treatment, the patient should be gently purged.

Distilled endive water, or the juice pressed out of the leaves, can be drunk several times a day in doses of three to four tablespoons. This is very useful in all feverish afflictions of the head, as well as inflammations of the chest, lungs, and stomach. It cools, refreshes, and strengthens the lungs, liver, and spleen, opens obstructions of the same, dispels jaundice, and is serviceable in treating all inflammations of the kidneys, matrix, bladder, and other viscera. It attenuates clotted blood, and strengthens weak babies while in their mother's womb. Endive water or juice mixed with mulberry juice, and employed lukewarm as a gargle, will defend against infections of the throat and tonsils.

Eyebright
Euphrasia officinalis
Sauer: *Augentrost* (1764)

European eyebright is not native to North America. Those species of eyebright that do grow here are generally found far to the north, and aside from Maine, grew quite outside the region that was settled during colonial times. Sauer's last remark, about not knowing if the plant grew in America, is evidence in itself that not only did he not grow it (the climate of Pennsylvania is probably too hot anyway), he must have dealt strictly with the imported dried herb, powders, or preparations already put up in sugar.

This is an elegant little herb which grows only a few inches tall. The flowers are white, blue, or have tiny yellow spots, and grow between the stem and the leaves. The leaves are dark green, crinkled, and small and all around rather deeply cut. As to taste, it is a little astringent and bitter. It grows in meadows and blooms at the beginning of autumn. If it grows upon mountains, it commonly has only one stem; in damp places, however, it develops many branches from the central stem.

Eyebright is warm and dry in nature and possesses the faculty to withstand all sourness, to warm gently, to open, to disperse, and to purify. For the eyes, it is a particularly effective herb.

The herb acquired its name because it is employed with good results for dimmed vision and for strengthening eyesight.

If a handful of this herb is infused in two quarts of white wine and drunk in the morning and evening, it will strengthen poor eyesight and prove serviceable against jaundice.

A powder that is useful and very strengthening to the constitution may be prepared thus: Take one loth of the leaves and flowers of eyebright, half a loth of cinnamon, a quint each of white ginger, cardamom, cubeb, mace, and fennel seeds, and twelve loths of loaf sugar. Grind all of this to a fine powder, then administer each morning and evening half a tablespoonful on a slice of bread that has been soaked in good wine—and enjoy it besides. This is an excellent remedy for strengthening the declining eyesight of the elderly, for purifying the head of cold fluxes, for strengthening feeble memory and a weak stomach, and for getting rid of dizziness. However, for those who have burning eyes, eyebright will not prove useful.

The distilled water of eyebright strengthens weak eyesight caused by cold fluxes, gets rid of jaundice, and breaks up stones. Take three or four loths in the morning before breakfast.

Eyebright sugar or conserve is prepared like rose sugar and is outstanding as an eyesight remedy, for it preserves it while at the same time strengthening the head. It purifies the head of cold fluxes, and serves well against jaundice, provided it is taken in nutmeg-size doses in the morning and evening.

Whether this herb grows in this country could not be determined. Should it not be found, one would hope that there are people who would obtain seed from Germany and spread it here far and wide.

Fennel

Foeniculum vulgare
Sauer: *Fenchel* (1765)

Sauer's treatment of fennel is long, but it did not cover all of the varieties grown among the Germans. Bronze fennel, which is perennial in Pennsylvania and rather invasive once established, was a source of both aniselike seeds and saladings. Florence fennel, which the Pennsylvania Germans called Schniddegraas, *"snipple grass," was raised more for poaching and for salads than for seed. Common fennel supplied the ingredients of medicine, and its seeds were often used in place of cumin in recipes where cumin was called for. Even the fresh flowers were chopped and worked into bread (Sauer mentions the addition of seeds but not flowers) or cooked in pancakes. Sauer's conserve or fennel sugar was also employed in dessert cookery in much the same manner as vanilla sugar, just as fennel comfits were incorporated into cakes and cookies.*

The sugar recipe for dizziness is worth noting, since Sauer and other Philadelphia apothecaries sold it under the name of Compound Cephalic Sugar. It was popular among young eighteenth-century ladies given to swoons and palpitations in the presence of suitors and handsome men, since recovery was assured and the taste was always pleasant.

The roots, leaves, and seeds of fennel can all be used. They possess the virtue of warming and drying gently, of strengthening the stomach, of dispelling windiness, and of easing breathing. Fennel also clears the eyesight, strengthens and improves the hearing, and opens obstructions. It cleanses the kidneys, stays nephritic colic and lumbago, and drives rheums from the head.

Externally, the distilled water of fennel is very good for treating acute inflammations of the eyes. It may be used alone or mixed with white vitriol. Moisten a piece of soft cloth with it and apply to the eyes.

The leaves of fennel boiled in water, and the decoction taken as a drink, is of service for all the above-mentioned maladies. But it is of special use for promoting milk in nursing mothers, for dispersing windiness, for ridding children of purples, and for purging the chest of phlegm.

Fennel seeds ground together with caraway seeds, juniper berries, and a little camphor, then put into a sachet and laid on the ears as hot as one can bear it, will dispel smarting pain in the same. It will absorb fluxes from the ears and restore poor hearing.

Take fresh, juicy fennel leaves and pulp them in a wooden or marble mortar. Add twice their weight in white sugar and let this sweat for several days in a well-stopped glass vessel set in the sun. This will yield an excellent fennel conserve.[88] Taken in doses the size of a nutmeg once or twice a day, it will strengthen and preserve the eyesight, and is beneficial to the matrix and stomach.

Others take one and a half loths of fennel seeds, a half loth each of dried eyebright leaves and prepared coral, and a quint each of cloves, cinnamon, mace, Indian long pepper,[89] and cubeb. Grind this to a fine powder and combine with twelve loths of well-skimmed honey fresh from the comb.[90] Prepare a salve from this which will strengthen the eyesight excellently, provided a dab of it is taken now and then.[91]

For dizziness, take one loth of fennel seeds, half a loth each of aniseed, coriander seed, and peony root, and a quint each of black masterwort, cubeb, clove gillyflowers, and marjoram. Grind it all together to a fine powder, then combine it with a half pound of white sugar. Take several pinches of this sugar every day.

The expressed, filtered juice of fresh fennel leaves administered lukewarm as eye drops from time to time will prevent the formation of cataracts, brighten dim eyesight, and dispel divers inflammations of the eyes.

When used in food and medicine, fennel is useful to those who are afflicted by phlegm in the lungs and chest, as well as to nursing mothers.

Some people are accustomed to kneading fennel seed into bread dough. This bread is quite useful to those who suffer from all kinds of eye ailments. It also absorbs windiness and is good for persons plagued by stomach pains, as well as for treating colic, iliac passion, pursiness, difficult breathing, mother fits, lumbago, and blockage and swelling of the liver. It is also good for those afflicted with stones and sand.

88. Sauer actually uses a word that implies wet and syrupy, but there is no comparable word in English for this. The sugar heats and becomes moist like wet snow. It is not liquid, which is why it may be eaten with a spoon in nutmeg-size doses.
89. This is *Piper longum* from India, not the New World capsicum.
90. Sauer calls it *Jungferhonig*, which literally means "virgin" honey. We would call it raw honey.
91. The salve is dabbed in the corner of the eyes, a point not made clear in the text.

When fennel seeds are chewed and eaten, they make a choice remedy for dissipating and driving out windiness of the belly.

Fennel seeds can also be made into comfits and chewed slowly, then swallowed, or eaten plain according to preference. Taken in this manner, they are a good remedy for foul breath. They also stop heartburn and the rising of hot bilious fluxes into the back of the throat. Fennel also dispels hoarseness and sore throat. And, eaten thus in the morning and evening, fennel seeds will promote clear eyesight. They are also very useful to pregnant women, for they strengthen the womb and fetus, stop casting of the stomach,[92] are good for dry coughing, strengthen the vital spirits, and are thus very useful to all sorts of feeble persons, especially when fennel seeds are ground to a powder, mixed with sugar, and then drunk in a glass of wine.

If fennel seed and sage are boiled in milk and sweetened with sugar, and drunk in the morning before breakfast, this is an excellent remedy for coughing and sore throat.

Distilled water of fennel taken in several spoonfuls a day will be of good use in treating all of the above-mentioned conditions. Likewise, the distilled oil of fennel, taken in doses of eight to twelve drops in a teaspoon of sugar, serves just as well for the same afflictions.

The seeds of fennel can also be ground and then boiling water poured over it. The decoction may be drunk very well like tea, since it possesses the virtue of strengthening the constitution in particular.

Fenugreek
Trigonella foenumgraecum
Sauer: *Bockshorn, Fönumgräcum* (1767)

For the gardener who has never grown fenugreek, the German name Bockshorn, *"ram's horn," may seem puzzling. It has to do with the seedpods, which are long and pointed and make the most perfect sets of miniature alpine ram's horns one is likely to get from a common herb. Otherwise, the plant is hardly interesting, and the tiny white pealike flowers are almost insignificant, except for their honeylike fragrance. Fenugreek is as easy to grow as clover, but a good deal of it must be planted if there is to be any kind of respectable harvest, since one plant will yield only a handful of pods. On that point, John Hill noted in his 1755 herbal that fenugreek was cultivated in fields in some parts of England, but he gave no hint about its uses, medical or culinary.*

In any case, this is a plant, like chickpeas and lentils, which is best treated as a crop for small fields. Whether it was raised like that in colonial America is a question for further investigation. There may not have been an economic incentive as long as fenugreek was easy to import from Spain or Portugal, or even from England. What we know for certain is that Philadelphia seedsman Bernard M'Mahon was selling seed for fenugreek by 1802 and that it was seed for the medical garden rather than for culinary purposes.

Fenugreek's close relative, blue clover (Trigonella caerulea) *was grown in colonial*

92. The vomiting in question is the common malady called morning sickness.

German gardens to flavor sapsago cheese, which was once very popular. When in bloom, it literally scents the garden with a honeylike aroma.

Fenugreek is warm and dry in nature and contains a large amount of mucilaginous substance. From this derives its capacity to soften, to dissolve, to dispel, to bring sores to a head, and to still pain.

For remedies treating people, the seeds are employed more externally than internally. If they are boiled in water and the water then strained through a cloth, this will heal runny scall, get rid of dandruff and mites, and make a good hair wash. Fenugreek seeds are also employed in emollient clysters.

For swellings of the chest, there is nothing better than the flour of fenugreek seeds mixed with celery or celandine juice and honey. Employ this as a plaster, and it will get rid of the swelling or bring it to a head quickly.

If fenugreek seeds are boiled and laid warm often over the joints, or if limbs of the body can be stuck into a warm dough made from fenugreek flour, or further, if a strong broth can be made with the seeds and then used frequently as a bath, this will prove quite effective to those whose nerves have become too sensitive due to flying gout or some other condition. It will also help limbs that are beginning to get crooked, although do not fail to rub and stretch them.

Fenugreek is a good horse remedy if the horse is plagued by iliac passion. It will clean out its stomach, stay the pain, and promote urine. But it should not be employed too sparingly because horses have strong constitutions and require a large dose. The seeds should be pounded very fine, but if that is too much trouble, they can be boiled, and both broth and seeds thus administered to the horse in doses of at least two ounces or four tablespoonfuls at a time.

Feverfew (Motherwort)
Chrysanthemum parthenium
Sauer: *Mutterkraut* (1773)

Keep in mind that in the case of this herb, Mutter *is the womb (uterus), so that while the herb is also known as motherwort in English, the mother is not the person but a specific part of her. This should focus our attention on the primary purpose of this plant: to heal maladies specific to women and women suffering from the preliminary and after-effects of childbirth.*

The Mutterkraut *of the Pennsylvania Germans, or more accurately, the* Wildes Mutterkraut *("wild motherwort," as opposed to the garden sort), was Oswego tea (Monarda didyma). According to Dr. Thomas Cooper, the red flowers were infused in brandy to create a pleasant cordial that tasted like peach schnapps.[93] However cheering that may be, it is not an hysterical water (a cramp remedy for women); thus it is important to keep these two very different motherworts separate, for their chemical properties are not the same—not to mention that mugwort (page 218) is also called motherwort.*

93. A. M. F. Willich, *The Domestic Encyclopedia*, edited by Thomas Cooper (Philadelphia, 1821), 3:267.

Furthermore, feverfew was eaten as a spring potherb by colonial Germans much the same way shungiku greens are eaten by the Japanese today. This point is mentioned by Sauer.

Feverfew is of a warm, dry nature. It possesses a sharp, volatile salt and volatile sulfurous elements. Thus it has the excellent virtues of dissolving all internal blockages, of thinning tough phlegm, of strengthening the stomach and matrix, of stilling colic and stomachache, of stopping fainting, and of promoting a variety of other things as well.

This herb should be highly valued by women, for it is used with special effectiveness internally and externally for all female complaints.

Feverfew is employed in cookery as well during the early spring when it is young and succulent. Very nice pancakes can be prepared with the greens, which make a healthy dish for both those men and women who, due to their cold natures, are plagued by colic or mother fits.

If feverfew is cooked in wine and a glass of the decoction is drunk in the morning and evening, this will prove good for dropsy. Many have been cured of this illness already by this very simple remedy.

When feverfew is ground to a powder and in the evening given to cattle with salt to lick, it will get rid of panting and bloating.

For lice, take four handfuls of feverfew, three handfuls each of agrimony, fumitory, and thyme, two handfuls each of the leaves of meadow saffron and wormwood, and one handful of water betony. Boil these ingredients in water and prepare it as a bath. Those infected with lice should bathe in this while it is warm every day, and prepare it fresh every other day.

If fresh feverfew leaves are pulped and laid upon the crown of the head, and this is repeated several times, this will draw up a fallen uvula in the throat and prevent dizziness and rheums of the head, as well as stop headache.

The distilled water of feverfew will warm a cold matrix, ease a difficult delivery, and kill worms, if a small glass of it is drunk often according to want.

The salt of feverfew prepared in apothecary shops, taken daily in ten-grain doses in a glass of wine, will serve excellently for treating dropsy.

A choice hysterical water may be prepared in the following manner: Take six handfuls of feverfew, three handfuls each of lemon balm and pennyroyal, two handfuls each of holy thistle and red field poppies, one handful of fish mint, and one quint each of cinnamon, cubeb, aniseed, and fennel seed. Chop it all together and pour one gallon of old white wine over this. Let it infuse for a few days well stopped. Then distill it. A woman who is plagued by mother fits may take several spoonfuls of this hysterical water daily. Those who do not find it too distasteful may also infuse a little piece of beaver cod in this water, which will make it more potent.[94]

94. Beaver's cod is explained on page 62.

Fig   141

Fig
Ficus carica
Sauer: *Feigen* (1775)

Imported dried figs were an article of commerce in colonial America, and while perhaps a bit expensive, they were not beyond the reach of most people who needed them for medication. Fresh figs, however, were found only in the gardens of the well-off, for the trees required the attention of winter protection and judicious pruning. Fresh figs were shipped up the coast from colonies in the South, but it is rather doubtful that such luxuries reached hinterland farmers. In any case, the ingredients for most of the remedies under figs suggest costliness, so they must be read in the context of an urban setting. The columbine seeds, which elsewhere in the herbal are styled as rare, would definitely suggest this. Sauer's religious fervor is of course reserved for the end as a kind of moral seal of approval in line with Johann Jakob Schmidt's Biblischer Medicus *(Züllichau, 1743).*

Figs are a noble and healthy fruit, particularly if they are eaten with grapes and almonds.

They are used, together with other simples, in potions for the chest in treating cold coughs and asthma. For example: Take one loth of licorice, four figs, eight Assyrian plums,[95] half a loth of locust pods,[96] and a quint each of anise and fennel. Boil this in one gallon of water for as long as it takes to hard-cook an egg. Let the patient drink this as thirst demands.

For colic: Take half a handful each of dried figs and white dog manure and boil it in one and a half pints of wine until reduced to one-third. Strain this, and add a little salt. Use this as a clyster.

Rembert[97] has written that if pregnant women eat some figs daily during the period before delivery, the delivery will be much easier. The women of Frankfurt follow this advice to the letter. If figs are boiled in water and the mouth washed out with the broth often, it will open the ingrown sores of the throat.

For those who are plagued by gravel, fresh new figs will promote urine and drive out the sand.

But if one eats too many figs, diarrhea will result, but it will soon pass.

For persons afflicted with shortness of breath, and whose chest is congested with phlegm, infuse figs overnight in brandy. Eat some of these every day in the early morning before breakfast. They will ease breathing and purify the chest.

If figs are boiled and children are given the broth to drink warm, this will promote the raising up of the purples and red measles, as well as hinder them from settling on the lungs and causing consumption, which in such cases commonly happens. It also stops blood-pissing under such conditions.

Simon Paulli[98] praised the following potion: Take one loth of shaved hartshorn, six dried figs, and a half loth each of columbine and fennel seeds, and bind it all up in a

95. Sebestan or Assyrian plums are explained under hyssop on page 175.
96. Locust pods or carob are treated on page 198.
97. Rembert is an alias of Rembert Dodoens (1517–1585), Dutch botanist.
98. Simon Paulli (1603–1680) wrote *D. Medeci Regii . . . de Simplicium Medicamentorum Faculatibus* (Strasbourg, 1667), which is the source of the material used here in the herbal.

sachet. Boil this in a gallon of water and give the broth to children when they are thirsty. Or, instead of this: Take twelve figs and one ounce of raisins together with a handful of barley, one loth of shaved hartshorn, and a tablespoon of fennel seeds. Boil this together in one gallon of water and let children afflicted with the purples drink the broth when thirsty. This will not only get rid of the purples completely, it will prevent them from leaving such deep pockmarks.

If a few figs are eaten in the morning before breakfast with a little pepper, they will purify the kidneys and bladder of foul matter and sand.

When someone has an inflamed swelling or abscess on the gums, there is nothing better than putting a piece of fig on it, or laid over it, for it will bring it to a head readily and open an abscess directly, however, not without preceding pain. Similar results may be had as well if figs are boiled in milk with marshmallow leaves, chamomile flowers, and saffron. Take the broth into the mouth often and hold it there. This will bring the sores to a head and open them up in quite a short amount of time.

Figs are employed quite effectively in emolliating plasters, for which reason the prophet Isaiah recommended a fig plaster, which he laid over the boils of sick king Hezekiah and made him well. Isaiah 38:21.[99]

Figs provide the body with fair nourishment, and for this reason they are very useful during famines—if you can get them.

The ash of fig wood mixed with oil of roses will yield a fine salve for burns. The lye made of fig ashes is excellent for getting rid of corruptions on the skin. The sap from the tree and leaves will take off warts. For those who consume dried figs in too large a quantity, the lice they harbor will make their skin scabby.

Flax
Linum usitatissimum
Sauer: *Lein, Flachs* (1767)

> *Flax was one of the earliest agricultural export products established in Pennsylvania. In fact, "Vinum, Linum et Textrinum" (Wine, Linen and Weaving) was the motto on the seal of the corporation of Germantown in the 1680s. Most of the old families that the Sauers knew were still or once had been involved in linen production. It was also an important cottage industry in the countryside, since many farmers devoted the winter months to a craft, especially flax processing and linen weaving.*

Only the seeds of this plant are generally used in medicine, and they are of a mild nature. They are discutient, they soften and ease, and they possess an oily, mucusy juice. They are have the faculty to loosen, to open, to still pain, and to ease difficult breathing.

If the leaves of flax are laid upon sores that have headed up, they will immediately create an opening so that it is not necessary to lance them.

---

99. Johann Jakob Schmidt discussed this very same biblical cure on pages 571–72 of his *Biblischer Medicus*.

An oil is pressed from flaxseeds that is not only employed by doctors but also by artists and other craftsmen, as well as burned in lamps (though this is not the healthiest way to get light). It is serviceable in treating cramps, stiff limbs, swellings of the hemorrhoids, and venereal boils, when mixed with rosewater or with the white of an egg and spread over the hurt often. This is also a good salve for burns. Furthermore, linseed oil is a good remedy for lumbago, sores, and difficult breathing when a few loths are drunk warm. It eases pain well, but it must be fresh because the old oil possesses a raw sharpness, warms too much, and induces casting of the stomach.

Gesner could not praise this oil enough for treating lumbago as well as coughs and asthma.[100] He administered six tablespoonfuls at a time. But due to its unpleasant smell, it is common that patients are a bit resistant, even though the results of this valuable cure are so much the greater. It is also employed by some in treating colic and gravel.

Flaxseeds boiled in water and the decoction drunk, or a loin bath prepared with it, will expel a dead fetus.

An excellent plaster that eases pain, softens swellings, and brings them to a head is made as follows: Take one once each of flaxseeds, fenugreek, and marshmallow root, and boil this in milk until it attains the thickness of a plaster. Then add a half loth each of chamomile and dill oils. Spread this between two cloths, warm it up on a hot platter, and lay it over the hurt.

Flaxseeds possess a special anodyne and emollient capacity if cooked well with milk or water and then spread several times over the hard, painful swelling or sore as hot as the patient can bear it. If the condition requires more treatment, remove the plaster so that it does not act further. Let the hurt shrink on its own and make a bandage for it. Flaxseeds brewed in water and drunk like tea are very soothing and healing to the stomach.

Linseed oil is very useful to both man and beast because of its anodyne and emollient faculties. If the oil is heated up in a frying pan and thinly sliced overripe apples are fried in it, then laid upon the base of the spine as hot as the patient can bear it, this will treat severe pains in the back, those caused by lumbago, or other painful conditions due to falls or internal injuries. When sweetened with rock candy, it is also good for coughing, raw throat, and other painful afflictions or sores of the chest.

Flixweed (Fluxweed, Herb Sophia)

Sisymbrium sophia
Sauer: *Sophienkraut* (1778)

There is a collection of closely related plants that have now been grouped together under the genus Sophia, *some being native, while others were naturalized from the Old*

---

100. Conrad Gesner (1516–1565) was a Swiss botanist and physician who wrote numerous books, most of which are now considered classics. This may come from his *De Raris et Amirandis Herbis* (Zurich, 1555), since Zwinger cited this work from time to time in his herbal.

World. Flixweed, which is sometimes called fine-leaved hedge mustard in addition to its other common names, is one of those species that came from Europe. Its introduction has been characterized as an escape from ship ballast, but it may have come in with grain. Since it was a medical plant of some importance, there is also the possibility that it was intentionally introduced into gardens. The Sauer herbal presumes that it is here already in 1778 and well established.

Flixweed possesses a strong, unpleasant odor and a disgusting, sharp herbaceous taste. It is of a middling nature, endowed with somewhat volatile salts together with a few oily elements but numerous earthy, fluid components. Therefore, it has the faculty to dry, to draw together gently, to glutinate, to still fluxes of the belly, to force urine, to heal wounds, and to cleanse sores.

If flixweed is boiled in a mixture of half wine and water, it will drive out worms and heal internal and external new and old wounds; indeed, it is a fine vulnerary. It is also usefully employed in vulnerary potions.

A useful powder for cancer sores that are open: Take four loths of flixweed, two and a half loths of water betony, two loths of sanicle root, one and a half loths of the bark from the root of a quince tree, and one loth of holy thistle. Grind it all to a fine powder and strew this over the sores, which have first been washed out with the water of water betony.

The powder of flixweed will heal deep sores on the shins if applied with fontanels made of writing paper.

The distilled water of flixweed is serviceable for all internal injuries and wounds if taken in four- or five-loth doses. Externally, it may be used to wash them, and in this manner employed to purify old injuries and sores.

The seeds of flixweed, or the dried leaves as well, may be ground to a powder and administered in a quint dose at different times to still diarrhea and fluxes of the stomach, indeed all manner of bleedings as well, provided it is taken with plantain water.

If flixweed is pulped and heated in wine, and then used as a plaster over injuries and wounds, and the decoction used to rinse out the injuries as well, this will heal them wonderfully.

French Mercury
Mercuralis annua
Sauer: *Bingelkraut* (1775)

This was also known as garden mercury, both because it was once cultivated as a potherb by the Germans and to distinguish it from the wild perennial (called dog mercury), which is poisonous. French mercury is an annual with very mucilaginous leaves and seeds that possess a taste similar to hemp. When cooked like spinach it acts as a thickener, and it was once employed much like okra to thicken soups. Otherwise, if eaten raw, its taste is also rather sharp and acrid. There have been reports of people dying from the consumption of dog mercury after mistaking it for good king henry (page 158). Before any attempt is made to use French mercury as a potherb, it would be advisable to learn the difference between it and dog mercury, to which it is closely related.

Common French mercury warms and dries moderately. It is endowed with a nitrous salt and a few sulfurous elements, together with a copious amount of watery sap. From these it derives its capacity to emolliate, to attenuate, to cleanse, to open the matrix, and to purify. It also promotes urine and stool. Due to these properties, it has been placed among the five most important emollient herbs.[101]

The leaves may be dried, ground to powder, and put in the porridge of young children in order to get rid of colic and to keep the bowels open.

The juice of this plant will get rid of warts, provided they are washed with it.

French mercury is quite useful when used in clysters, by which it loosens up constipation. For those who do not have stool for some days, administer this clyster: Take three handfuls of French mercury and a handful of mallow, and boil this in water. Measure out a quart of this decoction and add two ounces of rosemary honey and one ounce of chamomile oil, and mix together as a clyster.

A handful of fresh or dried French mercury heated in water, or in a mixture of half water and half wine, and then drunk will open up constipation and expel crudities and sand from the kidneys. Or, take one to one and a half handfuls of the herb and boil in meat broth, then take the broth and strain it. Add a pinch of cream of tartar or a spoonful of sweet almond oil and take it. This is a very serviceable remedy in many cases of constipation where, however, no other purgatives dare be employed.

Fuller's Thistle (Teazle)
Dipsacus fullonum, Dipsacus sylvestris
Sauer: *Kartendistel* (1774)

A native of the Old World, this teazle was introduced very early as an agricultural crop, since the stiff, thorny heads were used in processing cloth. Specifically, they were used for fleecing wool and for raising a nap on woolen goods. Many botanists now believe that the fuller's thistle is simply a variety of Dipsacus sylvestris, *since the distinctively crooked spines disappear on fuller's thistle if it reverts to the wild state. No matter, teazle is well naturalized in this country and is still raised in open-air museums to demonstrate its old craft uses. But as Sauer's herbal amply demonstrates, it was also a useful medical plant.*

101. The five *emollientia* are marshmallow, blue mallow, French mercury, pellitory-of-the-wall, and violet.

The root of fuller's thistle is dry in nature and very rarely used for internal remedies. It possesses an alkaline, coarse, purifying and healing salt.

If the root is heated in wine and then ground to a paste as for a plaster and laid over the hurt, it will heal fistulas and wounds in the privates. If it is stored in a copper box, it will remain good for an entire year. This paste will also get rid of warts.

The water that is found in the leaves of fuller's thistle is good for dim eyes and will also get rid of the yellow and brown spots under the eyes so commonly referred to as freckles or chits, if they are washed with it.

Fumitory
Fumaria officinalis
Sauer: *Taubenkropf, Erdrauch* (1764)

German colonists in colonial America are known to have introduced small herds of goats for their own use—there are actual records of goat keeping in several Moravian communities prior to the Revolution. Goat's milk was known to be safer than cow's milk for babies and young children, the milk of black goats being preferred above all others. This health benefit may lie behind the choice of goat's milk for the spring tonic made with fumitory noted below. Indeed, fumitory (like other herbs) was sometimes added to goat's milk cheese to make a species of medicinal food that could be eaten on toast by children and invalids.

The powerful action of fumitory may be due in part to its belonging to the poppy family. It is an attractive plant with blue ferny leaves that has escaped from colonial gardens and is now naturalized in most parts of the United States. It is a common weed in Pennsylvania, especially around abandoned farmhouses. It must have been well established by 1764, because Sauer used copious amounts of the fresh plants.

Fumitory is of a warm, dry nature. For use in medicine, it is gathered before sunrise in May and June. Fumitory possesses the capacity to dissolve, to open, to cleanse the blood, and to free it of salty melancholic humors. It also promotes sweat and protects against all types of poison. It is also very useful to the heart, liver, and spleen.

Chop and infuse fumitory in goat's milk and drink a tumblerful every morning during the month of May. This will cleanse the blood thoroughly and free one of the itch. The juice of fumitory is very useful to those who are afflicted with the French pox, if four loths of it are drunk each morning and evening every day for five to six weeks.

The juice can be preserved the whole year if it is pressed from the fresh herb and allowed to foment over a charcoal fire. Strain it through a cloth and put it in a glass vessel. Pour a little olive oil on top and stop it well.

The distilled water of fumitory, taken in six-loth doses before breakfast for several weeks in succession, will cleanse corruptions from the blood and get rid of scall, mange, itch, and bites on the skin.[102]

102. The itch, like the other skin conditions mentioned under fumitory, was largely the result of the custom of not changing the clothes during winter.

For those who are afflicted with the angry, inflamed, and spreading pain of scall, and who fear the onset of leprosy, take a quint of the best *Theriaca Andromaci* in six loths of fumitory water every month and sweat well. In addition to this, they must drink four loths of fumitory water mixed with two loths of hops water each morning and evening for at least three weeks during the fall and spring.

If fumitory water is snuffed into the nose, it will clean the brain of phlegm and restore smell.

An essence of fumitory can also be made with brandy, which is very good for the above-mentioned maladies, provided it is administered in twenty-five to forty drops each morning and evening for several weeks.

Galingale
Alpinia galanga
Sauer: *Galand-Wurtzel* (1766)

In the original Sauer herbal, galingale and birthwort were placed together for the obvious convenience of midwives. But galingale's uses were many; indeed, next to ginger and black pepper, it was one of the most common culinary herbs included in the Sauer herbal. Dr. Zwinger listed several types of galingale and even provided woodcuts of the most common sorts. All of these pictures show a dry root rather than a fresh one, for unlike ginger, fresh galingale does not travel well. We may presume that since the Sauer herbal deals only with this root, it is the dry article that is being discussed.

Galingale is a root that grows only in the Orient, particularly in China and a few places in the East Indies and nearby regions. It is employed quite effectively by the inhabitants there for sundry maladies of the stomach, and because this root is found in nearly every apothecary shop, it deserves a few words here.

The root of galingale possesses the capacity to warm, to open blockages of the internal organs, to dissolve thick humors, and to operate through the urine and sweat. It also strengthens the head, stomach, and matrix, and is employed very effectively in brandy bitters. Those who are accustomed to keeping such brandies in the house do well by adding half an ounce of finely chopped galingale root to each quart of brandy. This strengthens the stomach, drives out thick fluxes, awakens the appetite, and protects against miasmas and contagious fevers.

For those afflicted by dizziness, prepare the following cephalic powder, of which a few pinches are administered alone or in a glass of wine in the morning before breakfast or one hour before supper. Take one loth each of galingale, nutmeg, mistletoe from an oak tree, peony root, and cubeb. Grind this to a fine powder and combine it with one pound of powdered loaf sugar.

Galingale is very useful for colds of the head, for it strengthens the head immediately. It is also used effectively against cold and windy conditions of the stomach, since it warms the stomach and dispels vapors. For such conditions, the following effective stomach powder may be prepared: Take a loth each of galingale and cinnamon, and two quints each of anise, fennel, and caraway seeds, cloves, mace and nutmeg, and cubebs. Grind this to a fine powder and mingle it with one pound of finely powdered loaf sugar. Administer a half tablespoonful on a slice of bread soaked in wine each morning and evening. Some people put finely ground galingale in wine and drink a glass of this in the morning and evening. Others take half a quint of the finely ground root every day in a small glass of wine or brandy until the weakness is cured.

This powder is also quite useful against all afflictions of the womb brought on by cold, and will open blockages of the matrix, and expel that which has been retained there.[103] For such conditions, a very serviceable potion may be prepared in the following manner: Take one loth each of galingale and birthwort and a half loth each of sweet bay, cinnamon, and saffron, and grind this all to a fine powder. Add a handful of mugwort leaves, and then pour wine over this. Administer half a gill to the patient each morning and evening.

Garden Cress

Lepidium sativum
Sauer: *Gartenkresse* (1764)

While the Sauer herbal treats only one species, the discussion is based on material in Zwinger, and that covers quite a few different varieties. The reference to the Dutch using cresses in sandwiches should alert us to the fact that the best seed in Sauer's day was coming from Holland. The Dutch and Pennsylvania Mennonites engaged in active seed exchanges that are only now beginning to be appreciated by plant historians.

The varieties covered by Zwinger are more or less collapsed together in the Sauer herbal, but they are as follows: common garden cress, the frilly-leafed sort still grown today; Persian broad-leaf cress; and a ferny or carrot-leafed type very similar in appearance to the so-called Rishad cress of Iraq. All of these were used extensively in the omelets, soups, and Brockle *dishes favored by the German colonists.*

The seeds of garden cress as well as the fresh and dried herb possess the faculty of cleansing the blood, of opening internal blockages, of dissolving thick phlegmy matter, and of operating through the urine.

Garden cress is very good for scurvy. For this reason it is heavily consumed in Holland in sandwiches.

Half a quint of the ground seeds taken in plantain water will kill worms.

If anyone should fall and develop blood clots in the body, administer a quint of cress seeds in wine and let the injured person sweat profusely.

If garden cress is fomented in hog's lard, and rubbed over scaling itch on children, it will make a good remedy.

These seeds are also used in lye to keep hair strong and firm.[104]

For those who have lost the ability to speak due to apoplexy, they should chew cress seeds often.

---

103. This includes the removal of afterbirth and other things that have not been properly expelled during labor.
104. The German actually says that the hair will remain well rooted and stiff; this is perhaps an allusion to the custom of men pulling the hair back into a tail, as was the practice in Sauer's era.

The juice of this herb will cleanse and heal foul abscessed wounds.

People are also accustomed to making comfits with cress seeds, which are useful for expelling worms in old and young alike, for opening the mesenteric veins, for preventing apoplexy, for purifying the blood, and for expelling mucus and sand from the kidneys.

The distilled water of garden cress will open a blocked liver, spleen, and urinary vessels; drive grit and sand from the kidneys and bladder; cleanse the chest of phlegm; kill and expel worms; and is good for consumption. If drawn up into the nose, it will cleanse the head and cause vigorous sneezing. If it is held in the mouth, it will draw down phlegm from the head. When washed with it, all manner of corruptions of the skin, black moles, itch, pox, and abscesses will be healed. If a small piece of cloth is dipped into the water of garden cress and laid over these corruptions, it will cleanse the same. If a few loths of this same water are drunk, it will prove especially good for blood-spitting.

Most of all, garden cress can be used for all afflictions for which watercress is called for, and applied in the same manner.

Garden Poppy
Papaver sativum
Sauer: *Magsamen, Gartenmohn* (1770)

> *Sauer is vague about the manner in which this poppy is used in remedies. His caution is consistent with other potent herbs he felt were better handled by physicians or apothecaries than by laymen. If there is any hint, it is in the German* Magsamen, *which simply means poppy seeds, no particular type of poppy implied. It might be useful to point out that by suppressing the nerves or sensation of pain, the poppy was extremely useful during Lent in staving off the pangs of hunger. For this reason the seeds were widely employed in Lenten dishes. Poppy seed oil was also used as a substitute for butter among the Pennsylvania German Catholics. Both the white- and black-seeded varieties were grown in kitchen gardens.*
>
> *In* The British Housewife, *Martha Bradley published a recipe for poppy water in which two pounds of flowers are steeped overnight in brandy, then distilled with other ingredients.*[105] *This water could be purchased from apothecaries in colonial America and was highly opiate in its action.*

The garden poppy is cold in nature. The white seeded kind is safer to use than the black-seeded sort. The poppy has the ability to restrain the vital spirits, to suppress and to hinder their influence on the nerves, or to block them entirely. It can also ease all manner of pain, stop diarrhea and other discharges, induce sleep, and prevent coughs arising from sharp fluxes.

The field poppy possesses a capacity similar to the white-seeded poppy and therefore needs no further description.[106] Both must be used with great discretion, otherwise harm may easily be done by their employment.

105. Martha Bradley, *The British Housewife* (London, 1756), 2:123.
106. Sauer later changed his mind. Field poppies are discussed on page 117.

Garlic (Rocombole)
Allium sativum
Sauer: *Knoblauch* (1773)

*In Sauer's era there were not many varieties of garlic as we now know them, for gar-
lic did not play a large role in colonial American cookery. The Germans settlers, however, used garlic much more generously in the eighteenth century than later on, and
many country people considered the* Wald-Knoblauch *or* Ramseren *a healthful delicacy in spite of its strong smell. This is the wild onion known in colonial English as ram-
sins and better known today as ramps* (Allium tricoccum). *The diet of the German
settlers gradually became Anglicized as they adopted more and more American customs
and habits, but in remote areas the old preferences survived. The idea of "larding" a
roast of meat with garlic cloves was fully alien to the English palate, but quite acceptable to the Germans, which is why it is mentioned in the herbal as a healthy way to prepare meat.*

*If the herbal can be second-guessed regarding the garlic being employed, surely it
must be something very close to the garlic now called German red rocombole, an old
hard-necked type that is still cultivated by garlic collectors. Due to its rawness, it was
not considered appropriate for high-class cookery, and Maria Sophia Schellhammer
made a point of saying so in her cookbook under a short discussion on garlic. Yet the
rocombole fits the herbal, for it is indeed better when recently harvested. It does not store
well, and after a time, the desiccated cloves give off a rank smell in line with comments
made in the Sauer herbal. Zwinger's illustration of this type of garlic shows it prior to
developing a flower head.*

*Although garlic is now understood to contain many antiseptic constituents, histori-
cally the powerful odor of garlic appears to have been its primary
weapon against airborne disease. But internal applications were also
legion; indeed, many such remedies survived well into the nineteenth
century. Pennsylvania German herbalist Jacob Biernauer continued this
theme in his very bitter-tasting remedy against contagion: "Take garlic and rue and boil them in good-quality wine vinegar. Drink
mornings and evenings. This will help for certain."*[107]

Garlic is of a warm, dry nature and contains very
volatile, caustic, alkaline salts in its juices from which it
derives its faculty to drive out sweat and urine. It thins
phlegm and loosens up all internal parts, both above and
below. It also opens blockages and eases breathing.

Garlic is employed in cookery and medicine. It
warms and dries a cool, moist stomach, kills and expels
worms, and helps against the bites of snakes and mad
dogs. If garlic is eaten and worn outwardly, rats and

107. Jacob Biernauer, *Das unentbehrliche Haus- und Kunst-Buch*
(Reading, Pa., 1818), 20.

other noxious creatures will flee from it. If a snake or lizard should crawl into the stomach of someone during sleep, that person should eat garlic, for it will drive them out or kill them. In summary, garlic withstands all poison, for which reason Galen called it the farmers' cure-all.

Reapers and mowers who suffer from great thirst due to the heat of summer and are obliged to drink bad water should use garlic diligently, as was customary among the ancients.

If garlic is boiled a little in milk and then drunk, it will drive out worms, and will benefit those children whose stomachs have become extended due to the worms.

For loin stones, chop three heads of garlic into white wine. Let this boil up once, then strain it through a cloth. Drink this warm, and it will drive out the stone directly, promote urine, and much more.

Garlic will not bring the best benefit to those with a hot nature, or to those who are also plagued by gout, for it will stir up the general pains. It is also injurious to those who are afflicted by the French pox.

Newly harvested garlic does not give off as strong a smell as the old and is much more agreeable to eat. Some cooks lard meat with new garlic,[108] which is good for cold stomachs, and during times of pestilence, a very practical dish.

For children with stomach worms, take a head of garlic, grind it, and add a half loth each of aloe and ox gall. Heat it up, then press out the juice. Rub this juice over the navel of the child twice a day.

A good remedy for obstructed urine: Take three heads of garlic and bake them in hot ashes. Add half a loth of pepper together with a handful of juniper berries. Grind this all together and then boil it in enough red wine to form a plaster. Spread this warm over the balls and member or on the abdomen. A good piss will follow quickly.

When a horse cannot pass water, take skinned garlic and centaury and boil it well in white wine. Pour this down the throat of the horse.

Cook pulped garlic with olive oil, then stir in goose fat to form a salve. Spread this over the stomach where the kidneys are located, and this will promote urine as well as drive out sand and stones.

The Thracians, Turks, and Jews are great advocates of garlic, which they seek out as protection against poison and pestilence.

Garlic Mustard
Sysimbrium alliaria
Sauer: *Knoblauchkraut* (1775)

The English call this vitamin-rich herb by the quaint appellation jack-by-the-hedge, and this is also the name Sauer provided in his herbal. It is a close relative of flixweed (page 143), but is much easier to eat in salads due to its tenderness, especially when young. Garlic mustard does not make a very good potherb because cooking destroys its

108. The herbal uses the term *spicken*, which means that the garlic was drawn through the surface of the meat with a larding needle in a manner similar to bacon. Old paintings sometimes show meat roasted in this fashion, especially game.

nutritional value, but in the past it was indeed cooked, especially with cabbage or sauer-kraut, to which it imparts a mild garlic flavor. From a strictly culinary standpoint, the plant has many possibilities, and makes a fine addition to a shady corner of the kitchen garden. It is free of pests and reproduces abundantly, and even makes a respectable ground cover with an interesting leaf. In areas where winters are mild, the mustard is nearly evergreen, so it has the additional benefit of being available during a period when garlics are dormant.

Garlic mustard is warm and dry by nature, although it is not as powerful as garlic itself. The seed is spicier than the leaves. The plant possess a stinking, volatile, oily sharp salt, and from this derives its faculty to withstand all sourness, to penetrate, to expel by means of urine and sweat, and to withstand putrefactions. During April and May its powers are strongest. If the herb is dried, it loses its best properties.

The expressed juice of this herb is very serviceable in salves and plasters for burns. It is also mixed with other ingredients and employed very effectively for divers putrid injuries in which it prevents the putrefaction of the flesh, indeed all the same things for which water germander is employed. Let the leaves lie for one day so that they wilt, then chop and press out the juice. Pour some olive oil over this and keep it in a well-stopped glass vessel. The juice will keep well this way for an entire year.

Heat the leaves of garlic mustard with scabious, hyssop, speedwell, and elecampane root in a kettle of water well covered. Then add some spoonfuls of honey and drink a glassful of this often. It will dissolve phlegm in the chest, ease difficult shortness of breath, and dispel coughing of long continuance.

If the seeds are ground to powder and administered on occasion in doses of twenty to thirty grains in weight, this will not only loosen phlegm in the chest but also drive out worms, open blockages of the mesenteric veins, cleanse phlegmy matter from the kidneys and matrix, dispel jaundice and dropsy, and prevent atrophy in the young and old.

The herb is especially employed in clysters, or the expressed juice is mixed with the dosage. This draws out windiness and vapors, prevents colic, eases lumbago, and promotes the speedy passing of stones.

When the seeds are ground to a fine powder and worked into a plaster with storax[109] and a little wax, it can be spread on a piece of leather and laid thus upon a woman's abdomen. This takes away rheums of the matrix and stills its vaporous upheavals.

A powder made from the dried leaves and seeds can be mixed with the juice to form a salve. Spread this every day over proud, rotting ulcers that might soon change to cancer. This will purify and cleanse them, and promote their healing.

If the powdered seeds or the expressed juice is drawn up into the nose to cause a

---

109. Storax is a resinous substance, but it is difficult to ascertain what exactly Sauer was using. Solid storax came from a tree *(Styrax officinalis)* in Asia Minor and was a medical product used by the ancient Greeks and Romans. Liquid storax was obtained from another tree *(Liquidambar orientalis)* also in Asia Minor. Both were extremely expensive, but a similar less expensive product was available from Mexico as well as from local American sweet gum trees. Sauer's storax could be any of these.

little sneezing, this will draw out much of the water and phlegm, and purify the brain as well.

Gentian
Gentiana lutea
Sauer: *Entzian-Wurtzel* (1762)

The yellow gentian of Alpine Europe was the most common gentian employed in medicine during Sauer's era. The dried rhizome and roots were imported mostly from Switzerland or France, but three species of native American gentians could be used as substitutes. Its primary use was in stomach tonics. Gentian-flavored wine, which Sauer did not mention, was sometimes served at the beginning of meals as an aid to digestion. However, Sauer provides a recipe for just such a digestive under wormwood on page 360. Since gentian was widely employed to ease hysterics, its action on the uterus could induce miscarriage, the reason for Sauer's warning at the end.

Gentian is warm and dry in nature, resists putrefaction, dissolves hard phlegm, kills worms, and purifies sharp, putrid, salty blood.

When taken with sugar, powdered gentian kills worms.

One quint of the root taken in wine is good for quotidian and quartan agues, and treats difficult breathing in pursiness. It opens obstructions of the liver and spleen, and is also good for those who have fallen and injured themselves. It promotes urination as well.

Gentian root ground fine and mixed with *Theriaca Andromaci* will make a good plaster for drawing out poisons.

When a horse refuses to eat, give it gentian, bay leaf, and juniper berries mixed in its fodder.

Pregnant women should avoid the use of gentian.

Germander (Wall Germander)
Teucrium chamaedrys
Sauer: *Gamanderlein, Vergiss-Mein-Nicht* (1772)

Known as petit chêne, *"little oak," in France, this is a native of the Mediterranean area that has escaped and naturalized from old cloister gardens in most of northern Europe and England. The leaf resembles a miniature oak leaf and, when crushed, smells strongly of garlic. It possesses many of the same medical virtues as horehound, and prefers the same type of soil. The anecdote about Emperor Charles V is quite famous in herbal literature and is usually repeated any time wall germander is discussed. On the contrary, Sauer's allusion to the fact that the herb may be employed for improving male sexual performance is not found in other herbals.*

Germander possesses a bitter, alkaline salt together with some oily elements and thus has the faculty to dry, to warm gently, to withstand fluxes, to strengthen the brain and nerves, and to open all blockages of the liver, spleen, mesenteric vein, and matrix. It also absorbs all phlegm, and cleanses and heals wounds and injuries as well. It must be gathered during a full moon when it is in full bloom.

Heat two handfuls of germander in two quarts of wine, then strain it. This decoction is good for coughs of long continuance, for loosening up stoppages of the urine, for promoting the > = =,[110] for opening a blocked spleen, and for protecting against the onset of dropsy. It is also good for quartan ague, for dispersing blood clots in the body, and for killing worms. It is an effective remedy for women who have taken cold, and will heal ruptures readily.

If a quint of powdered germander is taken in centaury water every day for three days in succession, it will cure the tertian and quartan agues, but the stomach must first be purged.

Some people assign great reputation to this herb for treating gout, if it is boiled in wine and drunk warm in the morning before breakfast for sixty days in succession, although the stomach should be purged first and the patient should refrain from eating sour and salty foods. This remedy was sent to Emperor Charles V by the Genovese, who attested that it was found good by many men plagued by gout or pains in the joints, but in particular by Cardinal Doria, and that for many years thereafter they did not suffer from it any more.

Doctor Hoffmann[111] has provided the following receipt from his own experience for pains of the joints and gout, which should be employed repeatedly after the onset of pain for sixty days in succession. Take a handful each of germander, peas, and centaury. Boil this in a well-closed kettle with a gallon of water until reduced to one-half. Then strain it through a clean cloth, and store away for use. Take two tablespoonfuls of this every morning, midday, and evening before meals. Or, take two loths each of scorzonera root, shaved licorice root, two handfuls of germander, a half handful each of violets and rosemary flowers, four loths of lignum vitae, three loths of Zante currants, and six dates. Chop this all up and boil it in a well-covered kettle in two gallons of water until reduced to half. Strain it through a sieve and put away for use. Drink a glassful of this each morning, midday, and evening before meals.

The distilled water of germander is good for rheums upon the chest, difficult breathing, coughing and wheezing of long continuance, as well as for killing worms, getting rid of jaundice, healing ruptures and injuries of the stomach, purifying the blood, and for opening blockages of the liver and spleen.

---

110. As usual, prudish Sauer left out the condition. He meant the menses.
111. Dr. Friedrich Hoffmann (1660–1742). This is taken from his *Clavis Pharmaceutica Schroederiana* (Halle, 1675).

Ginger
Zingiber officinale
Sauer: *Ingwer* (1762)

Ginger was one of the first herbs to be included in the Sauer herbal, appearing as it did in the first installment of 1762. This alone should throw some light on its perceived importance to colonial Americans, German or otherwise. Indeed, ginger was one of the most common ingredients in colonial cookery, but for the rural farmer and his house-hold, it was dried ginger—dried root or powder—that figured in their food and medicine. Fresh ginger was expensive, and "green" ginger (a sticky preserve) was a confection only found on the tables of the well-to-do. Sauer's remedies confirm this indirectly in their consistent use of dried ginger, as in the ginger candy or brittle, which is delicious regardless of its medical purposes.

The Beauties of Creation (Philadelphia, 1796) made the costliness of green ginger abundantly clear: "Both the East and West Indies produce ginger: in the Antilles it is greatly cultivated, but the greatest quantities are imported from the leeward islands of Barbados, Nevis, St. Christopher, and Jamaica. Little is now brought from the East Indies, except what comes as confectionery and is called green ginger, which they prepare in India." In eighteenth-century terminology, green ginger was a "wet sweetmeat," ginger root cooked in a syrup then put up in jars. It was commonly served with dessert, or chopped into fruit pies. In the German community of colonial America, green ginger figured mostly in Christmas cookery.

Ginger, as the ancients customarily pointed out, is warm and dry to the third degree, and possesses numerous spicy, oily, and volatile salts. Thus it has the very same virtues as calamus, galingale, pepper, and other spices of similar warmth and dryness.

For those with a sanguinary nature, ginger should be used very little. Above all else, it is good for those with a cold stomach. It promotes digestion, awakens the appetite, takes off watery vapors, and strengthens weak eyesight.

A very healthful ginger candy can be prepared in the following manner: Take three loths of finely ground ginger, fresh lemon rinds well dried and ground to a powder, a half loth each of cinnamon and nutmeg, a quint each of cloves and mace, all of these ground to a fine powder. Then take two pounds of sugar and moisten it with rosewater. Put this in a new stoneware pot over a charcoal stove and let the sugar boil gently until it candies. Then stir in the ground spices and pour it into a pewter dish. When it cools, store in a dry place.[112] This candy makes quite a choice home remedy, particularly where there are children who otherwise resist being introduced to new things, but who also easily get stomachaches when they sleep naked.[113] This confection strengthens a cold stomach, promotes digestion, dispels crudities in the stomach

---

112. One would be tempted to call this "ginger brittle" because it is hard like modern peanut brittle. It is certainly delicious and easy to give to children.

113. The presumption that eighteenth-century children slept in quaint little nightgowns is somewhat false. Country people commonly slept naked, and very often many members of the same family slept not only in the same room but also together in the same bed.

and gut, and stays colic and all manner of stomachaches brought on by taking chill or by sleeping uncovered. It will discourage the recurrence of these maladies that arise in the morning, provided the candy is taken in a dose the size of a nutmeg upon awakening, or when otherwise needed.

Goldenrod (European Goldenrod)
Solidago virgaurea
Sauer: *Heidnisch-Wundkraut* (1769)

The European goldenrod is nowhere near as showy as some of the other American species, but it is also native to the New World, especially in New England. There were probably a number of other native goldenrods that could be used as substitutes, and perhaps some of these were even more effective in medical applications. But no goldenrod among the German colonists was valued more highly than Blue Mountain tea (Solidago odora), otherwise known as sweet-scented goldenrod. It grew in such popularity that by the 1830s there were herbalists well known throughout the countryside for their cures based on this plant. It was gathered in the summer and sold door-to-door, and even sold in large quantities to dealers outside the middle states.[114]

Goldenrod possesses a bitter, alkaline, mildly volatile, oily balsamic salt, and from this it derives its faculty to warm gently, to dry, to cleanse and heal wounds, to dissolve internal blockages of the liver, spleen, and kidneys, and particularly to expel stones, mucusy matter, and sand. It also dissolves clotted blood, withstands poison, and kills worms of the belly.

An essence may be extracted by infusing the chopped roots, leaves, and flowers in brandy. Thirty to forty drops should be administered often. It has the excellent virtues of sweetening all sourness of the blood, of opening blockages, of forcing urine, of dispelling sand and foul matter from the kidneys, and most importantly, of healing wounds and injuries.

Goldenrod is not only employed on external wounds, but it is also quite effective for internal ones as well, for it is easily administered in vulnerary potions. The leaves may be boiled in a mixture of half water and wine, then drunk several times daily. It will treat all of the conditions listed above, and provide a wash for rinsing wounds.

The leaves can be ground to a powder and strewn into old, runny wounds and injuries. This will absorb and dry out all putrid fluxes, refresh the wound, keep it clean, and heal it.

If the fresh green leaves are wilted a little, or the dried leaves are infused in good warmed wine and afterward pressed a bit, and then laid upon a wound, it will purify and heal it without a plaster or salve.

An infusion of the dried leaves taken daily instead of tea will cleanse the kidneys and bladder exceptionally well of all sand and foul matter.

114. "Sweet-Scented Golden Rod," *Vick's Illustrated Monthly Magazine*, October 1884, 310.

Instead of that, the root and leaves may be ground to a powder taken in a quint dose several times a day. This will prove very effective in driving out sand, stone, and thick matter from the kidneys and bladder.

The distilled water of this herb will promote urine, drive out sand, foul matter, and stones from the kidneys and bladder, and prove useful in treating bloody flux if taken in three- or four-loth doses often.

For injuries to the mouth it may also be administered effectively as a gargle.

Gold-of-Pleasure (False Flax)
Camelina sativa
Sauer: *Leindotter* (1775)

Gerard illustrated this herb under the common name gold-of-pleasure and gave its Latin name as Myagrum—*so did Sauer. The plant is a mustard and not* Leindotter, *the German name supplied in the herbal, for* Leindotter *is a colloquial name for* Calendula officinalis, *marigold (see page 203). The proper name in German is* kleiner wilder Leindotter, *or more commonly* Leinkraut *(flax weed), because it was often found growing among flax.*

The plant has naturalized in this country in areas where flax growing was once extensive (see flax, page 142). It was also grown for the high-quality oil that is expressed from the seeds. This was used as a cooking oil among the Germans, while the plant itself was employed as fodder for milk cows. The young leaves are edible and were once considered a valuable potherb.

This herb is of a middling nature, between cold and warm. It is endowed with an oily, mucusy juice containing somewhat mildly alkaline salts. The oil is found primarily in the seeds, which can be used in place of linseed oil. As a result we ascribe to gold-of-pleasure the virtue of softening, of easing, of staying pain, and also of healing wounds. If it is chopped fresh together with mustard and laid over a wound, it has the power to cleanse and heal it. The oil is used externally for softening hard tumors and stilling pain.

Goldilocks
Helichrysum stoechas
Sauer: *Stöchaskraut* (1777)

Even if this were the ugliest plant in the herb garden, it always wins with its name. But as it happens, the plant is quite attractive, with silvery woolly leaves that turn bright yellow as the plant matures. It can also be picked and dried as an everlasting, so it was common in the eighteenth century to use this herb in dried floral arrangements. Its pungent odor was an additional feature that gave rooms a clean, refreshing scent. Although it was grown in colonial German gardens, it does not seem to have naturalized here.

Goldilocks is of a warm nature. It is endowed with a volatile aromatic salt, from which it derives properties similar to hyssop and sage. It strengthens the head, chest, heart, and matrix, and will withstand all poison.

The handsome, short, tightly formed spikes of this plant are what is mostly employed in medicine as a cordial for the head and heart. Writers of old have already mentioned that goldilocks is useful for divers afflictions of the chest and lungs, as well as for opening all internal organs of the viscera. It is also highly praised for strengthening the head, and is effective for fainting, apoplexy, and the falling evil. It also withstands poison. It can be infused along with other herbs in wine and drunk thus, or placed in a flux-brandy or in an apoplectic water and used that way.

If the handsome flowers of this plant are boiled in wine and the decoction drunk, this will open blockages of the liver and spleen, will purify and strengthen the internal organs as well as the entire body, force urine and bring down the menses, block poisons, and aid in treating illnesses that are caused by cold. It also treats fainting, apoplexy, weak memory, falling sickness, palsy, and so forth. For injuries of the lungs and chest, it is also very useful, but for people of hot temperament, the internal use of this medicine will prove quite injurious.

If the leaves and flowers of goldilocks are smelled and laid upon the head, or poached in lye or infused in brandy and the head washed with this, it will strengthen a cold, feeble brain.

Good King Henry (Allgood)
Chenopodium bonus-henricus
Sauer: *Guter Heinrich* (1774)

Easy to grow from seed, yet difficult to transplant once established, this fine perennial potherb should be situated in a semishady bed where it can grow undisturbed for many years. The greens can then be harvested as needed in the spring and fall when they are at their very best. Spinach has more or less replaced this herb in cookery, although it was once an important plant in the kitchen garden. It was used extensively in sauces and purees of green vegetables, since it heightens the green color. It was also eaten as a sauce or side dish with rabbit and small game as well as with goose.

Good king henry is of a temperate nature, and possesses many watery elements combined with a few volatile nitrous salts and somewhat oily constituents. Thus it has the faculty to dissolve, to still pain, to heal, and to foster good blood.

Good king henry is an excellent vulnerary herb, which may be laid green on all angry rotten injuries.

For pain of the hemorrhoids, take the leaves, pulp them, then heat this up with butter and milk over a gentle charcoal fire. Press out the liquid, then swab it on the hurt. This will make a very good salve.

Long ago, people made a plaster of the leaves to treat the pain of gout, and experienced good results from it.

It is customary to cook the leaves, together with the stems and shoots, in meat broth with butter, salt, and a few herbs, and eat them thus. This dish is almost as nice as asparagus or hops cooked the same way.

Great Mullein
Verbascum thapsus
Sauer: *Wollkraut* (1769)

Great mullein was advocated in plasters by many early writers. As a treatment for fistulas, it was recommended by John Arderne in his 1376 work Treatise of Fistula. *Sauer recommends it for both plasters and poultices, and even employs the bright waxy flower in making an oil. Any remedies prepared for internal use, such as mullein tea, must be strained through a fine muslin cloth or bag, since the hairs on the leaves and flower caps are extremely irritating and may do more harm than good. Sauer wisely has limited his remedies to external applications, thus avoiding this problem. The plant itself is quite handsome and makes a good show during the summer in dry, hot spots in the garden where few other things will grow.*

The flowers and leaves of great mullein are endowed with numerous mucilaginous balsamic elements containing alkaline salts. For this reason, this herb possesses the outstanding capacity to still pain as well as to heal internal and external wounds.

If warts are rubbed with the juice of great mullein, it will get rid of them.

Should a horse be scratched or injured by thorns or brambles, boil great mullein in water and wash the wounds with the decoction. This will heal them.

If a horse steps on a nail, take great mullein, pulp it, and bind it into and around the hoof after the nail has been removed.

The oil of great mullein can be prepared in the following manner: Take fresh great mullein and put it in a glass vessel. Pour good-quality olive oil over this and let it stand awhile well stopped in the sun. Or, if a glass bottle is stuffed tight with the flowers and well stopped, and stood in the sun a few weeks without the addition of any other ingredients, an oil will result. This oil is very good for swellings of the hemorrhoids when they are swabbed with it. The flowers and the oil of the common mullein are used for emollient and anodyne plasters, for baths and clysters. The leaves may be boiled in milk or wilted over hot coals, and laid as a poultice over the hurt while warm. This will ease, emolliate, and stop the pain.

If great mullein leaves are boiled in water, poured into a bucket, and the patient is made to sit over this while naked, as hot as the person can bear it, the vapors will be very good for stopping the uncontrolled looseness that so commonly results from bloody flux and white flux, or from other breaches of the bowels. Some oak leaves can also be added to the boiling water.

Ground Ivy
Nepeta glechoma
Sauer: *Gundelreben* (1762)

This wild herb appears to be native to eastern North America as well as to Europe. It was a familiar plant to brewers, since it was used extensively for clarifying beer. It often took the place of hops in home brewing and was said to extend the keeping qualities of the beer itself. The German name means "creeping vine," which aptly describes the manner in which the plant runs over the ground.

The employment of ground ivy in brewing was due to the plant's strong antiseptic character in killing off certain yeasts while promoting others. Such a trait had obvious benefits in medicine, so ground ivy was also endowed—rightly or wrongly—with numerous healing powers. Its most widespread use was for consumption, and Sauer was quite in line with his times by including a cough syrup for tubercular patients. The plant was considered at its highest stage of potency when in full bloom in May. It was then that it was gathered and dried.

Ground ivy is warm and dry in nature and possesses the virtues of cleansing, healing, and promoting urine. It also dissolves phlegm in the chest and thick humors in the kidneys, as well as opening up all blockages of the body.

A few handfuls of ground ivy heated in wine and then drunk as a warm decoction will promote urine and prove beneficial to the female member. It kills worms, opens up congestions of the liver and spleen, dispels jaundice, and is beneficial for consumptives and those suffering from the stone.

To treat consumption, make the following cough syrup: Take one-half pound of ground ivy juice and add to it six ounces of powdered white sugar. Let this boil over a gentle heat until it becomes as thick as honey. Give the patient a tablespoon of this syrup frequently, along with a dose of conserve of red roses the size of a nutmeg.

To counter ringing of the ears, take ground ivy and put it in wine. Set this over coals so that it boils up vigorously. Then hold the end of a funnel in the afflicted ear and let the hot steam from the boiled infusion penetrate the ear.

For kidney stones, take dried ground ivy and grind it to a powder. Then add to this an equal weight of white sugar. Take a few pinches of this sweet powder in some ground ivy tea each morning and evening.[115] Old herbals say that it is difficult to believe how quickly this breaks up the stones.

An open wound cleansed with the juice of ground ivy and then powdered with the dried ground leaves will heal quickly. If the wound is an old one, then add a little verdigris to the juice; this will cleanse it thoroughly. This remedy is beneficial to both man and beast.

115. This tea was commonly called Gill Tea in colonial America and in England.

If one of your cattle is struck by iliac passion or worms, then add a generous amount of ground ivy to its fodder.

Groundsel
Senecio vulgaris
Sauer: *Kreuzwurz* (1777)

Groundsel is a very common Old World weed that is now fully naturalized in this country. The Latin name derives from senex, *"old man," in reference to the white down on the seeds. The German name refers to its use, the* Kreuz *being the base of the spine, the loins, and other spots in and around the "privities." It is also the pit of the stomach.*

Aside from medical uses, groundsel was once a popular potherb, and a rather important one for country people since it remained green for much of the year. Technically speaking, it is an annual, but since it reproduces so profusely it may be found in all stages of growth in any single garden. While it is also quite invasive and is spread far and wide by songbirds that relish the seeds, rabbits are quite fond of the greens. Rabbit cooked with groundsel and milk was indeed an old dish among the German settlers. The salad mentioned below was often eaten with groundhog, squirrel, and other small game.

Groundsel is of a middling nature, for its sap is endowed with some penetrating nitrous salts together with a few oily balsamic elements. For this reason, it has a bitterish taste and works as a gentle laxative. More than that, it opens blockages of the internal glands, and kills and expels worms. Only the leaves are used. The tender leaves of groundsel may be eaten by themselves or at times combined with other herbs in salads throughout the entire winter and in the spring. It is served with vinegar, olive oil, and a little salt. This dish is beneficial to those who have jaundice; it also awakens the appetite and kills worms.

If groundsel is cooked with mallow flowers in milk to form a plaster, then spread between two cloths and laid warm upon the hurt, it will disperse inflamed swellings of the bosoms and privates, and is of especially good service following a hard dangerous delivery.

When fresh groundsel is chopped with ivy leaves and fomented in fresh butter, then pressed through a cloth, this will yield an excellent green burn salve that may be applied to the place injured by fire or a burning object. It not only draws out the burn immediately, but also heals it readily.

Take two handfuls of groundsel leaves and boil them in two quarts of white wine. If this is drunk in the morning and evening, it will bring down menses that have lodged in the matrix.

The distilled water of groundsel is useful for treating blockage of the liver and for getting rid of jaundice, when taken in a half-gill dose with succory water in the morning before breakfast.

If the juice is pressed from the fresh leaves in a marble or wooden mortar and taken in four- to six-loth doses with meat stock every morning and evening, it will get rid of jaundice, open blockages of the mesenteric veins as well as the liver, kill worms, purify the blood, and heal scurvy.

A syrup can be prepared with the expressed juice and sugar in the same manner as other syrups. It is effective in treating blood-spitting, bloody flux, copious nosebleeds, fluxes of the matrix, and similar conditions if taken often.

The expressed juice of groundsel, applied externally, will heal fresh wounds, sores, injuries, scall, and itch when these conditions are washed with it often while it is warm.

If the fresh leaves are chopped and well ground with parched salt, and laid warm over the hurt like a plaster, it will stop the extreme pain of gout and aching joints. Freshly pulped groundsel worked to a thick plaster with barley flour and a little oil of roses, and laid warm over swellings in the private parts, will get rid of inflammation and ease the condition.

An excellent vulnerary plaster may be prepared with the leaves in the following manner: Take three-fourths of a pound of groundsel leaves, two ounces each of wake-robin and celandine, sixty earthworms, and two pounds of fresh butter. Chop and then pulp all the ingredients except the butter together in a mortar. Put this in an earthenware vessel and set it in the sun. Afterward, set it over a gentle charcoal fire to simmer until all the moisture from the herbs has evaporated. Work it vigorously through a cloth, then add half a pound of beeswax, a fourth of a pound of turpentine, and the same amount of resin, and melt this in the butter over a gentle heat. When this has cooled completely, add three loths of finely ground frankincense and stir it together well. Then store away for use.

Hart's Tongue
Asplenium scolopendrium
Sauer: *Hirschzunge* (1767)

This is a fern of very striking appearance, as can be seen from the woodcut.

Unfortunately, it is not native to North America, although maidenhair fern was often used as a medical substitute. Like maidenhair fern, hart's tongue was placed among the quinque herbas capillares *or five capillaries, since it acts on the small blood vessels. It was sold in dried form in colonial apothecaries.*

Hart's tongue is of a cold, dry nature. It contains many earthy elements mixed with alkaline salts, and thus possesses the faculty for withstanding all sourness, for sweetening sharp scorbutic blood, and for opening blockages of the spleen.

If hart's tongue is infused overnight in wine and then drunk the next day, this is very good for hypochondriacs.

A sugar or conserve can be prepared from the leaves of the hart's tongue in the same manner as for rose petal conserve. It is very good for hypochondriacs provided they take it from time to time in nutmeg-size doses.

The distilled water of hart's tongue opens blockages of the liver and spleen, operates by urine in expelling stones, protects against black jaundice, and resists nagging pain and the gloominess and sadness that, without particular reason, commonly plague melancholics and hypochondriacs. It is also good for quartan ague, provided a few loths are taken according to want. Furthermore, it is effective for curing a swollen uvula when used as a gargle, and will heal sores in the throat and injuries to the gums, if warmed and the gums are then rinsed with it.

Hart's tongue salts, as prepared in apothecaries, and administered in ten-grain doses in hart's tongue water, are good for all afflictions of the spleen. In many apothecaries, only the dried herb may be had, therefore it must be used instead.

Hazelnut
Corylus avellana
Sauer: *Hasselnuss* (1778)

The European species is not native, so the American species were the only shrubs available as substitutes. And for substitutes, there were only two choices, the American hazelnut (Corylus americana) *and the beaked hazelnut* (Corylus rostrata). *The leaves and fruit of both are distinctly different. These plants were not officially recorded until 1788 and 1789 respectively, so there is no way of knowing which plant was employed by country people. European hazelnuts are advertised in some of the German-language newspapers during Sauer's era, but they are of course imports, and they appear about the time of year one would expect to see such things in connection with Christmas. Thus the imported nuts were probably used in cookery, while the native ones were gathered for home remedies and countrified versions of hazelnut tarts, wine noodles with hazelnuts, and other dishes associated with the festive foods served during Christmas and New Year.*

In their kernels, hazelnuts contain an indiscernible sharp, raw, astringent salt within the milk. Thus they make the throat raw and cause hoarseness, especially when dried, for they contract the glands of the mouth so that they cannot release the necessary moisture to wet the throat.

When hazelnuts are burned to ash and mixed with hog's lard, then smeared diligently on the head, this will hinder the falling out of the hair and cause it to grow back.

If the reddish skin of the hazelnut shell is mixed with red coral and one quint of this is put into water of field poppies, it makes a proven remedy for pleurisy and likewise for diarrhea and bloody flux.

Some people fill an empty hazelnut shell with quicksilver and mix this with wax, or cover it with red velvet and tie it to a cord around the neck for protection against pestilence.

If hazelnuts are ground with rue and figs to form a plaster, which is then laid upon the wound, it will cure the sting and bites of venomous creatures.

The oil distilled from small hazel branches is highly extolled as a remedy for the falling evil, provided the afflicted person is given a few drops in water of linden blossoms. If a few drops of this oil are put onto cotton and this is then applied to a painful tooth, it will stop the hurt.

If several drops of this oil are taken in a few tablespoonfuls of centaury water, it will kill worms and drive them out with the stool.

When someone eats hazelnuts in excess, the nuts will clog the stomach and cause headache. This condition is caused more by the dry nuts than by the fresh ones, although eating too many fresh ones when they are not quite ripe will cause bloody flux.

Hazelnuts do not give as much nourishment as sweet almonds because the latter contain a milder balsamic oil.

Toasted hazelnuts eaten with a little black pepper will dispel rheums of the head.

Dr. Crato[116] writes that many people have been cured of the stone and gravel by eating nine to ten hazelnuts each time before the midday and evening meals.

Hazelnut shells slightly scorched and then ground to a fine powder and taken as medicine will drive out sand and corruptions from the kidneys through the urine. This is also useful to women in labor, for it promotes delivery.

The mistletoe that grows on the hazel tree, ground to a fine powder and taken frequently in half-quint doses, is a first-rate remedy for those afflicted by the falling evil. This mistletoe is considered more powerful than the mistletoe that grows on oak trees.

Hellebore (Black)
Helleborus niger
Sauer: *Schwarze Niesswurz, Christwurz* (1778)

The use of hellebore is not new to medicine. Marcus Porcius Cato discussed hellebore purges in his De Agricultura,[117] *and this appears to have been its primary use down through the centuries. However, its purging action is drastic, and it is also violently narcotic. For these reasons hellebore should be treated as a poison. The plant is still popular today as a garden ornamental, since it blooms in December; hence its other name in German:* Christwurz, *"Christmas wort." During Sauer's era, most of the hellebore prepared for medicine came from Germany.*

116. Dr. Joannes Crato (1519–1585) was a German physician.
117. Cato, *On Farming/De agricultura*, trans. Andrew Dalby (Blackawton/Totnes, Devon: Prospect Books, 1998), 177–78.

Black hellebore is of a hot and dry nature and operates by a sharp, caustic, vitriolic salt, from which it derives the virtue to purge forcefully, to attenuate, and to open.

Black hellebore should not be employed internally, but if it is, then only under the advice of an experienced physician. Nevertheless, some people have found that black hellebore extract made with brandy and then formed into pills, as well as the root used in purgative bitters, can prove useful.

Hellebore (German White)
Veratrum album
Sauer: Weisse Niessewurzel (1778)

The European hellebore of Sauer's herbal resembles the American hellebore, but the two differ greatly in chemical constituents. And since both are extremely poisonous, they should never be confused or misused. Indeed, German white hellebore was frequently employed during the Middle Ages to poison the tips of darts and daggers, and there was little that could be done as an antidote. The part preferred for medicine was the rhizome, which was sold dry in apothecary shops.

White hellebore is endowed with a sharp, caustic, vitriolic salt or poison, and for this reason it is of a warm, dry nature. It purges both the stomach and bowels, and thus should not be employed internally.

For those who are afflicted by somnolence to such an extent that they cannot be awakened, take powdered white hellebore in a dose the size of a pea, and blow it into the nose of the patient through the quill end of a feather.[118]

White hellebore should not be used internally because it promotes such violent vomiting that the patient may also choke on it.

If white hellebore is boiled in milk and set out to attract flies, all will die that eat it. The same result can be accomplished by mixing it with flour and giving this to mice, for they also die from it.

Hemlock (Poison Hemlock)
Conium maculatum
Sauer: Wütrich, Schierling (1771)

Poison hemlock naturalized everywhere in North America that Europeans settled, and evidently by the 1770s it was common enough that Sauer thought it appropriate to comment on its dangers and uses. The vernacular German name is Wütrich, *and the herbal alludes to the root meaning of this word as a way of explaining its deadliness. The*

118. This remedy is curious because it was well known that when snuffed, white hellebore would cause severe running of the nose. This would seem a dangerous method for awakening a patient, but it was also accompanied by violent sneezing. Given the fashion for snuff in this period, the sneezing was not viewed in a negative light.

term has several connotations: a bloodthirsty person, a bloodhound, in short, someone who is in a rage or fury. The root verb is wüthen, *to rage, rave, or foam at the mouth, all apt descriptions of the symptoms of hemlock poisoning.*

Poison hemlock closely resembles parsley, and when it is young, one can be easily mistaken for the other. It has quite often happened already, that by this error, people have lost their lives and that others have narrowly escaped with sickness and violent casting of the stomach.

This herb possesses an extremely sharp, caustic, oily salt that makes it quite dangerous and deadly when used internally. It justly bears the name *Wütrich* ever since the Athenians put world-wise Socrates to death with its juice. Some people who have mistakenly eaten its roots have either died or gone stark raving mad.[119] If geese eat this herb, they also go mad. Thus, it should not be used internally for either man or beast.

If the leaves are boiled in milk, or simply in water, and applied warm to hard tumors, this is said to soften and disperse them. Hemlock is especially praised as a treatment for swellings of the spleen when applied as a warm plaster over that place.

Henbane
Hycoscyamus niger
Sauer: *Bilsenkraut* (1766)

There are two sorts, one white, the other black, based on the color of the flowers. Both are ugly and so nasty smelling that it would be difficult to induce anyone to eat them, even accidentally, for the plant's other common name, fetid nightshade, is indeed well earned. Nevertheless, this plant has been employed since ancient times as a narcotic, a painkiller, and even as a love potion, though sometimes with deadly results. It is a very dangerous poison, for only twenty to thirty seeds will kill a child, and the seeds are quite small.

The plant was evidently brought to this country and cultivated in physic gardens, never anywhere that children might come into contact with it. Unfortunately, it has since naturalized and may be found growing in waste places throughout much of the country. The copious use of milk as an antidote to henbane poisoning appears in many other herbals, but goat's milk was considered even better.

Since henbane joins garlic, juniper, radish, and speedwell in using goose fat for preparing salves, it might be useful here to know how this fat was processed. The following recipe comes from Christine Knörin's Göppinger Kochbuch, *which was first issued in 1789. The remarks about using goose fat as a salad oil are also pertinent, since this substitution was quite common where olive oil was too expensive or unavailable.*

> *Goose fat is handled in the same manner described as pork lard except that rendered fat should be drawn from the loins, so that it has a better aroma. If*

---

119. This evidently refers to individuals who mistook hemlock root for Hamburg parsley, a popular vegetable among the Germans (see parsley, 236).

it is simply wanted for cold salads instead of using Provence olive oil, then it should only be cut from the belly and when made as cold as possible, melted over hot ashes. Let the fat run through a skimmer with very small holes into a porcelain vessel. The remaining fat in the cooking vessel should be allowed to heat completely and then brought to a full boil. For using this in cold salads, scoop out a little bit and let it dissolve in a small porcelain vessel, but not near a high heat. Use this instead of olive oil. It should be noted, however, that after washing the salad in the winter, it should first be brought into the room where it is to be served so that it is not so cold.[120]

This last remark makes a good point, for if the salad is too cold, the warm fat will chill and coagulate, which of course creates an unpleasant texture.

Henbane is of a hot nature, as its faculties prove. It has the capacity to contain the influence of the vital spirits, and after a time, to induce madness. It also stills pain, emolliates fluxes of the chest, induces sleep, and acts as an astringent. Only the seeds are used internally, about three to five grains, and that only rarely for stilling pain and stopping diarrhea and other fluxes of the stomach.

For blood-spitting, the following electuary works excellently: Take one ounce each of the sugar of red roses and violet sugar, half an ounce of quince paste, fifty grains each of prepared corals and hematite, twenty grains of cherry tree gum, thirty grains of henbane seeds, and enough quince syrup to make an electuary. Mix it all together well and administer a generous dab of this to the patient every three or four hours. This preparation is also effective against rheums upon the chest and hard coughs. It will induce good slumber and still all sorts of diarrhea, as well as pains in the limbs. The same results may be had from the following powder: Take twenty grains each of henbane seeds and white poppy seeds, forty grains of coriander, twenty grains of fennel seeds, ten grains of mastix, five grains of frankincense, one quint of powdered hematite, and one loth of sugar. Grind it all to a fine powder and mix it well. Administer thirty grains at a time.

An oil may be pressed from toasted, ground henbane seeds, which can be used externally for stilling all sorts of pain. For headache, it can be rubbed on the temples. It is also customary to mix this oil with other oils and apply this externally. If the pain caused by pleurisy is rubbed with this oil, it will prove of excellent use.

The fresh leaves of henbane wilted a bit on a hot hearthstone, and then laid over the swollen limbs infected with gout, will get rid of all the swelling and pain.

For severe toothache, take equal amounts of the oil of henbane seeds and the oil of cloves and put this on a little piece of cotton or directly on the gums beside the painful tooth. This will ease the pain quickly.

If someone wants to pull out a rotten tooth painlessly, take one and a half quints of henbane seeds, gum ammoniac, and sugar. Grind this to a fine powder and then mix it with a little goose fat, beeswax, and turpentine so that it forms a salve. Then

120. R. Christine Knörin, *Göppinger Kochbuch* (Stuttgart, 1798), 8–9. This was initially published as part 2 of Knörin's *Sammlung vieler Vorschriften*, although they may be treated as two separate books.

spread it on the affected gums several times. The tooth will loosen for easy removal.

However, henbane and its seeds should almost never, or only with the most extreme caution, be employed internally. There have been examples where man as well as beast have perished because they have accidentally gotten it into their stomach. If chickens are fed the seeds, they will die from it.

Should anyone, out of carelessness, eat henbane seeds or leaves in such a quantity that there is fear of injury, immediately drink fresh milk in copious quantities, or take onions or garlics and chop them very fine and drink this in a glass of wine.

Hoary Cress
Cardaria draba, formerly *Lepidium draba*
Sauer: *Türkischer Kresse* (1775)

Sauer, like Gerard, gave this as a species of the genus Draba, *which introduces confusion with whitlow grass, especially since the number of species belonging to that genus is quite large. Sauer mentioned whitlow in a few of the remedies, but his intention here is in fact something quite different: a mustard known in German either as* Babylonischer *cress or* Türkischer *cress. This plant is not native to North America, but has now naturalized in several places. Only the seed was used by colonial German apothecaries, and these were easily imported. This seed was probably the source of the plants that eventually escaped into the countryside.*

Hoary cress is of a temperate nature, possessing somewhat volatile salts together with numerous earthy and few oily elements. The seeds may be somewhat sharper and thus possess more volatile salts. From this, then, hoary cress derives its capacity to open, to purify the blood, to loose internal blockages of the liver, spleen, lungs, and mesenteric veins, as well as to purify the kidneys and to drive out urine and worms. The seeds may be administered for all of the above-mentioned afflictions in doses equal to the weight of one-half quint.

Holy Thistle
Cnicus benedictus
Sauer: *Cardobenedicten* (1762)

Holy thistle is a very handsome herb that can be grown as an ornamental. It is native to southern Europe, but has since naturalized in many other places, including North America. Many herbalists have treated it as a cure-all, and during outbreaks of the plague, it was considered a certain cure. Milk thistle (page 210) contains most of the same constituents, thus it may be used as a good substitute. If taken internally in too concentrated a dose, both of these thistles will act as strong emetics, thus defeating their purpose.

Holy thistle is of a warm and dry nature. It forces sweat, withstands sourness and poison in the body, dissolves hard phlegm, strengthens the stomach, promotes the appetite, opens internal obstructions, and cleanses the blood.

When a quint measure of powdered holy thistle is taken, it will force sweat and poisons from the heart, cleanse the blood, kill worms, and protect against contagion. It is also good for headache, dizziness, jaundice, and dropsy, and stills colic. It forces the surfeit of vapors from the stomach and matrix, and is good for the tertian and quartan agues, provided it is taken in a glass of wine an hour before the onset of the fever.

Villanovanus[121] remarked that he knew a man who had developed open holes and sores on his thigh right down to the bone. He had given over his entire wealth to doctors, and none could help him. He was in the end cured in the following manner: He beat holy thistle leaves to a cataplasm and then fomented them in wine. After that, he added melted hog's lard and let it foment again. Then he stirred in wheat flour until it thickened into a salve. Twice a day he spread this on the wounds and thus was fortunately healed.

The distilled water of holy thistle is also very useful against putrid fevers. It stops headache, protects against dizziness, cleanses sand from the kidneys and bladder, and is particularly good for pleurisy.

The finely ground seeds of holy thistle, taken in a pinch dose in the morning and evening, are an excellent remedy for all manner of fevers. They will even arouse the appetite. But it is preferable that first the stomach be cleansed with an emetic.

Hops
Humulus lupulus
Sauer: *Hopfen* (1767)

> *There were many varieties of hops brought to America in the colonial period, both from England and from Germany. Advertisements in period newspapers make it fairly clear that by Sauer's era, there was no shortage of hops for brewing or for baking. Indeed, many farmhouses had hop vines to supply the family needs, and some of these vines have now found their way into the wild.*
>
> *The herbal noted that eating hops shoots was healthful. They are also bitter and take some getting used to. Yet it was this very bitterness that appealed to the Germans in the spring. However, the shoots were not eaten raw, so some of the bitterness was carried off in the cooking water. Sophie Juliane Weiler's recipe for hops salad is typical:*
>
>> *Cut away the lower hard part of the hops shoots and poach the tops in salted water until tender. Drain in a sieve, and when cool, prepare them as a salad with vinegar, oil, pepper, and salt, all well mixed together.[122]*

121. Villanovanus was Arnoldus de Villanova (1240–1311), a Spanish herbalist and physician. His name is also written Arnaud de Villeneuve.

122. Sophie Juliane Weiler, *Augsburgisches Kochbuch* (Augsburg, 1790), 443.

Hops is of a temperate nature, having a sap endowed with few oily, thin, nitrous bitter salts. Thus it possesses the capacity to attenuate, to open, to operate by urine, and to sweeten and cleanse gently.

The foremost use for hops is brewing beer, for which it takes the place of a salt or spice. But if too much hops are used, they will make the beer quite bitter and prove troublesome to the head.[123]

Young hops shoots, eaten as food, cleanse the blood, heal the itch, and open obstructions of the belly, liver, and spleen.

Distilled hops water cleanses the blood of all unwholesomeness, opens an obstructed liver and spleen, and relieves them of their swelling and puffing. It is also serviceable for the itch, scall, and leprosy, and strengthens urination and the menses. Drink in doses of four or five loths in the morning before breakfast.

Horehound
Marrubium vulgare
Sauer: *Weisser Andorn* (1763)

> *In German, Sauer's horehound is very clearly indicated by the adjective "white." Yet lest there were any doubt, his opening line (below) further clarified what plant was intended. This was necessary because in German there is a "black" horehound (schwarzer Andorn). This herb was known in eighteenth-century English as ballote, or sometimes as stinking horehound (Ballota nigra), and is closely related to nettles. It is an ugly herb and foul smelling, but it was also used in folk remedies. By 1763, when Sauer published the segment on horehound, this plant had already fully naturalized itself in many areas of British America; thus there was a need to remind readers that black horehound would not work in the remedies discussed below. Regarding Sauer's conserve, which is quite easy to make, it has the familiar taste of old-fashioned horehound candy.*

The common white horehound (whose leaves are gathered in June) possesses the property of opening, of dissipating, of cleansing, of attenuating, of opening blockages of the lungs, liver, spleen, and matrix, and of promoting the cleansing and warming of the *vagina uteri*.[124]

Boil a handful of horehound in a quart of wine and an equal quantity of water. Strain this through a cloth, sweeten with sugar, and drink as needed. This opens obstructions of the liver and spleen, cleanses the chest of phlegm, furthers the cleansing of the *vagina uteri*, kills worms, and is useful against jaundice and injuries to the

---

123. A common bog plant called buck bean *(Menyanthus trifolata)* was used among some Germans as a substitute for hops in beer brewing. Its bitterness is even greater than hops, and it was often used in beers of a sweet or heavy character. But the herbal is right; it is the bitterness that can lead to a headache and flushed complexion.

124. Sauer left this space completely blank. He meant the vagina, a word he would not commit to print. The German word was *Mutterscheide*, which he sometimes indicated with the letters *M. S.* Woyt used the Latin. The opening to the vagina was called the *Muttermundloch*, to which Sauer's country readers applied numerous vulgar synonyms.

body. It also strengthens the stomach and awakens the appetite. However, those who suffer from injuries to the kidneys or bladder must refrain from using horehound.

The distilled water of horehound softens tough phlegm in the chest and lungs, dispels coughing, stops blood-spitting, and opens obstructions of the liver and spleen, provided a few loths are drunk from time to time. It is also good for women during childbirth, since it eases the travail.

Take a pound of fresh horehound leaves and add two pounds of loaf sugar. Pound this in a wooden or marble mortar until the sugar and herb is ground quite fine. This conserve can be kept for a whole year or longer in an earthenware vessel. It loosens tough phlegm in the chest, stills coughs, promotes expectoration, and is a useful remedy for the elderly who have difficulty breathing, and other infirmities of the lungs arising from cold. Take a tablespoonful at a time, once or twice a day.

Horseradish
Armoracia lapathifolia
Sauer: *Meer-Rettig* (1765)

> *Horseradish hardly requires an introduction, yet it is useful to remember that it was once much more of a vegetable and potherb than it is today. For the root was often boiled (which greatly weakens its pungency) and served like scorzonera (page 278) or carrots. The herbal provides a number of suggestions for preparing it for table use, including horseradish sauce made with grated horseradish, vinegar, and salt. All of these were popular with the Germans during the eighteenth century.*

Horseradish warms and dries very powerfully. It possesses the faculty to dissolve all thick, phlegmy humors, as well as expelling through the urine scorbutic sour salts from the blood. It purifies the matrix, carries off sand, gravel, and stones, eases difficult breathing, absorbs phlegm upon the chest, purifies the blood, and promotes digestion.

Horseradish possesses the same virtues as other radishes, except that in all its parts it is far more active, particularly in the expulsion of urine and stone. If horseradish is cut into slices and white wine poured over this, and it is allowed to stand overnight, then drunk in the morning before breakfast, this will expel urine and stones forcefully (good cider will serve just as well as the best wines in this case). However, it should be observed that if there is already an actual stone and of such a size larger than what can be expelled through the urinary passages, horseradish, like any other similar remedy, may easily cause injury. As long as it is nothing but sand and foul matter that is forced from the kidneys, horseradish will provide excellent effectiveness in loosening and expelling them.

Due to its volatile alkaline salts, horseradish has been found to be exceptionally useful for cold scurvy, because it powerfully alters the sharp acidity of scorbutic blood, sweetens the blood, and improves it. For this reason it heals all those illnesses and afflictions that are just arising from this condition. It is customary, to this end, to put the root in wine either alone, or with brooklime, watercress, scurvy grass, and chervil. This is then drunk several times daily for a continuance. A similar result may also be had by the water freshly distilled from horseradish.

Horseradish is also cooked with meat, for it excites the appetite and promotes digestion. But if it is employed too much, it will injure the eyes.

It is customary to shave or grate the root very small, and to eat this with salt and vinegar with meat or fish. Or, pour boiling meat stock over finely grated horseradish and let this stand well covered over coals. Then eat it with meat.

Some people pound the horseradish, add vinegar and honey, and then boil them together until it is as thick as an electuary. This is employed in cases of sharp, cutting kidney stones, and blockage of the matrix.

The juice expressed from the root mixed with the juices of watercress and scurvy grass, taken daily for several weeks in three- or four-tablespoon doses, will purify the blood, and cure scurvy arising from cold and sourness.

Horseradish can be grated fine, put into a bottle, and enough wine poured over it to cover it. Then stop it well and bury it in the ground for a week. After this, dig it up and administer a few tablespoons each time in the morning and evening. This is very good for women who are afflicted by wanness.

Pregnant women should never use much horseradish, for they rarely benefit from it.

For tertian or quartan agues, horseradish may be employed usefully when it is ground, mixed with rue and salt, and bound over the pulse and heels. The juice expressed from the root, rubbed over the back with pepper oil several times during fever chills, will provide an effective remedy for the same.

Ground horseradish root laid as a poultice over black measles will get rid of them immediately.

Fresh horseradish, cut into pieces and laid in fresh water, will yield a simple antilithic water for dropsical persons afflicted with sand and gravel.

Horsetail
Equisetum arvense
Sauer: *Schafftheu* (1770)

Horsetail is a wild herb found in wet, marshy places. It grows throughout the northern hemisphere and belongs to a class of plants that can be traced to prehistoric times. Its nearest relatives are the ferns; most of the rest of the clan are now fossils. The roots are perennial and may be grown in gardens near ponds or even in shallow water. Horsetail will also grow in deep shade or in any soil that holds water. There are ample references to horsetails in medical works from classical antiquity down through the Middle Ages (Galen being often cited), but the most mundane use—even among the Germans who settled in America—was that of a scouring brush. Because it is rough, horsetail makes an excellent material for scrubbing pots and pans.

Today, some gardeners raise horsetails for their ornamental qualities, since the stems, sometimes three feet tall, resemble giant bottlebrushes and thus lend an exotic or rather tropical aspect to the landscape. Judging from Sauer's strong convictions about the medical uses of horsetail, here is an herb that deserves closer scrutiny from medical science.

The virtue of common horsetail is that it thickens the blood, checking its flow, contracting the veins, and closing up sores and injuries. For this reason, the ancients said that due to these properties it is of a cold and dry nature.

The distilled water of horsetail is good for blood-spitting, and heals injured intestines, liver, kidneys, and bladder. It stops overflowings of the menses, and is serviceable for all sorts of ruptures, dysenteries, and diarrhea, provided four to five spoonfuls of it are drunk each morning and evening. This water will also heal putrid wounds and injuries, especially in the privates, provided you wet a small piece of cloth with it and then apply this as a warm dressing.

The tisane in which fresh horsetail is boiled is on all counts preferable to the distilled water because the best constituents are lost through the distilling process. This tea heals wounds of the mouth, gums, and throat when gargled warm. It is also useful to wash with a small quantity of the itch.

In New England, they have discovered that if you drink this tisane and continue the practice, it is supposed to provide a good remedy for kidney stones and gravel in the bladder. The trial is easy, and it does not cost much.

Houseleek (Great Houseleek, Stonecrop)
Sedum acre and Sedum album
Sauer: *Hauswurz* (1763)

This old-fashioned garden plant is more commonly known as hen-and-chicks, and very few people today know that it can also be eaten as a potherb. Sauer did not deal with the culinary side of its many uses, or with its applications in possets for agues, but he did dwell on two specific species, the common houseleek (Sedum acre) and the small houseleek often referred to as the white houseleek (Sedum album). The two cannot be confused, since the common houseleek has golden yellow flowers, while the small or lesser houseleek has white flowers. This distinction was important to Sauer, since there were other houseleeks under cultivation, and some of them had medical uses—ostensibly the reason for the remark regarding the remedy for nosebleeds.

In the horse remedy below, the herbal also made use of an unusual herb called stavesacre, but did not specify what part of it was to be employed—in all likelihood the seeds. Stavesacre must have been available in German apothecary shops in colonial America, since it was far more popular among continental physicians than among the English. While stavesacre is indeed an attractive herb and is as easy to grow as larkspur (which it resembles), it is also quite poisonous and should be treated with due respect.

Most houseleeks, but especially the common variety, operate by an indiscernible alkaline salt concealed in an abundance of watery sap. The houseleek derives from this its capacity to cool, to extinguish heat and burning, to quench thirst, and to ease divers pains.

A water can be distilled from houseleek, but because of its great coldness, it is not easily taken internally. If a small piece of cloth is moistened with it and laid on the forehead, it will be of good service to those who have become delirious due to fevers or otherwise from intense heat. It also serves well against all burning inflammations and swellings of the tender parts, such as the breasts of women and the privates of both men and women.

A half-teaspoon dose of the juice of houseleek taken with wine will expel worms.

For painful inflammations of the hemorrhoids, houseleek juice is useful when a cloth is moistened with it and then laid upon them.

When someone bleeds copiously from the nose, take cotton or linen lint, dampen it in the juice of houseleek, and press it into the nostrils. Yet the question here is only a matter of which works better: the great houseleek or the lesser?

The freshly pressed juice of common houseleek, when given on occasion in a tablespoonful dose with sugar, has been found particularly useful against the fits, gripes, falling sickness, and the startled frights of bad-tempered people—old and young—when awakened from their sleep.

For inflammations of the throat and tonsils, the juice of houseleek is exceedingly useful when taken as a gargle.

The distilled water of houseleek, or the juice of the same, is very good for inflammations of the eyes, when a small piece of cloth is dampened with it and bound over the eyes for the night.

If a horse has a swollen shank, take a handful each of houseleek, elderberry leaves, stavesacre,[125] and the leaves of rue and mullein. Grind this thoroughly, then foment it in vinegar and butter. Bind it warm to the horse's leg. When the plaster is removed, wash the leg with water in which pine cones have been boiled. (In this country, tar water will serve just as well as the pine cone decoction).[126]

The expressed juice of houseleek rubbed frequently on warts and corns will get rid of them.

For those who develop dry tongues during a serious illness, take a leaf of houseleek, peel off the outer skin, and hold it in the patient's mouth that it may be chewed a little. This is of great service.

The pulped leaves of houseleek fomented in unsalted butter or lard make a good salve for burns.

125. *Delphinium staphisagria* is an annual relative of the larkspur. It originates in Asia Minor. The plant, and especially the seeds, are extremely poisonous. Sauer called it *Wolfskraut*, "wolf's wort," but it has many other common names in German.

126. Although the herbal does not spell it out, it was the green or unripe pine cone that was boiled to make this decoction. They were often gathered green and dried specifically for this use. The reference to tar water is explained more fully under silver-leafed fir tree on page 290.

Hyssop
Hyssopus officinalis
Sauer: *Isop* (1763)

In Pennsylfaanisch this herb is known as Eisap, *and a firm distinction should be made between it and* wilder Eisap, *"wild hyssop," which is American hellebore. Due to our humid summers, true hyssop is much subject to wilt in the middle states; doubtless this problem was faced by many colonial gardeners as well. Nonetheless, it is a charming herb with blue-, pink-, and white-flowering varieties. There are also ones with variegated leaves, and rarer yet, a few with bicolored flowers. The only variety that Sauer knew was the common blue-flowering sort. Since it yields well to pruning, it was popular in colonial America as an edging plant around the beds of kitchen gardens. Furthermore, the flowers are quite attractive to pollinators, especially bees.*

Hyssop is of a warm, dry nature and operates by its numerous volatile sharp, oily salts. Hence it possesses the faculty to thin, to open, to purify, to dissolve, and to strengthen the head, chest, and stomach, and operates through urine and other things.

The foremost strength and virtue of hyssop is that of healing infirmities of the lungs and chest, such as obstructions of the lungs due to thick phlegm, coughs of long continuance, difficult breathing, and hoarseness. Take one loth of shaved licorice root, a handful each of horehound, veronica, and hyssop, and half a loth each of fresh figs and Assyrian plums.[127] Chop it all together, then boil it in a gallon of water for as long as it takes to hard-cook an egg. Let the patient drink this decoction at will.

Hyssop boiled in wine with sage and then drunk is good for those who complain that they have been lifting heavy things too much and have made themselves sore.

If hyssop is tied up in a small piece of cloth, boiled a little bit in wine, and then pressed firmly and laid lukewarm over closed eyes, it will dispel redness in the eyes occasioned by extravasated blood.

If hyssop is picked when the plant is running to seed, chopped fine, brandy poured over it, and then tightly stopped and set eight days in warm sand or the sun, it will yield an essence that can be strained off and sweetened with sugar. This can be administered to good effect for coughs, asthma, stomachache, loss of appetite, gripes of the intestines, and mother fits, as well as weakness of the limbs and nerves. Take a half tablespoon daily. This essence is also said to be of special benefit to those who are worried about attacks of apoplexy.

The distilled water of hyssop, taken in a dose of a few loths daily, will give excellent results in treating infirmities of the chest and lungs. It will expel worms, dispel dropsy brought on by cold, open blockages of a cold liver and spleen, and warm the stomach and all the inner organs. Held in the mouth, hyssop water often gets rid of toothache.

---

127. The Assyrian or Sebestan plum *(Cordia myxa)* might seem somewhat exotic were it not for the fact that it was greatly esteemed by German physicians. There are wild and cultivated sorts. In Sauer's era, most of this dried black, plumlike fruit came from the Near East, especially Syria. A paste or electuary called diabesten was also sold by apothecaries.

Indian Cress

Tropaeolum majus
Sauer: *Indianischer Kresse* (1764)

> *I should point out that there are two species represented by the name Indian cress,*
> Tropaeolum minus *and* Tropaeolum majus. *The first species was introduced into*
> *European gardens in 1576 and is the common sort discussed in herbals up to 1700. The*
> *latter one was introduced to Holland from Peru in 1684 by Dutch plant collector*
> *Hieronymus van Beverningk. This species more or less pushed out the other in popu-*
> *larity, and is indeed the one intended by Sauer.*
>
> *The date of Sauer's entry is also nearly contemporary with a 1761 letter sent by*
> *Thomas Lamboll to Philadelphia botanist John Bartram discussing this herb.*[128] *Lamboll*
> *called it Great Garden Cress, by which he meant the large-leafed vining variety.*
> *Sauer's comments about the plant expand our knowledge about its introduction, for it*
> *seems that his seed was coming directly from Spanish America. This would explain why*
> *the plants were still day-length sensitive and poorly adapted to northern climates. It has*
> *taken several centuries of selection to make this plant flower in short-summer areas. On*
> *the other hand, the large vining varieties do indeed bloom late in the season, even today.*
>
> *Finally, Sauer mentioned Indian cress and its various culinary applications with*
> *health benefits. One of these was the pickled seed. Maria Sophia Schellhammer included*
> *a very good idea in her Brandenburg cookbook: the seeds were not pickled separately but*
> *rather mixed in with small cucumbers when they were put down in brine.*[129] *This was*
> *done in two ways, Nuremberg style or French style. The former was achieved by layer-*
> *ing the pickle with sprigs of fennel picked together with the young seeds attached ("the*
> *more fennel the better") and then covering this with a mixture of white wine vinegar,*
> *springwater, and salt. The latter was also pickled in white wine vinegar, but the spice*
> *mix was different: bay leaves, fennel seed, cloves, and mace.*

Together with its earthy components, Indian cress operates not only by a goodly portion of its volatile, alkaline, caustic salts, but also by the somewhat balsamic oils in its
spirituous juices. From these it derives its capacity to warm and to dry gently, to
strengthen the heart and stomach, to open all manner of internal blockages, and particularly to cleanse sour scorbutic melancholic blood and to restore it to its natural
sweetness and temperature.

The leaves of this herb have been enjoyed in cookery for a long time, or else their
expressed juice is taken in drink. Or, lastly, the conserve made with the petals is mixed
with conserve of roses and powdered liverwort and taken in nutmeg-size doses three
or four times daily for healing consumption and coughing—if the afflictions have not
taken root too deeply, but more particularly, for those whose condition has as its
source sharp, salty, scorbutic fluxes.

If the flowers of this herb are boiled in milk, and then the milk is used for cooking children's porridge, this will prevent their atrophy or decline. It will open block-

128. John Bartram, *Correspondence of John Bartram* (Gainesville, Fla., 1992), 505.
129. Maria Sophia Schellhammer, *Das Brandenburgische Koch-Buch* (Berlin, 1732), 574.

ages of the mesenteric veins, awaken the appetite, repel all sourness of the gut, and heal colic.

Moreover, this herb can be prepared just like watercress, and used the same way for treating scurvy and other illnesses.

Take fresh leaves of Indian cress and chop them coarsely. Pour over them good-quality olive oil, then let this stand in a well-stopped glass vessel in the sun for a few weeks or even months. This will yield a highly valuable vulnerary oil that not only heals fresh wounds excellently, but also pox marks on the body with remarkable speed. This oil can also be administered orally for all manner of injuries to the internal organs. It is of particularly good service for bloody flux when a tablespoon dose is taken three or four times a day.

Because this herb originated in warm countries, it finds our summer in Pennsylvania much too short. Therefore it must be sown somewhat early and the seedlings covered when the nights are cold. Thus handled, it is easier to bring to flower than other cresses because ground fleas do not eat it.[130] And if it is set out so that it has room enough to spread, it will put out vigorous growth. The pretty orange flowers, which it produces in abundance, are not only very decorative, but also highly tasty and healthful for the body. They can be eaten in salads or as side dishes. The plant flowers in the late fall when there are almost no other flowers left in gardens, and continues until it runs to seed and is cut down by frost.

Ipecacuanha
Psychotria ipecacuanha
Sauer: *Ipecacuanha-Wurtzel* (1778)

Ipecacuanha was not employed in Europe until 1672, when samples of the root were introduced from South America. The French physician Adrian Helvetius experimented with ipecacuanha and determined its usefulness in treating bloody flux and other similar maladies. Helvetius patented his remedy, but it was later made public in 1688. Since the root was gathered mostly by Indians in the interior of Brazil, Colombia, and Bolivia, the true botanical nature of the plant remained under dispute until about 1800, when actual plants were brought back to Europe for analysis. We may judge from this that Zwinger's herbal was quite up-to-date, as it included such a cutting-edge remedy. Also evident is the total lack of association with humors, since the herb was introduced during a period when this approach to medicine had begun its decline. Which brings us to Sauer.

It is safe to presume that Sauer's supply came from South America, but botanically speaking, it could have been one of any number of similar roots that were sold under the name of ipecacuanha. In all likelihood, Sauer's plant was the greater striated ipecacuanha (Psychotria emetica), also called black or Peruvian ipecacuanha, which was traded out of New Granada and Lima.

130. *Grundfloh,* "ground flea," is old Pennsylfaanisch for flea beetles.

The root of this plant is very well known to the apothecaries in Germany as well as in England. It is ground to a fine powder and taken in doses of thirty to forty grains. The root works powerfully and with certainty as an emetic and sometimes also as a laxative. It is an excellent remedy for bloody flux, constipation, and other maladies. But primarily, it is used in most illnesses where an emetic is called for, and for this it is one of the safest. It is cheap and to be preferred over wild spikenard, *tartarus emeticus*,[131] and other vomitories.

Iris (Flower de Luce)
Iris germanica and *Iris pseudocorus*
Sauer: *Veilwurzel* (1774)

Sauer's discussion of iris must be prefaced with certain clarifications, since he made no scientific distinction between the sorts he appropriated for medicine. Furthermore, in each case, it was the root stock or rhizome that was used, and these resemble one another when sold in a dried state. It was therefore easy (and all too common) for druggists to commit frauds—one of Sauer's obvious concerns.

The iris that the Germans called Veilwurtzel, *"violet root," is generally equated with the orris root or* Iris florentina *of herbals, but in the Sauer herbal, it is evident that he had more than one species in mind. One of these was commonly called garden flower de luce or blue flower de luce in colonial America and is the common* Iris germanica *of horticulture. This handsome perennial, now raised mostly for its ornamental flowers, underwent so much improvement and hybridization during the nineteenth century that it is presently difficult to find the simple land race once familiar to herbalists. In any case, the plant has bluish green leaves and blooms in May through June with deep blue or purple-blue flowers on two- to three-foot stems. It is native to southern Europe, but may be grown in this country in a variety of soils.*

The large yellow flag of Sauer (which he referred to in German as a "water lily") is the Iris pseudocorus *of northern Europe. This is the myrtle flag of Culpeper and the fleur de lis of France, and is now fully naturalized in many parts of the United States. Normally called water flower de luce or simply yellow flag in old garden books, it has a bright yellow flower and prefers to grow in wet or moist locations, such as bogs or along streams. A variety with variegated leaves is now popular as an ornamental plant.*

Sauer's Florentine iris is the Iris florentina *of the old herbals, although technically it is only a variety of* Iris germanica. *It was often called white flower de luce owing to its distinctive color. It is a native of the Mediterranean from Spain to Cyprus, and there are some varieties that are indeed pure white. Florentine iris is the true orris root of trade, although in practice all of the species noted here were often sold indiscriminately by this name. This is probably why the herbal took pains to describe their different virtues. Sauer's concern should be obvious when we come to the native American blue flag, which cannot be used in medicine like the European species.*

131. This is also known as tartar emetic. It consisted of calcined antimony combined with cream of tartar and dissolved in spirits of urine. The recipe most commonly cited is the one that appeared in Louis Lemery's *Dictionnaire ou traité universel des drogues simples.* Sauer owned the Amsterdam edition of 1716.

The American iris, known as Iris versicolor, *is indeed still listed in American pharmacopoeia. It is a wild iris, now rather rare, found mostly in swamps and bogs. It can be brought under cultivation in damp, heavy soils, especially those rich in humus. However, as a medical plant, it is far more potent than its European cousins, and even a small quantity of it can act as a powerful emetic. Of all the irises, this one in particular should be treated as a mild poison, since its dosages in the hands of amateurs may lead to deadly reactions.*

Blue flower de luce is of a warm, dry nature and contains large quantities of sharp, aromatic, volatile salts. Thus, it has the virtue of dissolving corrupt phlegm, of loosening constipation, of fortifying the stomach, of drawing out discharges from the chest (making breathing easier), of opening the womb and kidneys, and also of purging sand from the bladder. However, the root of the large yellow flag possesses even more astringent, salty matter than the rest of the iris tribe, particularly more than the renowned and much recommended Florentine iris. Yet both cleanse the body gently and purge it well of watery humors.

The Florentine variety is somewhat gentler in its strength and properties than elecampane. If one partakes too much of it, especially while fasting, a violetlike odor will arise from the urine. This iris is also useful for inducing sleep, especially when mixed with saffron. For children, it is effectual against nightmares. Additionally, when cut into tiny cubes, the root can be administered to children that they may chew on it to ease teething.

An excellent purgative wine can be prepared in the following manner: Take one loth of Florentine iris root, half a loth of tamarisk bark, and one loth each of agrimony, brown betony, scabious, holy thistle, centaury, and wormwood; half a loth of good rhubarb root, and a quint each of anise and fennel seed. Chop all of this coarsely and place it in a small, clean linen bag. Pour over this two quarts of well-aged white wine and let it infuse twenty-four hours. Then drink a gill of the decoction every morning before breakfast, repeating the dose every hour until sufficiently purged. This laxative purifies the body of all evil humors and relieves those with phlegmatic chests and lungs who are constantly coughing or who have difficulty breathing. This is a good remedy for the onset of dropsy, and it checks obstructions of the spleen and liver as well. The dosage can be repeated every day for five or six days, or even for a week.

For children whining from colic, a condition that can easily change to bloody flux, take a quint each of Margrave Powder[132] (if you do not know where to get it, it can be procured from the printer of this herbal) and ground Florentine iris root. Give a pinch of this to the child in its porridge morning and evening after gently patting it on the stomach.

The large blue iris or rush root, which inhabits this country, dug up fresh, cut into thin slices, and infused overnight in half a teacup of rum, is an excellent remedy for a cold or for quaking fevers, provided one intends to drink the infusion while fresh each

132. Johann Jacob Woyt provided a recipe for Margrave Powder under the Latin name *pulvis epilepticus marchionum.* It contained peony root, ground coral, and other ingredients considered efficacious against seizures. See Woyt's *Gazophylacium Medico-Physicum* (Leipzig, 1784), column 1896.

morning before breakfast. However, the stomach should first be purged with a good emetic. If the fever continues after the first application, then repeat the remedy several mornings in succession.

Ivy
Hedera helix
Sauer: *Epheu, Eppich* (1769)

> *This herb was highly esteemed by the Greeks and Romans, who used it to adorn their gardens, not to mention the religious applications. The wreaths of ivy discussed below, as worn by the followers of Bacchus, were thought to prevent intoxication from wine; indeed, the plant was dedicated to that god. The great age of ivy-based remedies may be attested to by the burn preparation made with butter. This appeared in the medieval English* Leechbook of Bald *as a cure for sunburn.*

Ivy possesses a concealed volatile, alkaline salt with some balsamic principals. From these derives its capacity to heal, to cool, to still the pain of burns, and to heal them.

To honor their idol Bacchus, the pagans made wreaths of ivy for the head. Thus, during the time of the Maccabees, when the festival of Bacchus was celebrated, the Jews were forced to join in the procession and wear the wreaths in Bacchus's honor, as can be read in the Second Book of Maccabees, chapter 6:7.

This herb is not too safe for internal use in people, for it awakens dysphoria in the head and is injurious to the nerves. But drinking vessels made of ivy wood are said to be extremely useful to those suffering from splenetic disorders.

The green leaves of ivy cooked in wine can cleanse and heal all manner of livid sores, provided they are frequently washed with this warm decoction and the leaves are laid upon the affected parts.

Some women make little hats of ivy leaves and put them on the heads of children afflicted with running sores from scall. Due to its alkaline sap and moisture, the ivy operates well on this condition by countering the sharp, salty humors flowing from the sores.

Ivy leaves can also be used quite effectively with fontanels, because they not only draw out all angry humors but also strengthen the opening and prevent anything injurious from getting into it. All the more so if instead of peas made from the leaves, little pellets of ivy wood are inserted into the fontanels.[133]

Fresh ivy leaves pounded to a pulp and fomented in fresh, unsalted butter, then worked through a cloth, will yield a handsome green salve that is good for all injuries caused by fire.

If a cow is sick and no one knows what ails it, take a handful each of ivy, ground ivy, rue, and wormwood, and cook this in one quart of water until reduced to one pint.

---

133. Fontanels are soft spots on a baby's skull or surgical openings made to drain humors from the body. Sauer is clearly discussing the latter. It was normal to insert "peas" of paper into the openings to keep them clean and to allow a free flow of matter. The medical effectiveness was furthered when these insertions were made from materials with healing properties, as in the case of ivy.

Pour the decoction down the cow's throat by means of a funnel or horn. This has often produced good results.

Jalap
Ipomoea purga
Sauer: *Jalape* (1767)

A native of tropical America, and a near relative of the sweet potato, jalap should not be confused with Ipomoea jalapa, *which produces a vine bearing a handsome ornamental flower. The sliced root was the part used for medicine. It was dried and ground to a powder, which is how it was generally sold in apothecaries. Ginger was often mixed with it to prevent gripping. A tincture prepared with brandy was also sold in the shops. The primary center of gathering and processing the root was Xalapa, Mexico, which gave its name to the medicine. Judging from Sauer's remark, we must assume that the jalap of commerce in colonial America came here directly through trade with Mexico or via Havana.*

Due to its numerous gums and caustic purging salts, jalap is an excellent medicine for operating against superfluous watery humors. The dosage is from twenty to forty grains, or more for those of stronger constitution. It is a valuable remedy for dropsy. Dr. Zwinger reported that he had helped various men and women afflicted with dropsy by administering a jalap purge repeated four or five times. It is also useful for cleansing the head and chest of quantities of phlegm, for operating upon the fluxes, and for curing the afflictions and diseases of the joints from which they arise.

Jalap root is from a plant that grows at Xalapa in New Spain. Since it is indispensable in apothecary shops, it must be imported.

Juniper
Juniperus communis
Sauer: *Wachholder* (1768)

While the herbal focuses on the common juniper of Europe, Sauer's readers were able to mentally substitute the native Juniperus virginiana, *since it could be employed in the same manner. Huge stands of this American species may still be found in south Jersey, and in a region stretching south from Lebanon County, Pennsylvania, into Virginia and the upper South. Indeed, the American species is very common, and since the berries ripen over a period of two to three years, there is a constant supply of both the green and fully ripe blue fruits.*

These berries were widely employed in cookery among the German settlers and in preparations for keeping food over the winter.

The juniper tree and its berries possess a mild, volatile, balsamic salt. By means of these, they have the faculty to dissolve all thick fluxes, to moderate all sharpness, to loosen blockages of small veins, to enlarge the lungs and vessels of the kidneys, to open clots in the small veins, to strengthen the nerves, to force urine, and to strengthen the vision.

Take juniper berries and crush them a little, pour white wine over them, and then drink the infusion according to need. This is an invaluable remedy for gravel, since it drives out small stones and sand without inconvenience.

For colic: Take ground juniper berries and a little sour sots,[134] moisten with luke-warm water or sugar dissolved in water, and then cover it and let it stand in a warm place until it has begun to work. Distill this in a pewter or copper alembic. First will come a spirit or refined fluid, followed by a water, and with the latter, a balsamic oil. Both are good preservatives against gravel and stone. They are also excellent for coughs, asthma, fluxes of the chest, colic, swelling of the spleen, and similar conditions. Of the spirit, administer one to two tablespoonfuls per dose, but of the oil, give only ten to twenty drops in wine or meat broth.

This oil is also used externally in stomach and colic salves, when mixed with nutmeg oil, oil of wormwood, fresh butter, and beeswax and then smeared over the belly. Instead of the distilled oil, it is possible to prepare another oil from pounded juniper berries, adding warm olive oil, and then pressing it. The expressed oil is then mixed with capon or goose fat and a little finely ground saffron. This is rubbed over the chest, and will loosen and ease coughing, and cause expectoration. It will prove quite serviceable to those who cannot take the medication internally, or who refuse to, as is often the case with children.

A few drops of the distilled oil of juniper put into the juice of violets, or administered alone, kills worms, and will provoke a powerful piss.

A lye from juniper ashes boiled down until it develops a skin on the surface, then stored in the cellar and allowed to precipitate, will yield a good salt that may be administered in one-half or full quint doses. It will absorb all phlegmy humors, open the vessels of the kidneys, and force out water that has been retained by the body. It also loosens up the matter that transforms itself into the grittiness in stones.

If the ashes of juniper wood are put into a clean linen cloth, and wine is allowed to run through it, this will yield a good wine for forcing sweat and urine, which also dissolves all the phlegmy humors retained in the body, and expels them in the manner just mentioned.

Shred juniper wood to a powder and chop it together with yellow amber, storax,

134. The German simply says *Sauerteig*. What is intended here is one of two things: either the actual liquid starter or liquid yeast, which contains flour; or the reserved crumbs of dough from the most recent baking, which are also dissolved in water or milk

lily-of-the-valley, cowslips, and the flowers of betony, sage, lavender, and rosemary, as well as red roses. Grind this to a coarse powder and sew it into the lining of a linen house cap. If this is worn on the head, it will get rid of headache, warm and strengthen a cold, rheumy brain, drive out the fluxes, and preserve the wearer from apoplexy.

The Laplanders boil juniper berries in water just as we prepare coffee or tea. They drink this for pleasure or as a preservative. It forces urine, and hinders that which collects and forms into stones and grit in the kidneys or bladder.

If one-half or a full dozen juniper berries are eaten every morning before breakfast, they will strengthen the stomach and in particular the vision, clearing it and maintaining it; indeed, it also keeps one from seeing spots dancing before the eyes. But this must be kept up the entire year. They purify the chest, still coughing, stop swelling of the stomach, upheavals of the matrix, and cramps, and open the liver and kidneys. They also force urine and expel the stone, and protect from poison and pestilence. If they are boiled in water and the hot steam is allowed to rise into the eyes, this will get rid of inflammation and red spots in the same, strengthen the eyelids, as well as disperse those painless little growths that develop on eyelids from time to time, including infected sties.

An excellent remedy for the stone: Take one loth of juniper berries, bruise them, and put them in a glass vessel. Pour brandy over them so that they are evenly covered. Stop up the vessel and let it stand four days. Stir from time to time, then strain off the brandy. Press the berries well, and pour this again over the same amount of freshly bruised berries. Let this infuse again as before, then repeat for the third time. Strain and store away for use. To loosen up a stone, take one spoonful of this brandy, then sit in a loin bath in which a few handfuls of marshmallow, mallow, chamomile flowers, and flax seeds have been boiled. Sit in this from one-half to a full hour, and repeat this treatment several times. Do not sit in the loin bath soon after eating or in cases of constipation.

Where pestilence is raging, employ juniper wood and berries often in all fumigations of the house chambers where one lives. Also, according to one's inclination, chew the berries often.

If the distilled water of juniper berries is taken in a tablespoonful dose in the morning before breakfast, it will prove good for a cold stomach, and stop and disperse vapors and colic. This water is also used for gravel, for promoting urine, and for purifying the kidneys and bladder.

To warm and strengthen cold limbs: Take a generous handful of well-bruised juniper berries, a handful of lily-of-the-valley and lavender flowers, half a handful of marjoram and the flowers of rosemary, a tablespoonful of ground black pepper, and mix all of this together in a glass vessel. Pour one pound of double-rectified brandy over this and stop it up well. Let this stand in a warm place, then wash the affected limbs with it often.

King's Spear
Asphodelus ramosus
Sauer: *Afodillwurz* (1774)

The older name for this herb, Asphodelus, was corrupted in English into daffodil. Asphodel was a flower of the dead among the ancients, but it was not the daffodil of modern horticulture. The true asphodel is a tall, white, spiky flower that grows wild in many parts of the Mediterranean. A species from Sicily is yellow. The root of this plant is a source of starch that was used by ancient Greek and Roman cooks for starching the paper-thin tracta dough used in their pastries. It was also employed as a thickener like cornstarch during the Middle Ages, since it was allowed in meatless cookery. The boiled root yields a glutinous mass that can be used to make glue or even mixed with coarse flours for bread. Since Sauer does not mention uses of the live plant, we must assume that this was a stock item in his shop, but that it was probably imported in dry form.

Asphodel or goldwort is warm and dry and is endowed with a sharp, aromatic salt in its sap. From this derives its faculty to warm, to dry, to open, and to operate by the kidneys and salivary glands.

If asphodel root is boiled in wine and the decoction drunk thus, it will promote urine and other things.[135] It is good for convulsions, heals hernias, and eases pain from lumbago. It is also helpful against jaundice and the onset of dropsy.

When the root is burnt to ash, and mixed with honey to make a salve for the head, it will cause lost hair to grow back. Therefore, if the root is also boiled in lye with southernwood, and the head washed with this, it will prevent hair loss.

Asphodel powder and calcined alum, each mixed with an equal weight of honey, will heal leprous sores. (It may also be tried on scall.)

A fumigation made with this root will get rid of mice.

Larkspur
Delphinium consolida
Sauer: *Ritterspohren* (1766)

It is easy for larkspur to take over the garden, but the flowers are so cheering, and the colors so varied—especially the intense blues—that I often let them grow where they will. This is not the orderly sort of method proposed in Zwinger's herbal, but it is a good way to fill voids in the garden before the summer flowers come on. Unfortunately, larkspur contains toxins that will act as irritants to the skin of some people, and if eaten in even a moderate amount, the likely result will be violent vomiting. This is especially true of the seeds when they are ingested by small children. So it is somewhat surprising to see larkspur employed in the internal remedies suggested by Sauer, no matter how small the doses.

---

135. Sauer would not print the word, but in this case the "other things" were menses.

Larkspur is of a middling nature and is for this reason employed in both hot and cold illnesses. It possesses the faculty to open, to ease, to sweeten sharp sour humors, to strengthen the brain and nerves, to open blockages, to operate through the urine, and to kill worms.

If larkspur is boiled in wine and a glass of this is drunk in the morning and evening, it will open blockages of the spleen, purify the kidneys and bladder, expel retained urine, take out sand and gravel, improve dimness of vision, and kill worms.

Surgeons employ larkspur in their vulnerary potions as well, for it is a very healing plant.

The distilled water of larkspur is good for colic and iliac passion when taken in four- or five-loth doses. Young children should be given only one spoonful. It is also good for the gripes and fits, and when rock candy is added, it is good for coughs. When the eyes are rinsed with it, or when a cloth dipped into it is bound over the eyes for the night, it will take away redness and strengthen eyesight.

A sugar or conserve may be prepared from larkspur flowers in the same manner as marjoram sugar.[136] It is a proven remedy for heartburn when taken in doses the size of a nutmeg each time. It is also effective for gripes in young children, as well as iliac passion, if they are given a pinch of the sugar often.

When the seeds of larkspur are finely ground and infused in vinegar, this will kill lice on the head. Or, a comb may be dipped in it and the hair combed with the vinegar so that it wets the scalp.

The dried or fresh flowers of larkspur brewed in boiling water like tea, and then sweetened with sugar, will stay puking in small children when given to them to drink.

Lavender
Lavandula vera
Sauer: *Lavendel* (1773)

Theodor Zwinger designated this herb by the name Lavandula officinalis, *yet it is obvious from his botany that several lavender species were included. Today, lavenders are divided up rather differently. The one that Sauer had to contend with was a lavender brought here from England, which is why his herbal treated spikenard separately (page 305). English lavender does very well in Pennsylvania, and it is apparent that there were people during the colonial period engaged in distilling it.*

Thomas Nixon, a shopkeeper in Strawberry Alley, Philadelphia, advertised the "best spirit of lavender" by the quart, pint, and half pint in the Pennsylvania Gazette *for June 20, 1745—just about the time of year one would be harvesting the flowers.*

Lavender waters were not only important to physicians, they were crucial to bread bakers as well. This was particularly true of the German bakers, who added it to the slurry when setting sponge for bread. The purpose was to keep the bread from becoming moldy after it was baked. Jacob Biernauer published directions for this old-fashioned

136. Sauer provides an excellent working recipe under marjoram.

baker's trick years later in 1818: "Take a nut shell full of lavender water and add it to the water that you mix with flour when baking bread. If you bake the bread with it, the bread will not become moldy for as long as you want to keep it."[137]

Lavender, which possesses a faculty similar to spikenard and belongs to the same tribe, possesses a mild, aromatic, or oily volatile salt. From this derives its ability to strengthen the head, to control fluxes, to prevent apoplexy, and to strengthen the matrix and fetus.

Lavender and spikenard are two of the most valuable herbs for treating all cold distempers of the brain and nerves, such as dizziness, full and partial apoplexy, the falling evil, lethargy, convulsions, palsy, and numbness. They warm a cold feeble stomach, disperse vapors, force urine and other things as well. They also warm the matrix, open blockages of the liver and spleen, and get rid of jaundice, and the onset of dropsy. For all of these listed afflictions, boil a handful of lavender leaves and flowers in two quarts of white wine or water. Drink a few tumblers of this every day.

For difficult delivery: Take half a quint of lavender seeds, forty grains each of white amber and borax, and three drops of cinnamon oil. Grind this to a fine powder and divide it into three equal parts. Administer three times in white wine.

A good *lixivium* for cold distempers of the head: Take a handful each of lavender, rosemary, sage, chamomile, betony, red roses, and daisies. After they are all chopped together coarsely, put them into a sachet and lay the sachet in lye.

Agerius[138] has written about the special virtues of distilled lavender flower water: it is a good medicine for the elderly. It strengthens cold, rheumy heads, strengthens and warms the nerves, and dispels dizziness. A few tablespoonfuls should be taken in the evening and morning. When poured down the throat, it is also a valuable remedy for aged people in treating apoplexy, convulsions, and paralysis, both for those who are already afflicted or those who may be so inclined. For those who may have injured their tongues during such attacks so that speech is hindered, administer a tablespoonful of this water from time to time and have them hold it a while in the mouth. In this same manner it will often still toothache arising from cold fluxes. It also gives the mouth a pleasant odor, dries spongy gums, and reanchors the teeth.

If a few tablespoonfuls of lavender water are taken, this will prove effective against chilling of the stomach and all internal members. It will warm the liver, spleen, loins, and kidneys, as well as the urinary tract and the bladder. Furthermore, it opens and purifies them from cold phlegmy humors, forces urine, and promotes other things even more.[139] It is also good for barrenness in women.

Should anyone fall into a faint or be seized by weakness, swab their temples and nostrils with lavender water, for it will strengthen the heart and restore the spirits, and then administer a spoonful of it. Externally, if limbs have been lamed by apoplexy, the water can be rubbed over them warm, for it will strengthen these limbs greatly,

137. Jacob Biernauer, *Unentbehrliches Haus- und Kunst-Buch* (Reading, Pa., 1818), 28.
138. Nicolaus Agerius (b. 1568) was a German physician and author of several books on medicine.
139. The context suggests that this is also good for male potency, a fact confirmed by other herbals.

but particularly if sage water and juniper brandy are mixed warm in equal parts and the lame limbs are also washed with this mixture a few times each day.

An excellent oil can also be distilled from lavender. If it is swabbed on the crown of the head daily, it will prevent apoplexy, disperse rheums of the head, and get rid of dizziness, headache, and toothache. Yes, it will even kill or chase off lice in old and young alike.

Lavender can also be used with other cephalic herbs in baths for strengthening the limbs and nerves.

If lavender leaves and flowers are chewed, like other aromatic remedies, they will create a large amount of spittle and thus prove beneficial to those afflicted by cold fluxes, lethargy, lameness of the tongue, and similar conditions.

When lavender flowers are put in good-quality vinegar and then this is allowed to stand in the sun or on top of a warm stove, it will yield an excellent lavender vinegar for swabbing the face during weak spells or fainting, for headache, inflamed toothache, and for other distempers of the head.

Lemons, Limes, and Oranges
Citrus sp.
Sauer: *Limonen* (1774)

Genetic analysis of lemons, limes, and oranges has revealed that they are all natural hybrids of a common parent and therefore not strictly separate species. Lemon, for example, was once written Citrus pyriformis. *Today it is written* Citrus x limon. *This fact was not known to the learned world of Sauer's era, yet in an odd way, these fruits were often lumped together as though indeed they were half-brothers or -sisters. The reason for mentioning this is clear when the subject of limes is brought up.*

I have taken the liberty to insert limes into this entry of the herbal for one very important reason. The eighteenth-century mind did not often separate limes from lemons; they were viewed as different forms of the same thing. When limes ripen, they develop yellow skins; thus they turn into a type of fragrant lemon. In 1784, Johann Jacob Woyt made this interesting scientific distinction: lemon varieties were distinguished only by size and taste. Ripe lemons candied or preserved in syrup were called cit-ronat *because they imitated citron; unripe (green) lemons pickled in brine were called limes* (mala limonia). *The same word, Limonen, was used for both. This lack of distinction appears to have been customary among a large portion of colonial America's English-speaking population as well, so is it difficult to know from any given reference which types of fruit are being discussed. This means that everywhere Sauer uses the word lemon, it is also possible to read lime, or at least, ripe lime.*

Where the record is clear is in such advertisements as that by the Philadelphia French grocer M. Chevalier, who offered for sale fresh Portuguese lemons in Der Wöchentliche Philadelphische Staatsbothe *for March 28, 1763. This was an imported luxury fruit, and trade in such Portuguese or Spanish lemons was brisk during the eighteenth century. At the other end of the economic scale were the wild limes readily available in the Caribbean, a poverty food where they grew naturally and an acquired taste elsewhere. Their popularity in punch in the islands eventually brought them into fashion in American port cities, but limes as such are rarely mentioned in sales notices because, like strawberries, mangoes, bananas, and other foods brought in from the West Indies, they were not high-end in value.*

Oranges, however, were at the very top of the list, along with pineapples, because both carried considerable status. Some wealthy Americans maintained orangeries in which various kinds of lemons and oranges could be grown, but this had little effect on the marketplace, which is where Sauer's readers would have had to forage for this fruit. Yet we do know that a number of German farmers grew citrus trees in tubs and that these trees often supplied the neighborhood during medical emergencies. One late example from the July 5, 1819, issue of Poulson's American Daily Advertiser *is worth noting: a farmer in Lower Saucon Township of Northampton County, Pennsylvania, reported growing huge lemons on a potted tree. One of the fruits measured nine and a half inches in diameter and ten and a half inches from stem to blossom end. This is the earliest reference on record to the variety of lemon now known as Meyers.*

The recipes discussed by Sauer were not as difficult for country people to make as might be imagined, because even if there were no potted lemon tree in the neighborhood, the fruit and the juice could be bought readily from most local taverns where punch was served. Sauer's negative stance against this definitely upper-class, male-dominated drinking custom was in keeping with his Dunkard upbringing and pervasive suspicion of anything smacking of worldliness (medical arguments aside). His recommendation of the nonalcoholic beverage made with lemon juice, water, and sugar is one of the earliest American recipes for lemonade.

Lemons share with citrons a great similarity in their virtues, more so when they are fully ripe. They can be used quite effectively for fevers when cut into thin slices, sprinkled with sugar, and eaten according to want. They cool and refresh a hot mouth and stomach, quell hefty coursings of the blood, subdue bile, and quench thirst.

As with citrons, a syrup can be prepared with sugar and lemons. It also has the same curative properties. This syrup is credited with killing worms in the stomach, and with attacking sand and stones and driving them out. It strengthens the heart and dispels tremblings of the same.

When one writes on paper with lemon juice, nothing can be seen on the paper until it is held near a fire and the paper is allowed to turn a bit golden brown. Then the letters become visible.

Lemon juice, or sliced pieces of lemon, put into fresh water and sweetened with sugar to taste, makes a pleasant and healthy beverage for all ardent fevers, for contagious diseases in general, and particularly for those afflicted by gall bladder troubles and who, due to the dryness in their mouth, detect a bitter taste.

Just as the juice or inner fruit of the lemon and citron are healthy for fevers, contagious diseases, and the like, they are equally unhealthy and injurious to the healthy in the unceasing imbibing of punch.[140] Punch puts the circulation of the blood in too slow a motion when there is no heat, and through such inefficaciousness, the natural evaporation of its humors is hindered. The blood then becomes thick and sharp, and from this arise rheumatism or flying gout, gout, stones, colic, and similar vexing evils. And those who do not know how to curtail their pleasure are verily made to pay the price for it.

Thus, both of the above-described fruits make choice medicine, and an assured remedy against bilious contagious fevers and the like, for those who are afflicted with sundry feverish maladies, and yet a poison for both healthy and cold feeble stomachs, and the source of many painful afflictions, especially when partaken day to day or continuously.

Oranges, on the other hand, possess in their sundry parts a curative power similar to lemons and citrons, although to a more moderate degree. The juice is not as cooling because is it not as sour. It does not take off bile as well as the others, but it does strengthen the heart and stomach very much. And since they are not as cooling, and not as strong in their properties against feverish illnesses, oranges are therefore not as deleterious. Thus, they can be enjoyed as a comforting fortifier of the heart and stomach during various illnesses without fear of injury. The healthy of course enjoy them the most.

Lemon Balm
Melissa officinalis
Sauer: *Melisse* (1762)

This is an excellent herb to keep in the garden, for it is free of pests and will adapt well to a shady corner away from the mints. It is good for summer teas, and the infusion in white wine, as suggested by Sauer, changes the wine in an interesting and refreshing way. The taste is no longer suggestive of lemons, but of pears, and more of the pear skin than the sweet flesh. The overall effect is dry and perhaps medicinal, although the infusion could easily be used like dry white vermouth with a twist of lemon to start a meal. This is a far cry from the manner in which the Sauer herbal originally intended it to be used, but it is one of those herbs that invites trial. The lemon balsam cakes (which are really little pancakes) are delightful, and can be eaten with a salty cheese.

Lemon balm is one of the most splendid of the herbs, full as it is with the purest, sweetest, volatile, oily, aromatic

140. Punch derives from an Indian word *panch*, meaning "five." This refers to the five basic ingredients: arrack, water, sugar, lemon juice, and tea. The variations on this were many. In colonial America, the normal choice of ingredients included rum and/or brandy, water, sugar, lemon or lime juice, and green tea. Mint or sliced cucumbers were also sometimes added; juniper berries were preferred by the Germans. Well-made punch was clear and strained of all sediment or particles of tea and fruit.

spirit of salt. From this it derives its unrivaled capacity to warm and to dry, to strengthen the head, heart, stomach, and matrix, and to revive and enliven the vital spirits. It can also stop pain, absorb fluxes, and thin and dissolve tough phlegm in every part of the body, as well as open blockages of the spleen and matrix, stay windiness and vapors, and *****[141] The herb must be gathered in June and July, when the moon is in the sign of Taurus or Leo. Only the leaves are the part used.

Lemon balm is particularly efficacious for maladies of the head, heart, stomach, and matrix. This herb has stilled mother fits in many women simply when they smelled it. It can also be employed effectively in apoplexy, the falling evil, and dizziness. If a handful of lemon balm is put into a quart of white wine and the infusion drunk, it will prove good for all the above-mentioned afflictions. In many places, the women are accustomed to bake little cakes containing lemon balm for weak mothers who have just delivered. For these cakes, only the tender young shoots are chosen, then pulped and baked with eggs and sugar.[142]

If the leaves of lemon balm and chamomile flowers are fomented in wine, pressed between two plates, then laid warm upon the lower abdomen, they will stop mother fits very quickly.

When lemon balm is put into lye and the hair washed with it, it will preserve the natural color so that the hair does not turn gray as quickly as it would otherwise.

If beehives are rubbed with lemon balm, the bees will not abandon them.

If a few tablespoons are taken frequently, the distilled water of lemon balm will strengthen a cold, weak head, prove efficacious in treating dizziness and apoplexy, check swooning, allay the gripes, and will benefit a matrix that has grown cold. Indeed, it is also good for treating melancholy.

The conserve of lemon balm or lemon balm sugar is prepared in the very same manner as described under scurvy grass. It is supremely suitable for melancholic persons, for it dispels gloomy thoughts, fortifies a feeble heart, stays colic, and eases a cold head, stomach, and matrix, provided it is taken frequently in nutmeg-size doses.

Lentils
Lens culinaris
Sauer: *Linsen* (1778)

If we are to judge by the herbal's remarks below, lentil lovers may suffer dreadful consequences from their culinary inclination. Personally speaking, I not only eat lentils often, I grow them, and they have not dimmed my eyesight, "learned opinion" aside. Nor have I developed leprosy. Yet buried somewhere in these beliefs may be a thread of truth, since a heavy dietary dependence on lentils can result in lathrysm, a condition

---

141. Sauer intentionally left out a word that he considered offensive. Other herbals mention lemon balm in connection with bringing down the menses; this is probably what Sauer left out, given the reference to mother fits in the very next paragraph.

142. There were two sorts. One type was made with egg whites alone and resembled a crisp meringue, the other employed the yolks and resembled a small omelet or pancake. Both were sweet. They were also given to children recovering from illnesses and elderly persons too weak to eat heavy food.

that leads to partial or full paralysis. Lathrysm develops when the diet consists of 35 to 50 percent lentils; thus, it is more common among the desperately poor. Be that as it may, lentils were raised and consumed by the colonial Germans in quantities. They were primarily eaten during the winter, either in soups or in porridges of mixed ingredients, such as boiled grain or chickpeas. The most common method was to puree them, as in the following recipe from the Vollständiges Nürnbergisches Koch-Buch *(Nuremberg, 1691):*

> *Set the lentils in water and let them cook until soft. Force them through a sieve or strainer, then continue cooking. Add a little browned flour and pepper. Thereupon, chop rye bread and fry it in lard. Pour the boiling soup over this, and set over hot coals. Let it boil up again and just before taking it to the table, fry some chopped onions in lard and turn them out over the top.(44)*

This was the typical farmhouse method of preparation, for the list of ingredients is extremely short: water, lentils, browned flour, pepper, rye bread, lard, onions.

At the other end of the scale stands Johann Christian Wolf's recipe for lentil soup (he called it a coulis*), which appeared in his* Neues Leipziger Koch-Buch *(Frankfurt/Leipzig, 1779).*

> *Once the lentils are thoroughly cooked, take chopped onions, carrots, lemon peels, a little rosemary, bay leaf, thyme and minced ham. Sauté this in butter. Then combine with the lentils and a little water in a stewing pan. Cover and let this cook gently for one hour. Then rub the mixture through a hair sieve. Slice some dinner rolls and brown them in butter. Then it is tasty. Instead of ham, you can also serve up smoked eel or smoked salmon in the same manner.(22)*

The central idea in both cases was to pour the puree over the fried bread. Whether cooks followed the exact order of ingredients was of course a matter of taste and economic choice (naturally in rural households, the lemon, rosemary, and bay leaves would probably be left out). But the basic concept of cooking, pureeing, and serving the lentils over bread was indeed a common colonial German treatment. However, the medical dimension of lentils lay in what Sauer called the "first water" (erste Brühe). This was the initial cooking liquid poured off after the lentils were tender.

Lentils are middling between hot and cold, and thus dry only to a small degree. Like the other hulled grains discussed in this herbal, lentils are similarly endowed with many volatile salts. However, they are coarse and oily.

Lentils boiled and eaten in their cooking liquid will emolliate a stiff gut. But if the cooking liquid is saved and prepared with other broths, it will cause constipation. Lentils are thus a useful food for those afflicted with fluxes of the stomach and bloody flux.

If the cooking liquid of lentils is drunk, it will drive out worms in children.

Learned opinion is quite unanimous in allowing that those who partake of lentils too much will develop darkened eyesight, damage the stomach, bloat the gut, suffer from tormented dreams, and develop thick blood. Indeed, this may also lead to leprosy and cancerous sores.

Lesser Scabious (Scabious)

Scabiosa columbaria
Sauer: *Scabiosen* (1770)

The Sauer herbal is consistently vague about what is meant by scabious. First, there is field scabious (Knautia arvensis). *Then there is devils's bit* (Scabiosa succisa), *which is discussed separately on page 124. Finally, there is lesser scabious, the small plant discussed here. However, both field scabious and lesser scabious can be used in the same way in remedies, so it is evident from this that Sauer pragmatically meant both plants when he wrote* scabiosen *in German. Only the field scabious is naturalized in this country, and it was probably not introduced as a garden plant, but something that came in with grain or seeds for meadow grasses.*

Scabious possesses the faculty to warm and to dry. It expels through sweat, withstands all poison, opens, cleanses, and heals wounds and sores, and dissolves phlegm in the chest and promotes its expectoration. The herb is gathered at the end of May about the time of the full moon.

This plant is praised for treating many internal and external afflictions. It is used these days primarily for the chest and lungs, purifying them of all phlegm, softening and dispersing sores and internal apostemes of the chest. For these conditions, the following potion is very useful: Take one-half loth of shaved licorice root, five red Assyrian plums, three fresh figs, a handful each of scabious and rose hips, and a quint of aniseeds. Chop it all together and boil it in one gallon of water for as long as it takes to hard-cook an egg. Then add four loths of sugar. The patient may drink this according to want and take it instead of a fine ordinary beverage. It will take away severe and disturbing coughs, open the chest, and make breathing easy. It will disperse all internal tough phlegm in the chest and lungs, the bosoms and sides, and ease expectoration.

The root of scabious hung around the neck of children will prevent the purples from injuring their eyes.

When scabious is laid in lye and this is then used to wash the head, it will get rid of mites in the hair.

A good salve for scall: Take four loths of scabious juice and three loths of oil of sweet bay, and let this simmer together over a gentle heat until the juice has evaporated. Then press the mixture through a cloth and add a quint each of pure powdered brimstone and silver earth. Swab this salve on the place where the itch or scall has broken out.

For fistulas, old weeping sores, or cancerous injuries, the following vulnerary potion is quite effective: Take two loths of scabious root, one loth of avens root, half a loth of celandine root, two handfuls of scabious leaves, and a handful each of speed-well, agrimony, and sanicle. Chop it all together and put it in a new earthenware pot or stoneware jug. Pour over it one gallon of wine and two quarts of water. Cover the pot or jug tightly and stand it in a kettle of boiling water. Let this simmer for four hours, then take it out and let it cool while still tightly covered so that the contents cannot evaporate. Then strain off the potion and run it through a clean cloth. Store in a cool place and administer about half a pint to the patient every morning and evening.

The distilled water of scabious is very good for coughs, sores in the chest, and pleurisy. It will purify the chest and lungs of all phlegm and pus when taken often in four- or five-tablespoon doses. It cleanses the blood of all impurities, for which reason it is quite useful to those who are inclined toward leprosy or who are afflicted with the French pox. It will gently get rid of the purples and measles in children, provoke a mild sweat, and strengthen the heart against miasmas.

If a quint of the best-quality *Theriaca Andromaci* is taken in scabious water, it will prove excellent against the plague if the patient is made to sweat it out.

A quint of crab's eyes taken in scabious water a few times is good against pleurisy and sores of the chest.

Scabious water is a good healing remedy for wounds, injuries, and open sores in the privates of man and woman if a small cloth is dipped in it and laid warm over the hurt.

The scabious syrup and the conserve made of the flowers as prepared in apothecary shops can be used to good effect on all of the afflictions enumerated above.

Licorice
Glycyrrhiza glabra
Sauer: *Süssholz* (1772)

The ancient Romans called it radix dulcis, *"sweet root." The German name means "sweet wood," yet anyone who grows this herb will readily attest that the leaves smell like burning rubber. It is also an invasive plant with roots that spread in a ropy network underground. The root is the part used to make both the medicines and the candy. It was largely imported in the dry state. There is a native American licorice* (Glycyrrhiza lepidota), *but it is found primarily in the upper Midwest and Canada and was therefore not known, or at least not employed, during Sauer's era.*

Licorice is of a middling nature. It possesses a very sweet taste, and is endowed with volatile, alkaline salts. Thus it has the faculty to ease, to dissolve, to sweeten all sharp phlegmy matter and salty fluxes of the throat, chest, and kidneys. It also drives down sand and mucusy corruptions through the urine.

If a half-ounce of licorice root is chopped fine or grated, and boiled in four quarts of water for as long as it takes to hard-cook an egg, then drunk as needed according to thirst, this will ease a raw throat, stay coughing, dissolve tough phlegm in the chest, and modify the burning sharpness in urine.

A potion for the chest, for easing sharp coughs, and for freeing the chest of hard phlegm is prepared in the following manner: Take half a loth each of grated licorice root, nice figs and raisins, a half loth each of anise and fennel seeds, and pound and chop it all together. Bind it up loosely in a little piece of cloth and boil it in four quarts of water for as long as it takes to hard-cook an egg. Let the patient drink this according to thirst.

For those who want barley water for quenching the thirst, take a handful of barley, two loths of raisins, half a loth of licorice, and a quint each of anise and fennel seeds, and chop it all fine. Bind it up in a small piece of cloth and boil it in four quarts of water for as long as it takes to hard-cook an egg. Drink this when thirsty.

For those who have gotten Saint Anthony's fire, take dried licorice root and grind it to a fine powder. Sprinkle this over the sores. Some red bolus and a little camphor can also be mixed with this.[143]

It goes without saying that licorice is an excellent remedy for the chest, lungs, wheezing, asthma, lumbago, inflammation of the lungs, consumption, hoarseness, and raw throat. It dissipates, thins, purifies, eases, moderates, and moistens. Because it warms the stomach gently, it promotes digestion and strengthens the stomach, for it possesses a gentle astringency. Because it opens the liver, it cleanses and dissipates the tough humors. It affects the kidneys and bladder likewise due to the virtues listed above, and because it eases the cutting heat of burning urine.

When half a loth of grated licorice is boiled in a pint of wine with half a handful of linden blossoms, and the mouth is rinsed with this often, it will frequently stop toothache.

Licorice sap is very useful for coughs, asthma, raw throat, and other afflictions of the chest, if a hazelnut-size dose is taken in the mouth often and allowed to dissolve there gradually so that the melting sap may be swallowed.

Lignum Vitae (Guaiacum)
Guaiacum officinale
Sauer: *Französenholz* (1776)

This tree was first described in 1628 by Spanish botanist Francisco Hernandez and is native to both the West Indies and parts of South America. The wood was one of the products of commerce brought to Philadelphia from the Caribbean. Most of the lignum vitae sold here came from Santo Domingo, Haiti, and Jamaica. The use of the wood in medicine was quite popular in the seventeenth century, but by Sauer's era it was generally replaced by the resin. In this respect, the remedies below are somewhat old-fashioned. Since the wood and resin turn green on exposure to air and light, both produces were sold in black glass bottles. A related tree, the Guaiacum sanctum, *was also harvested for similar purposes. It was imported mostly from Saint Croix and Saint Benedict.*

---

143. Red bolus is a pill made from one of several types of greasy red clay. The red *terra sigillata* of Rheinfelden is a possibility here, although *bole armeniac* appears elsewhere in the herbal, and it too is red.

Lignum vitae is endowed with numerous oily, resinous elements together with an acidic volatile spirituous salt. It has the capacity to operate by urine and sweat powerfully, to dry up fluxes and wateriness, to free the blood of an overplus of injurious salts, and to resist all putrefaction. It is employed in treating jaundice, dropsy, all manner of fluxes, and in particular venereal diseases. For these, not only the wood but also the bark and resin are made use of.

For sundry eruptions of the skin or for old sores of long continuance that will not heal, or for the French pox, there is a potion, which is also an excellent purifier of the blood, which can be made in the following manner: Take eight ounces of chipped lignum vitae, two ounces of Chinese smilax (for those who do not have this, use as much dried burdock root instead), two ounces of the bark of sassafras root, three loths each of finely powdered antimony and Zante currants, and one ounce of fennel seed. Chop it all up fairly small and then boil it in one gallon of water in a well-covered vessel that has been set into another vessel of boiling water. Let this boil a few hours, then strain it off and administer a gill of the decoction each morning and evening. A gallon of water can be poured over the chips of wood that remain from this, boiled up a bit, and employed as a common drink for quenching thirst.

Drinks made with lignum vitae are also very good for coughs, consumption, and similar afflictions of the chest. This treatment is particularly good for gout, flying gout, scurvy, the falling evil, fits, and dropsy, as well as for the itch and other outbreaks of the skin. Such a treatment may be made in the following manner: Take one ounce each of round birthwort root and elecampane root, three ounces each of lignum vitae and sassafras, half a handful each of hyssop and speedwell, one handful of wormwood, and one ounce of fennel seed. Chop it all up and boil for one hour in two gallons of water. Strain and administer one gill to the patient each morning and evening.

Lily of the Valley
Convallaria majalis
Sauer: *Mayenblümlein* (1774)

> *It is a pity this fragrant flower so popular with brides is also quite poisonous. However, the toxins, in small doses, were once used in medical remedies. There were both pink- and white-flowering varieties known in Sauer's day, and both were cultivated in colonial America. The pink one has even naturalized in parts of southeastern Pennsylvania. However, the most interesting material here is Sauer's instruction for distilling lily of the valley. His description of the process is rather explicit and paints a relatively clear picture of how the other herbal waters mentioned in the herbal were prepared.*

Lilies of the valley possess a volatile, sour salt mixed with somewhat oily balsamic elements, which give it a bitter acidity. From this derives its capacity to dry, to warm gently, to strengthen the head and nerves, to thin thick humors on the brain, oftentimes opening up blockages of the same. If used externally, it will cause sneezing. The flowers employed in medicine must be gathered in May about the time of the full moon, early in the morning while still covered with dew. The roots are rarely collected, but will also cause sneezing. Nothing else of the plant is used.

For the pain of gout: Take fresh lilies of the valley and fill a clean vessel with the flowers. Seal it well, then bury it for a month in an anthill, after which a thick juice similar to an oil will be found. Rub it over the gouty limbs. It is also useful for treating iliac passion or colic in children, if it is rubbed warm over their bellies. Furthermore, it is good for treating the early stages of leprosy if the afflicted limbs are swabbed with it.

The distilled water of lilies of the valley, taken in one- or two-spoonful doses, will strengthen a weak head and heart, promote difficult delivery, withstand the falling evil, apoplexy, and dizziness, and restore lost speech. Those small children who are plagued by fits, colic, and worms should be given a tablespoonful from time to time.

The sugar of lilies of the valley is prepared like rose sugar. It strengthens a weak heart, turns back fainting spells, and is beneficial to a feeble head. It is also good for those who have come down with the falling evil, or who are worried about apoplexy, if it is taken in doses the size of a nutmeg as wanted.

A useful and fine spirit can be distilled from the fermented or soured flowers in the following manner: Fill a glass alembic with lily-of-the-valley blossoms covered with fresh morning dew, and if desired, a little sourdough sots may be added. Close the glass up tightly and set it for six weeks or two months in the cellar so that it ferments normally. Then distill it into a sand-cupel from the alembic. This will yield an excellent spirit that is extremely good for treating apoplexy, lameness of the limbs, dizziness, fits, the falling evil, and hypochondria.

During this distillation, the first waters to condense are trifling and normally thrown away, but the spirit that follows is especially valued. If it is rectified again, the inherent volatile salts will go off and collect on the sides of the glass. After this comes a very smooth, fine spirit that, as well as the salts, can be stored away for future use. Administer the spirit in fifteen- to twenty-drop doses each time. The spirit can also be used for external treatments.

Linden Tree (Lime Tree)
Tilia cordata, Tilia europaea
Sauer: *Lindenbaum* (1775)

The linden or European lime tree is not native but was introduced here early in the eighteenth century, for the American basswood, although related, does not contain the same medical properties. I well remember two very ancient lindens planted by the old Heinrich Weber house near Blue Ball in Lancaster County, Pennsylvania. They towered over the house and must have been planted there in the 1760s when it was built. Such trees rarely last that long, for linden makes excellent furniture. In any case, the dried flowers and powdered berries were imported. The herbal even refers to the equally valuable mistletoe that grew on it, which was important for making a Geist *or spirit employed in medicine. The tisane or tea brewed from aged, dried flowers is narcotic and will even produce a high, a property useful in anodyne treatments.*

In Europe, linden sap was harvested in the spring and boiled down to make sugar or an electuary that was highly prized during the Middle Ages, especially when combined with linden blossom honey.

The linden tree is of a warm and dry nature and possesses a sulfurous spirit combined with temperate sour, volatile salts in its flowers and other parts. Thus it has the capacity to strengthen the head and nerves, to purify the blood, to sweeten all sour, sharp humors, to control apoplexy and fits, to contain the irregular coursings of the bodily spirits, and to still pain in the limbs. The mistletoe of the linden possesses the same virtues as the tree. If the berries are allowed to ferment alone or along with the flowers, and then distilled, it is possible to obtain a rectified spirit.

The distilled water of linden blossoms, taken in spoonful doses, is highly praised for treating the falling evil, convulsions, dizziness, and other cold distempers of the head. It is also good for colic, and will benefit injured bowels following bloody flux. If someone has been struck by convulsions, administer often a spoonful of linden blossom water, lily-of-the-valley water, and black cherry water mixed together. When young children are afflicted with the fits, give them often a tablespoon dose of one part peony water and one part linden blossom water. Linden blossom water is also used by women to remove spots on the face. It will also heal blisters in the throat and a scurvied mouth.

If young children develop a large, bloated belly (which is commonly called cardialgy), they should be administered a tablespoonful of linden blossom water from time to time. A mucilaginous juice can be extracted from the inner bark of the linden tree when it is infused in plantain water or springwater. It makes an excellent salve for burns. The sap that flows out of wounds in the bark will make hair grow back when a bald spot is moistened with it.

The powdered seeds or berries of the linden are praised for treating diarrhea and similar fluxes of the belly, for which reason this powder was at one time kept on hand by military people. If some of the seeds are swallowed, they will still a nosebleed. They can also be ground with vinegar and stuck into the nose.

To prevent a horse from dying: Take mushrooms that grow on and about the base of linden trees and lay them in water.[144] Let the horse drink this and a contagious disease will not easily hurt him.

The mistletoe berries of the linden dried and ground to a powder are good for fits and the falling evil. Children should be given about twenty grains per dose, while adults should be given up to sixty grains often.

If linden leaves are boiled in water or milk, and a cloth is dipped in it and laid warm over the arse, it will stop looseness.

144. The text says mushrooms, but the fungus intended is really a tree fungus growing out of the bark.

Liverwort

Peligera canina
Sauer: *Leberkraut* (1773)

*The liverwort of Europe is a lichen that grows flat against the ground with odd-look-
ing, overlapping leaves. It is often found on mud banks and in wet, shady spots, doubtless the reason it was assigned a cold temperament by the old herbalists. The lichen was
gathered from the wild and dried. It was then sold by apothecary shops either as whole
leaves or as a powder. Both forms are mentioned in Sauer's herbal, and both were
imported from Europe, for the lichen is not native even though there are several species
similar to it. Nicholas Culpeper remarked that liverwort "fortifieth the liver exceedingly and makes it impregnable." It was therefore one of the key herbs in controlling
humors in the blood.*

Liverwort is of a cold, dry nature and possesses an oily, volatile, mildly alkaline salt.
Thus it has the capacity to withstand all sourness, to open, and to cleanse and heal.

The leaves of this plant are especially praised for opening blockages of the liver,
for strengthening a weak liver, and for cooling an inflamed liver. It also forces urine,
cleanses the kidneys and bladder, and heals injuries in the gut.

If pure liverwort is ground to powder and administered in white wine to little boys
who have suffered a hernia, this will heal the condition, but they must be kept well
bandaged for several weeks.

When the leaves are boiled in water and gargled around in the mouth, this will
heal scurvy of the mouth and reduce swelling of the tonsils and uvula.

The distilled water of liverwort possesses similar virtues, but in particular it will
cool an inflamed liver and withstand jaundice when a few tablespoonfuls are taken
several times a day.

Locust Pods (Carob or John's Bread)

Ceratonia siliqua
Sauer: *St. Johannesbrod* (1778)

*The medical preparations discussed below come from the sweet brown seed pods of an
evergreen tree that grows in many parts of the Mediterranean region. The tree is
known by various synonyms (charoupia and teratsia in Greek, for example), and in
ancient texts it has even been confused with the acacia or shendjet of pharaonic Egypt.
In any case, Sauer called it locust tree in English, which is the reason for placing it here,
rather than under carob, which is its most common name today. Indeed, this is the carob
tree of biblical reference, and among German pietistic physicians like Johann Jacob
Schmidt, the pod was imbued with considerable curative powers—mystical, physical,
and spiritual. This may explain in part why the Germans were such avid believers in
carob, much more so than the English.*

The pods preferred by German physicians came from Syria in the form of dried pulp,

but the colonial American druggists were supplied from Spain, where carob was sold under the name algaroba. *The Germans prepared a popular heartburn remedy from the pulp called* syrupum de siliqua. *Sauer published an approximation of it using violet syrup and plantain water.*

Locust pods possess a sweet juice that is mixed with an indiscernible oily spirit. From this arises the plant's capacity to dissolve, to attenuate, and to contain and to sweeten the effervescence of sharp humors.[145] Two ounces of locust pods boiled in two quarts of water and drunk thus will help against coughing, consumption, and difficult breathing, and promote urine.

Dried locust pods ground to a powder and a quint dose, taken dry because it is sweet, or taken with violet syrup and plantain water, will quickly take away heartburn, stop sharp burning of the urine, sweeten sharp phlegm in the chest, and ease coughing.

Lovage
Levisticum officinale
Sauer: *Liebestöckel* (1763)

The medieval herbal healer Hildegard of Bingen recommended lovage as a remedy for sore throat and swollen tonsils. The Sauer herbal recommends a lovage stem straw for treating the same thing. These stems were also candied like angelica or poached and served in spring salads, especially those made with scorzonera, carrots, asparagus, and other cooked ingredients. The flavor is a cross between parsley and celery, so it is especially good for flavoring restaurants made with turkey, goose, or duck stocks. The colonial Germans often cooked it with parsnips or root celery. Being hardy and a perennial, lovage is an herb that can be maintained in a garden without much trouble for many years.

Lovage is of a warm, dry nature and operates by its numerous oily, volatile, alkaline salts. From these it derives its faculty to penetrate, to open, to dissolve thick phlegm, to strengthen the stomach and matrix, and to expel urine, grit, and sand. It also cleanses the chest, eases breathing, and cleanses and heals wounds and injuries, as well as dispelling windiness and vapors. The root of lovage is gathered in March and April, the leaves in June, and the seeds when they are ripe.

Felix Würtz,[146] the celebrated surgeon, wrote: If lovage roots are dug while the sun

---

145. This bubbling up of acids is in the blood, one of the negative conditions warned against by adherents of humorial medicine.

146. Felix Würtz or Wirtz (1518–1574/76) was a Swiss surgeon and author of several popular books on surgery.

is passing into the sign of Aries, and they are fastened around the neck, they will make an approved remedy for atrophy and decline of the limbs.[147]

The distilled water of lovage is good for women in confinement. It dissolves blood clots in the body, expels blocked urine and menses, breaks the stone, and is serviceable to asthmatics, provided they drink a few loths of it.

The comfits made with the seeds of this herb eaten in a dose of as much as half a loth will likewise prove useful in all the illnesses cited above.

The raw seed ground very fine and taken in a quint dose in white wine will disperse windiness and the vapors, stop colic and mother fits, force down urine, and stay painful dripping from the bladder. It also will force out worms. The leaves, root, and seeds possess similar virtues, thus they can be boiled in wine and the decoction drunk.

Those who are plagued by windiness and the vapors can make for themselves the following spice sugar: Take one loth of lovage seeds, half a loth each of anise and fennel seeds, three quints of cinnamon, and a quint each of cubebs and mace. Grind all of this quite fine and mix the powder with half a pound of sugar. Take a half-tablespoon dose of this sugar frequently, either dry or sprinkled on a piece of toasted bread moistened with wine.

Boil the leaves and roots of lovage in water with licorice, elecampane root, figs, Assyrian plums, and raisins, along with a few spoonfuls of honey to sweeten. Strain this through a sieve, and take a tumblerful of this daily every morning and evening. This will loosen tough phlegm in the chest, provoke its expectoration, still coughing, ease shortness of breath, banish hoarseness, and cleanse kidneys clogged with phlegmy corruptions.

The leaves and root of lovage boiled with betony, veronica, and sanicle in an equal mixture of wine and water, and a few glasses of the decoction drunk daily, is a valuable potion for falls. For it dissolves clotted blood, cleanses and heals all manner of corrupt injuries, opens blockages of the liver, spleen, and kidneys, and expels the poisons of all sorts of snakes and bites of other venomous creatures.

The hollow stem of lovage, used as a straw, is useful against sore throat and throat ailments.

An essence of lovage may be extracted from the root and leaves in brandy. Administered often in teaspoon- to tablespoon-size doses, excellent results will be felt for all of the above-mentioned afflictions. For this essence, however, the leaves and roots must be dried in the shade before the brandy is poured over them.

This herb is also highly useful when employed in foot baths.

The water in which lovage leaves and roots were cooked is very useful for washing the skin. It not only takes away corruptions, but also makes the complexion soft, white, and beautiful, provided the skin is washed with it every morning and evening. A similar virtue is also ascribed to the distilled water.

For injuries of the throat and mouth, as well as swollen tonsils and gums, the distilled water is especially effectual, provided it is employed slightly warm as a gargle for the throat or wash for the gums.

147. I define this as witchcraft, since there is an implied unnatural transfer taking place, with or without a "witch." The point of the remedy is this: the roots of lovage gathered during a particular solar phase possess unnatural curative powers.

The root of lovage, together with sanicle, goldenrod, and ribwort plantain, chopped together and boiled in wine, may be used fresh to irrigate old wounds. This will cleanse them and promote quick healing.

Lungwort
Sticta pulmonaria and *Pulmonaria officinalis*
Sauer: *Lungenkraut* (1773), *Buchkohl* (1777)

The herbal is quite correct in alluding to the fact that there is more than one lung-wort, for this plant belongs to the borage family, and there are numerous closely related species. Some are even native to North America, but the old lungworts of medicine are the ones described here. Both are plants of Old World origin brought to America as a garden ornamentals and as medical herbs. Their importance may be gleaned from the fact that Sauer published two entries on lungwort, but essentially repeated in 1777 what he said in 1773, with some slight additions which I have melded together. The point is, both plants could be used interchangeably. Lungwort acquired its English name according to the doctrine of signatures because its speckled leaf resembles the shape of a lung. The Germans commonly call the official lungwort Bachkohl, "brook cabbage," since in the wild it grows along woodsy streams.

All kinds of lungworts or brook cabbages are dry and cooling in nature and are endowed with mildly alkaline salt intermingled with oily balsamic elements in their milky saps. They derive from this their goodly faculties to purify and heal all sores and wounds, to withstand all injurious acidity, to open internal blockages, and to sweeten sharp, salty, soured blood.

Surgeons use this herb very effectively in their vulnerary potions because it causes wounds to heal excellently. But it must be gathered in July and dried in the shade. The flowers are thrown away.

If four handfuls of lungwort are boiled in two quarts of wine with an equal amount of water in a covered vessel until boiled down to about one pint, then strained, it will yield a fine potion for all internal injuries of the chest, lungs, and viscera. It is also useful for treating pulmonary consumption and consumption if administered in half-gill doses in the morning and evening. Tabernaemontanus[148] wrote that there was no other nobler remedy to be found for these diseases, particularly if it is employed immediately upon their outbreak. It will then not only prevent pulmonary consumption from gaining the upper hand but will also root it out fully. This potion, used thus, will immediately open blockages of the liver, get rid of jaundice, heal all wounds caused by gunshots, stabs, or hackings.[149]

If someone develops fluxes upon the chest, and is worried that it may develop into pulmonary consumption, take one loth of pure powdered lungwort leaves and mix

148. Tabernaemontanus was otherwise known as Jakob Theodor von Bergzaben. He is discussed under asparagus on page 50.
149. This refers to military applications for treating battle wounds.

this with four loths of sugar. Add endive, ground ivy, borage, or corn poppy syrup, just enough to make an electuary. Administer in doses the size of a nutmeg.

Lungwort ground to a powder and given with salt to horses, cattle, or sheep to lick will get rid of constriction of their chests, wheezing, and coughing. For horses, it must be chopped into their fodder.

The distilled water of lungwort is good in all feverish afflictions of the chest, lungs, stomach, and liver. It is serviceable in treating pulmonary consumption and consumption, gets rid of jaundice, and heals fresh wounds. Take several tablespoonfuls each morning and evening. If used externally, it will control inflamed sores of the throat and mouth when used often as a warm gargle. If a cloth is dipped in it and laid over the hurt, it will heal injuries in the privates.

The syrup of lungwort prepared in apothecary shops is a valuable article for pulmonary consumption when a few spoonfuls are administered often. And finally, an essence may be extracted from the leaves in brandy and then mixed with the syrup of licorice, daisies, or violets. This can be given in spoonful doses for treating coughs, hoarseness, and asthma arising from cold fluxes and phlegm. Or it can be taken in thirty to forty drops for purifying and sweetening the blood and for healing sores and wounds.

Manna (Manna Ash)
Fraxinus ornus and *Fraxinus excelsior*
Sauer: *Manna* (1776)

> *Manna or manna ash is a small tree that grows in the Mediterranean region. The part used is the sweetish sap that exudes from the bark of two distinct species. Most of this sap was collected and processed for commerce in Sicily during the eighteenth century, so the manna sold in colonial America probably came from there. The sap was sold in the form of a dry gum that could be ground to powder or dissolved in warm water. This is the reason for warming the wine in one of the remedies given below.*

Manna is a gentle and agreeable laxative by nature, for in particular it carries off phlegmy matter and watery humors. It is also quite serviceable in treating afflictions of the chest, since it purifies the chest of all phlegm and stills coughing. Old people who are afflicted with asthma and coughing should take five loths of manna and let it dissolve in a glass of wine over a charcoal stove. Strain this through a clean cloth and drink it warm in the morning before breakfast.

If three loths of manna and one loth of cream of tartar are dissolved in boiling water, and then drunk warm, it will prove a very fine laxative and will keep the body open for a long period.

Manna is also a useful remedy for children if, according to their age, one-half to as much as two or three loths are dissolved in milk and worked to a pap with a little flour. Or, it can be dissolved in warm wine or meat stock. This will purify the chest and stomach, and at times cause the children to puke, and thus cough up the thick phlegm.

Manna can also be combined with other ingredients for preparing excellent laxative remedies, for example: Take two quints each of rhubarb, senna leaves, cream of tartar, and Zante currants and a fistful of violet flowers, and chop it all together. Let this infuse for twenty-four hours in one pint of water, then strain it off and dissolve four to six loths of manna in it. An adult may take eight to ten loths of this drink at a time.

Marigold
Calendula officinalis
Sauer: *Ringelblume* (1772)

In stark contrast to the German inhabitants, the English-speaking colonials used their marigolds in very different ways, at least when it came to cookery. Rochester seedsman James Vick reminisced in 1880 how, even as late as the 1830s, many rural Americans would never think to eat a leg of mutton without marigold sauce.[150] This rustic relic of baroque cookery lingered on here much longer than in England itself. But mint eventually won out as lamb became more fashionable.[151]

German cooks used marigold vinegar in salad dressings, or mixed with honey and drawn butter (or goose fat) as a sauce on parsnips, skirrets, and similar sweet-tasting root vegetables. It was also boiled with chicken, for chickens were fed marigolds to make their skin yellow, and used extensively in egg dishes. Most of all, the flower petals were dried and used as a condiment in soups; indeed, this custom was so pervasive that it is mentioned in many period accounts. The flower itself was also popular, since it will bloom through the winter if properly protected. Perhaps for this reason, it had a long-standing association with the New Year and rebirth. As a symbol of spiritual rebirth and resurrection, it was used by many German colonists to decorate graves, hence its other old name, Todtenblume, *"flower of the dead."*

The marigold is endowed with a balsamic, gently volatile alkaline salt. It possesses the faculty of warming gently, of drying, of strengthening the heart, liver, and matrix, and also of opening their blockages. It withstands poison, forces sweat and other things, and gives ease to the travail of difficult delivery.

If the leaves together with the flowers are heated in wine, and the decoction drunk, it will purify the chest of all phlegm, strengthen a feeble stomach, get rid of jaundice (provided there is no sign of fever), and take away palpitations of the heart.

When the flowers of marigold are boiled in lye, they will make the hair yellow. The salts of marigold as prepared in apothecary shops will open blockages of the liver and matrix and are useful for jaundice, provided fifteen grains are taken a few times in marigold water.

Marigold-flower vinegar, which is prepared like rose vinegar, is useful for ardent fevers when a small piece of cloth is dipped into it and bound over the wrists where

---

150. "The Calendula," *Vick's Illustrated Monthly Magazine*, October 1880, 308.
151. "Mint Chow Chow for Roast Lamb," *American Agriculturist*, September 1869, 344.

the pulse is taken, and over the soles of the feet.

As reported by Dr. Hoffmann,[152] if marigold flowers are rubbed on warts so that they become wet from them, then rinsed with horse urine and allowed to dry on their own, and this is repeated three or four times, the warts will fall off.

The seeds kill worms, and if a potion is prepared by boiling the leaves and flowers, it will get rid of jaundice.

The distilled water of marigold flowers is good for blockages of the liver arising from jaundice, promotes the menses, and is serviceable against contagion, if it is taken in three- or four-tablespoon doses often.

Marjoram (Sweet Marjoram)

Origanum majorana
Sauer: *Majoran* (1766)

The aroma of ham, onions, and marjoram cooking together was doubtless one of the prevalent smells of Sunday dinner on an eighteenth-century German farm. Marjoram was employed in flavoring nearly everything, from noodle stuffings to sauces and sausages. But it is such a tender herb that it must be protected in the winter or else grown in pots. I have no doubt that this was common practice in colonial America; of all the kitchen herbs, this one was most firmly believed to help women get pregnant, as the Sauer herbal readily confirms.

Marjoram possesses the faculty to warm, to dry, to thin phlegm, to strengthen the head, nerves, chest, stomach, and matrix, and to loosen internal blockages.

Foremost, marjoram is employed in treating old cold distempers of the head and matrix, for it possesses the special virtue of warming and strengthening the brain and the matrix.

This is also a fine herb for cookery, since it provides food with a pleasant taste.

For cold distempers of the head, take a half handful each of marjoram, sage, rosemary, betony, and lemon balm, and chop it all up. Sew this into a sachet, and pour a gallon of wine over it. Take the infusion in the morning and evening as you would a regular drink.

If marjoram is boiled in white wine and then the decoction drunk, this will prove good for treating the onset of dropsy, troublesome passing of the water, and colic. It is also good for dispersing bloating of the matrix and the corruptions that may be retained there.

Those who are accustomed to washing their head with lye will discover that if marjoram is added to the lye, it will strengthen the head.

When fresh marjoram is rubbed between the fingers and then stuck into the nostrils, it will cause sneezing, break up the snot, and purify the head.

If marjoram is boiled in wine and the steam allowed to rise through an inverted funnel, this will strengthen hearing and get rid of buzzing.

152. Dr. Friedrich Hoffmann. He is referred to several times in the herbal.

Fresh marjoram is very usefully employed on newly born babies. If their noses are stopped up, and they have difficulty drawing breath as though they are beginning to choke, rub fresh marjoram vigorously and hold it to their nose, or take fresh, unsalted butter and melt it in a skillet. Then add fresh or dried marjoram and let it foment in the butter. Then press the butter through a cloth and swab the baby's nose between the eyes with this salve. This same salve is also good for strengthening a feeble stomach in tender children if it is rubbed warm upon the navel and upward over the stomach to the chest.

The distilled water of marjoram is excellent for all cold distempers of brain, falling evil, fits, palsy, convulsions, and dizziness. It will restore lost speech, strengthen the heart, force urine and gravel, warm the matrix, and is helpful to those who are barren, provided a few loths are taken in the morning and evening.

If a small cloth is dipped in marjoram water and laid warm upon the head, it will get rid of headache arising from cold. If the water is drawn up into the nose, it will restore lost sense of smell and purify the head quite well.

A conserve or sugar of marjoram (which is prepared like rose sugar) is very good for all cold distempers of the head, stomach, and matrix. It strengthens a weak heart and opens blockages of the liver.

The marjoram conserve just mentioned may be prepared thus: Take one part marjoram buds just as they are beginning to bloom, and grind them very fine in a marble or wooden mortar. Then add two parts, or double their weight, in white loaf sugar and pound it fine again. Store away for use. This conserve may be administered each time in nutmeg-size doses. Rose, violet, and various flower and herbal conserves may be prepared and stored the same way.

If three drops of the distilled oil of marjoram are taken in wine, this will get rid of bloating of the matrix, and protect against apoplexy, the falling evil, convulsions, and headache of long continuance that has arisen from cold. It is also one of the foremost remedies for purifying the head of all angry humors.

Marshmallow
Althea officinalis
Sauer: *Eibisch* (1774)

The Greeks and Romans used the mucilaginous root of the marshmallow as a source of thickening for soups in much the same way okra is used today. It was also put into stuffings for the same reason. The old French confection, also made from the roots and called pâté de guimauve, *was used to treat coughs and sore throats. Modern marshmallow candy is its descendant, but contains no mallow, or anything else of medical value for that matter. In addition to the roots, the leaves were eaten as well, and the tender young shoots were put raw into salads. Likewise, the flowers are edible and can be employed in preparing an interesting conserve rather like the old* pâté *of the French.*

Sauer's mention of his 1770 almanac (below) was intended to direct the reader to his material on blue mallow (see page 66).

Aside from their earthy elements, the roots and leaves of the marshmallow possess a mucilaginous, thick, imperceptibly volatile nitrous sap. From this derives its ability to cool, to dry, to emolliate, to discuss swellings, to still pain, and to purify the kidneys and chest.

Because marshmallow and blue mallow possess the same virtues throughout, they may be used in similar ways. (Refer to the almanac for the year 1770.)

If marshmallow roots and flaxseeds are mixed in equal amounts and boiled in milk to form a plaster, which is then laid on the hurt, this will emolliate and bring sores to a head, especially those that form on the neck and chest.

When someone is burned or scalded, it is customary to brush marshmallow leaves with oil and lay this on the burn.

If a horse develops a crop on the throat, take a handful each of marshmallow, rue, ground ivy, wormwood, and flaxseeds and pour water over this. Let these ingredients simmer together, then foment the injury, and afterward swab it with a mixture of sweet bay oil and fresh butter.

Marshmallow root may be gathered in the spring, cleaned of all dirt, and then chopped fine and wine poured over it. Let it infuse awhile until the virtues are drawn out. Then use the infusion. It will heal injuries of the lungs and bowels injured by bloody flux, purify the bladder, and stop blood-pissing.

The syrup of marshmallow prepared in apothecary shops is very good for chest sores and consumption. It is also serviceable in treating burning and dripping piss. For kidneys anguished by heats, foul matter, sand, and pains, take a few tablespoonfuls of the syrup according to taste and repeat this every four hours.

A useful poultice can be prepared from marshmallow roots and leaves together with chamomile flowers. Boil these in milk for emolliating hard wounds and swellings.

Marshmallow salve or so-called Althea Salve,[153] which one finds in apothecary shops, possesses a special faculty for emolliating, for discussing swellings, for bringing them to a head, and for healing them. It also eases pain and is used very much in treating stiff and crooked limbs.

Dried marshmallow root, ground to a fine powder and then taken in forty-grain doses with rock candy several times a day, will loosen thick humors from the chest, stop coughs of long continuance, heal consumption, ease burning piss, and expel sand and stones from the kidneys. The remedy is particularly effective when poppy, caraway, wild carrot, or celery seeds are also added.

Masterwort
Imperatoria ostruthium
Sauer: *Meisterwurz* (1770)

> *Masterwort is described in the Sauer herbal largely as it appeared in Zwinger.*
> *Zwinger's material traces to Tabernaemontanus, who called the plant* Imperatoria.

---

153. This is more accurately called *unguentum de Althea*. Dr. Woyt made the interesting observation that when it is smeared on the soles of the feet, it will stop coughing.

Zwinger also gave the French name as otruche, *so there is not much doubt about the true genus and species in this case, even though several previous authors who studied the Sauer herbal identified the plant as American masterwort* (Angelica atropurpurea). *This is quite impossible because it was not known to Tabernaemontanus or even to Zwinger's son, who tried to revise the old nomenclature. American masterwort was not officially classified until 1753.*

Although European masterwort was cultivated in England as a potherb and medical plant, the herb originates from central Europe; thus it was much more firmly established in German botanical medicine than in English. The plant is perennial, with dark green leaves, and somewhat resembles angelica. Like angelica, it prefers moist situations and is therefore not as easy to grow as smallage or some of the other old garden greens. It was evidently brought here by the Germans for the reasons given below. The most powerful recommendation, however, was its ability to cure barrenness in both women and men, a sexual elixir firmly believed in by the country people who used it. The only problem was the bad taste, which disappears when the herb is distilled. Whether it caused babies or not, water of masterwort at least made them merry.

Masterwort possesses a large quantity of volatile oily salt and is so hot that it exceeds all other herbs in sharpness. It has been observed that while the root is somewhat hot, the sap from it is much hotter and drier. Masterwort withstands poison, operates through the sweat, loosens all phlegm in the chest, kidneys, and matrix, abates windiness, kills worms, cleanses and heals sores, and promotes urine and the menses.

Masterwort is especially good against all contagion, and is particularly employed when the plague is raging.

If masterwort is chewed, it will cleanse the head of rheums and get rid of stinking breath.

The distilled water of masterwort warms a cold stomach and strengthens the same. It is good for barren men and women, it forces down gravel and loin stones through the urine and menses, and is very good for cramps of the matrix and the pain following delivery, when administered a few tablespoonfuls at a time.

If half a quint of ground masterwort is taken in white wine at the onset of quartan fever, and repeated several times, it will get rid of it, although the stomach must be cleansed by purging beforehand.

If the fresh root of masterwort is cut into little round slices and sewn on a string, then hung around the neck, it will drive out quinsy and inflammation of the throat. If the sliced root is bound around the throat and hands, this will prove effective in drawing out the heat of fevers.

When powdered masterwort is mixed with hog's lard, and ringworms are swabbed with this salve, it will drive them out of the skin.

For colic due to vapors or sharp humors, there is nothing better than eating one or two slices of fresh masterwort root from time to time. This will also still swelling of the matrix and strengthen a cold feeble stomach.

The essence of masterwort, drawn out in brandy and taken from time to time in fifteen- to twenty-drop doses in an herbal water, will strengthen digestion, purify and warm a cold phlegmy matrix, abate windiness and swelling of the gut, stay colic and stomachache, promote sweat, dissolve phlegm in the chest, and promote its expectoration as well. It will also get rid of stinking breath and still tertian and quartan fevers, provided the essence is administered one or two hours before each outbreak of fever. It will prevent apoplexy, fits, and the falling evil, and purify the kidneys of all sand and scummy matter. Similar results may be had for all these afflictions by boiling the root of masterwort together with the leaves in white wine.

Dried masterwort, ground to a powder and administered in thirty- to forty-grain doses in white wine several times, will prove effective against the poison of crazed animals and venomous creatures, such as mad dogs, cats, foxes, snakes, otters, spiders, and scorpions.

To prevent the plague and other contagious diseases: Take one loth each of masterwort and prepared hartshorn, three quints of sorrel seeds, half a loth of scorzonera root, and one loth of sugar. Grind it all together to a fine powder. This may be administered every day or every other day in thirty- to forty-grain doses in a glass of wine.

Similar results may be achieved with the preserved root of masterwort, which should be eaten in one-half-loth doses or greater every morning before going outside. This will strengthen a feeble stomach as well, and ease difficult breathing.

For lethargy and apoplexy, shave the hair from the crown of the patient's head, then pulp fresh masterwort together with an onion or a head of garlic to form a thick puree. Spread this on a cloth and sprinkle salt over it, then lay it over the shaved spot. After this, blow dried powdered masterwort into the patient's nose.[154]

Mastic Tree
Pistacia lentiscus
Sauer: *Mastixbaum* (1778)

> *The sweet licorice-tasting resin from the bark of this Old World tree is still used in cookery and medicine. The Romans and Greeks flavored fruit with the berries; the resin is used to flavor Turkish delight. In Sauer's era, the preferred mastic of commerce originated from the island of Chios in the Aegean Sea, a place long devoted to mastic orchards.*

In all of its parts, the mastic tree possesses an astringent binding balsamic gum, and thus has the capacity to glutinate and to dry. However, true mastic is the resin exuded from the bark, which is endowed with a highly aromatic, temperately volatile spirit of salt. Thus mastic has the capacity to sweeten all sharp, putrid, corrosive humors, and as a result, due to its gently balsamic power to bind, it can check dangerous eruptions and hemorrhages.

Mastic resin is quite useful to the stomach. If three small grains of it are swallowed every evening, this will still stomach pains.

---

154. This was normally accomplished with a miniature bellows.

One loth of mastic together with a little orange peel boiled in two quarts of fresh water, and then taken as a drink, will prove good for diarrhea and especially for bloody flux.

If mastic is chewed, it makes pleasant breath, draws down phlegm from the head, and promotes expectoration.

To treat all manner of fluxes of the stomach, take one loth each of mastic and fish mint[155] or even common balsam oil, and rub this over the stomach while the lotion is quite warm.

Mastic pills may be made as follows: Take one loth of mastic, one-half loth of agaric, and two and a half loths of aloe and grind this together to a fine powder. Stir in a little rose honey until it forms a thick mass from which the pills can be formed as needed. Pills weighing twenty to twenty-five grains should be administered in one dose. They will gently purge just like Frankfurt Pills.[156] They will protect persons from all manner of cold apoplexies and rheums upon the lungs. They also strengthen the head, expel fluxes and pain from the same, sustain the brain, eyes, and ears in their natural powers, and cleanse the female member of all foul immoderate fluxes.

For those plagued by strong fluxes and coughing, and who have a sore in the lungs, stomach, or the gut, take one quint of good-quality mastic and mix it with two loths of rose sugar. Take a dose of this the size of a nutmeg when wanted. Likewise, from time to time the patient should take a few grains of mastic dissolved in a lightly boiled egg.

If mastic is ground to a powder and spread on a linen cloth well warmed and then stroked with the blade of a knife, this will make a plaster that, when laid upon the stomach and abdomen, will stop vomiting and diarrhea. If it is laid upon the temples or behind the ears, it will still a toothache.

To treat sciatica and other pains of the joints arising from cold fluxes, take one loth each of mastic, myrrh, caraway, sage, pennyroyal, and sweet bay and grind this to a fine powder. Add a little brandy and honey and form this into a plaster. Lay this freshly made and well warmed upon the hurting hip or joints.

A spirituous water can be prepared from mastic in the following manner: Toss little lumps of mastic onto glowing charcoals and catch the smoke in a new earthenware pot. When it is quite full of smoke, fill it at once with fresh springwater and cover it well, for in this manner the water will absorb all of the properties of the mastic. Indeed, the spirituous balsamic oil will fully unite with the water. This is an excellent remedy for those who are

155. *Fischmünz* has not been identified. This may be a colloquial term for *Mentha aquatica* or calamint. The context would suggest this since it was similarly used to treat diarrhea and other internal ailments.

156. Frankfurt or Beyers Pills were a patent medicine. They were popular in the eighteenth century and imported for sale to the German community in America, often under the Latin name *pilulae Angelicae*, one of the key ingredients being angelica.

afflicted with diarrhea or bloody flux, provided they drink of it continuously as thirst requires.

To treat severe upheavals of the stomach, take one quint of good-quality mastic, a handful of red rose petals, one-half quint of cloves, and foment this in one pint of wine. Strain it through a cloth and give this to the patient once or twice, depending on the severity of the condition.

Melilot (Yellow Sweet Clover)
Melilotus officinalis
Sauer: *Steinklee* (1773)

Melilot is rather weedy and untidy in its habit, far better suited to pastures than a kitchen garden. However, it is a wonderful bee plant, so it was often planted in or near orchards where the hives were kept. It was also grown as a fodder crop or as green manure; thus it was provided with many avenues of naturalization in this country. It is still very much in use among rural herbalists.

The common melilot is middling in nature, although more warm than cold. It operates by means of its numerous oily balsamic mild components mixed with an alkaline salt. Thus it possesses the faculty to thin, to emolliate, to ease pain, to dispel, to strengthen the head and nerves, and to purify the kidneys and bladder. The leaves, flowers, and seeds are used in medicine.

For swollen privates in men, take a handful each of melilot flowers, chamomile flowers, flaxseeds, and fava bean flour, and also a little wormwood. Boil in milk to form a plaster, then spread it between two cloths and lay it warm upon the balls.

For inflamed swellings of the female subject, the arse, and privates: Take one loth each of marshmallow root and leaves, a quint each of mallow, melilot, and chamomile flowers, a half loth each of barley flour and the flour of flaxseeds, and boil this in milk to form a plaster. Spread it between two cloths and lay this warm over the swelling.

From firsthand experience, people long ago attributed to the distilled water of melilot in particular such virtues as strengthening the head and memory and purifying the kidneys and bladder of sand and gravel, when three loths of it were drunk in the evening before going to bed.

The melilot plasters prepared in apothecary shops will soften and dispel hard swellings and ease the pain of the same. They will also get rid of swollen tonsils when laid over them externally.

Milk Thistle or Saint Mary's Thistle
Silybum marianum
Sauer: *Mariendistel* (1764)

Milk thistle has recently undergone a revival, and well it should. This is an attractive herb that is both visually ornamental and highly useful for its medical properties, espe-

cially for liver ailments. It is also a tender annual, thus unlike many thistles, is not at all invasive. Due to its short height, it can be used as a border plant or in patches as landscape accents. In fact, during the seventeenth and eighteenth centuries the stalks were eaten like asparagus, and the unopened flower heads were cooked like artichokes. Milk thistle was once esteemed as a very good vegetable, and it is evident from the Sauer herbal that it was still treated this way among the German colonists.

This is a handsome, tall but prickly plant whose leaves are ornamented with white flecks. According to its nature, it is warm and dry and is similar in all its components to holy thistle. Nevertheless, it is not as bitter, even though it possesses the same faculties. For this reason, it is not necessary to write too much about it, since in the almanac for 1762 I have already discussed holy thistle. The distilled water of milk thistle is very effective in treating pleurisy and complaints of the chest. It is also good for the plague, ardent fevers, jaundice and dropsy, and for expelling blocked urine, gravel, sand, and so forth. It also helps increase the milk in wet nurses and nursing mothers, and should be employed in doses of three to four loths at a time.

The fresh juice expressed from milk thistle heals cancer in its early stages on the nose and bosoms if the affected places are swabbed with it often.

Millet
Panicum miliaceum
Sauer: *Hirse* (1777)

There is not much documentary evidence concerning millet growing in colonial America, but it was definitely raised to some extent by the German-speaking settlers, especially those of Swiss origin. The Futhey and Cope history of Chester County, Pennsylvania, mentions early attempts at millet growing and even a description of a type of pancake made with the flour.[157]

Millet, barley, and oats formed the old medieval grain triumvirate among the peasantry of south Germany and Switzerland, and to some extent this was brought to America by the Swiss Mennonites, especially the more conservative groups. It has been suggested that the reason why the Pennsylvania Germans preferred yellow cornmeal over white was the visual (and perhaps also taste) similarity to the old yellow millet mush dishes of Europe. The idea that millet was more healthful when cooked in milk also stems from the Middle Ages and was carried over into cornmeal cookery in the New World. Indeed the very same passage recommending this combination, as it appeared in the herbal, was reprinted in Der Hoch-Deutsche Americanische Calender *for 1830 under an article on millet. Yet most interesting of all are the comments in the herbal about storing medicines and foods in chests of millet. This is definitely an ancient concept that actually works, but no one seems to have explored the reasons why.*

---

157. J. Smith Futhey and Gilbert Cope, *History of Chester County, Pennsylvania* (Philadelphia, 1881), 340.

Millet is cold and dry in nature and possesses a somewhat temperate volatile oil and salt. Thus it has the faculty to nourish well and to sweeten the sharp humors in the blood.

Millet provides less strength to people than other grain foods. Those who wish to eat it should boil it in milk, for it will thus be easier to digest.

Wet nurses who have watery milk should find millet meal cooked in milk a good remedy.

A choice anodyne sachet may be prepared thus: Take two handfuls of some slightly toasted millet, one handful of parched salt, one and a half handfuls each of vervain and chamomile flowers, one ounce of rosewort,[158] and one loth of zedoary. Chop and grind it all together and sew it up into a sachet. Warm the sachet often, and according to one's preference, sprinkle it with Hungary water[159] or some other apoplectic water, and lay it upon the forehead to get rid of the pain. If bound over the ears, it will relieve and get rid of ringing and buzzing, and restore hearing to good order. When laid upon other painful limbs, it will dispel the cold painful fluxes that have collected there.

The water distilled from millet is very serviceable for treating gravel and stones of the kidneys and bladder when taken in a gill dose in the morning and evening. It will drive down the stone quickly, and purify the kidneys and bladder of all scummy matter.

To make a potion for treating tertian fever: Take one pound of hulled millet and boil it in three pounds of water until it puffs up and colors the water. Strain off the broth and administer it at room temperature on the day the patient begins to shake with fever and when the ensuing temperature ends. Cover the patient well to sweat it out.

This potion is also very useful in treating ardent fevers, the pox, and smallpox, for it not only cools and drives out infection through the sweat but also protects the lungs from contagion and stops and heals bloody flux.

If such medicines as rhubarb, Mechoacan jalap,[160] camphor and the like are stored in millet, they will keep longer undamaged. Also, if meat is wrapped in a thin cloth and covered with millet, it will not spoil as quickly. Likewise, all manner of fruit will keep longer if they are stored in millet.

Mint (Spearmint)
Mentha spicata
Sauer: *Balsam, Müntze* (1763)

> *The herbal treats mint plurally in this entry, but the herb Sauer mostly had in mind was spearmint, for the remedies agree with prescriptions given in other herbals of the period. This point becomes acutely clear when we consider the entry for mint that appeared in the 1777 installment of Sauer's herbal. I have not reproduced it because Sauer reprinted the text below, so there was no need to repeat it. But he did shorten it*

---

158. Rosewort, formerly *Rhodiola rosea*, now *Sedum roseum*, is a perennial sedum both native to northern and Alpine Europe as well as to North America. Sauer's supply came from a large native habitat on the Nockamixon Rocks along the Delaware River.

159. Hungary water, or the Queen of Hungary's water, as it was also called, was distilled from rosemary flowers almost exclusively. See rosemary on page 000.

160. Mechoacan jalap is a weak form of jalap from the state of Michoacán in Mexico.

a bit and made one or two minor alterations: for example, instead of lemon balm in the last line, he used feverfew.

Where he sowed confusion was in relabeling the 1777 entry for Krauser Balsam *or curly mint* (Mentha crispa), *which he also quite incorrectly called* Bachmünze (calamint). *Curly mint, which was commonly called English mint in colonial Pennsylvania, will work well in the remedies, but calamint* (Mentha aquatica) *will not. Indeed, its use will have dreadful consequences when applied in any of the remedies dealing with pregnant women or even little girls. Nicholas Culpeper put it rightly when he said of calamint, "Let no woman be too busy with it, for it works very violently upon the female subject." Culpeper even went so far as to add that simply by smelling it, calamint will hinder conception in women. The truth of that has not been demonstrated, but for any reader who takes the opportunity to refer to the original German text, do not let the reference to calamint lead one astray.*

Mints are warm and dry in nature, resist astringencies, dissolve tough phlegm, stay swellings of the bowels and matrix, stop colic, open blockages, and warm the stomach, liver, spleen, and matrix, as well as a cold brain and nerves.

All varieties of mint strengthen the stomach, promote digestion, and stay puking, powerful upheavals of the stomach, and violent hiccups, as well as ease its ability to take food. They can be used fresh or dried, but they should not be used too strong, otherwise they will make thin watery blood and readily bring on biliousness. For this reason, those who are overly bilious should employ mints sparingly.

Mint essence made by infusing dried mint in brandy will bring comfort to all manner of feebleness of the stomach and matrix.

If mints are boiled in water and used for washing the head, they will heal foul runny scall. The distilled water of mint will warm a cold stomach and stay puking, provided it is drunk now and again. It is very good for children who have a stomachache. It will kill their worms and heals scall when the head is washed with it. If mint water is warmed and a small piece of cloth moistened with it, then laid over breasts that are swollen from clotted milk, this will dissolve the clots and open the glands.

If the leaves are boiled and laid warm over the stomach of children, this will stop stomachaches. When fomented in butter, pressed, and the butter then rubbed in the bellybutton of children, this will strengthen a feeble stomach and stay vomiting.

If mint is boiled in wine and a good draft of it taken thus, it will promote urination, disperse windiness, and kill worms.

If the fresh leaves are rubbed hard and then smelled, this will strengthen the brain and bodily spirits. It is also good for fainting spells.

Mint, lemon balm, and chamomile boiled in wine and laid warm over the belly of a woman in confinement will stay the pain following her travail without injury.[161]

161. In the 1777 installment, lemon balm was changed to feverfew, and measurements were given: two handfuls of each herb. Sauer further instructed the reader to chop the herbs very fine and to place them in a small sachet that was then boiled in one quart of wine. The sachet was pressed between two plates and laid on the belly of the woman as warm as she could bear it. This later expansion of the text provides some insight into how Sauer paraphrased and rewrote material from other herbals—or added clarifications at the request of his readers.

Mistletoe
Viscum album
Sauer: *Mistel, Mispel* (1778)

Mistletoe is a perennial evergreen parasite that does not grow in Pennsylvania, so it is unlikely that Sauer had direct access to fresh plants. Mistletoe does grow in the South, however, so it is quite possible that it was gathered there and sent to apothecary shops in the North. In any event, it was powdered mistletoe that was sold in shops, so it could be imported just as easily. It was evidently very common, or Sauer would not have included it. In fact, one did not simply buy mistletoe; rather, various kinds of mistletoe had to be specified, such as oak tree mistletoe, linden mistletoe, and hazelnut mistletoe, all of which are mentioned in the herbal under their respective trees. The Zwinger herbal illustrated mistletoes of differing sizes and habits of growth. Such pre-Linnaean images are somewhat difficult to identify since they are not always actual species but often the product of localized growing conditions. Zwinger's Swiss mistletoe, for example, is notable only for its large clusters of berries.

Most of the following discussion is devoted to a cure for falling sickness (epilepsy). This is paraphrased from a pamphlet by Sir John Colbatch called The Treatment of Epilepsy by Mistletoe *(London, 1720). The powder was administered by dissolving it in water of black cherry, an important point, since Sauer did not explain how to get it into the patient.*

All mistletoes, but especially those from the oak, linden, and hazel bush, contain mucilaginous sap and an alkaline volatile salt. From these originate its capacity to sweeten all sourness, to open obstructions of the mesenteric glands, to control falling sickness, and by the by to stop it altogether, as well as to check atrophy.

For the falling sickness, the following remedy is used in England: Take mistletoe from an oak tree—stems, leaves, and berries—and dry them gently in a bake oven. Grind them to a fine powder and give a full-grown adult as much as will fit upon a sixpence each morning before breakfast and each evening upon going to bed. But children should be given less according to their size or strength of constitution. Administer this three days before and three days after a full moon, and continue in this fashion for several months. This treatment has already helped many people, though they must first purge the stomach well with a good emetic. Furthermore, before being treated, the plethoric abounding in an overplus of blood should not neglect being bled.[162]

When a child has worms, give it mistletoe of oak in fresh milk in the morning before breakfast. Repeat this several days before the light of dawn.

162. Specifically, being leeched or cupped by a bleeder.

Monk's Rhubarb
Rumex alpinus
Sauer: *Mönchs-Rhabarber* (1775)

This is often equated with garden dock or patience dock (Rumex patienta), its old Latin name being Lapathum sativum patientia, *but the species are quite separate. The leaves may be used in cookery just like spinach, and they are much milder than sorrel. According to Hieronymus Bock's 1546* Kreütterbuch *(Strasbourg), monk's rhubarb was first observed during the Middle Ages on a mountainside on Black Forest lands belonging to the Lords of Stauffen. Carmelite and Carthusian friars in the area brought it under cultivation in their monasteries, using it as a potherb because it was one of the first greens to appear in the spring. It later spread from the monasteries into general cultivation, hence the popular name. Sauer's initial comment seems to indicate that monk's rhubarb was not widely cultivated in colonial America, but that he at least had seen it in gardens around Philadelphia. The dock has since naturalized in North America, and due to its rich nutritional properties it is undergoing a revival among serious gardeners.*

This plant can be grown in this country easily and in abundance. The root is endowed with somewhat watery sap that is sulfurous or oily, together with a nitrous, caustic, gently purging salt. From this it derives its faculty to warm gently, to dry, to dissolve internal blockages, to operate through urine and stool, and to cleanse the blood. It also prevents jaundice and dropsy.

The dried powdered root may be taken in a half-loth dose as a laxative, or infused together with whole roots in wine or beer, or mixed with a purgative wine bitters, and the infusion administered daily.

Moss (Oak Moss)
Evernia prunastri
Sauer: *Baum-Moss* (1773)

Sauer is at first somewhat vague about what he means by mosses, but it gradually becomes clear from his text that he is actually dealing with lichens of the family Usneaceae. In particular, his so-called oak moss has been employed since ancient times as a leavening agent in bread—this use was well known to the Egyptians and is still practiced by the Copts. In northern Europe it was employed in bread baking to add flavor and as an agent for retaining flavors of other added ingredients. Extracts made from this lichen are still employed today in flavorings for various food products. During Sauer's era, oak moss was imported both in the dry and powdered state.

The moss that grows on small trees, as well as many other mosses, possesses a drying, astringent power and faculty. It is uniquely endowed with numerous earthy and few coarse sulfurous elements.

Those afflicted with bloody flux or diarrhea should boil tree moss in water or red wine and take this in drink. Employed in this manner, especially when prepared with oak moss, this decoction will protect women from premature birth. It can also be dried for powder and administered in raw egg. Rich women can add a little prepared pearls to it.[163]

Some take oak moss, infuse it overnight in wine, then drink the infusion for jaundice.

If tree moss is boiled in white wine, and the gums rubbed with this, it will strengthen wobbly teeth. If used as a gargle, it will get rid of swelling of the uvula.

Mouse Ear (Hawkweed)
Hieracium pilosella
Sauer: *Mausöhrlein* (1770)

It would be wrong to describe this plant as a miniature dandelion, but that is how some people would view it. The tiny leaves are hairy and often grow flat against the ground. The plant spreads by means of creeping scions or runners, very much like a strawberry. It thrives in dry, sunny locations and is not the sort of herb that easily grows in herb gardens because it does not like cultivated soil. Thus, in the past, it was largely collected from the wild.

Mouse ear is also found in North America because it has naturalized here as an adventive weed. If native mouse ears were employed as substitutes, there were indeed several to choose from, Maryland hawkweed (Hieracium marianum) *and rattlesnake weed* (Hieracium venosum) *being two of the most common. They grow in dry woods and can be coaxed into adapting themselves to shady rock gardens. It is evident that one of our native plants was widely used because in most of the remedies the leaves had to be employed fresh; and not only fresh, but picked in the late spring.*

Mouse ear has the capacity to warm gently, to dry, to draw together, and to block. It also cleanses and heals wounds and sores. It is gathered in May and June when it is succulent and milky.

Heat a handful each of the leaves of mouse ear and wild strawberry in two quarts of white wine and drink a gill of this decoction each morning and evening. This will open blockages of the liver and take away jaundice. This is a good drink for kidney and bladder stones.

Take the fresh leaves of mouse ear and goatsbeard gathered in May and June, pulp them, and press out the juice. If taken in four-tablespoon doses mixed with sugar each morning and evening for a few weeks running, it will prove a good remedy for the

---

163. Sauer does mean pearls. Prepared pearls were ground to a fine powder. But he is also being extremely sarcastic, in line with the remarks about rich women under sugar on page 313.

falling evil. It will also heal all internal and external injuries, sores, and wounds, and stop blood-spitting. These same herbs can also be pulped and boiled together as required in good red wine, strained, and taken by the glassful in the morning as well as in the evening.

Take the leaves of mouse ear, goatsbeard, periwinkle, plantain, and centaury and boil them in wine. With this vulnerary wine, rinse wounds and putrid angry sores as well as fistulas each morning and evening. After rinsing, dress the injury with pure finely powdered dried mouse ear if the wound is weeping, otherwise moisten the powder with rose honey and turpentine mixed with the grated yolk of a hard-cooked egg. This will heal it admirably and in a very short time.

Mouse ear ground to a fine powder and given in twenty-four-grain doses in a soft-cooked egg will revive people who have been weakened by wounds and loss of blood just as if they had been brought back from the dead. For this reason surgeons hold this herb in high esteem. It possesses such a potent faculty for blocking that when sheep eat it in the meadows, their stomachs become so bloated that oftentimes they die from it.

A handful of mouse ear leaves, boiled in two quarts of wine and taken in a glassful dose each morning before breakfast and again in the evening, will stop overflowing of the terms in women, prevent the violent puking of gall, and prove serviceable for bloody flux as well as strong fluxes of the stomach. It heals wounds and ruptures, for which reason it is added to potions for wounds and ruptures.

Mouse ear and its root are gathered in May, washed, and then dried in the shade. They are then ground to a fine powder, which is a good remedy for ruptures in young children. Administer it to them in doses the size of a hazelnut in their porridge each morning and evening. Or else give it to them with something they like, and keep them tightly bandaged.

If someone has a thorn or splinter in their skin, take fresh or dried mouse ear, grind the leaves very fine, and mix this with rabbit suet to form a salve. Lay this over the affected place, and it will draw out the thorn.

Take a handful of mouse ear and boil it in half a quart of water and half a quart of wine. Then wash the mouth with the decoction. This will heal sundry injuries of the mouth and scurvy of the gums, as well as stop toothache. If the dried herb is ground to a fine powder and snuffed, it will stop nosebleed. Put the same in fresh wounds, and it will stop the bleeding.

The distilled water of mouse ear is serviceable for blood-spitting; checks dropsy and jaundice, bloody flux, and fluxes of the stomach; heals injured intestines; stops overflows of the menses; and kills worms. Take each morning and evening four- or five-tablespoon doses. This is also useful for treating sores and abscesses of the mouth, gums, and throat when employed frequently as a warm mouthwash and gargle.

Mugwort (Motherwort)

Artemesia vulgaris
Sauer: *Beyfuss* (1763)

> *Mugwort, like wall fern (page 338), is one of the key herbs in Pennsylvania German folk medicine. Above all else, it is an herb devoted to the reprieve of womankind, but since the early Middle Ages, it was also used in cookery, especially with game. Under the medieval name* cingulum sancti johannis *(girdle of Saint John the Baptist), it was once used extensively with venison dishes and infused to flavor vinegar. It was also commonly fed to geese and prepared in stuffings for green goose.*
>
> *The English name is said to derive from the fact that the flowers were placed in mugs to flavor drinks and used with ground ivy (page 160) in the fermentation of ale. The German name* Beyfuss *refers to the "goosefoot" tracks made by witches, and the magical lore surrounding the plant is indeed large. It is called* Aldi Fraa, *"old woman," in Pennsylfaanisch, in reference to the goose mother whose origins may trace to the female consort of the Gaulish god of war. Because it was employed both in cookery and in medicine, mugwort was commonly planted in the kitchen gardens of the colonial Germans. It escapes readily, and is now naturalized throughout much of the eastern United States. It is also difficult to eradicate, even when harvested ruthlessly.*
>
> *Lastly, Sauer refers to two distinct varieties, the red and the white. The red possesses a dark tinge to its leaves, while the "white" is the common green one. There is also a variegated mugwort, although it is somewhat rare.*

Mugwort possesses the capacity to warm, to dry, to open, to disperse, and to cleanse foul matter from the matrix. It also has a faculty to expel. In general red mugwort is considered better than the white variety.

A small glassful of mugwort boiled in wine, and the decoction drunk each morning and evening, is an especially good remedy for sickly women, both young and old.

Dry or fresh leaves of mugwort given to cattle in their fodder, along with some salt, is good for their coughs.

The expressed juice of fresh mugwort combined with an equal quantity of wine is a choice remedy for treating people who have been wounded by a bullet. Give two-tablespoon doses to the patient several times each day, and also put some of it into the wound itself, for it possesses a strong faculty for allaying the pain and mortification caused by gunpowder burn. If no fresh mugwort is on hand, then take the dried leaves and boil them in equal portions of wine and water, and administer as directed above.

For quartan fever, take two handfuls of mugwort, and one handful each of holy thistle and Saint-John's-wort. Boil this in white wine until reduced by one-third. The patient should then drink a small mug of the decoction in the morning and evening.[164] It is also good if an emetic is taken first to thoroughly clean out the stomach.

Mugwort is an excellent herb for foot baths for sickly women. Indeed, it is generally acknowledged that this herb is the very best for patients recovering from con-

164. The word "mug" *(Becher)* would not have appeared here unless something specific was understood. This probably refers to an ash or ivy wood mug. The medical properties of these woods are discussed on pages 47 and 180 respectively.

finement and who are not back to normal. And this is particularly true for cases where neglectful injuries have occurred during birth. It is also good for young women whose health has been affected by taking a chill, by palpitations from frights, or other shocks to the system.

The herb should be boiled in equal parts wine and water, and a copious glassful drunk every morning and evening. Also, for a period of time each evening, make a foot bath, and soak the feet in it until the bathwater is lukewarm. Then dry off the feet thoroughly and go directly to bed, lest the feet become chilled. Otherwise, the injury that follows the foot bath is often greater than the usefulness hoped for from the treatment.

Mulberry
Morus nigra and *Morus rubra*
Sauer: *Maulbeere* (1775)

There are three types of common mulberries, but the Sauer herbal is mostly concerned with the black and red. The European white and black species were introduced here during the colonial period, the white especially in the 1600s in connection with early attempts at silk culture. Both the black and white mulberries have naturalized, but it is not clear how readily available they may have been during Sauer's era. Nonetheless, it is very clear from the Sauer herbal that fresh leaves and fruits are necessary in some of the remedies, so Sauer must have judged the native red mulberry a practical equivalent. It was extremely common, especially in rich bottomlands along rivers and large streams.

It is no secret that mulberries were a great favorite of German cooks. Maria Sophia Schellhammer included several recipes in her Der zufälliger Confect-Tafel, *including the jelly recipe here, which also served a medical purpose similar to the syrup recipe in Sauer's herbal:*

> *Rub the mulberries with a wooden spoon until broken very small, then set this overnight in the cellar so that they throw their juice. Then pour off the clear juice through a hair-cloth. Once you have gotten two* Maas, *dissolve and boil one pound of sugar until it reaches the thread stage. Add the mulberry juice and stir this together well. Let it boil up one more time.*[165]

The leaves of mulberry and the bark from the roots contain numerous watery elements mixed with mucusy, volatile, sour salts. They derive from these elements the faculty to stop, to ease, and to draw together. But the fruit, when it is ripe, is endowed with much watery juice, which at the same time pos-

165. Maria Sophia Schellhammer, *Der Wohl-unterweisenen Köchin zufälliger Confect-Taffel* (Berlin, 1732), 102.

sesses sundry sour, subtle salts. Therefore the fruit has the special capacity to cut through all thick phlegms of the throat and its glands, to cool them, and to prevent inflammation of the throat.

Mulberries in particular promote a good, sharp, strong stomach, for which reason they are healthy. The ancients were accustomed to eating them early in the morning before sunrise and for a cooling repast at the end of the midday meal.

A useful syrup may be prepared from mulberries in the following manner: Take six ounces of mulberry juice, twelve ounces each of blackberry juice and honey skimmed and strained clear, and three ounces of sweet wine. Let the juices together with the honey and wine simmer slowly over a gentle charcoal fire until it thickens to a syrup.

This syrup is generally mixed with gargle waters and makes a powerful remedy for all sores, corruptions, inflammations, and quinsies of the throat and mouth. It will draw up a fallen uvula, and prevent the occurrence of fluxes. Take with each ounce of this syrup three ounces of all-heal water. Heat it until lukewarm and then gargle with it.

A water is distilled from mulberries that are not quite ripe. It will dissolve all tough phlegm in the chest, get rid of internal sores, and heal burning coughs. It is a good gargle water for an angry, sore, swollen neck and injured throat. It will clear the eyes if from time to time they are rinsed with it while warm.

If sugar is dissolved in the pressed, strained juice of mulberries, and then boiled over a gentle heat, it will yield an acidic syrup, which is not only serviceable in juleps for quelling internal heats, but also sores or blisters on the tongue and mouth, which its sharpness penetrates and heals.

The leaves and bark boiled in water, or half water and half vinegar, and held in the mouth, will still toothache.

Mustard (Black Mustard)
Brassica nigra
Sauer: *Senf* (1768)

Like flax, mustard was one of the early export crops grown in colonial Pennsylvania. Thus there were fields upon fields of mustard everywhere. Benjamin Jackson and Company, whose well-known Mustard and Chocolate Store was located in Letitia Court, Philadelphia, during the 1760s, operated the Governor's Mill in Philadelphia's Northern Liberties—a mill built for William Penn, for the sole purpose of grinding and manufacturing mustard for domestic use and export. Jackson sold his mustard in black glass bottles with William Penn's coat of arms as his trademark. This mustard, both ground and prepared, went out all over the British colonies, and was readily available to Sauer's readers. It was advertised in all of the colonial newspapers, often showing a picture of the mustard bottle so that potential customers would readily recognize it when at market.[166] Sauer, however, provides a recipe for prepared mustard (mustard sauce), so that his readers could make it at home.

166. For example, refer to Jackson's advertisement in the *Pennsylvania Journal* for September 16, 1762.

Aside from culinary mustard, the Sauer herbal also mentions a mustardy compound called the Cure of Mithradates quite a few times. The mustard specific to it was penny cress (Thlaspi arvense), *which is also known in many old herbals as Mithradate mustard. It has naturalized in North America, and I have found a strain of it from Pennsylvania's Mahontongo Valley called shallot cress due to its shallotlike taste—most penny cress is quite garlicky. It is biennial in that the fall plants overwinter and bloom the following season. The cress is nearly evergreen and provides an excellent source of winter salad greens when raised in cold frames or under straw. Penny cress can be used medically like the black mustard discussed by Sauer.*

Mustard warms and dries powerfully and possesses a sharp, volatile, alkaline salt containing somewhat oily elements. For this reason it has the faculty to dissolve, to absorb retained phlegm, to strengthen the stomach and promote digestion, and to expel through the kidneys and bladder. Externally, it will draw up the flesh and turn it red, open sores that have come to a head, and cause sneezing.

For common and quartan agues, take one quint of ground mustard in a glass of wine or meat broth right before the outbreak of the fever.

For meat dishes, a very good mustard sauce may be prepared in the following manner: Take vinegar and put it in a glass bottle with enough ground mustard to make it thick. Add a little sugar and let it stand twenty-four hours. It is then ready for eating. If the bottle is kept well corked, this mustard will keep for many weeks, especially during cool weather. This mustard sauce may be enjoyed with food, but it also purifies the head, warms the stomach, absorbs the immoderate overflow of thick tartaric humors arising from hypochondria, promotes urine, clears the chest, and promotes expectoration from the same. It is also useful for asthmatics, but does not do much good for the eyes when used too copiously.

For inflammation, pain, and redness of the eyes, the following mustard plaster will be found useful: Boil some dried figs in water until they are soft, then pound them in a stone mortar to make a paste. Take half a loth of this and an equal quantity of powdered mustard, a quint of Solomon's seal, three quints of Venetian soap, and as much honey as is necessary to make a plaster. Spread this thickly on a cloth and lay it over the nape of the neck. After a time, refresh the plaster, and repeat until the skin becomes quite red. This will draw out fluxes from the eyes and ears so that hearing will return.

Mustard employed internally as well as externally is particularly useful to those afflicted with hypochondria. When used internally in cookery, as mentioned above, it absorbs all internal sourness and the swelling of the spleen caused by it. It also treats anguish and dismay, and absorbs all of the thick humors of the stomach and gut. For blockages and bloating of the spleen, however, ground mustard should be mixed with urine and thus applied as a plaster over the region where the spleen is located. The volatile elements in the urine together with the volatile salts of the mustard penetrate powerfully and will dissolve and dissipate sour phlegmy humors in the bloated spleen.

For this reason the mustard sauce mentioned earlier possesses a strong faculty for purifying scorbutic blood, and for stopping scurvy of the mouth, even if only the seeds are chewed. It also protects against apoplexy, dizziness, and all afflictions connected with sleep. For this reason, some elderly people eat it with sugar every day.

If powdered mustard is mixed with honey and a little sharp vinegar to make a salve, and then spread on a cloth that is laid over a shaved head, and left there until the scalp turns red, this will dispel lethargy, dizziness, and apoplexy.

A valuable blister plaster for toothache can be prepared in the following manner: Take one loth each of pigeon manure and powdered mustard, half a quint of black pepper, and grind it all to a fine powder. Add a little pitch and turpentine, and stir it to a thick, sticky plaster. Spread this on leather or taffeta the thickness of a *Thaler*, then lay this on the temples and behind the ears. Leave it there until it falls off by itself. It will draw out the fluxes in the eyes, ears, and teeth, and dispel the pain in them as well.

Mustard seeds mixed with honey and dissolved gum traganth (dissolved in white lily water) and spread over moles, spots, and freckles on the face and other parts of the body daily will take them away and make the skin soft and beautiful.

If mustard and cress seeds are ground and bound into a small bundle and old white wine poured over it, and this is taken as an aperitif before meals, it will strengthen the stomach, purify the blood, and dispel all colds and scurvy arising from sourness, without fail.

If powdered mustard is mixed with a little sourdough sots and pulped rue, then moistened with vinegar so that it forms a plaster, which is then spread on a cloth half a finger thick and bound to the soles of the feet, this will prove effective against the hotness and head pain of ardent fevers, as well as the fables told by patients.[167] This is proven.

Myrrh
Balsamodendron myrrha
Sauer: *Myrrhen* (1771)

Myrrh is a yellow resin exuded by the bark of a bush native to the Arabian peninsula and Somalia. It was sold in dry form in brittle, reddish brown lumps. It is easily ground into powder or dissolved in liquids, although it becomes sticky when wet. Sweet cicely is also called myrrh by country people, but the two should not be confused. True myrrh was once extensively employed in midwifery, especially among the German colonists. The Kurtzgefasstes Weiber-Büchlein *(Reading, 1802) advised, "When a woman commences to labor, bind the root of henbane to her left hip. Grind myrrh to a powder and give it to her in wine. This was said to help promote delivery."*

In myrrh there are numerous oily, balsamic, salty, sharp, bitter, caustic-smelling elements. From this resin derives its faculties for opening, for softening, for bring-

167. This is Theodor Zwinger speaking, as parroted by Sauer. We must presume that Zwinger considered this cure a lot more intelligent and effective than some of the folk remedies told him by his patients. Of course, the plaster is also very painful; he may have gotten even with a gossip this way.

ing sores to a head, for dispersing, for withstanding all putrefaction, and for restoring thickened blood to its proper consistency and circulation. Furthermore, due to its earthy components, it draws together gently, and eases and improves conditions aggravated by sharp, sour, corrosive humors. It gets rid of choler, and strengthens the liver and stomach.

The following essence is excellent: Take two ounces of the best myrrh and three ounces of cream of tartar, and let this stand for a few hours over warm ashes well covered. Then pour a pint of tartarized brandy over it. In a short time, this will draw out the essence, which is then strained off and put away for further use. An adult may be administered up to fifteen drops, but for children, only two, three, or even six may be given them. This is effective for those old people who suffer from stomachache or mother fits and rheums upon the chest. It will kill worms, force out the purples, open blockages of the liver, and cure jaundice.

The oil distilled from myrrh, administered often in two, six, or eight drops, will kill and drive out worms, protect the blood from corruption, keep away the plague and other contagious diseases, and open a blocked matrix and liver.

A good protective remedy for the plague: Take half a loth each of myrrh, aloe gum, *bole armeniac*, diaphoretic antimony,[168] and prepared hartshorn; a half quint each of mace, cloves, and saffron; and two loths of rock candy. Mix and grind it all together to a fine powder. Take two pinches at a time with wine or honey. A quint of sublimated flower of brimstone may also be added to this powder.

To heal scurvy of the mouth, take myrrh, tormentil root, birthwort root, red roses, plantain, rosemary, frankincense, and a little alum and boil this in water. Use this to wash out the mouth. If there are loose teeth, and the gums are rotting, take the ingredients just enumerated and boil them in red wine, then add a little rose honey or mulberry juice and use this as a mouthwash. After that, rub the following salve over the gums: Take four loths of rose honey, a quint each of mastic, myrrh, frankincense, columbine seeds, and calcined alum. Mix it all together very well.

To get rid of the humors of tumorous fluxes, the following plaster is very valuable: Take a handful each of mint, marjoram, and speedwell; a half handful of elder flowers; a half loth each of sweet bay, juniper berries, myrrh, mastic, and frankincense; and a quint of brimstone. Boil all of this together with fresh rainwater or water of limestone, or in a mixture of half wine and half vinegar, until reduced to one-half. Strain it off, and warm it up often, dipping a cloth into it that is laid as hot as the patient can bear it over the swelling.

Twenty grains of ground myrrh taken in water of purslane will kill worms. Those afflicted by quartan fever may take a quint of ground myrrh in warm white wine one hour before the fever commences. This should be done three times, but not before the stomach has been cleaned out by a purgative.

Myrrh is added to those medicines that can be used against poison, thus it is employed as well during pestilence.

---

168. A diaphoretic is a remedy that causes profuse sweating. There were some five basic preparations made with antimony specifically for diaphoretic applications. The herbal does not specify which of these should be employed, although it was probably *antimonium diaphoreticum simplex*.

If myrrh and alum are boiled in water and the feet washed with this, it will take away the foul odor.

Nettle (Stinging Nettle)
Urtica dioica
Sauer: *Nesseln* (1763)

Although it is now naturalized in this country, stinging nettle is nowhere near as common and abundant as it is in Europe, where I have seen entire pastures covered with it as thickly as mint. The herb is deservedly cursed by anyone who is luckless enough to walk through it, yet it is also rather handsome in its own way, especially when in full bloom. In spite of a reputation in league with poison ivy, nettle is still firmly accepted by herbalists, and teas made with it can be found in most health food shops. Nettle tea is often taken to treat prostate problems, for which it is deemed quite effective.

In line with Sauer's penchant for moralizing, Johann Jakob Schmidt noted that nettle was mentioned in the Book of Job. While its biting leaves may have symbolized Job's many torments, Schmidt allowed that the plant was only useful in remedies, for which he assigned it the faculty "to open and to purify, particularly the lungs and kidneys. It is a good remedy for stilling fluxes of the blood. As a vulnerary, it is effective in treating old injuries, scall, and so forth."[169] His comments have the ring of Zwinger, but in fact Schmidt's introduction stated that he consulted the works of Dr. Friedrich Hoffmann, to whom Zwinger also attributed many of his remedies. In essence, all three books overlap since they share the same material.

Nettle is of a warm, dry nature. It is opening, discutient, purifying of the blood, healing, and useful for driving out urine and stone.

The root of the large nettle possesses the special faculty of preserving people from developing stones, provided it is powdered and one-half or a full quint is taken from time to time.

If this root is boiled in wine and sweetened with sugar, it will be good for those with coughs arising from thick phlegm.

If the root of the nettle is washed and ground together with a little saffron, and some white wine is then poured over it and expressed from the mass, this infusion will prove effective for jaundice of long continuance when a few tablespoonfuls are taken for several days in succession and the patient is made to sweat profusely.

For the prevention of gravel and stone, it is very good if in the spring, the tender shoots are boiled in water and

169. Johann Jakob Schmidt, *Biblischer Medicus* (Züllichau, 1743), 704.

the broth drunk every day for a period of time. It is also healthy to eat the boiled greens.

If a quint of nettle seeds are ground fine and taken with wine, this will prove a good treatment for lumbago and sores of the chest. If nettle juice is snuffed up into the nose often, it will stop nosebleed.

The distilled water of nettle leaves is also good for lumbago, for promoting expectoration, and for purifying wounds.

Freshly pressed and strained nettle juice, taken in four- to five-loth doses twice a day for several weeks, is excellent for tertian and quartan fevers, as well as for blockage of the mesenteric veins, the liver, and kidneys; and for jaundice, dropsy, and foul matter in the kidneys. It will also purify sharp, thick blood, get rid of lumbago, and cleanse external wounds.

If a handful of nettle root is cleansed and chopped fine, and an equal amount of dock root and juniper berries added, then boiled in one gallon of water until reduced to one-third, this will yield an excellent remedy for dropsy and jaundice when sweetened with a little sugar and taken regularly as a drink.

Nutmeg and Mace
Myristica fragrans
Sauer: *Muscatnüss, Muscatblüthe* (1770)

The nutmeg is a tropical tree that produces both nutmeg and mace. Mace is the outer shell of the nut, which is dried and processed separately after they are harvested. Both have been articles of commerce since the Middle Ages, and both figure largely in the cookery and medicine of the colonial Germans. Nutmeg was so commonly used to flavor food that most households had it on hand. For this reason, throughout the Sauer herbal, measurements are often given as the size of a nutmeg, a useful point of reference in kitchens where weights and measures were not always available. For the reader today, this is relatively easy to translate, for it approximates two level tablespoons.

Nutmegs and their outer shells possess an aromatic or spicy principle that is quite warming and drying. They strengthen the head, stomach, and matrix, and glutinate gently. They bring sleep, stay pain, dissipate vapors, promote digestion, prevent fainting and palpitations, stop vomiting and diarrhea, and strengthen the eyesight and the nerves.

A nutmeg ground together with twelve loths of rose honey and four loths of brandy, then gently cooked until the brandy evaporates, is good for stopping stomachache and gripes arising from cold or from vapors. Take three tablespoons every morning before breakfast.

Where there is no temperature present in those suffering from the flux and diarrhea, nutmeg grated into a glass of old wine may be administered with good results.

If pregnant women suffer from weakness, toast a slice of bread over hot coals and then rub it well with a nutmeg, and dip it in good wine or a strengthening herbal water and lay it as warm as they can bear it on their navel, this will allay gripes and all kinds of dysentery, strengthen the fetus, and prevent premature birth. If laid on the navel following delivery, it will be an excellent remedy for stilling the pains of her travail.

A good stomach powder can be made in the following manner: Take eight loths each of aniseed, fennel seed, coriander, caraway, and ginger; two loths of the finest stick cinnamon, one loth of calamus root, and half a loth of nutmeg. Grind all of this to a fine powder, then take one or two pinches in the morning before breakfast.

If nutmeg is chewed and eaten, it will strengthen the head, give a sweet-smelling breath, clear the eyesight, and strengthen a weak heart, stomach, and liver. It will also prevent swelling of the spleen, promote urine, block and ease the discomfort of fluxes of the stomach, bloody flux, vomiting, and squeamish stomachs, and disperse vapors in the gut.

To make a useful stomach plaster: Take the best-quality Cure of Mithradates, spread it very thickly on a strip of leather, then scatter powdered nutmeg over it. Lay this on the stomach to stop vomiting and nauseous eructations.

The oil pressed from nutmegs is good against pains in the limbs and nerves arising from chills. A little of this oil dissolved in warm broth and eaten thus is serviceable against vomiting, gripes, gravel in the loins, and a feeble matrix. It is particularly good for children who are plagued by colic when it is smeared on their little navels.

Similar uses have also been found for distilled oil of nutmeg, provided three drops are taken in a glass of wine. This will warm a cold stomach, strengthen the same, take off all corrupt vapors from the body, dissipate windiness, ease colic, give a sweet-smelling breath, and serve well against ailments of the bladder.

Mace gives off a pleasant aroma, has a sharp taste, and will yield a yellow dye. It has the same virtues as the nut, but because it is of a more subtle composition, it is also more effective for all of the above-mentioned maladies. Mace dissipates vapors and serves well against trembling of the heart. Above all else, mace is celebrated for warming and strengthening a cold feeble stomach, for aiding and promoting digestion, and for dissipating corrupt vapors from the stomach.

Oak Tree (White Oak)
Quercus robur and *Quercus alba*
Sauer: *Eichbaum, Eicheln* (1775)

While the herbal deals exclusively with the common European oak (Quercus robur), the ancient oak of the Druids, American readers found an equivalent in our native white oak. During the colonial period, all white oak trees in Pennsylvania were supposed to belong to the Penn family, according to their colonial charter. In practice, the white oaks ended up as barrels and ships, but many ancient trees were preserved due to their huge size or historical associations. The Treaty Oak under which Penn negotiated the purchase of Pennsylvania was a popular icon even in Sauer's day. Another Treaty Oak from the same period still survives at London Grove near Kennett Square, Pennsylvania. I mention these old trees because years ago, the leaves, acorns, and galls were collected from them by practitioners of folk medicine due to the perception that they held special healing powers. One such oak has stood in my own garden for over two hundred and fifty years.

The oak tree possesses in all of its parts a gently vitriolic, astringent sour salt, combined with a large quantity of earthy elements with little oil. From this, the oak derives its capacity to stop and to draw together, and to block all manner of bloody and dropsical fluxes, diarrhea, bloody flux, and involuntary flux of natural seed.[170] It provides thin, watery blood with a better consistency, and checks rheums of the head.

The mistletoe of oak contains an insensible, sharp, volatile, sour salt, from which it derives its capacity to open, to penetrate, and especially to eradicate the noxious origins of fits and falling evil.

The thin outer skin of acorns, dried, parched in the oven, and then ground to a powder, will prove especially serviceable for bloody flux if administered to the patient from time to time in half-quint doses mixed with nutmeg and calcined hartshorn. An effectiveness similar to oak mistletoe may be derived from the acorn itself.

If oak leaves, the leaves of wild tansy, chamomile flowers, and great mullein are chopped together, placed in a small bag, and then boiled in milk or water in which a hot, glowing iron has been plunged,[171] and the poultice thus laid over the arse while warm, this will still looseness from bloody flux in young and old.

When the mistletoe of oak is dried and ground to a powder, then administered in one-half or up to one full quint, it will prove effective not only for the falling evil, but it will especially stop diarrhea and the immoderate coursing of the menses when taken in a soft-boiled egg from time to time.

Fresh oak leaves laid over inflamed blisters will draw out the heat and heal them. If the leaves are chopped and laid over fresh wounds, they will not only stop bleeding but promote the healing as well.

Oak leaves picked fresh in May, chopped, and then distilled will yield a useful water that, if drunk often, will stop heartburn and expel sand and foul matter gently from the kidneys and loins. It will also restrain diarrhea and other looseness of the body by the by, and stop blood-spitting. Indeed, it will moderate all hemorrhages of the blood and give ease. In particular, when oak water is mixed with some quince or plantain water and spread warm over hot, burning blisters on the feet, it will reduce and heal them.

Oak bark ground to a powder and boiled in red wine or in smithy water,[172] and the steam from this allowed to rise over the abdomen, will not only stop looseness of the body during both bloody and white flux, but will also heal a fallen end gut and hysterocele in women.[173]

---

170. Sauer merely made a vague reference to other fluids, but since this passage is taken from Culpeper, I have restored what Culpeper actually said. In common parlance, this is called a wet dream. Sauer was too prudish to allow this in print.

171. This was accomplished with a long iron commonly used for heating slings and other hot drinks.

172. The herbal actually calls it *Schmiedlöschwasser*. This is the red rusty water used to temper hot irons in a smithy.

173. Ulceration of the uterus.

If acorns are dried and ground to a powder and then taken as a remedy, they will stop common and bloody fluxes, as well as blood-pissing, nosebleed, and other hemorrhages.

Oak galls, due to their drying and astringent faculty, are useful for treating many external afflictions. They are especially effective in treating scurvy of the mouth and mouth sores when red roses, acorn skins, and galls are ground together and boiled in wine or water. The mouth should then be washed with this frequently. A little rose honey may also be added, for this will be all the more healing.

Take one quint or half a loth each of oak gall, nutmeg, mastic, *terra sigillata*,[174] cinnamon, and cloves. Grind these together and combine with melted beeswax, turpentine, and a little oil of quinces to make a plaster. Spread this on a piece of leather and lay it warm over the stomach. This will cure it of refusing to keep down food, the rising up of vapors, casting of the stomach, diarrhea, and looseness of the body, as well as strengthening digestion.

Surgeons also find powdered oak gall useful in their treatments. They strew it into rotten wounds, for it cleanses and dries all corrupted flesh and other putrid humors very well. It is also good for stopping blood.

If oak leaves are boiled in wine or water and the decoction drunk, this will stop blood-spitting, various fluxes of the stomach, and severe anemia in the female sex, and will also heal internal sores.

Rainwater that has remained in an oak stump will heal the weeping sores of scall when they are washed with it. It will also get rid of warts.

Water distilled from oak leaves is a healing remedy for coughing blood, and in particular for those children who are afflicted by bloody flux. Oak water will also break up and expel stones and drive gravel from the loins. It prevents pissing blood, and for this reason is quite effective in treating such that commonly experience blood-pissing after using Spanish fly.[175]

This water also heals scurvy of the mouth and other injuries of the throat as well as inflamed hot swellings in the privates of both men and women.

Those who have brown or black fever blisters on their legs may take a small piece of cloth and dip it in this water and lay it lukewarm over the sores.

Oak water poured lukewarm over a cloth and laid upon an inflamed limb will cool it and heal it. If old wounds are washed with it and allowed to dry on their own, this will also heal them.

Oats

Avena sativa
Sauer: *Haber* (1770)

Oats were associated with poverty food in Germany, so this was one of the grains the German settlers consciously avoided once they became well-off in this country. Yet oats did

---

174. A clay commonly called red bolus. The type used here probably came from Rheinfelden in Germany. It is mentioned on page 193 under licorice.

175. Spanish fly was a notorious aphrodisiac that caused an intense prickling sensation in the genitals. Obviously, such kinkiness carried with it certain risks.

retain certain respect as a health food, especially after the publication of Johann Gottfried Fiedler's tract on oat cures in 1714.[176] This rather obscure work looms large in our discussion because its theories and cures were incorporated in the revised 1744 edition of Zwinger's herbal—which Sauer copied—and Sauer himself printed excerpts from the tract in his almanacs and newspaper. Oat porridge was the sort of modest fare that Sauer approved of. Its appeal to him was in part due to his own moral asceticism, something that surfaces in his discussion of tea on page 321. In fact, the entries on tea and oats might best be viewed together, since water oats and oat flour soup offer an alternative to the pleasurable lifestyle of punch cups and dainties that Sauer so vehemently detested.

Oats possess more temperate volatile, oily, and less watery elements than barley, therefore it is valued for its warmer nature.

A generous portion of oats ground with juniper berries and parched in a frying pan, then put into sachets and laid upon the stomach as warm as the patient can bear it, will stop colic. When the sachet becomes cold, reheat it on a hot bake stone and lay it upon the stomach again. Women also use such a remedy for mother fits.

Soups and broths prepared with oat flour make excellent food and nourishment for the sick, for they strengthen and nourish them, and children acquire a healthy rosy color from eating it.

Oat flour soups are particularly useful for afflictions of the head, dizziness, coughing, maladies of the lungs, liver, and spleen, bloody flux, tertian and quartan fevers, as well as gravel and the cold evil.

Ewes and wethers become very fat when foddered on oats if they are given two handfuls a day. But sometimes when they are fed with it, they become so fat that the caul of their stomach bursts and they die from it.

When the sheath of a horse is swollen, prepare a vapor from boiled oat straw and place this under the horse. After a time, drop a red-hot stone into straw water so that steam rises again. This will help the horse.

An excellent potion may be prepared from oats, which has already been published for the second time in this almanac, yet so little accounted for even though it has already performed many excellent services.[177]

For pleurisy, and cold painful fluxes, warmed oats have already proved useful. They are first toasted in a frying pan, then poured into two little linen bags. Lay one on the pained place and the other on a hot hearth stone so that it is warmed to replace the first one when it cools. Continue in this manner until the pain has disappeared.

Olive Tree and Oil
Olea europaea
Sauer: *Oelbaum* (1777)

Olive oil was one of the most frequently mentioned import products in colonial American newspapers, but the quality was varied and always expensive. The rawness

176. Johann Gottfried Fiedler, *De Cura Avenacea/Von der Haber-Kur* (Halle, 1714).
177. This refers to Fiedler's oat cure, which evidently Sauer published some years prior to 1769.

referred to by Sauer is obviously a reference to the coarser types of olive oil, and especially to the noticeable differences in national preferences, Portuguese and Spanish olive oil tasting much more bitter than that of Italy, for example.

Country people in colonial America did use olive oil, but consumption varied greatly from one ethnic group to another. The ample references in the Sauer herbal to salad dressings and other similar specialized culinary applications point rather clearly to specific German eating habits, medical remedies aside. However, olive oil was not used as an everyday cooking oil, except perhaps by the well-to-do and by the small community of German Jews who lived in this country during that period.

There were many attempts to find substitutes for olive oil. It was not until after the revolution that Chinese oil radishes were introduced expressly to answer the purpose of expensive imported olive oils. The American Republican *for April 17, 1810, carried a long article discussing Moravian experiments with oil radishes both in Pennsylvania and North Carolina in 1807 and 1808. Seed was available for sale through Christian David Senseman at Nazareth, Pennsylvania. Later, in the 1830s, considerable experimentation was undertaken with sunflower oil, which remained popular among the Pennsylvania Germans until the Civil War. But olive oil always remained a culinary ingredient for the well-off, and as it is today, it was very much a symbol of economic status when used in cookery.*

Finally, the preparation called Samaritans Balsam, mentioned in the text below, deserves a few words, for this remedy was indeed popular among the German element. It served as the framework or theme of Eliam Baynon's Der Barmherziger Samariter *(Hanover, Pa., 1798), an advice book on healing.*

The leaves as well as the fruit of the olive tree are put to use in various ways, but we do not have these trees here in this country. Thus I will only mention what is usefully done with the oil, which we call *Baumöl.*

Olive oil possesses the capacity to soften, to ease, to act as a laxative, and to make all the interior passages supple. It eases dryness of the chest, sweetens the sharpness of fluxes, and heals wounds. Indeed, this oil possesses a certain caustic sharpness that is applicable to many conditions, particularly for diarrhea or injuries to the chest. But it is far better when boiled a little to cook out this rawness.

If someone has taken a hard fall, take three to four tablespoons of cooked olive oil each day so that it disperses clotted blood and restores it into circulation.

For someone with a hoarse voice, or with thick phlegm in the chest, or who is afflicted by hard coughs and asthma, they will benefit very much if they take a tablespoonful of boiled olive oil mixed with rose honey often. This will dissolve the phlegm in the windpipe so that it can be expectorated.

Olive oil is used externally in quite a few vulnerary plasters and salves, particularly in the valuable wound balm prepared in the following manner: Take half a pound of olive oil and a fourth of a pound of turpentine, and put it together in a clean vessel. Fill this with two parts Saint-John's-wort flowers and one part mullein flowers. Pour over this two quarts of wine and boil until the wine is reduced. Then put the mixture in a glass bottle and set in the sun for one month. Or, take half a pound of olive oil, a fourth of a pound of turpentine, a fourth of a pound of earthworms, and a handful each of red beet chards, chamomile flowers, and Saint-John's-wort flowers. Thoroughly boil the earthworms, beet chards, and flowers in the olive oil, then press it well through a cloth. Put the liquid in a glass vessel and add a fourth of a pound of turpentine to it. Stand this in the sun until it yields a fine balsam, which is wonderfully healing for all wounds and open injuries.

Some people also prepare a good wound balsam from only olive oil and wine. They boil them together until reduced to a thick balsam, which they call Samaritans Balsam, after the example of the Good Samaritan in the Gospel of Luke, chapter 10.

In Italy and Spain, where olive oil is common, persons of quality are accustomed to bathing in it when they are afflicted by gravel, lumbago, and the stone, for it softens all of the passages. Children and adults who are plagued with consumption and atrophy also bathe in it often.

If a slice of bread is toasted by the fire, brushed thickly with olive oil, and then eaten, it will open the body very nicely, and is quite useful to pregnant women if they employ the remedy often.

Olive oil is above all else a very useful article in clysters. In cases of strong stomach grips and colic which are coupled with constipation, a clyster of plain olive oil is generally effective.

For various internal injuries brought about by a fall or similar occurrence, a tablespoon of olive oil taken often will prove an effective treatment.

When the legs and arms are rubbed with olive oil every morning, this is very good for those who easily take skin allergies during mowing and hay making. It goes without saying that olive oil is an excellent remedy against all sorts of poisons. If a person or an animal is bitten by a snake, put plain warm olive oil on the injury immediately and repeat this every hour. It will help for certain. If someone is stung by a wasp, bee, or some other insect, there is no more effective a remedy than olive oil rubbed over the hurt. Or, according to the person's constitution, take a square cloth and moisten it with olive oil and bind it over the spot.

Fresh wounds rinsed with wine and then dressed with olive oil will heal very well. If there is no water to mix with the wine, it will heal well just the same.

For those who cannot pass water, be they adults or children, take olive oil and stand it over hot charcoal until it becomes warm. Then smear the patient's abdomen with it very thoroughly and warm the hands over the same coals. Rub the stomach vigorously with the hot hands so that the oil and heat are absorbed into the skin. By means of this remedy, some already have been fully cured of dropsy, by repeating this daily about two or three weeks in succession. Those who want to do this twice a day, so much the better. Every time after massaging the stomach, a woolen cloth or piece of flannel must be laid warm over it so that no cold air can affect it.

Onion
Allium cepa
Sauer: *Zwiebel* (1771)

The herbal's discussion of onions makes a bit more sense when it is viewed in the context of the original onion illustrations in the Zwinger herbal. The descriptions of the various onion types are keyed to those woodcuts, which depict the typical range of types then available. I would like to point out that Sauer's long onion is very much like the so-called Florence or "torpedo" onions that are coming back in fashion today. The herbal is right. They are much stronger than the round ones.

Common onions are warm in nature and possess numerous volatile, sharp salts that withstand astringency. From these, onions derive their capacity for opening obstructions of the liver and kidneys, and for expelling urine and gravel. But they are of greater service to those of a cold, dropsical nature than to those of an ardent, dry one because for the latter, onions easily excite a powerful ebullition of the blood, thus resulting in headache and sore eyes.

Long onions are more biting than the round ones: red more so than the white, dried onions more than the green, and the raw more so than the cooked.

If boiled onions are eaten, they will expel blocked urine. In particular, the juice pressed from onions roasted under hot ashes will cure the same condition if taken in doses of one-half to a full tablespoon.

Many people eat raw onions with bread and salt as protection against miasmas. Experience has demonstrated that this is a good remedy. Garlic and onions are commonly the farmers' panacea. However, weak and sickly people should avoid onions even when cooked, since they often induce sleeplessness.

For difficulty in breathing, roast onions under hot ashes and eat them every evening and morning. Some people add sugar or honey to the onions, which furthers expectoration and opens the chest.

For killing tapeworms in children and expelling them, chop raw onions and lay them in fresh water overnight. Give this infusion to the child in the morning.

When young children cannot pass their water, cook onions to a pap consistency and lay this warm over the lower belly next to their privates. This can also be administered to adults with good results. It is even better when the onions are fomented in oil of chamomile and then laid over the lower belly as warm as the patient can bear it.

Take an onion and remove the center part. Fill the cavity with *Theriaca Andromaci*. Roast it, mash it, and spread it as a plaster between two cloths. This is a fine remedy for emolliating pestilential boils.

For emolliating abscesses and furuncles so that they head up and burst, mash together onions and figs and spread them warm between two cloths. Lay this over the affected place. The onions can be fried by themselves and laid warm over the abscesses for softening and opening the sores quickly.

During times of pestilence, peel a large onion and hang it in the room. It will absorb miasmas and swell up.[178]

Should anyone be burned by fire, scalding water, or anything else, immediately take an onion and some salt. Mash this fine and spread it on the burn, or wash the burns with the juice of an onion mixed with salt. This is an excellent remedy, but it must be administered at once before the burn turns ulcerous, otherwise it will increase the pain and introduce inflammation.

To make an excellent salve for burns, heat some onions under warm ashes, then chop and foment them in fresh butter and olive oil. Then add quicklime or silver earth and oil of egg.

A first-rate ointment for swollen hemorrhoids: Hollow out an onion and fill it with oil of bitter almonds, then roast it in hot ashes. Press out the juice and smear the hemorrhoids with it.

Take equal amounts of onions, rue, and mint and pulp them together in a mortar. Add salt and smear on the bite or sting of a poisonous creature or snake. It will draw out the poison or act as an antidote to it.

If a horse has a split hoof, make the following hoof salve: Take four onions and chop them fine. Add one ounce of turpentine, a fourth of a pound of wax, a little resin, and some sheep's tallow. Let this dissolve and combine by the fire, then let it cool. Smear the affected hoof with it diligently.

Opium Poppy
Papaver somniferum
Sauer: *Magsamen* (1770)

The use of opium is of course illegal today, although in Sauer's era it was readily available. It was widely employed as a painkiller, but its narcotic and addictive characteristics were also well understood, and many sad tales were circulated about people who were in fact destroyed by their medicine. However, the opium poppy is really very beautiful and is still cultivated as an ornamental. The white sap from the green seedpods produces the drug, but the seeds were the part most used by colonial physicians. As the herbal points out, there were white- and black-seeded varieties.

The opium poppy is of a cold nature. The white-seeded sort is safer to use than the black. It possesses the faculty of restraining and repressing the bodily spirits, of blocking their influence on the nerves, or of staying them completely. It eases all manner

---

178. This folk practice may be considered magic since it depends upon an unnatural transfer. In essence, the onion was thought to act like a magnet for absorbing contagion. This very same practice was employed with sea onions or squill (page 283).

of pain, stops diarrhea and other uncontrolled fluxes, brings sleep, and prevents coughs arising from sharp humors.

The field poppy possesses all of the same virtues as the white-seeded opium poppy and thus no separate description is necessary.[179] However, both must be used with great caution since they may easily cause injury.

Orach
Atriplex hortensis
Sauer: *Zahme-Melden* (1775)

The picture of orach in Zwinger's herbal is rather sad, for it shows a weedy-looking branch covered with seeds. The plant is used in cookery when it is much younger than that, indeed, while it is hardly a foot tall and the leaves are still large and succulent. Today, the brightly colored seedlings often show up in mixed salads in high-end restaurants, but the larger lettucelike leaves have not yet come back into fashion.

Unfortunately, Zwinger's botany is a bit confusing, for as with the docks, where he listed sixteen different plants all called the same thing, orach has likewise undergone strange associations. I say this because his beets run into amaranths and his amaranths run into orachs, yet it all makes sense if they are grouped simply by their leaves. Somehow, Sauer managed to sort it all out correctly on his own: obviously he knew what the plants looked like.

Zwinger gives fourteen kinds of orach, but from these I can only extrapolate four that are really orachs. A few of these were actually grown in colonial kitchen gardens. I give them here in the order that they appeared in Zwinger's herbal: "white" orach, a green sort with silvery underleaves; red orach, actually purple-red; a wild sort with gray-green leaves; and a wild sort with narrow, pointed leaves. Zwinger also lists the plant called strawberry spinach, but this belongs to a different genus and species. The dark green and red varieties were definitely grown in our gardens, and by Sauer's era there was also a yellow one with chartreuse leaves and stems. The two wild sorts have since been brought into cultivation and improved through breeding. Thus it is possible to obtain seeds for all of these plants today.

Orach is of a moist, cold nature. It possesses divers watery juices together with somewhat nitrous volatile salts. It derives from these its faculty for attenuating, for opening, for promoting stool, and for forcing urine.

It is generally held that the leaves of orach do not particularly agree with the stomach, except in cases of acute fever, for then it is very serviceable in cooling and opening the stomach. In this respect it has its uses. But for those with cold, feeble stomachs, it could well lead to the onset of dropsy and jaundice.

This herb is employed usefully in emollient clysters and plasters, as well as in cooling foot baths.

179. On second thought, Sauer included material on the field poppy in the 1774 installment. It is now out of original sequence, since the herbs are arranged alphabetically in English.

Oregano (Wild Marjoram)
Origanum vulgare
Sauer: *Dost* (1777)

> *There is a lot of herbal literature in the United States claiming that true oregano was not known here until the Greeks brought it in during the 1920s. The Sauer herbal would suggest otherwise. Oregano did not receive much space in the herbal because it was grown primarily for medical reasons, especially for the distilled water, yet its antiviral characteristics were well understood. The difficulty with any discussion of oregano is taxonomy. All of the oreganos, including marjoram (now called* Origanum majorana*), have undergone reclassification. Indeed, an international conference was held in 1996 devoted entirely to oregano, its genetic makeup, and its threatened extinction in its wild habitats.[180] True oregano is now divided into three subspecies, only one of which is considered ideal for cookery. Sauer's* Dost *is certainly oregano, but we cannot determine which of these subspecies was being grown.*

Oregano is somewhat warming and drying. It is endowed with an aromatic oily salt and possesses the faculty to discuss swellings, to open, to strengthen the head, heart, stomach, spleen, and matrix; to relieve the chest, and to dry out rheums of the head.

If half a quint of the dried flowers of common oregano and an equal amount of plantain seeds are administered in wine, this will still bloody flux.

A good remedy for all fluxes of the stomach: Take the leaves of oregano, dry them, and then grind them to a powder. Take a couple of fresh eggs, make a small pancake with the powder, and then eat it.

If oregano is boiled in wine and the steam is allowed to rise up into the ears through an inverted funnel, this will get rid of buzzing and ringing.

The distilled water of oregano is good for asthmatics and consumptives. It strengthens the stomach, warms the matrix, and promotes the menses when three or four loths are taken in the morning before breakfast. If it is slightly warmed and the mouth is gargled with it, this will take away all corruptions of throat and gums, still toothache, and draw up a fallen uvula.

Herbal bitters, among them bitters of oregano, are very effective in treating all people who are plagued by rheums of the head that have descended into the chest and lungs, causing constant coughing, for these wines also promote expectoration. Likewise, they are beneficial to persons with jaundice and to hypochondriacs.

Oregano boiled together with other herbs in bathwater and foot baths for strengthening the limbs will have a good effect.

If a water is distilled from oregano, an oil will swim on the top. Several drops of this oil swabbed over a painful tooth with cotton will ease and dissipate the pain excellently. As an internal remedy, a few drops of this oil may be mixed with sugar in the water of oregano and administered from time to time to those who are plagued by rheums of the head, apoplexy, stomachache, bloating of the matrix, colic, and vapors.

180. Stefano Padulosi, ed., *Oregano: Proceedings of the IPGRI International Workshop on Oregano* (Rome, 1997).

Parsley
Petroselinum sativum
Sauer: *Petersilien, Peterlein* (1765)

English horticulturist Philip Miller observed in The Gardener's Dictionary *(London, 1731) that "every old Woman in the Country, that hath a Garden, knows how to cultivate a Parsley-bed." We must read this comment on several levels. First, Miller lumped parsley and soup celery together under the term* smallage, *even though they are a different genus and species. For many gardeners in the eighteenth century this was a convenient way to deal with two plants that were physically similar and used in much the same manner in cookery and folk medicine. Indeed, they were often considered different forms of the same thing and they are treated this way by Theodor Zwinger in his herbal.*

By this rationale, the Great Garden Parsley of Miller was both the large, flat-leafed sort we generally call "Italian" today, as well as the green tops of the root parsley now commonly called Hamburg parsley. Add to this true smallage or leaf celery (Zwinger called it "water parsley"), both the flat and curled sorts, and we may form a better picture of what the German gardeners were planting in colonial America under the name of parsley or smallage. The Sauer herbal confirms rather clearly that the Hamburg sort was preferred, since it provided a parsniplike root as well as greens—in short, two foods from one plant. This was especially important to country people because in Sauer's day, parsley greens were still being cooked and eaten like spinach. The dainty, ornamental mossy sorts were only grown by the well-to-do.

Yet what Miller said about old ladies and their parsley beds was absolutely true, so much so that contemporary writers often left out critical information (to posterity) on the grounds that the cultivation of parsley was so well known it need not be repeated. We are grateful, therefore, under the entry for broad beans (page 69), to learn that the ashes of those plants make excellent fertilizer for parsley and can be used effectively to force the germination of parsley seed, which is the starting point of any parsley bed. The importance of the parsley bed to Miller's old ladies is best appreciated when one reads through Sauer's huge list of treatments in which this humble plant was employed.

Parsley is of a warm, dry nature. It is used by almost everyone not only in cookery, but internally and externally in medicine as well. In particular, the seeds and the root possess the faculty of opening, of loosening, and of expelling urine, crudities, and sand. It also reduces windiness and all manner of swellings of the liver, spleen, and corrupt flesh. If the root is to be used in medicine, it must be gathered in the spring.

Because parsley is so commonly employed in food, it would not be useless to mention those afflictions for which it is most suitable and those for which it is injurious.

Parsley possesses the faculty for warming, opening, and strengthening. It will warm and strengthen cold livers, kidneys, and bladders. It opens blockages of all the viscera, particularly the liver. It drives out jaundice, forces urine, and purifies the kidneys, urinary vessels, and bladder. For this reason it serves excellently when cooked with meat and fish, in soups, and other dishes that strengthen and warm a cold, weak, dull liver. It is also good for treating dropsy and jaundice and similarly in all cold distempers of the liver, spleen, kidneys, bladder, and matrix. For all of these afflictions just mentioned, both the root and the leaves may be used to good effect. On the other hand, for all maladies of the eyes and head, parsley should be abjured.

Carolus Stephanus[181] has pointed out that there are people who have become freed of the falling evil, but whose condition returned anew just by eating parsley. Nursing women should also refrain from eating it, for it will reduce the flow of milk. Women in confinement should carefully avoid parsley in their soups, for not only will it injure the baby greatly by the diminishment of the mother's milk, but also some have held the opinion that on occasion babies have gotten the fits as a result.

Those whose natural color has not returned following a lengthy illness should eat parsley roots and greens in all their foods.

Parsley root and greens used generously in cookery will protect people from the stone, for it carries off all sand and gravel.

If a frisky horse is wanted, give him parsley root and greens mixed in his fodder often.

The water distilled from parsley greens and root at the beginning of spring will open blockages of the liver, purify the kidneys and bladder, carry off sand and stones, and force down trapped urine. Drink half a gill in the morning before breakfast.

The juice expressed from fresh parsley greens and roots, strained and taken in half-gill doses every day continuously for ten to fourteen days, will not only heal blood-spitting and bloody piss but also purify thick, sour, salty blood. It will also open all internal blockages, force down urine, and carry off all corruptions of the kidneys. Furthermore, it will heal jaundice and dropsy.

Parsley eaten raw or with the sugared seeds[182] will clear the breath of the smell of garlic, tobacco, wine, stinking vapors, and other such causes.

When parsley seeds are ground to powder and a quint dose is taken each morning and evening, this will not only promote urine but also clear up jaundice and dropsy, atrophy, blockages of the mesenteric veins, and all manner of worms in the gut. It is also good for treating the bites of venomous beasts, and the injury done by mercury poisoning.

For pains in the kidneys and lumbago, for thick corruptions of the matrix, and for stoppages of the mesenteric veins, take two loths each of parsley root and greens, asparagus root, and wild spikenard,[183] a handful each of pennyroyal leaves, lemon balsam leaves, agrimony, and horehound; half a loth of juniper berries; and a quint each of fennel and aniseeds. Chop and grind it all together, then put it in a sachet and pour two quarts of white wine and one quart of water over it. Stop it up well and let it stand without heating. Take a gill dose every morning and evening.

If fresh parsley is pulped and mixed with fresh white bread and egg white to form a plaster that is applied lukewarm often, this will get rid of inflammation and pains in

---

181. Carolus Stephanus or Charles Estienne (ca. 1504–1564) was a French physician.

182. Sauer does not say that these are parsley comfits, but that is what they would be called in English medical books of this period.

183. Wild spikenard (*Asarum europaeum*) is also known as hazelwort and cabaric. It is called *Haselwurtz* in German.

the eyes and chest, as well as Saint Anthony's fire on the arms and legs.

When parsley greens are boiled in lye water with southernwood and willow leaves, this will prevent the hair from falling out if used as a hair wash.

For throbbing toothache due to cavities, take one loth of parsley seeds, one and a half quint of black pepper, a quint of henbane seeds, and grind it all to a powder. Add one-half quint of opium gum rubbed with wine and work this into a dough. Form this into tablets. When a toothache commences, stick one of these tablets into the cavity and keep it there for one hour. Keep the head warm, and the pain will soon stop. These tablets often draw out a great deal of pussy matter and spittle, which should not be swallowed, rather spit it out directly.

If parsley is pulped and mixed with honey, and spread on a cloth like a plaster, then laid over the bosom, this will dissolve clotted milk and the painful swellings lodged there. It will also get rid of the hotness and inflammation. A similar result may be had by pulping parsley together with chickweed, then fomenting this in a skillet with butter. Apply this like a plaster.

Take parsley, garlic, and juniper berries in any amount that suits and pound them together. Then cook this with red wine to form a salve. Spread this thickly on a cloth and lay it warm over the lower abdomen. This will promote a mighty piss.

Parsnip
Pastinaca sativa
Sauer: *Pastinachen* (1766)

The Pennsylfaanisch word for parsnip is Baschtnade, *and in spite of the short entry devoted to this vegetable in the herbal, this—along with turnips—was one of the most important of all the cold-weather vegetables in the colonial German kitchen garden. Sauer pointed out that parsnips were best employed in cookery, and the range of preparations was long: purees, soups, puffs, fritters, or simply boiled like carrots, to name a few. They were even cooked and mashed, and then mixed with spelt flour and flour corn to make a type of muffin once popular in the middle colonies.*

The importance of the parsnip lay in the fact that it could be left in the ground and harvested as needed over the course of the winter. Furthermore, during the winter, when other remedies relying on fresh herbs were not possible, parsnips provided nursing women with a means for increasing milk. The herbal goes even farther by claiming that parsnips will help increase the chance of pregnancy, a fact that may be more folkloric than proven, although the phallic shape of the root may point to the origin of this belief. In any event, the seeds were also employed in remedies (as Sauer points out), as well as in cookery. They taste very much like dill seed and can be ground and used in their stead.

Parsnips are of a warm, moist nature. The wild ones are stronger than the cultivated sorts, for which reason they are used more in medicine. The root possesses numerous sweet, nourishing, succulent properties, and is thus employed most profitably in cookery.

Parsnips are very useful as food for those who have trouble giving milk. They promote urine, dispel the cold evil and dripping piss, and are useful for barren women. They will increase milk in nursing mothers, and are beneficial to emaciated people because they provide solid nourishment.

A quint of parsnip seeds boiled in water, and the decoction thus drunk, promotes urine and is therefore also quite serviceable to those afflicted by dropsy.

Peas (Common Garden Peas)
Pisum sativum
Sauer: *Erbse* (1776)

We might presume that the varieties of peas grown by the Germans in America during Sauer's period would be mostly German, but in fact the situation was quite mixed. In a 1791 issue of the Dillenburgische Intelligenz-Nachrichten *(Dillenburg news intelligencer), an official weekly published in Hessia, Germany, an apothecary in the town of Hadamar offered a long list of spring pea seeds for sale. These included such varieties as Early White Sugar Pea, English White Sugar Pea, Wide-Podded Sugar Pea, asparagus pea, crown peas, English shelling peas of various types, Dutch shelling peas, Apple Green Bush Pea—in short, most of the varieties of peas also readily available in Holland, England, and America at that time.*

The sickle pea is one of the eighteenth-century English shelling varieties still surviving among the Pennsylvania Dutch; two very old German varieties, the Danziger Golderbse *(Danzig golden pea) and the Breslau pea, were popular as split peas and are also still grown by heirloom gardeners. Unfortunately, Sauer did not mention which varieties were best suited to his remedies, but one thing is quite clear: his discussion centered on dry peas. The pea broth he mentioned was either prepared from pea flour or from dry peas cooked and pureed; its consistency was thin, not thick like pea soup.*

Common garden peas are of a rather middling nature between cold and dry. They are endowed with a fairly large amount of volatile, alkaline salt together with somewhat sulfurous elements. Thus they have the capacity to purify, to expel through the urine, and externally to cleanse and heal.

Peas provide better nutrition than beans, thus they are commonly found in the cookery of rich and poor alike, for they satisfy hunger and give good nourishment. Yet they must be well cooked, otherwise they will give rise to numerous vapors.

In some places a pea broth is employed when purgatives have been taken. Also nurses in attendance of women who have just delivered give the mother pea broth in which parsley root has been boiled, this for the cleansing of the matrix of impurities that remain there.

Peas boiled in water and lye and used for washing the head will heal runny scurf on the scalp. If itching limbs are washed with this, it will heal the onset of mange.

Peas boiled in water to the thickness of porridge, and the steam from it allowed to rise over the face when the purples begin to dry out, will prevent the pox scars from remaining, if the treatment is repeated frequently.[184]

Peach Tree
Prunus persica
Sauer: *Pfirsching* (1770)

Culpeper stated that Lady Venus owned this tree, and that it was an ideal source of remedies for children. The Sauer herbal confirms this, but warns women against eating the fruit raw. Due to its laxative action, the raw fruit was thought to injure their sexual organs and perhaps induce miscarriage or abortion. Stewing was the best mode for female consumption of the peach, and we are given a recipe suggestion in order to carry through on that advice. Needless to say, peaches were introduced into the Delaware Valley in the seventeenth century, and by the time Sauer published his herbal, they were growing abundantly everywhere.

Peach schnitz, or sliced dried peaches, were one of the most common of all the dried fruits eaten by the Germans in the middle colonies, and they were often combined with dried apple schnitz and other dried fruits in winter recipes. The use of cinnamon and ginger, as mentioned below, may be read as more or less rote for peach cookery during this period, although it was also common to use peach blossom water as an additional flavoring agent since it was cheaper than real bitter almond. But flavoring was also extracted from the kernels, which were once widely used in medicine as well.

The herbal devotes considerable attention to peach kernels, one of the ingredients in noyau, a brandy liquer made from peach or cherry kernels. Noyau was quite fashionable in eighteenth- and early-nineteenth-century American cookery to flavor desserts and mixed drinks. Peach kernels, however, contain prussic acid (among other dangerous constituents) and must be treated as toxic. There are ample references in period newspapers to deaths resulting from cakes or other desserts flavored with peach kernels instead of bitter almond. One would have thought this would have acted as a deterrent, but evidently prussic acid affects some people more strongly than others, so it was easy enough to point to individuals who suffered nothing more than the pleasure of enjoying a well-flavored pie.

The flowers and young leaves of the peach tree yield an oil that is similar to bitter almonds and much safer to use. Undoubtedly, the remedies discussed below and made with these ingredients were highly fragrant of bitter almond. One can only conjecture whether they killed or cured.

184. *Purples* is a colloquial term for rush or purple fever, which resembles chickenpox. The word is also used for scarlet fever and diseases with similar rashes. Its correct medical name in German is *Friesel*.

Although the peach is a delightful fruit and useful in treating hot stomachs, they should be eaten in moderation and not all the time. In the morning before breakfast, they are too cooling on account of their watery nature, and can thus easily cause angry fevers, blockages of the urine, and for those of the female sex, a source of injury. Cooked and seasoned with a little cinnamon and ginger, peaches make a pleasant dish, and may be enjoyed without injury. When raw, they should be avoided entirely on cold, foggy, or rainy days, because they are then greatly harmful.[185]

A few handfuls of peach blossoms boiled in a pint of water, sweetened with molasses, and then taken as a drink, will produce an excellent laxative of special service to those afflicted by dropsy. If the flowers are eaten in salads, they will open the belly and benefit those who are plagued by constipation. The water distilled from peach blossoms serves as a children's laxative and will kill their worms.

Six to seven peach kernels skinned and eaten will drive down stones and counter-act drunkenness, if they are taken before meals.

The oil pressed from peach kernels and a few drops put in the ears will ease ear-ache and improve hearing. If it is rubbed on the temples, the oil is good for headaches. A few loths of the oil taken before breakfast will stop colic and gravel. It is also serviceable for painful hemorrhoids, if they are smeared with it, and a small piece of cotton is moistened with it and laid over them.

For headache, take half a loth of the expressed juice of vervain that has been cooked until thick, and a quint each of poppy seed oil and the oil of peach kernels. Mix this together thoroughly to make an ointment that can be rubbed frequently on the scalp and temples.

Young shoots from the peach tree, dried in the shade and bound warm to the fore-head, should also be of good service for headaches.

Pear Tree
Pyrus communis
Sauer: *Birn* (1769)

We might wonder where Sauer got his figure of 288 pear varieties; it was taken from the Zwinger herbal, and Zwinger actually listed each of those varieties by name. Since Zwinger's list really dates from the 1690s, there were probably twice this number of varieties by the time Sauer published his herbal. Not much research has been under-taken into the various sorts of pears cultivated in colonial Pennsylvania prior to the 1780s, but we do know that several Germans specialized in the importation of fruit trees. Christian Lehman of Germantown, not far from where Sauer lived, operated a small nursery and advertised imported tree stock during the 1760s. If Lehman did not have a particular variety on hand, he was ready enough to order what was wanted through factors back in Germany.

We do know that the St. Michael's pear was popular. St. Michael's was an old but-ter pear that is said to have produced a seedling about 1805 called the Hosenschenk or

185. This is because according to the system of humors and sympathies, cold foods were deemed unhealthy when eaten on cold days.

Shenk's pear.[186] *This was a variety with small, brown-skinned fruit that ripens in late August. St. Michael's is considered extinct in Pennsylvania, but the Hosenschenk survives.*

There are at least 288 varieties of pears, and they all have very unequal virtues, for which reason I have divided them into the following common types: the sour, the raw or tart, the sweet, the winey, and the unsavory watery pears. All share in common the astringent faculties of the apple, and all thicken the blood, as well as draw up the tiny vessels of the viscera. Indeed, the crab and other wild pears, as well as all the sour, tart, and raw varieties,share this faculty to a much higher degree than the sweet and winey types, which when they are fully ripe contain a smooth juice that is mixed with many sulfurous and spirituous elements. For this reason, they strengthen the stomach and heart. The watery pears, however, are of little use, and red pears injure the stomach.

Dried pears, particularly the dried wild pears, when cooked, are quite effective in treating fluxes of the stomach, as well as bloody flux and the whites.

Anyone suffering from the gripes and sand should abjure pears altogether.

If tart or raw-tasting pears are cut up into pieces and cooked to a sauce in red wine, then a couple of ground nutmegs, a spoonful of powdered mastic, and a handful of ground dried fish mint or curly mint are added along with a few spoonfuls of sourdough sots, this pap may be spread warm between two cloths and laid over the belly. It will prove effective in treating stomachache, casting of the stomach, colic, and bloody flux. But as soon as it dries, it should be reheated and freshly moistened with red wine.

Preserved pears provide a nice reviving repast for the ill, particularly those who have refused food or who are afflicted with fluxes of the stomach. A preserve can be prepared either with sugar or honey and various spices in the following manner: Take good well-tasting, winey ripe pears, pare them, and take out the cores. Cut them into thin slices and mix cloves and bits of cinnamon bark with the fruit. Prepare a syrup in a separate pan with white sugar and water, then lay the spiced pear slices in this. Let it boil up a few times, then set away from the fire and let it cool. Let this stand for twenty-four hours so that the juices of the pears combine completely with the syrup. Then pour off the liquid and cook it again until it thickens. Then pour it again when lukewarm over the fruit. Repeat this daily until the syrup attains the consistency of molasses, for this will preserve the fruit uninjured. Instead of sugar, honey well skimmed of particles and cooked down until thick may be poured over the fruit to preserve it in the same manner as for sugar. This preparation must be carried out in an earthenware vessel. In a similar manner, apples, quinces, cherries, and various other fruits may be preserved and stored.

---

186. Jacob B. Garber, "Seedling Fruit," *Pennsylvania Farm Journal*, October 1852, 197–98.

Pennyroyal

Mentha pulegium
Sauer: *Poley* (1765)

The name of this herb is more commonly written Poleiminze *in German, but its other common name* Flohkraut, *"flea plant," aptly describes its usefulness in ridding the body of vermin. The odor of the fresh or dried leaves is quite pungent. Not surprising, Hildegard of Bingen wrote that pennyroyal had the virtues of fifteen herbs combined (she listed them) and therefore could be used as a potent remedy against fevers. The tea made from the fresh leaves is specially good for upset stomachs. The* Kurtzgefasstes Weiber-Büchlein *(Harrisburg, Pa., 1799), advised, "If pennyroyal is eaten, it is good for women who have been so neglected by the midwife that the afterbirth has remained in them too long, whereby some women would soon die" (19). Eaten as directed, the pennyroyal acts to expel the afterbirth. We may also conclude that if it acts that strongly on afterbirth, it will do likewise to a fetus. This is an herb that pregnant women should take special care to avoid, as the herbal clearly warns.*

Pennyroyal is of a warm, dry nature and possesses the capacity to attenuate, to disperse, to promote urine and sweat, and to remove vapors from the intestines and matrix. It strengthens the head and heart, takes the phlegm from the chest, and stops pain. Only the leaves and the young shoots of the herb are used, and should be gathered in June.

A handful of pennyroyal boiled in a quart of wine with a little saffron, and a gill of this decoction drunk every day, will prevent stones, restore deficiencies of the weaker sex, restrain jaundice and dropsy as well as the gripes, and frequently colic as well. However, pregnant women should refrain from using pennyroyal entirely, yet it is necessary during their delivery.

When someone must drink impure water, put pennyroyal into it. It can then be drunk without harm.

When pennyroyal leaves are set on fire while still green, and used as a fumigant, they will drive away fleas.[187]

If pennyroyal is pulped with a little burnet and vinegar, bound in a small piece of cloth, and then held before the nose, it will revive those plagued by sleepiness and prevent swooning and mother fits.

The distilled water of pennyroyal is in particular an excellent water for uterine pain, strengthening the matrix, and so forth. But pregnant women should not use it, for otherwise, it warms the stomach, promotes urination, and is serviceable in cases of green sickness. A dose of half a gill can be taken in the morning before eating.

The expressed juice from fresh green pennyroyal, which is then strained and mixed with an equal quantity of loaf sugar and made into a syrup without boiling, is excellent for dissolving tough phlegm that has lodged in the chest and for stilling the coughing that results from it. It also strengthens a feeble stomach, awakens the

---

187. This fumigation was accomplished by dropping the leaves into a chafing dish of coals.

appetite, dispels clammy humors, dries fluxes, and opens internal parts congested with phlegm.

A conserve may also be prepared from the young shoots that is serviceable in treating all the above-mentioned conditions.

An oil distilled from pennyroyal leaves and given in doses of six to twenty drops in sugar possesses an unusual capacity for treating all manner of gripes, mother fits, headaches and body pains, sleepiness, apoplexy, coughs, dizziness, and toothache. However, it is just as serviceable when rubbed externally in anodyne and discutient salves.

The leaves of this herb can be used in all elixirs intended for strengthening the matrix, stomach, and head, as well as in waters for uterine pain. The essence of pennyroyal leaves drawn out in brandy or rum can be used to good effect in all of the above-mentioned maladies.

Peony
Paeonia officinalis
Sauer: *Peonien, Gichtrosen* (1766)

Sauer's peony is not the opulent double-flowering kind that we know today. It was a low plant, with single pale red or rosy-purple flowers. The herb is named after Peon, healer of the gods in ancient Greek mythology, but the German name means "fit roses," Gichtern being fits or convulsions. Thus the herb was commonly used to treat epilepsy and a host of related children's diseases. An important article in these treatments was the peony water mentioned by Sauer. It was evidently produced by a number of distillers in colonial America, for recipes often appear in old manuals. Michael Krafft published one for a Compound Peony Water in his 1805 distilling book, but by the 1830s such remedies were considered quite old-fashioned, and peony disappears from popular medicine.

The root of peony possesses the faculty to strengthen the head and the nerves, and to open the matrix and other parts thereto. It is distinguished by male and female plants, of which the male is valued in medicine as much more effective than the female.

The peony flower, together with its roots, leaves, and seeds, represents a peculiar and not well understood power against the falling evil, but from which the famous Margrave Powder derives its reputation.

The root of the peony, dried and ground to powder and administered in doses of a quint weight, will take away that which in newly delivered mothers is most important.[188]

The famed herbalist Mattheolus[189] advised that if a half loth of beaver cod and three handfuls of peony flowers are boiled in four pounds (that is, in two quarts) of wine, and a child is bathed in it as soon as it comes into this world, then as long as it

188. Specifically, to rid the womb of afterbirth.
189. Pier' Andrea Mattioli (1500–1577), a well-known Italian physician during the Renaissance.

lives, it will not be afflicted by fits or the falling evil. This remedy was firmly proved in the case of eight children from one mother, who did not employ this remedy on the first two, who died of fits. But after that, the mother applied the remedy on the surviving children, and they all remained free of the malady.

In the apothecary shops of Lübeck, the following powder for young children is prepared, of which a pinch is administered in their porridge for pain in the internal organs, colic, and vapors: Take one loth each of peony root and Florentine iris, forty grains of saffron, one loth of the best grade of sugar, three quints of rock candy, and grind it all to a fine powder.

If the ground seeds or kernels of the peony are finely powdered and given to young children in their porridge, it will protect them from the stone.

The distilled water of peonies will benefit young children where there is worry that they may become afflicted by fits. It will also protect them from the falling evil, if they are given a tablespoon-full of this water from time to time.

The conserve of peony or peony sugar is very good for the falling evil, dizziness, and other weaknesses of the head that originate from cold; it also serves well against hysterical passion, jaundice, and blockage of the liver and kidneys, if a nutmeg-size dose is taken on occasion.

Peony syrup is effective against apoplexy, the falling evil, and fits, in particular in young children, when a spoonful dose is administered.

Pilewort (Lesser Celandine)
Chelidonium minus
Sauer: *Feigwartzen Kraut* (1768)

> *This small herb with its rather embarrassing name bursts into flower in March and covers parts of my garden with a carpet of yellow. The small, intensely green leaves are indeed good in salads (as the herbal suggests), and during colonial times were doubtless much appreciated as a spring tonic. The important part, however, is the root, which acquires small round swellings very much resembling piles themselves. This was the part prized for curing the condition, and there are still country people today who swear by it.*

Pilewort operates through its numerous mucilaginous balsamic and mildly volatile alkaline components. Thus it possesses the capacity to purify and to sweeten the blood, to provide good nourishment, and to expel gently through the urine and sweat.

Experience has demonstrated that this herb possesses the remarkable capacity to get rid of piles (from which it derives its name), when the fresh roots and leaves are pounded to a pulp and applied as a poultice, or as a powder if they are dried.

If the root is well mashed and mixed with baked sweet apple, and this is applied like a plaster, it will stop the pain of piles very much.

Dr. Hoffmann[190] has praised the expressed juice highly when spread on a cloth and then laid warm over piles or hemorrhoids.

190. Dr. Friedrich Hoffmann appears several places in the herbal. His particulars are given on page 11.

If the fresh leaves of this plant are eaten in mixed salads, they will prove effective in treating scurvy. If the fresh root is worn from a string between the buttocks, it will stop the overflow of flux from piles.[191]

Plantain
Plantago major, Plantago lanceolata
Sauer: *Wegerich* (1768)

Sauer deals with two distinct species, although both may used in a similar manner in herbal remedies. The first is broad-leafed plantain (Plantago major); *the second is ribwort plantain. Ribwort plantain is easily distinguished by its long narrow leaves. Both are now common weeds in American lawns. Zwinger's herbal also mentioned a third variety with red leaves, a subvariety of the broad-leafed plantain. It was mostly gathered from the wild, but some people cultivated it to increase the size of its leaves, which could be used like chard in cookery.*

One of the most important applications of plantain was the manufacture of plantain water. This is probably one of the most commonly employed waters mentioned in Sauer's herbal, normally as a medium for administering other medicines. If the Sauer herbal is any measure, then vast quantities of plantain water must have been consumed by the Germans in America during the eighteenth century. But like peony water, which was also important to the German community, plantain water had fallen out of fashion by the early nineteenth century. However, the herb itself still remains a feature of folk remedies, and the greens continue to be eaten to this day.

Both the broad-leafed and ribwort plantains cool and dry, for they possess a mildly volatile alkaline salt mingled with somewhat mucilaginous balsamic elements in their copious saps. Thus they have the capacity to purify internally corruptions of the blood, to stop ebullition of the same, to sweeten soured fluids in the body, to open internal blockages and force out corruptions through the urine, to control all fluxes of the blood, and to stop diarrhea. Externally, they are used to cleanse and heal wounds and injuries.

Those who are afflicted by copious pissing of blood may be freed of the condition if they take a few loths of plantain syrup with shepherd's purse water or fresh juice often.

When a horse has been ridden too hard during the heat of summer, or begins to flag, as so often happens when they are galled, or when gripped by the so-called wolf between the legs, there is nothing better for their healing than a poultice of fresh and somewhat wilted plantain leaves applied often.

If plantain leaves are used in cookery, they will stop fluxes of the stomach and heal internal injuries, particularly those of the kidneys and bladder. They will also help treat blood-spitting, blood-pissing, and the immoderate coursing of the menses. A

---

191. The action of walking bruises the root, which then releases juice that treats the condition. Although it is not stated, common sense would require wearing something akin to a diaper under such circumstances.

similar effect may be obtained with the seeds, when taken in a half-quint dose in a soft-cooked egg.

Plantain is also useful in treating all injuries of the lungs, liver, spleen, and matrix because it possesses a remarkable faculty for curing internal wounds.

It is this herb in particular that is praised so much in treating bloody flux. When administered to an adult at the onset of the condition, the following potion should be given: Take one quint of finely ground rhubarb, one ounce of rose syrup, half a gill of plantain water, and give this mixture to the patient. Let the patient fast until midday, then administer a quint of ground plantain seeds in plantain water or plantain juice each morning for three days in succession. Administer to children in a proportion according to their age.

If plantain leaves are bruised and applied as a poultice, this will prove serviceable in treating all old, runny, angry, rotten injuries that are spreading.

If a woman wants to remove milk from her breasts, she should swab her nipples with the juice of water plantain.[192]

If the root of plantain is boiled and the decoction used for rinsing the mouth, this will stop toothache.

Plantain juice will cleanse sores of the mouth and will prove very effective when poured into fistulas.

If plantain is pulped and mixed with egg white, then laid as a poultice over a wound, it will stop the bleeding. The same treatment will heal burns on the limbs. Furthermore, if the leaves of plantain are picked fresh and rubbed a little until they are bruised, then laid as a poultice over the place inflamed by burning nettle, this will stop the burning immediately.

If a gill of distilled plantain water is drunk every morning and evening, and this is kept up for several days, it will not only cure both tertian and quartan fevers but purify blood as well, remove jaundice and dropsy, prevent nosebleed, and heal wounds and injuries.

If the feet become swollen from too much walking or fatigue, take plantain leaves and vinegar and mash them together. Apply this as a poultice over the swelling.

Should a horse become raw from riding, feed him plantain leaves together with the roots mixed into his fodder.

A very fine herbal water can be distilled from plantain if it is chopped, some water poured over it, and then distilled. This water is especially powerful for cooling all unnatural heats, internal as well as external. For internal treatments, drink it in half-gill doses. For external treatments, dip a small piece of cloth in it and lay this over the hurt. This will prove effective for cooling, drying, and healing inflamed swellings, wounds, and injuries. It is also good for burns and for reducing burning blisters. Internally, it is very good for blood-spitting, fluxes of the liver, blood-pissing, bloody flux, and fluxes of the stomach. It is also useful as a gargle when taken for scurvy of the mouth and inflammations and corruptions of the mouth, and it will remove swelling at the onset of dangerous throat sores. It also firms up the gums.

192. Mad dog weed (*Alisma plantago*) or water plantain is native to both Europe and North America. It grows in swamps and ponds.

Plantain water can also be used externally in eye remedies, especially for the inflamed swelling of the same. Taken internally, it will prove serviceable for treating divers internal injuries, particularly those of the kidneys and bladder. It gets rid of worms in young children. When someone's uvula becomes swollen, they should take plantain water in their mouth and gargle with it. This water is also good for those who are worried that they may be contracting consumption.

A syrup may be prepared from plantain juice that is especially good for treating blood-spitting, bloody flux, diarrhea, fluxes of the liver, blood-pissing, and internal injuries.

Nota bene: What has been said here about broad-leafed plantain may also be understood to apply to ribwort plantain, because they possess exactly the same virtues.

Plums and Prune Plums
Prunus domestica, Prunus institita, Prunus sp.
Sauer: *Pflaumen, Zwetchken* (1770 and 1771)

Nicholas Culpeper wrote that plums were like women, some better, some worse. His metaphor was based on the fact that he placed plums solidly under the oversight of Venus. Strange science perhaps, yet it is interesting that most of the plum-based remedies discussed by Sauer were intended for women—an emphasis totally avoided by Culpeper. Sauer's euphemistic expressions are sometimes difficult to unravel, especially in matters dealing with sex and genitalia, yet his meaning is sometimes baldly clear. His Hitze, *for example, is an old medical term for sexual orgasm, but of course that is not a malady. What he meant were "the heats," that uncontrollable condition in women known as hot flashes. For this, prunes come to the rescue.*

Sauer discussed plums and prunes twice in his herbal, once in 1770 and again in 1771. This repeated appearance should attest to the importance given to plums by the German element in America. There is also a clear differentiation in the original German between plums intended for table use and prune plums, those varieties developed specifically for drying. Both of Sauer's entries have been collapsed into one, with the repetitive material edited out.

Regarding the species of plums discussed, all were of European origin. This includes Prunus domestica, Prunus institita *(the damson plums), and the various gages that some pomologists believe constitute a distinct species. Most plums grown today, aside from true heirloom varieties, are hybrids of American, Asian, and European species.*

I will not venture to guess what varieties Sauer had in mind because the stock of plum trees sold in the colonies at that time was highly mixed, consisting of imported English, French, Dutch, and German trees. For various reasons, few of them did well in North America, a recurring lament in our early agricultural literature. But I will point out that all of the Germans who settled in the middle colonies and who claimed southwest Germany, Alsace, or Switzerland as their homeland (this would include the Sauers) held prune plums in great esteem. The famous plum butter of the Rhineland, nothing less than a symbol of regional cookery in those parts, was quickly replaced in

America by apple butter, since apples thrived here much better. Yet it should come as no surprise that Sauer should include remedies with plums in his herbal. This was not only comfort food for the German element, it was health food and medicine for German wives and mothers.

On this last note, let it be said that the German love of plums was based on an intuitive understanding of what worked. Science has recently discovered that plums and prunes contain the highest proportion of antioxidants of any of the common foods we eat today.

There are many sorts of plums, and one variety is always proclaimed to be healthier than the other. All claims aside, when the fruit is fully ripe and eaten in moderation, no plum can be condemned. But when eaten unripe and sour, plums are highly injurious and unhealthy, causing dangerous eruptions and bloody flux, yet they do purge gently. From the dried plums various useful preparations can be made for the sick, especially for persons burdened by hot flashes and constipation. For this, the following remedy is quite efficacious.

Take one ounce of senna leaves and half a loth of anise. Tie them up in a clean piece of cloth and put this into an earthenware pot. Pour over this one pint of water and an equal quantity of red wine, then add a fourth of a pound of good-quality prunes. Let this cook over a charcoal stove until it is reduced by one-half. Then add four loths of white sugar and a *quintlein* of ground cinnamon. For constipation, eat five, six, or seven spoonfuls of this laxative in the morning before breakfast and then drink some of the juice afterward.

Those who would prefer a laxative of senna leaves but cannot because of its bitter taste will manage better by taking half an ounce of senna with a small handful of prunes or sweet plums and boiling them with the leaves in a pint of water until the prunes are soft. If the liquid from this is drunk, a gentle laxative will result, particularly beneficial for women who have just delivered as well as for those of weak constitutions.

In cases of high fever and quinsy, it is beneficial for the sick to boil some prunes and repeatedly take one in the mouth and hold it there for some time. The cooked fruit moistens the mouth and eases a dry tongue, as well as quenching the thirst brought on by fever.

Prunes poached in white wine and sprinkled with sugar are good for keeping the bowels open when the juice of a lemon is added to the fruit. This is also a pleasant refreshment for the sick, since the fruit cools the mouth and keeps it clean.

Sage and hollyhock leaves stewed in a broth of one part wine and one part water, or the same proportion of vinegar and water, and then mixed with a little honey of roses, and used frequently as a warm gargle, will cut and dissolve mucus on the tonsils and uvula, thus reducing their swelling.

Primrose
Primula veris
Sauer: *Schlüsselblume* (1772)

The German name for this herb means "key flower," and it is applied without distinction to primroses, cowslips, and oxlips, all of which have flowers of somewhat similar shape. The primrose was formerly employed in cookery and the flowers fermented to make primrose wine, or infused in brandy to make a sedative drink much favored by women for cramps. It is an old garden flower normally grown along borders and paths, and unfortunately much relished by slugs. They are doubtless attracted to its succulent leaves due to the subtle fragrance that pervades the entire plant, and which becomes concentrated in the flowers when they bloom in April and May.

My grandfather's primroses, which I now grow, came from a very old garden in Lancaster County, Pennsylvania. They are the plain pale yellow sort, which appears to be the variety most commonly found in country gardens. They bloom at exactly the same time as the sweet violets (page 316), so the two together can easily fill a garden with a wonderful heady fragrance. Sauer repeatedly used the term wohlriechend, *"fragrant," in describing this herb, which leads me to suspect that he must have experienced it firsthand. The roots, which were also employed in medicine, were dug in the fall from plants that were over two years old.*

Primroses are warm and dry in nature. They operate by means of a volatile, balsamic, alumish salt, from which they derive the capacity to dry, to open, to strengthen the nerves and brain, to reactivate the bodily energies, and to halt fluxes. The petals and the flowers are employed in particular, although the roots are used at times.

The dried root of primrose, ground to powder and given to children, will kill their worms. Sometimes the root can also be infused in vinegar, then drawn up into the nose in order to dispel toothaches.

Simple distilled water of primrose is quite serviceable when apoplexy strikes or when afflicted by fits. It will warm a cold head, restore lost speech, and strengthens the fetus as well as a feeble heart. Take a few tablespoons of it repeatedly.

Primrose sugar possesses a similar efficacy, which will be described below. Take a dose of it the size of a nutmeg all at once.

An excellent remedy for painful joints may be extracted from the full-blown flowers and petals in cherry brandy. As an internal remedy, take half a tablespoonful. For external uses, wash the affected limbs with it. It will stay the pain in those who are struck by cold fluxes. Indeed, it is also good for those whose limbs are paralyzed by apoplexy. If the condition has not continued too long, it will restore movement to the affected limbs.

If the fragrant flowers are taken with an equal weight of loaf sugar and bruised and rubbed to a pulp, then left in the sun, it will develop into a conserve. This conserve can be administered as stated above under primrose sugar.

Purslane
Portulaca oleracea
Sauer: *Burtzel* or *Burgel* (1764)

The herbal takes pains to describe a variety of purslane that is not exactly like the common one found growing as an invasive weed in our gardens today. It resembles this weed in coloration, yet in habit it was tall or upright; after reaching a height of about six inches, it fell over and rambled across the ground. This is probably the "red" variety mentioned in some of the old garden books, semicultivated but, through constant selection, more succulent than the small wild kind. It was one of the most important summer salad herbs in colonial German cookery.

In that context, a salad was understood to be a type of side dish, sometimes quite ornamental when served on the tables of the well-to-do. It was not a course by itself but could form part of any series of courses, depending on the elaborateness of the menu. For this reason, many salad recipes are quite simple, rather than mixtures, since they were intended to compliment the other dishes served with them.

Purslane was very popular in this regard, its lemony flavor highly valued, and its nutritional qualities well understood. There were several other kinds cultivated by the colonial Germans, aside from the one mentioned in the herbal. The most sought-after of these were the tall green and the golden (both still available). These are erect-growing varieties developed for their large, succulent stems. The leaves were removed and the stems neatly trimmed into finger-length pieces, then poached in salted water like asparagus. Thus cooked, they were served at room temperature.

Maria Sophia Schellhammer suggested laying the stems on a dish so that they radiated outward from the center. Raw leaves could then be scattered over this—a mix of the green and yellow to give higher visual effect. Olive oil, wine vinegar, and pepper served as a dressing. Country people, for whom olive oil may have been too expensive, substituted bacon drippings and employed apple, pear, peach, or even watermelon vinegar in warm dressings.

This herb has a brownish red, succulent stem, and commonly grows a span high.[193] It then bends over and sprawls across the ground. It has smooth, thick, succulent leaves, brownish red above, but whitish and shiny beneath. It produces numerous small branches with which it runs across the ground from each joint. At the far tips it produces tiny pale yellow flowers. The plant does not bloom until late summer, at which time it produces black seeds. It mostly grows as a weed in fine gardens, and on other well-tilled lands.

Purslane is of a cold and moist nature, and thus possesses

193. The span in this case is the distance between the tip of the thumb and the tip of the index finger when stretched apart. In other words, about six inches.

the fine virtues of cooling, of stilling powerful effervescence of the blood, of cleansing the kidneys, and of cooling the liver.

If purslane is eaten raw as a salad or cooked, or its boiled juice drunk, it will make an excellent remedy for heartburn and upset stomach. It is likewise good for inflamed kidneys, injured bladders and matrix, and sharp, burning urine, and will dispel lewd passions. It kills stomach worms, helps against blood-spitting, bloody flux, and immoderate bleedings of the hemorrhoids, as well as overflowing of the terms in women.

A half quint of purslane seed ground fine and given to children in milk will kill worms and drive them out.

For those plagued by burning and trickling urine, ground purslane and lettuce seeds mixed with sugar should be employed frequently in their food and drink.[194] They will experience good relief.

The distilled water of purslane can be drunk to quench and cool all internal and external heats brought on by fever, and afflictions of the liver, stomach, and other internal organs. It also checks bloody flux and other fluxes of the stomach, cools inflamed kidneys, and eases burning urine. It stills immoderate bleedings of the hemorrhoids and so forth, and controls blood-spitting. When small children cannot sleep on account of a high temperature, or if they have worms, they should be given several tablespoonfuls of this water.

In cases of ardent fever and headache, when the patient cannot sleep, take two loths of sweet almonds, a half loth each of watermelon and pumpkin seeds, and six loths each of purslane and lettuce waters. Grind the almonds and seeds very fine, and rub them through a cloth with the waters to yield a milk. Give a generous drink of this to the patient toward evening. This milk both strengthens and cools the patient thoroughly, so that he may sleep.

Quince
Cydonia oblonga
Sauer: *Quitten* (1772)

Quince is not an apple, and it is not a pear, but it is related to both. The large white flowers, which are charged with a pink blush, are far more beautiful than those of the apple tree, and they are fully edible—a luxurious addition to spring salads. However, it is the fruit that is used, and it has been used as food and medicine for many, many centuries. But the fruit must be cooked in order to unlock its exquisite flavors.

In her Book of Marmalade *(New York: St. Martin's/Marek, 1985), British food historian C. Anne Wilson traced the origins of modern orange marmalade back to quince and the* melomeli *and* cidonitium *of classical antiquity. Those ancient preparations were preserved in many areas of Europe during the Middle Ages. In the German Rhineland, they evolved into something commonly known as* Quittespeck, *or*

---

194. Lettuce seed has played a role in medicine since ancient times. Lettuce was sacred to the Egyptian cult of Amun-Min. The opiate nature of lettuce sap and the medicinal uses of the seeds were known even then.

as it was called in genteel cookbooks, Quitten-Confect.[195] *It was brought to America by German settlers, and medical benefits aside, it is still a classic Christmas confection among the Pennsylvania Dutch. Sauer's recipe for a highly spiced version would please any palate that appreciates the taste of gingerbread.*

Sauer also mentioned quince schnitz (dried slices of quince), which were once highly prized by early American cooks. The Yankee Farmer *for May 8, 1840, confirmed this many years later by noting that peach schnitz pie was "unrivalled" when quince schnitz were mixed in. It would do no harm to bring some of these old flavor combinations back into fashion.*

Quinces have the virtue of astriction, yet they improve digestion. They can be prepared in a variety of ways so that the taste is pleasing to both the sick and the healthy. And they are quite grateful to the stomach.

If quince pips are pounded in a mortar, and rosewater (lacking rosewater, pure springwater) is poured onto them, the mixture will produce a mucilage that relieves inflamed eyes and heals the cracked nipples of nursing mothers. This mucilage is especially useful in treating all types of burns resulting from fire. When taken orally, it is also a good remedy for quinsy and divers inflammations of the throat.

To make quince paste, take ripe quinces that are not too hard and gritty, pare them, and cut them up into large pieces. Remove the cores and seeds, and put the fruit in a fresh earthenware pot. Pour water (or if you please, red wine) over this and let it cook until the fruit is as soft as porridge. While still hot, press this through a hair sieve with a wooden ladle so that all the hard and gritty particles are removed. Then, to each two pounds of this puree, take one pound—or if you want it very sweet, two pounds—of white sugar. Let this mixture boil until it reaches the consistency of a stiff paste. Pour it hot into small, round wooden boxes lined with greased paper to cool and set.

Divers agreeable spices can also be added to this electuary, for example, cinnamon, cloves, mace, ginger, and so forth. In this way it becomes very pleasing to the palate, and when taken morning and evening, it strengthens the stomach, promotes digestion, enlivens the appetite, quiets a queasy or upset stomach, is good for diarrhea and bloody flux, and agrees well with pregnant women. A liqueur can also be distilled from quinces that is effective for all the above infirmities, provided four spoonfuls of it are taken in the morning and at night.[196]

Quince juice cooked to a syrup with sugar and taken frequently by the spoonful will calm the effects of bloody flux and strengthen the stomach so that it can retain nourishment.

To put up quinces, pare them and cut into thin slices. Boil them in water until they become slightly soft, then remove from the liquid. Add cinnamon, cloves, and brown

195. Friederike Löffler's *Quitten-Confect* was not only typical of this period, her recipe was reprinted many times in this country. It is rather charming, since she recommended pressing the quince paste into little molds of the wine god Bacchus. See her *Ökonomisches Handbuch für Frauenzimmer* (Stuttgart, 1795), 542–43.

196. Quince water, also called *Gwittegortschel* in Pennsylfaanisch. It was once a popular Pennsylvania German schnapps.

sugar to the liquid, and bring this to a boil until the sugar is cooked to the thickness of a syrup. Put the cooked fruit in glass, stoneware, or earthenware jars; pour the syrup over this, and seal. Quinces put up in this fashion are extremely good for the stomach, strengthening it, and especially good for controlling loose bowels. Ripe quinces can also be pared and dried like other sliced fruits and thus cooked as needed for the benefit of the sick or the healthy by adding brown sugar, cloves, and a little cinnamon.

To make quince syrup, take the best ripe quinces, pare them, and shred them on a vegetable grater. Press the juice through a cloth. Measure the juice, and add half the quantity of white sugar. Let this boil in a new earthenware pot over a charcoal stove until it attains the thickness of honey. Then seal it up in glass or stoneware vessels. This syrup strengthens the stomach, stimulates the appetite, aids in digestion, and calms queasiness, windy stomachs, and vomiting; it binds the belly, and is very useful in cases of bloody flux.

Radish
Raphanus sativus
Sauer: *Rettig* (1766)

In volume 8 of his Cours complet d'agriculture (Paris, 1789), the Abbé Françoise Rozier discussed the numerous varieties of radish then popular on the Continent. These included the white-skinned winter radish of Strasbourg (much like a parsnip in color and shape) and the large, rooty black radish commonly called Long Black Spanish—both sorts are still available today. These two varieties were definitely in Sauer's mind when he chose the radish remedies for the herbal, since the radishes in question had to be large, long, and tapered in order to make the poultice as directed.

German physician Johann David Schoepf, during his travels through Pennsylvania in the early 1780s, suggested that it was the German troops brought here by the British who first introduced the black radish to America shortly after the revolution. Schoepf's comment has been quoted often by plant historians, when in fact it may only be half right.

It is quite evident from Sauer, not to mention evidence in other colonial sources, that long black radishes were relatively common. Schoepf may have been thinking of the small, round black radishes that were more delicate for table use and at one time a great favorite with beer drinkers. It is difficult to imagine that the eighteenth-century German radish known as Schifferstadt Long Black, a variety raised in the Palatinate as well as in Schoepf's native Hessia, would not have found its way to America with German settlers. It was highly valued for its medical properties and is still raised in the region around Schifferstadt as a cash crop.

Whatever the case, radishes are extremely rich in vitamin C, which may explain why they were so important to winter diets deprived of fresh fruits and greens. It would also explain why radishes worked so well against so many common maladies afflicting the working people of the 1700s.

The temperament of the radish is warm and dry. It has the virtue of loosening and drawing up hard phlegm from the chest, thus easing respiration, and of expelling sand from the bladder, and of dissolving kidney stones so that they pass out as sand. Radishes also fortify digestion and loosen blockages of the spleen and liver. Yet whoever eats too freely of them will be oppressed by windiness.

Generous drafts of freshly pressed radish juice will cause moderate vomiting in some persons. For those who may require this emetic, take one gill of the juice, add a little barley water to it, and drink thus. Not only will this purge the phlegm from the stomach and carry it off in the discharge (thereby relieving trapped airs), it will in addition free the kidneys of sand and mucus. For a similar result, others take one-half to one ounce of radish seeds, grind them to powder, and pour barley water over this. Stir thoroughly, then press the mixture through a fine cloth and drink the juice. Young children should be given proportionately less according to their age. For just about anyone, this is a harmless and mild-acting emetic, especially suitable for those of weak constitutions.

Indeed, for patients with strong constitutions, this remedy may not be effective. It should also be noted that when you want to purge yourself with radish juice, no salt should be added to it, since this will restrain vomiting.

Eating too many radishes is not good for the eyes, since the sharp fumes can easily weaken eyesight in patients of weak constitutions. Radishes also cause foul breath.

When pressing the juice from radishes, sweeten it with rock candy, and drink warm from time to time. This dissolves phlegm in the chest, casts it up, relieves asthma, and cleanses the kidneys. A quint of radish seeds ground and taken in a glass of red wine will provoke the urine.

In case of the ague, it is customary to cut a radish into slices lengthwise, strew them with salt, and bind the slices to the soles of the feet in order to draw the fever down from the head and heart. This is effective when repeated frequently.

Radishes are also valuable for curing corns. Bathe the feet in warm water during the waning of the moon. Cut away the corns without causing them to bleed, then put radish juice on the incisions so that the corns do not grow back. Radishes dressed with goose fat and laid upon the skin will draw out thorns.

You can distill a liquor from radishes that is highly recommended for kidney and bladder stones. But before making use of such internal remedies, the body should first be well cleansed with an appropriate purgative, otherwise the condition may go from bad to worse. This treatment promotes the opening of blockages in the liver and spleen, the dissolution of phlegm in the chest, and proves effective for those suffering from dropsy. It also kills worms in the gut. Patients who suffer from ulcerated kidneys or bladders ought to drink a few loths of this liquor on an empty stomach each morning before breakfast.

Ragwort
Senecio jacobaea
Sauer: *Stendelwurz* (1777)

Also known as ragweed, this common herb is responsible for many of the allergies and hay fevers suffered by people during the summer. The plant is toxic to many grazing animals, especially when it is in bloom, for during flowering, the toxins increase in the leaves. Nonetheless, it was once widely employed in poultices and horse remedies (especially for staggers), and yields both a green and a yellow dye.

Ragwort is of a warm, moist nature, and operates by its mildly gluey spirituous fluid sap, which possesses the faculty of enlivening the spirits and strengthening the heart.

The ancients cooked the root of this plant like other kitchen vegetables and prepared it for the table. But in our times, the root is only preserved in sugar and sold in apothecary shops. It is very useful for consumptives and those who are weak and thin. It also strengthens weak kidneys and bladder, and dispels blocked urine.

The essence extracted from the root in brandy, combined with the essence of ambergris, then administered a few drops at a time in betony water every evening and morning, will strengthen the brain, memory, and nerves.

Rampion
Campanula rapunculus
Sauer: *Rapunzel* (1777)

The Rapunzel of German fairy tales is really a personification of a plant, rapuncula being the feminine diminutive of the word for turnip. And like turnips, rampions were cultivated in kitchen gardens both for their greens and for their roots, which were eaten cooked or raw. In spite of its widespread popularity since the Middle Ages in German-speaking countries, it is not easy to find actual working recipes for rampion or for the sort of dishes noted by the Sauer herbal. But Maria Sophia Schellhammer did include a one-line recipe in her cookbook, which at least provides a sketch: "Pare them, then boil them in pea stock with butter and herbs."[197] The small roots were eaten raw with vinegar and oil.

Since rampion is not native, and there is no evidence that it has in fact naturalized in a large way, two other plants must figure in this discussion. One is star of Bethlehem (Ornithogalum umbellatum), *which was imported and planted here in great quantities, and the other is spring beauty* (Claytonia caroliniana), *a native plant. Star of Bethlehem was probably imported as an ornamental, but it quickly naturalized, and the bulbs were gathered and cooked much like rampions. Spring beauty yields tiny tubers that are rather starchy, like potatoes. These were highly valued by the Indians and were also harvested by the German settlers as a wild potherb, especially in frontier areas. Spring beauty was so heavily foraged that it became extinct in many of its original habitats. For this reason it has become quite rare.*

197. Maria Sophia Schellhammer, *Das Brandenburgische Koch-Buch* (Berlin, 1732), 478.

Rampion is of a fully temperate nature, possessing a mild, temperate, volatile, balsamic, salty sap. From this derives its capacity to provide good nourishment, to renew the blood with pleasantly nourishing moisture, and to dispel via the urine that which is unhealthy and corrupt in the stomach.

Rampion is employed as food either raw or cooked, and in the spring it appears on the table prepared as salad with oil, vinegar, and salt. Rampion excites the appetite and benefits the stomach. It also expels urine quickly. Small rampions mashed, to which a little black pepper has been added, will produce milk in wet nurses. The roots can also be cooked with fresh butter and herbs and enjoyed thus, or they may be employed in herb soups.

Red Currant
Ribes sativum
Sauer: *St. Johannesbeere* (1776)

> *Of all the small fruits, the red currant received the most attention in colonial German books on farming and agriculture. There are probably two good reasons for this. Unlike gooseberries, currants thrive exceptionally well in the middle states. They were planted here early on, and they are mentioned often in nursery advertisements. Secondly, a very respectable red wine can be made from the fruit, and this probably took the place of imported wine for many people. The native American red currant* (Ribes triste), *which is found in bogs in New England and the upper Midwest, grows outside the colonial settlement of the Germans and thus was not available. Sauer's currants were cultivated plants.*
>
> *This role as a grape wine substitute is readily substantiated by the large number of recipes for red currant wine that appeared in colonial newspapers and almanacs. One of the most widely printed and recopied recipes for red currant wine may be found as an addendum or insert to the back part of the* Amerikanische Goldgrube.[198] *It is too long to reproduce here, since it involves several pages, but the quantities given are telling; they are based on one acre of berry bushes, with the note that this will yield fifty gallons of wine.*

Red currants possess a somewhat volatile sour salt in their juice, which cools, quenches thirst, renews the digestive juices of the stomach, induces appetite, draws together gently, and thus shares in common all of the faculties of lemon or pomegranate juice.

If red currant syrup is drunk together with succory and sorrel water, it will prove good for treating those afflicted by ardent fevers, fluxes of the stomach, and the pox. It quenches thirst, settles a stomach that refuses food as well as strengthens it, and may be administered effectively to those who are suffering from looseness of the belly above and below. This syrup is also helpful for blood-spitting, if it is administered with gargle water. For those whose throats are swollen within, take a tablespoon of

---

198. "Anweisung Johannes-Beeren Wein zu Machen," *Die Amerikanische Goldgrube* (Lebanon, Pa., 1810), 198–200.

this syrup often. If this syrup is made into a julep with fresh water, it will serve well against drunkenness, particularly the next morning. But those who may have a cold nature and who are subjected to colic should abjure currants altogether.

Red currant syrup is prepared in the following manner: Take one and a half pounds of white sugar and dissolve it in eighteen loths of water in a new earthenware vessel over a gentle charcoal heat. Boil it until the sugar runs from the spatula or can be drawn into threads, then pour the syrup into a pewter bowl. Add one pound of red currant juice, mix, and store in a glass or earthenware vessel. This is serviceable for inflammations and fevers, for it enlivens inflamed viscera, quenches thirst, protects against choler, prevents puking, and strengthens the stomach.

Red currants may be preserved in white sugar in the following manner: Take one and a half pounds of the best sugar and let it dissolve in eighteen loths of springwater in a new earthenware vessel over coals. Let it boil for as long as it takes to run from the stirring spoon as mentioned above. Then add one pound of red currants and let it boil up. After that, store away for use. If the sugar becomes thin or watery, pour it off and cook it again until it becomes as thick as honey. Pour this back over the berries. They will keep thus for a year or more. These preserved currants will quench thirst, moisten a dry mouth and parched tongue during ardent fevers, ease heats of the stomach and viscera, and excite the appetite. They are good for such pregnant women as are possessed by desires to eat strange things, as well as for comforting the ill.

An electuary of red currants can also be prepared as follows: Take two pounds of red currant juice, and one pound of white sugar, and let this cook gently in a new earthenware vessel over a charcoal heat until it achieves the thickness of a paste. This electuary possesses the same virtues as red currant preserves. It cools and strengthens viscera exhausted by high fever, quenches the thirst and the heat of fevers, strengthens the stomach, prevents the puking of gall, stops bleeding and diarrhea, is effective during pestilence, and prevents fainting.

Red Raspberry
Rubus strigosus
Sauer: *Himbeeren* (1767)

While red currant bushes were imported, red raspberries were not. The native red raspberry was readily available in the wild, and in such large quantities that many farmers made a living by gathering them for market. Raspberry vinegar was especially well liked among the Germans and often drunk as a summer beverage in the fields. Raspberries were also dried for use during the winter, a fact well documented by linen bags of dried berries listed in household inventories of the period. I mention under turnips (page 328) that these dried raspberries were sometimes employed in preparing the Gumbis *pickles that were once such a part of the winter diet. Sauer, however, provides a number of delightful confectionery recipes that were used both as foods and as medicines.*

Red raspberries possess the capacity to cool, to strengthen the heart, and to withstand the corrosive noxious humors of the blood in all ardent fevers.

The distilled water of raspberries is useful in treating all hot distempers and is very comforting to the ill, who like its rich aroma and pleasant taste. They may be administered a few loths at a time according to their wants. From the juice of raspberries it is possible to prepare a valuable syrup that quenches the hotness of fever, prevents dizziness, strengthens a weak heart, and stops fluxes of the belly. It can be administered as a julep mixed with fresh springwater or with vinegar water. But since the juice from which the syrup is made is very much subject to fermenting, the juice must first be allowed to ferment and the syrup made with it carefully stored.

If good-quality vinegar is poured over raspberries, and this is used for swabbing the temples and pulse, it will prevent fainting and weakness of the heart. Or, a small piece of cloth may be dipped into the raspberry vinegar while warm and applied often to the parts just mentioned. Vinegar can also be poured over raspberry leaves to make a good cooling poultice for the pulse and temples.

A raspberry preserve may be prepared in the following manner: Take one part well pressed raspberry juice and let it stand a few days. Then pour off the thin liquid that rises to the top. Mix the remainder with twice its weight in good, dry sugar. While this is boiling, scum off the foam, and continue to cook it for as long as it takes to become like honey. Pour this thick syrup while very hot over fresh raspberries and store it thus.

To make an electuary or paste of raspberries: Boil a good measure of pressed, filtered raspberry juice until thick. Then dissolve a little sugar in it, and when it is reduced to the thickness of honey or even thicker, pour into shallow glasses so that the syrup jells into a delicious electuary.

The essential salts of raspberry are sometimes employed in a pleasant-tasting remedy that is prepared in the following manner: Take the juice of freshly pressed ripe raspberries filtered through blotting paper and boil this until it forms a thin scum on the surface. Set this in the cellar so that the coolness there will cause crystals to form on the sides of the vessel. The remaining liquid must be poured off carefully and boiled again and allowed to stand again in the cellar to form more crystalline salts. Finally, gather together all the salts, dry, and store tightly. If these essential salts of raspberry are administered from time to time in fifteen- to twenty-grain doses, they will cut through all thick humors in the stomach, quench the hotness of gall, get rid of the same, and expel it through urine and stool. They will also take away all the overplus of febrile humors in the blood, keep the liver open, and excite the appetite. For fevers, a small dose of these salts can also be dissolved in ordinary drinking water, for this will quench thirst completely.

Rhubarb
Rheum officinale
Sauer: *Rhebarbara* (1773)

Sauer's rhubarb is not the culinary rhubarb eaten today, but rather a related species that is too toxic for general consumption. Only the root is used, and this was imported in the dry state from Turkey or China during the eighteenth century. It was also grown in physic gardens or as an ornamental, but medical rhubarb was not cultivated in kitchen gardens by common farmers. Culinary rhubarb was first introduced into Pennsylvania by John Bartram in the 1730s and remained a curiosity for quite some time. Its general use in pies and puddings did not spread in the United States until well after the 1830s.

Rhubarb is by nature warm and dry. It opens, discusses swellings, and gently promotes stool without nature's call; it also strengthens after performing a purge, astringes, and blocks. It possesses somewhat oily elements together with numerous earthy, volatile, and mildly purging salts. From this it derives its capacity not only to purge gently and to restore the blood to its natural state and consistency, but also to open internal blockages of the glands. If the root is laid in the sun, or boiled, it will lose its purgative qualities and become useless.

Rhubarb is always a completely safe remedy for young and old. It can be administered to children and pregnant women without danger.

Take three quints of chopped good-quality rhubarb root, one quint of cream of tartar, and eight loths of succory water or fresh springwater, and let this stand overnight in a warm place. Afterward, early in the morning, press it through a cloth and administer the expressed liquid as a drink to the patient. The patient must then fast until midday. This potion is a fine, gentle remedy for all internal viscera, for it purifies and strengthens all at the same time the stomach, liver, and spleen; opens divers blockages; and gets rid of colic, jaundice, bad skin color, the early stages of dropsy, and all putrid fevers. It will also purify the blood, and carries off the surfeit of charred choler through the stool.

A quint of well-ground rhubarb taken with one ounce of sorrel water in the morning before breakfast, then followed by fasting until midday, will prove good in treating the afflictions just enumerated. Furthermore, when employed in this manner, rhubarb is especially renowned for treating all manner of fluxes of the stomach, bloody flux, and so forth, when someone is worried about an ulcer in the stomach or liver.

For stomach worms in children, administer ten to twelve grains of ground rhubarb in one spoonful of centaury water. This will kill and expel the worms.

Rhubarb is such a safe remedy that it can be administered without injury to people who are close to death. But it will not benefit those who cannot retain their water, or those who experience dripping urine.

The root of rhubarb is of such excellent use for all maladies of the liver that many who are thus afflicted may be administered a tincture of the same called Heart of the Liver or *anima hepates*, of which thirty to sixty drops, or still more as well, can be given in water, tea, meat stock, and other such broths.

Rhubarb syrup as prepared in apothecary shops is an excellent laxative for the elderly and for children. The elderly may be administered four to six tablespoonfuls, children one tablespoonful or more depending on their age. This will purge very gently without causing gripes in the stomach.

For tertian and quartan fevers, the following is a very good purgative when administered often: Take three quints of oil of tartar previously prepared, and pour a glass filled with fresh milk over it. Cover well and let this stand overnight in a warm place. Strain and press out well the next morning and drink the liquid thus. This will prove a gentle laxative and will reduce a fever very much.

For fluxes of the stomach, bloody flux, and the whites, rhubarb may be toasted, ground, and given in a quint dose.

Lozenges or tablets may be made from rhubarb with sugar and gum traganth and usefully employed in treating colic, diarrhea, and similar conditions.

For nosebleed or other hemorrhages, powdered rhubarb may be used to good effect because it sends into the gut and expels from the body all the sharp salty humors that on occasion give rise to bleeding—after which it constrains and astringes the bleeding.

Rice
Oryza sativa
Sauer: *Reis* (1776)

By the time Sauer began publishing his herbal, rice was becoming relatively cheap in the middle colonies. The rice plantations in South Carolina began shipping rice north on a regular basis after the 1740s; thus many Europeans traveling in America were surprised to note that even farmers could afford rice on their tables. Certainly, rice was not treated as an everyday food, and among the German element at least, it was more likely a Sunday dish or something associated with a special occasion. The rice pudding mentioned by Sauer would fall into this category, although it could also be treated as invalid cookery. Christine Knörin's plain pudding recipe may be viewed as typical for this period:

Wash about one half Vierling *of rice and cook this very slowly with sweet milk so that about half a* Maas *is used; a little sweet cream may also be added. At the beginning, a small piece of cinnamon should be cooked with it, and at the end, some sugar added until it is well sweetened. Once it has cooked down to a porridge consistence, let it cool. Beat about six to eight egg whites until stiff, then gently fold this into the rice. Pour the rice mixture into a porcelain platter or else into a baking vessel. Scatter sugar thickly over the top. Set this into a cake pan and let it bake gently in a slack oven so that it develops a nice golden crispy crust on top.*[199]

Rice was also used to strengthen homemade punch. Christian Fischer included this advice in his collection of old household receipts published for sale in America: "When the required water for punch is boiled with a handful of rice two or three hours before it is needed, and the punch then prepared with it, the punch will be much improved, that is, stronger and sweeter than when the water is not first prepared in this manner."[200] *This is somewhat similar to the use of wheat flour to thicken* kalte Schalen *(page 347).*

Rice possesses much temperate volatile salt combined with balsamic-sulfurous elements. It is thus mild, warm, and dry. It provides the blood with excellent nourishment and strength.

For both the sick and the healthy, rice is a very useful food. It is of particularly good service to those who are afflicted with headache, rheums of the head, immoderate nosebleeds, blood-spitting, blood-pissing, and the like. Furthermore, it is useful to those who are suffering from coughs, consumption, and jaundice, as well as to people whose mouths are overflowing with spittle. Beyond this, it is good for all fluxes of the stomach and sores of the stomach, gut, kidneys, and bladder. It gets rid of tenesmus of the stool, and strengthens feeble kidneys and a fallen end gut.

Rice pudding is beneficial not only to people who are healthy, but also to the sick who are afflicted with pains of the stomach.

Rosemary
Rosmarinus officinalis
Sauer: *Rosmarin* (1769)

I still have my grandfather's hoary old rosemary bushes. After his death, they were left to themselves almost twenty years unattended along the south side of a wall and managed to survive several intensely cold winters. I am sure that in colonial Pennsylvania, indeed anywhere there were German settlements, someone maintained a large tub or two of this very pleasant herb. It was not just a requirement for good cookery, it was also something of a medicine chest capable of producing a wide range of home remedies. But there was also another use now forgotten.

Rosemary had another name in German: Weihrauchskraut, *"incense plant," for it was used in churches. In colonial Pennsylvania it was customary at funerals to give out*

---

199. Christine Knörin, *Göppinger Kochbuch* (Stuttgart, 1798), 56–57. A Stuttgart *Vierling* equals 125 grams. One Stuttgart *Maas* equals 2 liters.
200. Christian Fischer, *Approbirtes Kunst- und Hausbuch* (Reutlingen, 1830), 380.

sprigs of rosemary tied with black ribbons. The Sauer herbal states that rosemary strengthens the memory, and due to this popular belief, it was employed as both an aid to the mind in recalling the deceased and a symbol in itself of remembrance.

If swooning and other such distempers of the mind could be characterized as afflictions lurking about funerals, there was always Hungary water for rescuing those who had succumbed. Hungary water was itself made from rosemary, and John Hill noted in his herbal that it was the flowery tops that contained the greatest virtues. He explained: "The famous Hungary Water is made also with these flowery Tops of Rosemary. Put two Pound of these into a common Still, with two Gallons of Melasses Spirit, and distill off one Gallon and a Pint. This is Hungary Water."[201] As a matter of clarification, rosemary only blooms on its uppermost shoots, so those who keep their plants neatly pruned will rarely see flowers.

Rosemary possesses its most excellent virtues in its leaves and flowers, which contain a balsamic oil together with a somewhat volatile salt. From this derives its capacity to thin thickened blood; to open blockages of the brain and other parts of the body, especially the small arteries; to enliven the bodily spirits; to purify the blood; and to strengthen the memory.

Because rosemary, by virtue of its powers, strengthens the head, reduces cold rheums, and proves effective in treating the falling evil, apoplexy, tremblings, and insensiblities of the limbs, thus it is employed in sundry ways.

The leaves of rosemary, together with the flowers, scattered on a slice of bread with a little salt and eaten in the morning before breakfast, will give good sharpness to the eyesight and dispel reeking breath.

During times of contagion and pestilence, dried rosemary leaves and flowers may be used as a fumigant, or if there is stench abounding, rosemary will serve for fumigation as well as a smoldering piece of juniper wood.

If a handful of rosemary is boiled in two quarts of good wine or in a mixture of half wine and half water, strained, and taken as a drink by the glassful each morning and evening for a period of time, this make a proven remedy for the whites in women, as well as for strengthening the heart, stomach, nerves, and limbs.

A handful of rosemary, hart's tongue, and celandine infused in two quarts of wine and drunk by the glassful in the morning and evening will prove a good treatment for jaundice.

If a large handful of rosemary is boiled in two quarts white wine until reduced to one-half, and then four or five tablespoons of good-quality honey are added, this will prove beneficial to those who are asthmatic as well as giving a clear voice, provided the decoction is drunk at night before going to bed.

Rosemary sugar, or conserve of rosemary (which is prepared in the same manner as succory sugar), is effective in treating all cold distempers of the head, in strengthening the memory and a weak heart, for increasing the vital forces, and for dispelling windiness. It is also useful in treating a cold stomach and matrix, for driving away melancholy, and for protecting against miasmas when taken in nutmeg-size doses

201. John Hill, *The Useful Family Herbal* (London, 1755), 313.

according to taste.

The distilled water of rosemary, if taken in one- or two-spoonful doses, will warm the entire body, strengthen the vital spirits, absorb cold fluxes, and prove beneficial to the head. It will restore lost speech, and is good in treating lameness in the limbs. Rosemary is also commonly employed in clysters for colic, stomachache, and pains of the matrix, since it expels thick humors, choler, and winds without nature's call. For such conditions, take half a pint of cow's milk, six loths of rosemary honey, and three loths of chamomile oil, and mix it all together for a clyster, which should be used several times until the pain subsides.

If four or five drops of the distilled oil of rosemary are taken in water of holy thistle, this will prove a fine remedy for tertian ague, provided it is administered to the patient half an hour before the onset of the chills. However, the patient must first be purged a few times and bled.[202] This treatment will also prove useful against dizziness, for removing headaches resulting from cold rheums, for preventing apoplexy, and for strengthening the memory. It can likewise be employed externally when swabbed on the crown of the head and temples.

The most excellent and renowned cephalic and nervine Hungary water is prepared from rosemary. It is both cephalic and cordial, and is useful in treating fainting and pounding headache when smelled, snuffed into the nose, rubbed on the temples and pulse, or a little is poured on the crown of the head. For strengthening the heart, a teaspoonful dose may be administered. It draws air into the chest and is good for frights of the heart and apoplexy when taken as aforesaid.

Rue
Ruta graveolens
Sauer: *Raute, Weinraute* (1765)

During the Middle Ages, rue was widely used as a remedy against the plague, since it was one of the well-known ingredients in the antipoison Cure of Mithradates—which Sauer explains in some detail. Mithradates Eupator, king of Pontus, lived between 123 and 63 B.C. His remedy was preserved by several Greek physicians in antiquity. Because it was considered an effective deterrent against the plague, the powers of rue were later directed against other diseases in colonial America, including cholera, but especially the yellow fever epidemics of 1699, 1741, and 1762.

Rue is not difficult to grow, and being an evergreen, it makes a handsome addition to the winter garden, for its leaves are finely cut and steely blue-gray. If it is given a warm dry location near a fence or someplace where its roots are well protected, the bush will last for many years. The Germans often planted it near gates since it was thought to protect such entrances from witchcraft, and sprigs of rue were even nailed above doors for the same purpose. But the plant was especially valued by those who raised chickens and other poultry, since the leaves could be boiled in molasses and given to the animals as a cure for croup.

---

202. Accomplished by cupping or with leeches.

Rue is of a warm, dry nature. It possesses the virtue of withstanding all poison, of protecting against pestilence and all malignant illnesses. It can brighten the eyesight, resist lewd desires, and reduce windiness. The leaves employed in this fashion must be gathered when the plant is in bloom, then dried in the shade.

If a few leaves of rue are eaten daily with meals, they will remove dimness from the eyes and clear the vision. Therefore, it is not unreasonable to add it to food eaten by painters, woodcarvers, and others who have need of a keen sight. Such persons that have eaten rue with their food for three weeks have noticed a marked strengthening of their vision. It was custom among the ancients to poetize rue with these verses:

Es kan der Rauten Kraft die Augen helle machen,
durch iher Hüllfe siehe der Mensch die schärffste Sachen.
Die Raute frisch vom Stock genommen und gekäut
befreyet das Gesicht von aller Dunckelheit.

Rue is empowered to make the eyesight keen,
for by its help men may view matters sharply.
When taken fresh from the stem and chewed,
it frees vision of every obscurity.

And another:

Der Fenchel und das Einsenkraut,
Die Roos, das Schellkraut und die Raut,
Sind dienlich dem Gesicht,
Das Dunckelheit ansicht:
Hieraus ein Wasser zubereit,
Das bringt den Augen Heiterkeit.

Fennel and vervain, rose, celandine and rue
are all servants to the sight, for penetrating the obscure;
prepare from them a water that brings light into the eyes.

A costly medication for poison is still prepared from rue these days, which ages ago King Mithradates kept in constant use to protect himself against all kinds of poison, and which this king wrote into a book in his own hand. It reads as follows: Take twenty rue leaves, the kernel of two walnuts, as much salt as one can hold with two fingers, and two figs. Grind it all in a mortar to form a paste and partake of this each morning before breakfast. No poison will be able to cause injury for the entire day.

This remedy is not only used against poison, but it is especially high-praised for protecting against pestilence, which is not unreasonable, since it has been found effective through daily use. Thus, the electuary of Mithradates should be highly recommended to the common man, so that he may be best protected from contagion. It does not cost much, and can be prepared by anyone easily. Much more benefit is derived from it than from the fake cure-alls of street hawkers.

If rue is taken in the morning before breakfast with a little salt or eaten on a slice of buttered bread, it will prove a good protection from the plague. However, pregnant women should abjure rue.

When a few sprigs of rue are eaten with a clove of garlic in the morning before breakfast, this will kill worms.

If rue is put into drinks, it will counter any injurious things that may be in them. For this reason the ancients were accustomed to say:

Lege Salbey und auch Rauten,
eh du trinckest, in den Wein,
so kanst du vor vielem bösen
sicher und verwahret seyn.

Lay sage and rue in wine
before you drink it,
and thus stay safe and sound
from many evils.

Another useful prophylactic against the plague: Take two loths of rue leaves, half a loth of figs, one and a half loths of juniper berries, one loth of walnuts, and two loths each of rose and rue vinegars. Mash it all together and take a dose the size of half a nutmeg in the morning before breakfast before going out into the air.

Those who possess an ardent nature should avoid rue, for it will easily give them a headache.

If rue is dried, ground to a powder and then taken in a half-quint dose with wine before going to sleep, it will help those who commonly piss in bed.

When rue is pulped and mixed with *Theriaca Andromaci* and formed into a plaster, it will heal the evil thing or felon.

If a sprig of rue is laid under the head of a baby, it will protect it from fits.

To prevent fainting, rub rue into vinegar and hold this under the nose.

If a rue bush is planted in the garden, it will drive away all noxious beasts, because they cannot bear the smell of it.

Should a dead sheep be found among the herd, fumigate their stalls by burning dried rue each morning and evening. This will protect the sheep from contagion.

If a horse develops a film over the eye, grind rue to a powder, and blow this into the horse's eye. Others take a half loth each of the juices of rue and fennel, and a quint of cock's gall, and mix it together, then swab it into the corners of the horse's eye.

To rid open wounds of horses of maggots and worms, and to keep them clean, take a handful each of rue, trefoil, flixweed, peach leaves, wormwood, baldrian, and agrimony. Boil this in wine, wash the wound with the decoction, then dip a cloth into it and lay it over the injury.

If the distilled water of rue is drunk in tablespoonful doses, it will especially strengthen weak eyesight and guard against lasciviousness. When the hands are washed with it and allowed to dry in the air, this will prove good for treating palsy.

To strengthen dim, feeble eyesight, take equal quantities of rue, vervain, fennel, celandine, and red roses, and distill this. Every day, put a few drops of this in both eyes. This will brighten and sharpen the eyesight very much.

The distilled oil of rue possesses excellent virtues when applied externally as an ointment and taken internally against convulsions, the plague, fainting, mother fits, colic, fits, the falling evil, and so forth.

The oil extract of rue is prepared thus: Take one pound of fresh rue and pulp it. Pour one pint of olive oil over this and let it stand three days. Afterward, simmer it over a gentle heat until the oil no longer spits and smokes when a little of it is allowed to fall on the hot coals. Then strain it off and store away for later use. This oil, spread warm over the stomachs of elderly people or children, will prove effective in treating gripes and colic. It will warm the livers of young children completely, when nothing else could accomplish it.

Take fresh or dry rue, wormwood, tansy, lemon balm, and marjoram in equal parts and mince them fine. Then put this in fresh unsalted butter and foment it in a pan over a gentle heat until the herbs shrivel away from the fat. Then strain off the fat, and store away for use. This will yield an excellent salve for children and old people. If a child has taken cold in the stomach from fruit, cold water, or something else, so that no food will stay down, or for whom food causes pain, smear this salve over the navel often and keep the child away from the cold. This will strengthen their weakened stomach and stop the pain. If the navel and lower belly are smeared with this salve as warm as the child can bear it, this will get rid of worms, stop gripes in the stomach, and strengthen those internal parts that have been injured by a chill.

If rue is ground together with juniper berries, then mixed with bread crumbs, good-quality vinegar, and salt so that it forms a wet pulp, and is then bound into a linen cloth that is laid over the forehead, pulse, and soles of the feet, this will stop headache, and diminish the heat of malignant fevers.

If the fresh juice expressed from rue is gargled often, it will prevent the purples from spreading into the throat.

When rue sugar (which is prepared like rose sugar) is taken often in pinch doses, it will not only prove effective against all malignancies but will also expel rank airs, as well as protect from apoplexy, fits, and the falling evil.

Rye

Secale cereale
Sauer: *Rocke* or *Rogge* (1774)

Rye was both a cause and a cure. It was one of the basic food grains of the German element, often combined with spelt flour and cornmeal for baking bread, but it was also a source of disease. A fungus can develop on rye that causes ergotism and Saint Anthony's fire in those who consume food made with the infected grain. This direct connection was not understood in the eighteenth century; thus the very rye that may have been administered in remedies of the sort Sauer describes may also have introduced maladies far worse than the patient already had. The various references to Saint Anthony's fire throughout the herbal must be taken in this context. The prevalence of Saint Anthony's fire also suggests a high dependence among the poor on one grain as a source of food. People with a highly varied diet were less apt to be affected severely by the disease than those who derived most of their nutrition from a limited source.

Rye does not possess as many volatile elements as wheat or spelt, but is endowed with rather more thick watery components, and for this reason it is of middling warmth. It is not as warm as wheat and is less nourishing than wheat, although it is warmer than barley and more nourishing than barley.

The flowers of rye are quite bitter, and are used by many people for treating tertian fever. This is administered as a tea.

Those who have acquired a stinking breath due to fever or some other illness, should eat well-salted rye bread made with fresh springwater before breakfast three mornings in succession.

A goodly quantity of rye boiled in water that is then given to horses to drink will get rid of their worms.

A water distilled from the green stems of rye grass is good for treating loin stones and hotness in the kidneys.

An excellent vulnerary plaster is prepared by surgeons from the juice of young rye grass. It is called Saint George's plaster and is prepared thus: Take one quart of the expressed juice of fresh rye grass and one pint of olive oil, and let this boil together over a gentle fire until the juice is boiled down. Then strain it through a cloth and, while it is still hot, dissolve into it half a pound each of turpentine and beeswax. Stir until it becomes cold, then it is ready.

For a felon, take the tender inner membrane of an eggshell and lay it over the painful spot. Then prepare a pap with rye flour and brandy or rum. Spread this thickly over a rag and wrap this over the egg skin so that the painful finger is completely covered.

Should a horse twist its foot, boil rye bran in vinegar until it forms a pap, then spread this warm as a plaster around the foot.

For earache, take a loaf of rye bread as hot as it comes from the oven, then cut it in half. Hold this to the ear as hot as the patient can bear it. This is also useful when hearing has been lost due to a loud noise.

When the crumbs of rye bread are mixed with vinegar to form a dough, and laid upon a horse that is swollen from being galled by the saddle or collar, this will prove an excellent remedy.

If the crumbs of rye bread are mixed with salt and this is bound over the spot for three or four nights, it will draw out the worm.

If rye flour is parched in a frying pan and laid warm over such limbs that are afflicted with Saint Anthony's fire or some other inflammation, this will both ease the pain and reduce the swelling. For those who may have elderberry blossoms and a little camphor, add these and it will work so much the better. Or add finely powdered clay smoking pipes. This is also good for expelling inflammations of the chest.

Rye flour is also employed in emollient poultices, either mixed with honey or boiled with milk.

Rye bran mixed with salt, parched in a frying pan, and then put into a sachet and laid on the hurt as hot as the patient can bear it will remove pleurisy. But it is necessary to make two sachets, so that one can be warming while the other is being used. Laid on the belly, the hot sachet will dispel the vapors and assuage the gripes that arise from them.

When the crust of rye or some other bread is toasted, then moistened with warm vinegar or red wine, strewn with ground nutmeg and cinnamon, and then laid hot over the stomach, this will still eructations, casting of the stomach, and diarrhea. When laid on the lower abdomen, this will stop pain following delivery thoroughly.

Saffron
Crocus sativus
Sauer: *Safran* (1768)

When Johann Jakob Schmidt came to saffron in his Biblischer Medicus, *he noted that it was placed among the cordial herbs for strengthening the heart: "It is beneficial to the chest and for apoplexies, and promotes monthly purification of the female sex. It grows so much the better when it is tread upon, and for this reason it is held up as a symbol of the humility and forbearance of Believers."[203] I rather think that it does much better when planted in very sandy soil and left to itself. Saffron has plenty enough to contend with, for its long evergreen leaves are greatly relished by rabbits and squirrels.*

Saffron grows extremely well in Pennsylvania, and its culture was introduced by the Schwenkfelders, a religious sect from Silesia, in the 1730s. For a long time it was a cottage industry managed by housewives who were able to derive a profitable income from it. The work of growing saffron is labor-intensive and comes all at once, since the herb blooms for a short period during the first or second week of October and must be picked by hand. But while it is in bloom, the soft violet flowers fill the garden with color and the rich scent of honey, drawing bees from far and wide. The fragrance is so strong that the bees often act as though they are drunk, but I have never known saffron to make people hilarious, as Sauer claims.

203. Johann Jakob Schmidt, *Biblischer Medicus* (Züllichau, 1743), 704.

Because it was a local product and readily available, saffron also became a notable feature of the cookery of the Germans who settled in Pennsylvania, a holdover from the Baroque era, when saffron figured highly in the cookery of the well-to-do. The Zwinger herbal provided a recipe for a saffron-flavored cook powder, but Sauer did not include it, either for space constraints or simply because he thought it unlikely country people would find it useful. But since he published cook powders elsewhere in the herbal, I thought it appropriate to reproduce it. When used with stewed chicken or fowl, it gives the dish a unique flavor, and of course the yellow color so well liked by the Mennonites, even today: "A Useful Powder for the Kitchen, to be Used in Food. Take eight loths of cinnamon, three loths of ginger, two loths of cloves, one loth of black pepper, and half a loth of saffron. Grind it all to a fine powder."[204] This makes a rather large quantity, but it can be kept for some time in an airtight container.

Saffron is warm and dry in nature and possesses a somewhat volatile salt combined with various oily elements. It derives from these its faculty for easing pain; for strengthening the liver, heart, spleen, and matrix; for purifying the chest; and for easing difficult breathing.

Saffron is an excellent and desirable remedy for treating many parts of the body when used in cookery or when powdered and taken in ten-grain doses in a small glass of wine. First of all, it is extremely effective in treating the heart, for it strengthens it, brings joy to the spirits, withstands corruption, and is good for treating palpitations, trembling of the heart, fainting, and weakness. Furthermore, it promotes digestion. Thirdly, for those afflicted by asthma, wheezing, and consumption, it will for the most part prove beneficial to the chest and lungs. Fourthly, it opens the liver and removes jaundice. When mixed with rosewater and rubbed warm over the eyes, it will prevent smallpox from entering the eyes. If a child commences to cry and refuses to suckle, and has green or yellow stool, this is a sign that it has a tear in the stomach. For this, administer a few grains of finely ground saffron in its porridge.

If ten to twenty grains of saffron are ground and taken daily in warm wine, this will prove very beneficial to asthmatics and consumptives.

For asthma, take a sweet apple, core it out at little at the top, and put half a quint of saffron in this, as well as an equal amount of frankincense. Bake the apple and give it to the patient to eat. This remedy has benefited many asthmatics very much.

For ardent fevers arising from asthma and anxiety of the heart that often plague patients, it is quite effective if a pinch of ground saffron is administered in their broth.

A very effective powder for bloody flux: Take one and a half quints of calcined hartshorn and new pipe clay, a quint each of tormentil root, *bole armeniac*, and pike's jaw, a half quint each of sorrel and plantain seeds and mace, and ten grains of good-quality saffron. Grind it all to a fine powder and administer a pinch of this in plantain water every two hours.

If a small bundle of saffron is worn over the chest, this will prove good in treating melancholic sorrow.

When someone is attacked by fits or convulsions, and lies speechless due to

204. Theodor Zwinger, *Theatrum Botanicum* (Basel, 1744), 420.

apoplexy and lethargy, take saffron and beaver cod mixed with sharp vinegar and dab this in the nose with a feather.

If saffron is used too strongly, it will provoke so much mirthfulness that people may think themselves about to die from laughing.

For headache that often results from ardent fevers, take three loths each of house-leek juice, nightshade juice, vervain juice (or the distilled waters of these same herbs), and rosewater. Mix this with half a quint of finely ground saffron. Warm it up often and dip a small piece of linen in it and lay this several times over the forehead. This will not only relieve headache, but stop deafness and insensibility.

If saffron is put into good brandy with camphor, this will yield a fine anodyne and discutient remedy called camphor brandy.

Sage
Salvia officinalis
Sauer: *Salbey* (1762)

The Sauer herbal mentions two kinds of sage, the "red" sage, which Zwinger called Salvia hortensis, *and the white or narrow-leafed sage, which Zwinger called the Sage of Virtue. These are not separate species but simply varieties of the same plant, although their physical characteristics are noticeably different. The red sage is the common sage of today, a large, rangy bush with purple flowers that grow in whorls. There are also plants that produce true red flowers as well as pure white ones. All of these were used in medicine.*

The narrow-leafed white sage, which is a smaller plant as well, is still considered the best sage for culinary purposes and was often employed in sage and onion sauce by the English.

Sage is warm and dry in nature. The small sage is more powerful than the large. It has the capacity to resist all corruptions, to cleanse, to gently draw together, and to quicken the vital spirits.

Sage is excellent for a cold brain, for it strengthens the nerves and is good for treating all cold weaknesses of the head. It also warms the stomach and encourages the appetite.

Some people imagine themselves safe, that by eating a few sage leaves with salt in the morning before breakfast, they will be protected the whole day from contagion and miasma.

Foods that are prepared with sage agree well with those who possess a cold nature.

When sage is chewed, it will cleanse a rheumy head of fluxes and make the breath pleasant smelling.

Take sage leaves and blossoms dried in the shade, as much as can be grasped between five fingers, and infuse this in hot water. When drunk as tea each morning and evening for a continuance, and sweetened with equal parts milk and rock candy, this will prevent fluxes of the head, take away hoarseness—even when it has lasted for a long time—ease breathing, and strengthen the nerves.

Boil sage and mullein in wine and sit over this while it is still hot. This will cause a dangling end gut to draw back into the body.

The distilled water of sage possesses a wonderful power against all cold maladies of the head, protects against apoplexy, the falling evil, and fits, and takes away dizziness. It is also good for coughs and warms the stomach when a tablespoon dose is taken from time to time.

Persons who have been rendered speechless due to apoplexy should be given a few tablespoonfuls of this water, for it often restores lost speech and strengthens a feeble tongue. When snuffed into the nose, this water purifies the head. Rubbing the hands with it when it is lukewarm, then letting them dry in the air, will dispel trembling.

An excellent essence can be extracted from freshly chopped sage put in brandy. Pour enough brandy over it in a glass vessel so that it covers the sage to the height of a finger. Then let this stand in the sun for several weeks. This is a capital prophylactic against apoplexy. It also strengthens and warms cold nerves, brain, stomach, and matrix. It improves the memory and dispels dizziness.

Saint-John's-wort
Hypericum perforatum
Sauer: *Johannes-Kraut* (1762)

All of the hypericums are rather handsome herbs and make delightful garden plants if they can be coaxed into cultivation. Most of them prefer the wild and thrive on uncultivated ground. I have planted Saint-John's-wort many times in spots where I wanted it to grow, only to have it die there and reemerge elsewhere in some inopportune corner of the garden. One must learn to let these things take their course.

While there are numerous native species, this one has been introduced from Europe, and doubtless this was done intentionally, since the herb has had a long association with herbal cures going back to pagan times. Indeed, there was a carryover of this among some of the Germans who settled in America, for they would pick Saint-John's-wort on the twenty-fourth of June (Saint John's Day) and hang it in their houses as a charm against storms, thunder, and evil spirits. Sauer makes no mention of this, but he was rather proud of his St. John's oil, which he mentioned often in both his almanacs and newspapers. The tea made from the leaves tastes very much like Blue Mountain tea made with sweet goldenrod (page 156), and the two can be harvested about the same time.

Saint-John's-wort possesses the capacity to warm, to cleanse, to heal, to ease, to still pain, and to dissolve thick, congealed blood. An excellent vulnerary balsam is made from this herb in the following manner: Take four loths of Saint-John's-wort from a plant whose flowers are not yet fully open, and two loths of the young shoots of great mullein. Chop these very fine, then pour twelve loths of double-rectified brandy over them. Let this stand a few days until the brandy has drawn out the color. Press this through a cloth, and then add two loths of turpentine. Let this stand three days and nights in a warm place, and thus you will have an excellent balsam for external use on wounds, and for use when taken orally for internal injuries. The dose for the latter is one teaspoonful at a time taken two or three times daily. This remedy is incomparably good for diarrhea and other sharp fluxes of the belly, provided the body is first given a laxative with rhubarb or *panacea antimonii*.[205] About the very excellent St. John's oil, refer to this almanac for the year 1760.

Sanicle
Sanicula europaea
Sauer: *Sanickel* (1769)

The leaf was the part used in eighteenth-century medicine, and much was claimed for its curative powers. Dr. John Hill noted, "It has been vastly celebrated for the Cure of Ruptures, but that is idle."[206] The Sauer herbal takes quite the opposite position, for most of the remedies do indeed treat breaches of some type. Sauer's final remark is somewhat interesting because the sanicle of his medicine was the European species imported in dry form, or gathered from local gardens. It is not an American woodland plant, but black snakeroot (Sanicula marylandica) *appears to have served as a native substitute since the seventeenth century. Sauer does not seem to have known about this, or else he would not have recommended self-heal as a substitute.*

Sauer's reference to a saucerful of liquid is worthy of mention because it was common practice in his era to pour hot tea or similar beverages served in china cups into the deep bowl-like saucers that accompanied them, and then sip the drink from that. This was a way of cooling the beverage, but these saucers were also somewhat standard in size, so most people would easily recognize the quantity intended. Some cookbooks even measured flour and other loose ingredients this way. The custom of drinking from saucers lasted well into the 1840s, but then died out once china manufacturers began changing the design of saucers to resemble the shallow sorts we know today.

Sanicle operates through its numerous alkaline salts, combined with balsamic elements. Thus it is warm and dry by nature and possesses the virtue of purifying, cleansing, and sweetening the blood; and of opening, cleansing, and healing all sour, sharp salty humors.

Among all the vulnerary herbs, sanicle is most employed by surgeons, for they use it daily in their vulnerary potions and prepare many other remedies with it. Boil one handful of sanicle in two quarts of fresh springwater for as long as it takes to hard-cook an egg. This decoction will heal internal injuries of the

---

205. Also written as *antimonium laxativum*. This was a commonly sold laxative powder consisting of antimony and saltpeter.

206. Dr. John Hill, *The Useful Family Herbal* (London, 1755), 324.

chest, viscera, and the gut, and will stop the uncontrolled loss of blood.

The distilled water of sanicle is a healing remedy for those with internal ruptures and injuries, for it heals internal wounds completely when taken daily in four- or five-tablespoon doses each morning before breakfast. It will heal scurvy of the mouth and sores of the throat when gargled with it lukewarm. For injuries and wounds in the privates, sanicle water will heal them completely when they are washed with it often, and a small piece of linen cloth is dipped in it and laid over the hurt.

An essence of sanicle can be drawn off in brandy. It is excellent for healing all wounds and injuries. Take twenty to thirty drops several times each day in a warm tea made with the same herb. If this essence is reduced to the thickness of honey, it will yield the Extract of Sanicle that is so serviceable in treating the whites and bloody flux.

To make a vulnerary potion for the wounded, the following will prove effective: Take four handfuls of sanicle; three handfuls each of lady's mantle, wintergreen, speedwell, and periwinkle; two handfuls each of betony, agrimony, germander, ribwort and broad-leafed plantains, and red roses; and a handful each of mugwort, mouse ear, and wild tansy. Chop it altogether very fine, and when it is needed, take one handful of this mixture and boil it in two or three quarts of water. If no fever is present, add a little wine to it. When it has boiled for a while, strain it off through a cloth and give more or less one saucerful to the patient or injured person two or three times daily. (Should this herb not be found in this country, or not in some places, the leaves of self-heal may be used instead, which in many instances possess nearly the same virtues.)

Sassafras
Sassafras officinale
Sauer: *Sassafras* (1768)

Sassafras was also known in German as Fenchelholz, *"fennel-wood," in reference to its fennel-like taste. The logs, dried roots, and bark were sold in apothecary shops. It was customary to sell the wood shavings "to order" so that they would be fresh. Medical works of the period often refer to sassafras as the* panacea catarhorum, *the sure cure of catarrh, but the most famous use of sassafras was in its treatment for venereal diseases. Godfrey's Cordial, made with sassafras, anise, and several other ingredients, was another popular commercial remedy sold in Sauer's era. Somewhat in line with the cordial idea, Germans in colonial America often added sassafras to beer, both to enhance the taste of the beer and to take advantage of the added medical properties. This evolved out of the old medieval custom of adding fennel seed to beer for similar reasons. Sassafras flavoring is still added to Pennsylvania Dutch root beer today.*

Adding the flowers to salads, as the herbal suggests, is an unusual concept, but not without its parallels, for the young leaf buds, while still gray and fuzzy, are dried and ground for the gumbo filé used to thicken soups in the Deep South.

The root of the sassafras tree is the most useful part, and the bark of the root is the most powerful, thus for medicine it is most widely employed. It possesses the faculty to dry up all fluxes, to purify the blood, and to expel through the urine and sweat all excess corruptions. It is especially useful for expelling the French pox from the blood.

It is customary to prepare all sorts of medicines from sassafras root. For those who want to boil a good sudorific potion, take two and half loths each of rasped sarsaparilla root, lignum vitae, Chinese smilax, and the bark of sassafras root; two loths of Hungarian antimony; four loths of Zante currants; and a half loth each of fennel seed and cinnamon. Grind and chop all of this together and then put it in an earthen, pewter, or glass vessel and pour a gallon or more of springwater or rainwater over it. Cover this tightly and let it simmer several hours. Strain off the liquid, and administer one or one and a half gills of it warm to the patient in the morning and evening. This potion will force out all sharp, salty humors through the sweat and stool, improve the condition of the blood, and prove serviceable in drying and healing old injuries, for it fosters healthy flesh in the same. It also promotes the normal circulation of the blood.

The learned Mynsicht poured hot springwater over rasped sassafras root (or one can also use a good old wine), and then let this simmer or digest over hot ashes. It will produce a reddish tincture to which a little cinnamon may be added, and then cooked down to make an extract as thick as honey.[207]

The distilled water of sassafras can be administered in spoonful doses, but if it is double-rectified, give the patient no more than sixty drops. However, if dosing the balsamic oil, then give the patient only four to ten drops in wine or sugar. Both of these treatments open blockages of the liver and spleen, remove windiness and painful swelling of the gut, strengthen the stomach, and absorb thick humors from the same. They expel gently through the urine and sweat, for which reason they are very useful in treating venereal afflictions, yes indeed, even scorbutic blood.

The distilled oil of sassafras possesses the special virtue of easing difficult deliveries by expelling the child. After delivery, it will purify the matrix of all corruptions that remain there, and if taken regularly, it will make barren women fruitful.

For those afflicted by salty blood and the itch, the following diet drink may be taken with good benefit: Take one loth each of Chinese smilax and the bark of sassafras root, and half a loth of rasped hartshorn, and chop and grind it all together. Simmer this in three quarts of water for one-half to one hour. Those who want it a little more agreeable-tasting may add a small piece of licorice or a little anise or fennel seed. After it is boiled, strain it off through a clean cloth. This potion is also very helpful to those who are laid up by gout or pains in the limbs. Indeed, it is good for anyone plagued by thick, cold fluxes, whether they be upon the chest or in the limbs.

A salad can be prepared with sassafras flowers when they are quite fresh. If they are eaten daily, this will prove very healthful. Or, the flowers may be dried in the shade and drunk instead of tea for a period each day. This is very helpful to those who are dropsical by nature.

207. This was sometimes sold under the commercial name of Mynsicht's Extract of Sassafras. Adrian von Mynsicht (1603–1638) was a German mystic and Rosicrucian as well as a physician.

Savine

Sabina cacumina
Sauer: *Sevenbaum* (1770)

Savine is a tall, pyramidal evergreen tree native to both Europe and North America. For medical purposes, it is best when used fresh. But since it is not common in America, at least in the middle regions settled by the Germans, native red cedar (Juniperus virginiana) appears to have served as an equivalent in poultices, for red cedar was generally called savine among country people. The fresh, prickly young shoots are the part used, and Dr. Zwinger described and illustrated the two types found in Europe. Both of these were also dried and exported for the powders mentioned by Sauer.

The savine tree is endowed with an extremely sharp, balsamic salt. From this derives its capacity to thin the blood forcefully; to sharpen and open the veins of the matrix in particular, but also other easily opened veins as well; and to release blockages of the urinary tract, provided that those who undergo these strong purges accompany them with bleeding.

Powdered savine mixed with cream will yield a very healing salve for scall in young children. Some heat savine in cream and smear the affected scalp with this.

If ground green savine is spread as a poultice on the stomach, it will kill worms.

If a small piece of cloth is dipped into savine water and wrapped around a finger throbbing with pain, this will kill the worm in it. If it is drunk, it will bring down the menses in women.

The greens of savine are also employed effectively with other vulnerary herbs when used in treatments for falls, because they diminish malignant clotted blood forcefully, but where there may be a concern about severe bleeding from the injuries, this treatment ought not be employed. But if savine is boiled in wine and then used to wash out old injuries on the legs, it will purify and promote their healing.

Dried leaves of savine ground to powder and mixed with Venetian glass[208] in honey, then put into a nutshell and bound over the navel, will kill umbilical worms.[209]

Savory (Summer Savory)

Saturea hortensis
Sauer: *Saturey, Bohnenkraut* (1769)

It was once customary in the German farm markets of Maryland and Pennsylvania to sell string beans together with little bundles of fresh savory. One did not eat beans without savory, which is why the Pennsylvania Dutch call this herb Buhnegreidel, *"bean herb." This custom is still maintained in the Palatinate of southwest Germany, from which many of the Pennsylvania Germans originated, but the truth of the matter is,*

208. *Vitrum Venetum* was a specific for treating worms prepared from rock crystal or some other exceedingly pure substance finely ground.

209. Worms that infect the area of the navel. This is not a specific kind, for there were several sorts that made their way into the body by this means. This is a condition that mostly affected newborn babies and small children prior to the era when regular bathing became fashionable.

the "bean" eaten with savory was originally the fava bean, not the New World bean eaten with it today.

In the Middle Ages, the Germans ate fava beans in the winter, in preparations very much like French cassoulets, and it was in those baked bean dishes that savory was added in generous amounts. The reason for eating savory with beans was medical as well as nutritional, as the Sauer herbal explains rather bluntly: it takes away the vapors that cause swelling, in short, gas.

Savory is of a warm, dry nature. It operates through its mildly volatile oily salt, and possesses a faculty somewhat similar to hyssop. It works particularly well in expelling through sweat, in loosening phlegm in the chest, and in proving beneficial to the head.

Savory is employed usefully in cookery, particularly with young meats and fish. It is the spice of the poor, excites the appetite, warms the stomach, promotes digestion, strengthens vision, and is very usefully employed in making sausages, for it makes them more tasty and healthy. It is also quite good when cooked with peas, beans, and other podded vegetables because it takes away the vapors that cause swelling. Additionally, it is good when cooked with cabbage and other potherbs on the grounds that it provides them with a nice aroma and a pleasant flavor.

If two handfuls of savory are infused in two quarts of white wine and the infusion then drunk, it will strengthen a feeble head and weak vision, prove beneficial to asthmatics since it dispels phlegm and promotes its expectoration, and expel urine and other things.

When savory is boiled in water and the decoction drunk often, it will loosen phlegm in the chest, ease difficult breathing, and get rid of coughing. If the broth is employed as a gargle, it will get rid of the pain and swelling of the tonsils and glottis.

Cold, dropsical people should use savory diligently, by infusing it in wine and drinking this often, for it will protect them from convulsions. On the other hand, pregnant women should use this herb sparingly or not at all, for it will not do them any good.

Savory possesses all of the virtues and faculties of thyme and wild thyme, for which reason one may be administered or used in place of the other in medicine.

For lethargy, indeed for those people who cannot be awakened, take a few handfuls of savory and boil this in wine. Dip a cloth in this often and lay it warm over the head. If desired, a sachet filled with savory may be laid warm over the head in the same manner.

Saxifrage
Saxifraga granulata
Sauer: *Steinbrech* (1774)

The saxifrages are a very common genus indeed, but this species is not native to North America. Its German name derives from two words: Stein, "stone," and brechen, "to break." This refers to its ability to break up stones in the kidneys and bladder, and this is the meaning of the Latin name as well. Sauer evidently sold this herb in the dried state imported from abroad, for it is not clear that any of our native saxifrages operated with a similar medical action. None of them are listed in any of the common household materia medicas in the nineteenth century, and none of them were sold by the Shakers, who specialized in native medical plants.

The only native saxifrage that was employed by the Germans seems to have been the lettuce saxifrage (Saxifraga micranthidifolia), which was gathered as a spring health food. Since it can only be found near cold springs and brooks, its distribution was never widespread. Salads made with it were thought—by country people—to produce results similar to saxifrage water, but this is not substantiated in medical literature of the period.

Saxifrage operates through its bitter nitrous, mildly volatile salts and thus possesses the capacity to warm gently, to thin and dispel thick humors, to open blockages, to expel through the urine, and to cleanse and heal wounds and sores.

Saxifrage is considered a valuable remedy for gravel, sand, and stone in the kidneys and bladder, for which reason it acquired its name, since it stands in front of all other herbs in breaking up and expelling stones. Take one handful of the leaves and boil them in two quarts of white wine. Take this decoction often as a drink.

The distilled water of saxifrage taken in half-gill doses in the morning before breakfast will promote urine and purify the kidneys and bladder of gravel, sand, foul matter, and stones. The essence drawn out from the leaves and root in brandy is very good for all of the conditions enumerated above. It also promotes the healing of wounds and injuries.

Some people also boil the leaves in water and use this in baths for treating the loins and kidneys.

The following is a valuable antilithic gravel powder: Take one loth of saxifrage seeds, a half loth each of cress seeds, medlar pits,[210] and fennel seeds; a quint and a half each of prepared crab's eyes and salts of holy thistle; and a loth and a half of sugar. Grind all of this together to make a fine powder. Administer it often to people who are particularly burdened with gravel and foul matter in the kidneys, but during the new and full moon, let them take a quint of the powder at each meal in boiled licorice water. This will purify the kidneys powerfully, and get rid of the cold evil and cold piss.

Scorzonera
Scorzonera hispanica
Sauer: *Haberwurtz* (1772)

Sometimes called Vipers Grass in old herbals, this is a very useful garden plant in several respects. Its leaves and roots are edible, and the plants can be left in the ground to increase in size from year to year, unlike salsify. Furthermore, the greens appear early in the spring and then again in the fall, so that during cool weather the plant is quite

---

210. Medlar *(Mespilus germanica)* is a small tree with brown, apple-like fruits. The seeds are larger than apple seeds.

generous in providing ingredients for the kitchen.

The herbal refers to scorzonera as Haberwurtz, *"oat root," for it does indeed taste like oats—or oysters or clams; opinions vary. It is now more commonly called* Schwarzwurtzel, *"black root," in German and may be considered one of the basic root vegetables of the German and French kitchen garden. Likewise, it was cultivated extensively by the Germans in colonial America, but much less so among the English. German cookbooks of Sauer's period abound in recipes for scorzonera, the sorts of pleasant dishes referred to in the herbal. Christine Knörin's preparation from 1783 is typical:*

> *Once the roots are pared, put them directly into water to which a little flour has been added so that the roots remain white. Then put the scorzonera in cold water with a small piece of veal that has been previously soaked in water to draw off the blood. Add a small piece of butter worked to a paste with a little flour. When this begins to boil, add hot meat stock so that the ingredients may become quite tender. Also add salt according to taste. When the ingredients are tender, add another piece of butter worked to a paste with flour so that the sauce achieves the necessary consistency, and add a little nutmeg. N.B. Once the scorzonera is cleaned, it should be cut in half lengthwise and sliced into pieces not quite half the length of a finger.[211]*

Knörin put the scorzonera in water because when it is pared and exposed to the air, it will turn brown.

Scorzonera, or snakes bane, is endowed with an alkaline sweet-and-sour salt mixed with mild balsamic elements. From these it derives its capacity to withstand poison, to purify the blood, to strengthen the heart, and to give rise to a happy disposition.

Garden-cultivated scorzonera is prepared in cookery as a very pleasant and healthful dish with salt, butter, and herbs. It furnishes the stomach with good nourishment and improves the blood.

If a small cloth is moistened with the milky juice expressed from the leaves and roots mixed with fennel or lovage water and laid warm over the eyes often, this will get rid of inflammations, pain, and red spots, as well as strengthen weak eyesight.

The dried root can be boiled in water either by itself or together with other ingredients and administered as a diet drink to those patients who have been bitten by poisonous creatures, or who have been attacked by ardent pestilential fevers and other such contagious diseases.

From the root, and sometimes from the leaves, flowers, and seeds, it

211. Christine Knörin, *Sammlung vieler Vorschriften* (Stuttgart, 1783), 46–47

is possible to create an essence and extract in divers ways, namely: Boil the fresh, young succulent roots, leaves, and seeds in the water distilled from this plant in a closely covered vessel. Then strain it through a thick cloth, and further cook it to reduce it somewhat. This yields the essence, but if it is boiled until it is as thick as honey, it becomes an extract. These are far easier to keep than if they have been prepared with brandy, albeit those too are very useful.

The distilled water of scorzonera is good for malignant or pestilential fevers. It strengthens a weak heart and matrix, protects against dizziness, and opens up blockages of the liver and spleen, provided a few tablespoonfuls are taken as desired.

Scorzonera root preserved in sugar will open a blocked liver and spleen, dispel sadness, give protection from contagion, and prove serviceable against the falling evil, cardialgy, trembling of the heart, dizziness, and mother fits, provided a few pieces are eaten according to want.

Fresh scorzonera root possesses the same faculty for all of the illnesses enumerated above, and in general purifies the blood, and sweetens it as well. Furthermore, with or without the addition of other ingredients according to each person's tastes and preferences, it will reinvigorate and provide excellent therapy when boiled in meat broth or milk, then pressed out well and a pint or more of this juice drunk every morning before breakfast several weeks in succession according to a moderate, orderly way of life.

Scurvy Grass or Spoonwort
Cochlearia officinalis
Sauer: *Löffelkraut* (1762)

Both European scurvy grass (spoonwort) and upland cress (Saint Barbara's cress), as well as several closely related mustards, were all sold under the name of scurvy grass in colonial markets. Thus it is not always possible to interpret period references to these herbs any more specifically than that. The German name, which means spoonwort, is a little more specific because at least the name hints at the leaf shape. However, Sauer's herb is not in doubt, since his discussion is based on Zwinger, and Zwinger provided a picture of the plant.

Its importance to colonial Americans is revealed by its English name, for even a casual perusal of Sauer's herbal will reveal a consistent concern about scurvy and its cures. This is a disease that results from poor diet, specifically a deficiency of vitamin C, which in itself should tell us something about the shortcomings of colonial nutrition, especially during the depths of winter when fresh greens were scarce. Scurvy grass was generally planted in the fall so that it would remain green all winter, even under the snow. It tastes very much like watercress, and as with watercress, cooking it destroys a lot of its nutritional value. For this reason, its medical and dietary virtues are best when it is fresh, so in the past it was generally used as a salad herb. Otherwise, it was infused in beer to create an antiscorbutic tonic.

Scurvy grass water, or spirit of scurvy grass, as it was also called, was equally impor-

tant for correcting vitamin C deficiency. It is often mentioned in colonial newspaper advertisements. Charles Osborne, for example, advertised it for sale from his shop at the Golden Pestle in Second Street, Philadelphia, in the Pennsylvania Gazette *for February 15, 1759. The late winter timing of this advertisement could not have been more appropriate, since this was the period of the year when scurvy began to show up. The production of spirit of scurvy grass continued well into the nineteenth century, at least until lemons and limes became more widely available.*

Scurvy grass is warm and dry and operates by means of its copious sharp, volatile spirituous salts, together with a small quantity of oil in its juice. It therefore exhibits a great similarity to watercress in its capacity to dissolve thick, tough phlegmy humors, to open blockages of the spleen and the veins of the chest and lungs, and to purify the blood.

This herb is a splendid remedy for scurvy, yet it is sometimes too fiery, in which case it requires a cooling supplement. To this purpose, a little saltpeter can be added, either mixed with the juice or taken separately.

A useful conserve or sugar of scurvy grass can be made as follows: Take as much fresh scurvy grass as you want and add to it twice the quantity of dry white sugar. Grind this in a wooden or marble mortar until it is quite fine and soft. Put this up in a well-glazed earthenware vessel. This is a valuable and pleasing remedy for scurvy and blockages of the liver and spleen, when taken from time to time in doses the size of a nutmeg. A similar result may also be had from the distilled water of scurvy grass, if administered frequently in half-gill doses.

For those who suffer from great extremes of pain due to scurvy, especially about the shins and feet, the following steam bath should be prepared: Take four loths of marshmallow root, two handfuls each of wormwood, mallow, scurvy grass, brooklime, mugwort, and chamomile flowers, and half a loth of caraway. Chop it all up and boil it in springwater. Let the warm steam rise over the affected limbs.

The expressed juice of fresh scurvy grass along with the pulped leaves, applied as a cataplasm upon the face for the duration of a night, will take away blemishes, spots, and impurities on the skin. But the following morning, the face should be scrubbed thoroughly with water in which bran has been boiled.

The expressed juice of fresh scurvy grass is also very useful against putrefaction of the gums, provided they are rubbed with it. A similar result may be obtained with the distilled waters of scurvy grass and brooklime, or, if these waters are not available, then take the herbs and boil them in milk and rub and rinse the gums with this.

If the expressed juice of fresh scurvy grass is combined with rose honey and calcined alum, and then smeared over putrid scurvied gums, it will heal them completely and reset wobbling teeth.

For an excellent gargle for scurvy of the mouth: Take a gill each of self-heal, plantain, and scurvy grass waters, a quint of alum, and three loths of rose honey, and mix this together thoroughly. Gargle with this in the throat and mouth.

Fresh scurvy grass infused in beer for three or four days, then put up in a well-stopped vessel, will impart all of its virtues to the beer. Persons afflicted with scurvy, or who suffer from ailments of the spleen, will find great usefulness in this if it is drunk daily.

If the leaves of scurvy grass are chewed frequently, they will keep the mouth pure and safe from all types of scurvy.

The expressed juice from the fresh leaves, taken in one- to one-and-a-half-loth doses in the morning and evening, will not only cleanse scorbutic blood of superfluous salts, but will also treat consumption, atrophy, and tertian and quartan agues, as well as jaundice and dropsy.

Sea Holly
Eryngium maritimum
Sauer: *Mannstreu* (1770)

The herbal uses Mannstreu *as a general term for several species and subspecies of the genus* Eryngium, *all used for more or less the same purpose. While Sauer is not altogether specific, he is probably discussing* Eryngium maritimum, *which is the species most commonly touched upon by herbalists of his period. It was also the species most commonly sold in dry form by colonial apothecary shops, both the seeds and the roots.*

The root was considered a powerful male aphrodisiac, more so than ginseng, which was only then coming into fashion. It was sold dried for tea or candied for more convenient use. The aphrodisiac action is alluded to by Sauer in the references to "other things" below. Woyt was less coy in his approval, remarking that it was an excellent herb for helping old men get erections. We might have gathered that from the herb's German name, which implies something that men may depend upon.

Nearly all members of this genus make nice rock garden plants because they thrive in dry, alkaline soil. In the wild, sea holly grows on the beach above the high tide line. I have seen it in Cyprus covering acres of ground along the beachfront, an impenetrable wall of sharp thistles blocking all access to the water. Not even goats venture near it, although it has a charming pale blue-white flower that is quite inviting to the bees.

Sea holly possesses splendid virtues for thinning all manner of phlegm, for loosening internal obstructions, and for promoting urine, and other things. Only the roots and seeds are used. The water distilled from sea holly purifies the blood, helps against ague and quartan fevers, opens obstructions of the liver and spleen, is serviceable against jaundice, and promotes urination and other things. It is also useful to those who complain of kidney stones.

The roots of sea holly can be preserved in sugar like succory. This is a good remedy for those with liver complaints, jaundice, and dropsy. It also takes away colic and falling evil, and strengthens a feeble stomach and matrix.

Sea Onion (Squill)

Urginea maritima
Sauer: *Meer-Zwiebel* (1772)

Squill is native to the Mediterranean and grows near the coast, indeed often within a few hundred feet of the water. It is also an odd-looking plant because the leaves die down during the heat of summer; then in late August or September long, wiry flower stalks shoot up to as high as four feet. The tops are covered with small white flowers. It is still customary in parts of Greece to hang the bulb in the house to prevent miasmas or to draw off diseases in the same manner that Sauer uses onions (see page 232). Stored in grain, the bulbs are said to keep out damaging insects.

As the Sauer herbal points out, it was the bulb that was used in medicine. Due to its pungency, it was necessary to prepare it prior to use. Baking it in the oven was one common treatment. Squill or sea onion honey was at one time a well-known medicine usually sold under its more impressive Latin name, oxymel scilliticum. *This was a popular cold and cough remedy, for which Sauer provides the recipe.*

Sea onion possess a sharp, volatile, bitter salt, which however evaporates when it is dried. It dissolves all manner of tough phlegm, frees the viscera of all overflowings of gluey humors, forces out urine, eases breathing, and induces expectoration from the chest.

Raw sea onion cannot be used internally without injury. For this reason it must be prepared thus: Take a whole sea onion, remove the outer skin, and wrap it in bread dough about one finger thick. Bake this in the oven, then remove the onion. Slice it with a bone or wooden knife, and thread the pieces on a string. Hang this in the air until they dry completely. From these then a sea onion vinegar can be prepared in the following manner: Take four loths of the prepared dried onion and pour sixteen loths of good quality vinegar over this. Let this stand fourteen days over a gentle warmth or else in the sun. This vinegar was very highly esteemed by the ancients; indeed, it was held up as a universal cure.

Those who take a tablespoonful of this in the morning before breakfast will be safe from scurvy of the gums and throat. It will strengthen the stomach, force out urine, and sweeten the breath. It will also give a clear voice, brighten the vision, improve hearing, and promote a healthy complexion. It aids in the digestion of food and will see to it that there may be no internal blockages, swellings, or hardness. In fine, sea onion vinegar is an outstanding remedy for maintaining good health. It is also serviceable against the onset of the falling evil, and when held in the mouth, it will reset wobbly teeth. When used as a gargle, it will draw out rheums of the head. For the difficult breathing of a person who commences to choke, let them lick slowly from a tablespoonful of the vinegar. This will dispel the clotted phlegm powerfully.

For those who find sea onion vinegar too sour, a sea onion honey may be prepared, or have someone else prepare it as follows: Take one and a half pounds of honey, and let it boil until foamy in water. Continue boiling until it becomes a little thick, then add one pound of sea onion vinegar. Boil this a little more until it attains the thickness of syrup. This honey preparation is very useful for the head, stomach, and internal afflictions of the viscera, especially those arising from cold.

It is also possible to make a useful wine from sea onions: Take eight loths of sea onion prepared and dried as mentioned above, and pour four gallons of good white wine over this. Keep this in an earthenware vessel. Take a gill of it in the morning before breakfast, and it will dispel phlegm from the chest. It is also useful to the kidneys and bladder, and gets rid of gross fat on the body, thus maintaining people in good health.

For asthma and coughing, sea onion honey may be employed in the following manner with good results: Take one loth of the honey and as much sweet almond oil, and two to three loths of violet juice. Mix this together well and administer to the patient a tablespoonful every six hours.

Dried sea onion is to be had in nearly every apothecary shop, so it is not necessary to go through the trouble of the first-mentioned step of wrapping it in dough and baking it in an oven, rather it can be purchased ready-made and the vinegar or honey prepared at home. But it is also certainly true that these two items, namely the vinegar and honey, can be obtained in almost every shop as well, provided they are not too old and partially or completely gone off.

Self-Heal (Brunella)
Prunella vulgaris
Sauer: *Brunnellen-Kraut* (1764)

The German name, as well as the English common name brunella, are thought to derive from Bräune, *"quinsy," the primary malady for which this herb was used. The herb was heavily employed by the military, since this condition was common among soldiers. No doubt, as the armies moved, so moved self-heal, for it followed Europeans to North America and is now naturalized here. That it was common in Pennsylvania by the 1760s is evident from the Sauer herbal, although the dried herb was also sold in shops. The dry herb was often employed as an infusion like tea.*

Self-heal possess a thick four-sided stem about one foot in height. The leaves are rough, dark green, and closely resemble mint. At the top of the stem and on the lateral branches grow spiky flowers of a purple or sky-blue color. The plant grows in the woods and in dry pastures.

Self-heal has the capacity to cool, to dissolve, and to remove inflammations, as well as to cleanse and heal. It is gathered in May or June about the time of the full moon.

Self-heal is not surpassed as a vulnerary, for it heals gently and eases all manner of injury. Hence it can be used in vulnerary potions.

In some localities, the young leaves are eaten in salads.

The distilled water of self-heal is an excellent medicine for all injuries of the mouth, particularly quinsy and scurvy of the mouth, provided one gargles with it often. Or, prepare the following gargle: Mix together six loths of self-heal water and plantain water, and one loth each of rose honey and mulberry juice.

A small piece of cloth dipped in self-heal water and repeatedly laid warm upon the affected place until it dries will prove exceedingly beneficial against all inflammations of the privates in both men and women.

The expressed juice of this herb put into fresh wounds, and a cataplasm of the pulped leaves bound over them, will heal them quite readily. It protects against all infections, and stanches bleeding as well as stilling the pain.

Those who do not have the distilled water of self-heal, or cannot get it, just use the freshly pressed juice during the summer, or in the winter boil the dried leaves in water and use this instead.

Senna
Cassia acutifolia
Sauer: *Seneblätter* (1775)

Senna is a desert shrub native to Egypt and Arabia and neighboring regions. It was first brought into use as a laxative among the Arabs, and was discussed by several medieval physicians, including Masawayk al-Maridini (called Mesue the Younger), whose apricot remedy is discussed on page 46. The leaves were the part gathered for medical commerce, and most of this in Sauer's day was exported from Alexandria under an Egyptian monopoly, with considerable adulteration along the way. The leaves lose their purgative virtues when boiled, and powders made from them must be used immediately, for they absorb moisture and thus go off. Nonetheless, senna was considered a woman's best friend, and its leaves are also mentioned in connection with laxatives under plums and prunes on page 249. Because senna has a nauseating taste, it is normally mixed with other ingredients to make it more palatable, hence the various preparations noted by Sauer.

The most famous (and supposedly best-tasting) patent remedy made with senna was Daffy's Elixir, which was also known simply as tincture of senna. During the 1740s Hannah Glasse, eighteenth-century cookbook author, became involved, along with Dr. John Hill, whose herbal is mentioned several times in this book, in a scam surrounding Daffy's Elixir. Both of them ended up in bankruptcy court, which gained them as well as their elixir considerable notoriety.

The leaves of senna possess a caustic mild salt with numerous mucusy elements. They are a very useful laxative for young and old, and can be employed safely by all classes of people.

Senna leaves have the greatest reputation for purgative medicines, since they can be used safely by everyone; yes, even by pregnant women. They purify dense, blackened melancholic blood, take off the gall, and open blockages of the internal organs, in particular the liver and spleen, provided a serviceable laxative sachet is made with them.[212]

212. The sachet in this case is used like a tea bag so that the infusion is free of the dust and other impurities that may be adhering to the leaves.

It is always good when using senna to combine it with cream of tartar, because this will hinder the fibrous parts of the leaves from sticking to the gut and giving rise to colic.

Those who want to take senna as a powder should prepare thirty to sixty grains per dose; indeed, it is always improved by the addition of cream of tartar, cinnamon, ginger, anise, fennel seed, and so forth, as for example: Take two or three quints of senna leaves, forty grains each of pure rhubarb, anise, crab's eyes, and cream of tartar, and half a loth of powdered sugar, and grind all of this together to make a powder. Administer a quint in the evening and in the morning as needed, and it will keep the body open.

A very useful laxative resin may be prepared in the following manner: Take four ounces of fine senna leaves, eight grains each of cinnamon and ginger, a quint of cream of tartar, and a quart of water. Put these ingredients in a new earthenware pot and let them stand overnight. Then boil the mixture and press it through a cloth. To this decoction, add four ounces of white sugar and one pound of clean Zante currants, or just as many pitted prunes. Boil it a little bit longer until it thickens to a proper electuary. Then store in glass vessels. Administer one to two loths of this per dose. This is an excellent and gentle laxative.

Mix together two to three loths of senna leaves, one loth of peach blossoms, half a loth of tansy, and one and a half quints of cream of tartar. Pour over this half a pint of boiling water and let it stand overnight. Then cook this down to a syrup consistency with honey or sugar in an earthenware vessel. This will yield a laxative and worm syrup of which as much as two tablespoons or more may be administered according to the age of the patient or other considerations.

Servis (Sorb Apple)
Sorbus domestica
Sauer: *Sperwer, Speyerling* (1777)

This is an Old World orchard fruit of which there are a number of varieties, some shaped like apples, others like pears. It is treated like the medlar in that the fruit is harvested only after it has been exposed to frost or when bletted (allowed to overripen).

It is evident from the herbal that this tree was cultivated among the colonial Germans, but doubtless the dried fruit was also imported for medical purposes. Sauer further noted that where the domesticated sorb apple was unavailable, wild ones could be substituted. In Sauer's era, this would be the North American mountain ash or rowan tree (Sorbus americana), which was once quite common in eastern woods. Like the medlar and sorb apple, its fruits are best after they have been nipped by frost. The instructions for hanging branches of fruit upside down in a dry room for use over the winter are noteworthy. This was an old method for keeping food fresh well into the depths of January. Corn left on the stalks, ground-cherries still attached to the uprooted bush, indeed, many sorts of garden products, could be stored in this manner.

The sorb apple is of a cold and dry nature because it contains numerous earthy, sour, salty principles, with little or no sulfurous components. Thus its fibrous flesh glutinates as well as restrains and blocks.

If branches of the sorb apple are bound together in bundles and hung up in a dry room, the fruit can be preserved for a long time. The fruit can then be administered when one wants it in treating all manner of internal disorders, bloody flux, and the like.

The fruit can be pared and the core removed, then boiled in water and sugar like quinces, and thus preserved. In sweetmeat, the apples strengthen the stomach, revive its enfeebled nerves, awaken the appetite, and quell casting of the stomach and diarrhea.

The unripe apples can be cut apart, dried in a bake oven, then ground to a powder. This powder can be used in treating the above-mentioned internal afflictions.

The fruits of wild servis trees will provide similar results for the various conditions enumerated above when the domesticated sort is not to be had.

Sharp-Pointed Dock
Rumex acetosa
Sauer: *Grindwurtz* (1777)

In the chaotic final year of his printing career, Christopher Sauer tried to bring closure to the herbal, but in his evident rush, this entry became a nightmare for plant identification. First, Grindwurtz *(scab or scallwort) is more commonly the name of scabious in German, an entirely different herb. However, Sauer picked this term up from Zwinger, who used* Grindwurtz *as a designation for anything vaguely resembling sour dock (as opposed to cultivated garden sorrel, which is related). Therefore Zwinger listed sixteen plants called* Grindwurtz, *which made identification of the herb here somewhat difficult. The key was in Zwinger's Greek: oxylapatham, which means a dock with pointed leaves. Based on that, I have assigned this herb to* Rumex acetosa, *also sometimes called* Rumex acutifolium. *This is called "common" dock by Zwinger and Sauer alike. However, the plant depicted by Zwinger is not a sheep sorrel or sour dock, which have distinctly pointed leaves, but something akin to* Rumex hydrolapathum, *or great water dock. My point is that the dock discussed by Sauer cannot now be identified with certainty. This issue may have been moot in Sauer's mind in any case, since all of these various docks can be used more or less the same way in the remedies he provided. They are also excellent for treating common dandruff.*

Common dock, together with its leaves, possesses a middling temperament lying between warm and cold, for which reason it is drying and absorbing in its action. It is endowed with somewhat balsamic oily elements with a large quantity of gluey watery sap together with a mildly volatile, nitrous salt. Therefore it has the faculty to cleanse, to purify, and to nullify all sour, caustic salts in sores, wounds, and itchy scabs, and thus it promotes their healing.

The root also possesses a purgative capacity, but it must be taken in such a large quantity that, due to its unpleasant taste, it is seldom employed in this amount—especially since there are plenty of other things that are better to use. However, if a laxative is wanted, then simply boil the root in wine and drink this until it purges. This is useful for forcing the sourness from the stomach that is caused by diarrhea, and thus stopping it properly. For a surfeit of strong fluxes from the hemorrhoids, this root can also be boiled in water and the decoction drunk on a daily basis.

If the fresh leaves are wilted on the hearth and pulped in a warm mortar, then laid over the affected place as a poultice that is renewed every eight or ten hours, this will draw out heats, still Saint Anthony's fire, inflammations, ringworms, and itch, and heal rotten, spreading sores and injuries. It is also useful in treating the bites of venomous beasts, in treating all manner of wounds, and for promoting their healing readily.

When the leaves and root are fomented in fresh butter or hog's lard, pressed through a cloth, and mixed with sublimated flour of brimstone, they will yield an infallible itch salve, which can be swabbed warm on the patient in the morning and evening. This cure will take effect even more rapidly if the scabs and flaking skin are first well washed with wine or vinegar in which a little alum, egg white, and sulfur have been boiled.

The root of this herb possesses the special virtue of healing all kinds of mange and scurf, for which it has received its name.[213]

Another salve for mange or the itch can be prepared in the following manner: Take dock root, grind it to a fine powder, and mix this with vinegar. Some people take honey and the powdered root, mix them together, and then smear this over the affected parts while at bath. Others boil the leaves and root together with a little sulfur in wine, add some vinegar, and then wash the patches of scabious skin with it while warm. The same benefit may also be had from the water distilled from dock root, provided the skin is washed with it.

The seeds of dock are very good for treating bloody flux, if half a quint are taken in a glass of red wine in the morning before breakfast.

If the dock leaves are cooked in meat stock and eaten thus, they will emolliate a hard stomach. This dock broth also benefits gouty persons plagued by blockages of the body.

When the root is boiled in vinegar or wine, and the mouth is washed out with the decoction, this will prove very good against scurvy and scurvy of the mouth. It firms up the teeth and heals the gums. If it is employed as a gargle, it will heal sores in the throat and glottis. When old or fresh wounds are washed with it, it purifies and heals them.

If any cattle should become mangy, wash the infected places frequently with this warm decoction, and it will get rid of the condition as well as heal the skin.

213. This refers to the German *Grind*.

Shepherd's Purse
Capsella bursa-pastoris
Sauer: *Tächelkraut* (1775)

The young plants of this herb were formerly sold in the markets of New York, Pennsylvania, and Maryland during the early spring. The leaves grow out radially from a central root, and when the plants are small and tender, they make a delicious and decorative addition to spring salads, but are also just as good cooked in soup. Shepherd's purse was introduced from Europe during the seventeenth century, and was probably planted in gardens from which it escaped, for it was useful in both medicine and cookery. In Pennsylvania, it is well documented as a market garden plant even in the eighteenth century. Its popularity was due to the fact that it could be overwintered under straw, and thus provided a source of vitamin-rich greens when other potherbs were unavailable.

The aroma and taste of shepherd's purse is indifferent, although one may detect an astringency along with a certain dryness. For this reason, this herb is assigned a dry, cold nature, as experience has shown. It is thus endowed with many earthy, raw salty elements and possesses its highest virtues in April and May.

For blood-spitting, bloody flux, bloody piss, and immoderate menses, take a handful of shepherd's purse and boil it in two quarts of white wine (water is also good). Strain this through a cloth and give a tumblerful to the patient in the morning and evening.

By taking the fresh, green, pulped leaves or dry ones cooked in wine with ribwort plantain,[214] country people are accustomed to heal their fresh wounds, and not without good results, when the herb thus prepared is bound over the injury as a plaster.

If a steer starts to fail too quickly, give him shepherd's purse to eat. For horses, it should be cut small and mingled with the fodder.

For tertian ague, pulp shepherd's purse with a little vinegar and bind this over the wrists and ankles after first purging the stomach two or three times. For those with a nosebleed when the blood will not stop flowing, put shepherd's purse in the patient's hand on the same side of the body from which the nose is bleeding. As soon as the herb is warm, it should stop the bleeding. If the dried or fresh root is held under the tongue, it will produce the same results. One can also dip cotton into the juice of shepherd's purse and press this into the nose. In summery, this herb stanches all bloody fluxes more powerfully than all other sanguinary herbs, for which reason some call it blood root. Namely, for such fluxes, pulp the fresh leaves alone or the dry ones with vinegar and bind this over the abdomen as well as under the buttocks and soles of the feet.

Some would have it that shepherd's purse takes away jaundice provided the leaves, seedpods, and flowers are placed in the shoes, which are then worn without socks.

The expressed juice of this herb possesses an excellent faculty for cooling, stopping, and staying diarrhea and other fluxes of the stomach, and for healing bloody

214. Ribwort plantain was called *Spitzenwegerich* in German.

piss. Administer five- to six-tablespoon doses of the juice in the morning and evening. If this juice is held in the mouth, and then rinsed with, it will strengthen wobbly teeth. It will heal all inflamed injuries of the throat provided it is used as a gargle faithfully. A small cloth dipped in this juice and laid warm on the breasts of women when they begin to redden will reduce the swelling.

Silver-Leafed Fir
Pinus abies
Sauer: *Füchtenbaum* (1776)

The pine tree discussed in the Sauer herbal is in fact a European species not found in North America. Its other German name is Edeltanne, *and this is one of the trees that has made the Black Forest famous. The North American balsam fir* (Abies balsamea) *is probably the only tree that comes close to the German one in physical resemblance, and this is the tree that Sauer had in mind when he said that fir trees were not everywhere common. The reason for that remark was simple: balsam firs only grew in swampy colder regions of colonial America, and in Pennsylvania, that put them well beyond the mountains in what was then Indian country.*

But this point was really not important, for as Sauer well knew, the basic remedies could be made to work with almost any pine tree. Regionally, these would have been the Jersey pine (Pinus virginiana) *and the pitch pine* (Pinus rigida). *But Sauer goes even further than this by recommending tar as a good substitute. Tar water cures became quite popular in the nineteenth century; thus Sauer was somewhat ahead of his time in promoting this very innovative idea.*

In the bark as well as in the young shoots, the pine tree possesses numerous balsamic, oily elements mingled with a sour volatile, temperate salt. From this derives its capacity to sweeten all sharp, salty humors, to improve salty scorbutic blood, to heal injuries, and to gently expel foul matter and sand through the urine. It also stops diarrhea and fluxes of the stomach. The green pinecones, however, possess a mild, fatty, milky substance that gives them the virtue of tempering sharp, salty fluxes and of aiding in the treatment of hoarseness and coughing, as well as easing the cold evil and sharpness in the urine.

If the first, or young, outermost shoots of the tree are boiled well, and a glass of this decoction is drunk in the evening and morning, it will heal all scurvies exceedingly well. But most of all, the small green cones of the pine tree are useful in medicine when they are fresh. If they are dried, then ground to a powder with rock candy and some licorice, then taken in tablespoon doses several times a day, this will prove very good for hoarseness, for stopping coughs, and for sweetening sharp fluxes that have sunken into the chest.

Due to its balsamic oils, the resin that flows from the spruce tree possesses the virtue of bringing swellings to a head, and in time of discussing them. It forces out urine, foul matter, sand, and stones when administered in pill form. When boiled in water and the broth used warm for washing itch that has attacked the limbs, it will heal them.

This resin is likewise a very good remedy for the itch and scab on cattle. It also heals all manner of wounds on cattle, for in particular, it prevents flies from doing mischief, as when they leave their eggs or dung in wounds and then worms appear, thus making the wounds almost impossible to heal.

But because these fir trees—or as the English call them, pine trees—are not found in all places in this country, farmers can obtain all of the benefits mentioned above from tar. A certain English doctor has written an entire book about the virtues of tar. Proceed with it thus: Take one quart of tar and put it in a clean iron pot. Pour two gallons of water over it and let it boil. When it has boiled for a quarter of an hour, take it from the fire and let it cool. Pour off the water from the tar completely, strain it through a thick, clean cloth, and store away for use. A half pint of this tar water may be administered warm in the morning before breakfast as well as in the evening before going to bed (for children, administer less). If this is kept up for several weeks, it will act as an anodyne, purify the blood, expel gravel and sand from the kidneys and bladder, and prove useful in treating backaches and lumbago. It is also a valuable remedy for all maladies of the chest, and is useful in treating the onset of pulmonary and common consumption.

When someone has taken a cold drink during harvest or during a great heat, and feels injury from the chill, they should not tarry in getting this remedy as soon as possible and continue with it daily for a space of time. A small piece of cloth dipped in tar water and laid warm over wounds and injuries will heal them well in both man and beast. If the skin is washed with warm tar water conscientiously, it will get rid of the itch and similar outbreaks. For coughs, consumption, injury from a cold drink, and all injuries of the chest, some licorice may be chopped very fine and boiled in this water. Fennel or anise may also be added. After it is boiled, add some sugar so that it takes on a better taste. This remedy is simple, useful, and never injurious. But it does not perform many cures or miracles, because it is unknown to most people, and tastes so nasty, or even disgusts them, that once they try it, they soon give it up.

Skirret
Sium sisarum
Sauer: *Wassermark* (1776)

The long, narrow root, the part used in cookery, tastes like parsnips and was one of the most commonly eaten winter root vegetables during the Middle Ages. Its German name means "water marrow," and it was especially well liked with fish for fast days. But as Sauer pointed out, skirret greens were also commonly employed in the spring in pottages of greens, what he called Kräuter-Musse, *"herbal mushes." The greens fell out of fashion in the seventeenth century, but remained an important food source among country people. The plant is extremely hardy and prefers to grow in moist, sandy soils.*

Skirret is of a warm nature, as its aroma and taste demonstrate. It brings sores to a head, opens, and expels, for it operates by means of numerous volatile, balsamic alkaline salts. Thus it possess the fine virtues of sweetening and purifying scorbutic, sharp, salty blood; of strengthening the stomach, liver, and matrix; of opening blockages of the internal parts; and of freeing up tough phlegm. It also forces urine and sweat, eases breathing, and stills coughing.

When skirret greens are still young and tender, they can be employed in cookery in thick porridges of green potherbs, in soups, or in salads. All of these flush the urine, bring down the menses, force out stones and worms, take off yellowness from the skin, and protect against the onset of dropsy.

If the seeds of skirret are ground to powder and taken in a quint dose in white wine, this will force out urine and purify the kidneys and bladder of thick corruptions and stone. Skirret may be usefully employed externally for douches and loin baths.

Skirret will dissolve the clotted milk in the breasts of women if it is pulped and laid on the breasts as a plaster.

Horse doctors boil the leaves with salt or saltpeter and use it for divers swellings or itchings on horses.

The distilled water of skirret taken daily in four- or five-loth doses promotes urine, drives down stones, is good for dropsy, and opens the liver and so forth.

Skirret juice is an excellent purging medicine for putrid sores and wounds when mixed with rose honey or made into a salve in the following manner: Take one and a half loths of the juice of skirret, three loths of rose honey, three quints of barley flour, and half a loth of turpentine, and mix all of this together to form a salve.

The excellent virtues of this plant notwithstanding, it must be employed cautiously and with care, for it is injurious to the eyes and unsuitable for all maladies of the head. It also damaging to the milk of nursing mothers, and very dangerous to small children because they can easily take fits from it.

Sloes (Blackthorn)
Prunus spinosa
Sauer: *Schlehen* (1775)

While this is an Old World plant, various North American sand cherries, beach plums, and similar wild fruits were used in its place. When eaten raw, sloes were much preferred after having been "bletted" or touched by frost. Thus softened, the fruits were popular among the German element for kalte Schalen *(page 347). Sauer's technique for making sloe wine is identical for the method he suggested for elderberry wine on page 131.*

The entire sloe plant possesses numerous coarse, unfermented, costive salty elements, and is therefore an astringent. The flowers are endowed with more volatile, sulfurous elements combined with somewhat sharp, caustic salts, from which they derive the faculty to act as a laxative and, due to their bitterness, to kill worms.

If sloes are boiled in red wine, they are useful for diarrhea and bloody flux.

Some people take the flowers of sloes, dry them, then grind them to a powder. If a quint of this powder is taken in warm white wine, it will be found quite effective against the stone.

A syrup from sloe flowers is prepared in apothecary shops in the same manner as violet syrup, which opens the body quite gently as a laxative. It also serves well as treatment for pleurisy and coughs, and for purifying the kidneys of foul matter, sand, and gravel. Adults should be given a dose of up to six loths while young children should only be given half that, up to two or three loths. This will dissolve phlegm in the chest and drive out worms.

Before sloes begin to turn blue, they can be broken up small in a mortar and tossed into wine that has turned viscous. Stir well and stop tightly. This will restore the wine quickly. The mashed sloes may also be dried in the open air, for they will keep over a year for this use.

The gray, whitish moss that is found growing on the limbs of sloes can be boiled in red wine. If laid over the hurt, they will hinder the increase of a rupture. If this moss is dried, ground to a powder, and taken in half-quint doses, it is effective in stilling nosebleed, and other bleedings and hemorrhages.

The distilled water of sloe blossoms is good against sores on the body and chest illnesses. It is also useful to drink for all oppressions of the heart and stomach.

If the juice of sloes is rubbed over the place where no hair is wanted to grow, it will make the skin bare and smooth.

If the end gut should come out, rub it with the juice of sloes or powder it with ground sloes. Then press the gut back in with a small piece of warm cloth, and sit on a little sack of warmed-up oats.

If a healthful sloe wine is wanted, take ripe sloes, pound them in a mortar, and form them into round balls. Dry the balls on top of a warm stove, then toss them into a keg and pour wine over them. This wine will acquire a beautiful red color and a delightful aroma. It is a comforting drink for those with hot stomachs, for it strengthens and cools. It is also useful for sundry stomach fluxes, blood-spitting, and immoderate terms. It promotes urine, and purifies the kidneys and bladder of scummy matter and sand.

When a handful of dried sloe blossoms is boiled in wine or water, then drunk, this will act as a laxative quite gently. They can also be employed for this purpose when boiled in fresh milk.

Warm up some water of sloe blossoms and dissolve rock candy in it. Take one tablespoon of this warm often, and it will prove good for hoarseness in the throat. It will dissolve phlegm in the chest, stop coughing, and ease asthma in young and old.

Smallage (Soup Celery)

Apium graveolens
Sauer: *Sellery* (1768)

Now naturalized in many temperate areas of the United States, smallage has even invaded the salt marshes of California, a habitat not unlike its original home in Europe. This Old World plant should not be confused with native wild celery (Vallisneria spiralis), which migrating ducks feed upon in our brackish marshes. The seed and leaves of this latter plant imparted a delightful flavor to canvasbacks much prized by colonial gourmands.

Smallage is not difficult to grow, since its culture is similar to that of parsley. It even looks like the flat-leaf or so-called Italian parsley preferred by cooks for the intense flavor. Smallage is likewise intensely flavored, but the taste is that of celery, with a distinct overtone of saltiness. Its use as a pot and soup herb in eighteenth-century America was ubiquitous because the herb is hardy and normally overwinters with minimal protection. A little straw thrown over it in the fall will yield a crop all winter, one reason why it could be relied on for home remedies. Like parsley, smallage is biennial and produces seed the following season. The yield of seed is copious and may be used in cookery or in any remedies where celery seed is called for.

Parsley and celery have the same faculties for warming, drying, expelling urine and stones, and purifying the kidneys. They also strengthen the stomach, mesenteric veins, heart, and matrix; ease difficult breathing; purify salty blood; and open internal blockages.

Smallage is used in two ways in cookery—raw and boiled—and is healthy when prepared either way.

The root and leaves strengthen the stomach, promote digestion, make good healthy blood, and open all internal blockages of the liver, lungs, spleen, matrix, and kidneys. Smallage dispels sadness and melancholy, and is thus a completely healthy food that can be employed in treating many illnesses.

If the water distilled from smallage is taken in a gill dose daily in the morning and evening, or the expressed juice is taken in half-gill doses, and this is kept up for a long time, it will get rid of consumption and hypochondria, as well as kidney pains and pains in the loins. It expels urine powerfully, eases shortness of breath, quells coughing, gets rid of jaundice, and promotes good digestion. It also purifies gross thick blood, particularly that which is overflowing with sour scorbutic salts. This remedy can also be employed externally as well as internally for purifying, cleansing, and healing all manner of putrid injuries and sores to good effect.

A similar result may be had from smallage soup, if boiling hot meat stock is poured over the freshly chopped green leaves, allowed to stand covered for half an hour, and then drunk warm daily. Besides other benefits, this restorative will encourage a happy disposition.

When the root of smallage is boiled in meat stock, or mixed with an herbal wine, and this is drunk daily, this tonic will open sundry internal blockages of the liver, spleen, matrix, kidneys, and lungs, and prove useful in treating all of the maladies introduced above.

Smartweed (Arsemart)
Polygonum hydropiper
Sauer: *Flöhkraut* (1766)

> *Smartweed is native to Europe, where it grows in wet soils or upon cold clayey ground. It has now naturalized, but several native smartweeds may be used in the same manner. One of its old English names is arsemart, which is how it is identified by Culpeper, who further noted that when the plant was strewn in rooms, it would kill the fleas there. This is the common use employed by German country people, who scattered it among willow leaves in the summer (see willow on page 354) to keep the household animals from bringing in fleas. The German name for the plant is* Flöhkraut, *"flea plant," in reference to this custom. There were also a great many folk beliefs associated with the herb, Sauer's wound and toothache remedies providing two good examples. Indeed I consider them witchcraft, since by my definition they depend for their success on the unnatural transfer of a disease or condition to a plant, which is then destroyed.*

Common smartweed or "water pepper" warms and dries. It possesses the faculty to thin all thick phlegm, and to cleanse through the urine all salty scorbutic sharp humors of the blood. It cleanses the kidneys and opens internal blockages of the liver, spleen, and mesenteric vein. It possess the most power in May toward the full moon.

The leaves of smartweed are a wonderful vulnerary for horses, if they are boiled in wine or vinegar, the wound rinsed with the broth, and the boiled leaves laid over it. When a horse has been galled by a saddle, there is nothing better for the injury than to wash it with fresh urine and then to apply a poultice of pulped smartweed.

Various surgeons have written that if this herb is drawn through fresh water, and then bound over an old, open wound until it is well warmed, and the bandage then buried in a damp place, this will have the remarkable power to heal the wound as the herb rots in the ground.

For hypochondriacs, those afflicted by scurvy and venereal disease, there is nothing better for the purification of sharp blood than the essence of smartweed made with brandy. Administer twelve to thirty drops in fumitory water each time and do it frequently.

A water may also be distilled from smartweed that, if drunk often, will cure jaundice completely, drive out all the scummy matter and gravel retained in the kidneys, and cleanse and sweeten sharp scorbutic blood as well. Externally, this water is very useful for all manner of old, proud, stinking wounds and fistulous sores if they are rinsed with it or irrigated with it while it is warm.

For toothache, some people have ascertained that there is nothing better than when fresh smartweed is infused in water, then laid on the painful tooth. Or just as well, it can be applied externally by infusing it in water and laying it as a poultice on the cheeks until the herb becomes warm. Then bury the smartweed in a manure pile. The pain will completely stop as soon as the leaves begin to rot.

Snakeweed (Bistort)
Polygonum bistorta
Sauer: *Natterwurz* (1778)

The herb takes its name from the shape of its root, which is twisted and snakelike. It was known to the ancients and figured largely in pagan beliefs and medicine due to its very high astringency. The root also contains a large amount of tannic acid and thus can be used quite effectively in tanning leather. The leaves and young shoots were eaten as greens in the spring, especially around Easter. In England, they served as ingredients in Easter puddings; in Germany they went into egg Brockle *or* Dummes. *In colonial America, only the imported dried root was available in apothecaries, since the plant is not native and is difficult to maintain in gardens. That is why Sauer made no mention of its culinary uses.*

Snakeweed possesses coarse, caustic, alkaline particles from which it derives the virtue of glutinating, of stopping, of healing, and of dissolving clotted blood. It is cold and dry in nature, and should be gathered when the sun passes into the sign of Cancer.

To treat all manner of fluxes of the belly and severe menses, take one loth each of snakeweed and tormentil and boil them in one gallon of water for as long as it takes to hard-cook an egg. Let the patient drink of this potion according to need. This decoction is also serviceable to those who have been taken down by contagion, or to those who believe they may have been infected.

Powdered snakeweed root taken in a dose equal to as much as ten peppercorns in weight, and eaten with a soft-cooked egg in the morning before breakfast for several days in succession, will preserve pregnant women from miscarriage, and also checks powerful menses.

Snakeweed is particularly effective for stopping blood flowing from fresh wounds, and not only that, the root powder also dries up the wounds completely, and promotes their healing.

Distilled snakeweed water stops bloody flux and diarrhea, and withstands poison and contagion. If you drink two or three loths of this water, it even has the power to stop bleeding, and will promote the healing of old, corrupt, stinking, spreading sores if they are bathed with it frequently. In this same manner, snakeweed water can even be used for cancers of the back and the nose.[216]

216. Perhaps it should be noted here that the conditions referred to resulted from exposure to the sun. The face and neck of people who worked in the fields were often severely sunburned even though they wore hats and work shirts. Skin cancer is not a new problem.

Sorrel

Rumex acetosa
Sauer: *Sauerampfel* (1768)

Maria Sophia Schellhammer discussed sorrel in her Brandenburg cookbook and noted that there were three sorts: the Spanish, which had large leaves; the round-leafed variety, which was considered rare; and the wild or wood sorrel, which was eaten during times of food shortages. The common French variety of sorrel called de Belleville, which became popular in the latter part of the eighteenth century, did not appear in garden literature until about 1749, so it is doubtful that Schellhammer knew about it. The distinction here between cultivated sorrel and the sharp-pointed dock discussed on page 287 is purely horticultural and economic. Cultivated sorrels were refined and therefore representative of a different economic level than the wild sorts, which were foods of the poor.

Schellhammer also pointed out that among the Germans sorrel (as well as the wild docks) was mostly used in soups and in what she described as "green stocks." This is her recipe for a green stock made with garden sorrel: "Take wheat greens, sorrel, and parsley and pound them together in a mortar. Then add finely grated bread and press this through a hair sieve with a little ground ginger."[217] Her puree is then thinned with water, white wine, or meat stock. The wheat greens are young shoots of wheat akin to wheat sprouts eaten today. They were quite useful medicinally and are mentioned under wheat (page 345).

In spite of the fact that Schellhammer ranked wood sorrel with famine or food shortages, country people did indeed eat it and use it in remedies. Her attitude may be attributed to her well-to-do upbringing and to class attitudes held by citified Germans at that time. In fact, wood sorrel is treated generously by the Sauer herbal (page 359). Furthermore, the last line of Sauer's discussion of sorrel below—which promises to take up wood sorrel separately—is itself evidence that he had an overall plan for his herbal. Sauer carried through on this promise and turned to wood sorrel in 1773, five years later.

Sorrel cools and dries, and possesses numerous gentle, mildly volatile salts in its sour juice. For this reason, it has the faculty of tempering all internal effervescence of the blood during fevers, of quenching thirst, of dampening the fiery fermenting gall in those excited to anger, and of resisting pestilential contagions.

To make an everyday drink, instead of wine, for use in treating all sorts of fevers: Take one ounce of sorrel root, half an ounce of strawberry roots, and one ounce of rasped hartshorn, and boil this in two gallons of water for as long as it takes to

217. Maria Sophia Schellhammer, *Das Brandenburgische Koch-Buch* (Berlin, 1732), 485.

hard-cook an egg. Instead of the root, one can take a few handfuls of fresh sorrel leaves.

Sorrel seeds are an excellent remedy for treating bloody flux if the patient is given them ground to a powder. Yet it appears that this virtue and effect does not only derive from astringency of the seeds, but also, in certain circumstances, their oily milk absorbs and mellows the sharpness of the flow.

For those who have lost their appetite due to the strong heat of gall, first take an effective purgative, then eat sorrel in salad or cooked in meat broth. This will restore the appetite.

Sorrel, lettuce, and endive prepared as a salad and thus eaten will assuage an unsettled stomach and open blockage of the liver brought on by the overflow of burning gall.

Those burdened by great thirst, and who possess an ardent nature, should use sorrel in cookery and in salads.

If a quint of sorrel seeds are ground and administered to children twice, this will get rid of tapeworms.

Take the leaves of garden sorrel or a mild-tasting wild one and distill them without other ingredients. This will yield a useful, strongly cooling water that will prove a certain quencher of heat in all types of inflammations. If this water is drunk in the morning and evening as well as during the day, and one's daily drinks are mixed with it, it will powerfully lessen all internal and external heats arising from pestilential and other types of fever. It will cool an inflamed liver and stomach and take away all the corruptions that are caused by such inflammations of these organs. It will also quench thirst, excite the appetite, reduce jaundice, counter the welling up of gall, drive away malignancies from the heart, and cool the same during all hot distempers.

Take the well-strained juice pressed from the fresh leaves and pour this over steel filings in a glass vessel. Let this stand awhile in warm sand. This will yield an excellent tincture of steel, which may be taken in twenty- to thirty-drop doses in fumitory or borage water. This is an excellent remedy for those who are afflicted by hypochondria, scurvy, the falling evil, and the upwelling surfeits of fiery gall and by strong anger as well. It purifies the blood, maintains the regularity of the body, quells internal heats, dampens gall forcefully, and awakens the appetite.

If sorrel juice as mentioned above is allowed to cook down to half its quantity over a gentle fire, and then stored in an earthenware vessel in the cellar, the essential salts will precipitate on the sides of the vessel. These salts are an excellent remedy for all of the conditions mentioned above, but particularly useful during the summer when carried on journeys so that it can be mixed with one's drinking water as a cooling tonic.

If a syrup or conserve of sorrel is prepared, it will also prove useful when mixed with fresh water for making a cooling julep, and may be employed for all manner of heats.

Wood sorrel may be used in nearly every instance in just the same manner as garden sorrel, and a little more will be said about it later.

Southernwood

Artemisia abrotanum
Sauer: *Stabwurz* (1775)

Another common German name for this herb is Eberraute, *"boar's rue," because it was used during the Middle Ages as a culinary herb with brawn or wild boar's meat. Sauer's name means "rodwort," although the* Stab *can be rendered into English many different ways, such as stick, wand, or as some herbalists have suggested, the "wane" of Gaulish mercury. The import of the name is that the wood of the stem was once employed in spells and charms, perhaps owing to the fact that when a branch of southernwood is stuck into the ground it often takes root, thereby seeming to have a life of its own. For this reason, it figures rather highly in Pennsylvania German* Braucherei.

My first brush with this occurred many years ago when I first acquired my southernwood plant from the yard of a 1790s farmhouse near Graterford in Montgomery County, Pennsylvania. There was a long row of it growing along the base of an old stone wall. When I asked why there was so much southernwood—a good 100 feet of it, far more than anyone could possibly use in one household—I was told that it been planted there by the owner's great-grandmother to keep away the copperheads. I quietly accepted this explanation and thought no more about it until I began translating the passages below from the Sauer herbal. I am now sorry that I never bothered to ask whether it worked.

Southernwood is of a warm, dry nature. It possesses divers volatile, salty elements combined with a balsamic oiliness. Thus it has the capacity to dissolve and to dissipate remarkably, to oppose all poison and corruption, to heal the poison bites of scorpions and spiders, to kill worms, to force urine, and to open blockages of the liver, spleen, and matrix.

The young tops of southernwood together with their round yellow flower buds and blossoms may be fomented in water, wine, or good-quality beer. Drink a gill of this each morning and evening. This is a useful remedy for those who are plagued by difficult breathing. It serves exceptionally well against jaundice, opens blockages of the liver, promotes urine, warms a cold matrix, and purges it of all uncleanness. It dispels pain in the loins, hips, and spine resulting from cold.

The pulverized root of southernwood drunk in half a quint of white wine from time to time will kill all types of stomach worms.

When a person cannot pass water due to the stone, administer a quint of southernwood leaves with a little saltpeter in white wine often.

The powdered seeds of southernwood taken in a quint dose with white wine will kill worms and drive them out. This can be given to children in their porridge or in soup.

For those whose nose is blocked up so that they cannot smell, lay the dried leaves of southernwood on glowing charcoals and let the smoke rise into the nose. Smell will soon return.

Experienced surgeons are accustomed to mix southernwood in their plasters for drawing out thorns, splinters, and other things that remain stuck in the flesh.

Snakes can also be driven away with southernwood, for where it is planted, no snakes will appear. And where they are already found, it will drive them away if the dried leaves are laid on hot coals to make a fumigant.

If southernwood is laid around and upon grains that are stored in the attic, it will protect them from all vermin.[218]

The distilled water of southernwood will heal sores in the privates, if a cloth is dipped into it and laid upon the hurt. If it is drunk with a little grated nutmeg, it will get rid of the cold evil and promote a forceful piss.

Sowbread (Ivy-Leafed Cyclamen)

Cyclamen hedereaefolium
Sauer: *Schweinbrod* (1773)

A native of Italy and Greece, this attractive plant was introduced into European gardens at a very early date and has since naturalized in many places far beyond its original habitat. The part used is the root or tuber, which is said to be at its optimum powers when the plant is in full bloom. Sauer's remedies presume that the root is fresh, from which we must conclude that this cyclamen was well established in some colonial gardens. Pigs do in fact relish the tubers, and this does not seem to cause them the same extreme reaction it induces in humans. Ivy-leafed cyclamen was also said to act as an aphrodisiac, but given its strong purgative action, I cannot see how this would throw one into a fit of passion. Quite the contrary, it is a powerful abortant, as the herbal warns.

Sowbread is warm and dry in nature and possesses a somewhat sharp, penetrating salt mixed with slightly sulfurous elements. Thus it has the faculty to sicken or to act as a powerful emetic, to open blockages of the viscera, and to reduce all manner of tough, phlegmy swellings.

This herb should not be used so readily for internal remedies, because it is much too strong in its action. For when the stomach is only rubbed with the juice or the juice is put into the navel, it will cause passing of stool. Pregnant women in particular should abstain from using it, because it will do them great harm.

A good remedy for ringing, buzzing, and deafness of the ears: Take one and a half loths of sowbread root, shred it fine, and pour over it the same quantities of chamomile oil, oil of roses, and almond oil. Boil this until reduced to one-half, then strain it through a cloth. Put six to nine drops of this oil on a little cotton and press this into the affected ear. Leave it there overnight. This may be repeated every evening until the condition improves.

---

218. This refers to the old custom among the Pennsylvania Germans of storing grains in the attic, a practice that was common in the eighteenth and early nineteenth centuries. Since grain was valuable and was as good as cash in the barter system that then prevailed, grain was treated like money. Therefore it was also safest from theft when stored in the attic.

The juice expressed from sowbread root cooked to a plaster with gum ammoniac, and then laid over the hurt, will prove excellent in treating hardness of the spleen and all sorts of other hard, phlegmy swellings. The dried root of sowbread, together with its own juice and any kind of gum, may be boiled to form a plaster and used for the same kinds of hard swellings. Some people also mix butterwort with the juice.[219]

Sow Thistle
Sonchus oleraceus
Sauer: *Hasenkohl* (1777)

The German name means "hare's cabbage," which is sometimes rendered into English as hare's lettuce. It looks more like lettuce than cabbage, and has been used as a potherb since antiquity. From a culinary standpoint, it is similar to dandelion and succory, and as John Hill pointed out, "The Leaves are to be used fresh gathered, a strong Infusion of them works by Urine, and opens Obstructions. Some eat them in Sallets, but the Infusion has more Power."[220] The problem with sow thistle is that it varies greatly due to soil and environment and, when brought under cultivation, changes into an altogether different plant—and much for the better. The leaves resemble lettuce, although they have tiny spines. Yet there are some varieties that are smooth and almost spineless. When very young and tender, it was gathered by country people and eaten in soups and salads. Sauer's herbal lists many ways in which it was prepared.

The characteristic of all of the *Sonchus* plants like goose thistle and sow thistle is their mixed watery and earthy nature and their cooling effect. What may be said of one can also be understood for the others, and so they may be employed interchangeably. They contain a nitrous, bitterish salt mixed with few oily elements, and for this reason, they provide the blood with good nourishment. They force urine gently, cool effervescent choler, and, due to their soapiness, open blockages of the liver and spleen.

It was customary for people of old to enjoy sow thistle like endive and plantain leaves in cookery, and it is still used today by many people in Germany and Italy. But this herb is employed particularly in salads and vegetable dishes while it is still very young, and is good when boiled with meat or chicken. It is effective in treating all illnesses of the liver that owe their origin to heats or blockages. It is also good for inflammation of the stomach, and will get rid of the gnawing brought on by choler. Sow thistle is also useful for treating blockages and inflammations of the chest.

219. *Schmeerwurtz*, "butterwort," is generally given as *Pinguicula vulgaris*. It is not native to the mid-Atlantic region, but it is found in the Adirondack area of New York and in parts of Canada. It was often used as a botanical agent for curdling milk.
220. John Hill, *The Useful Family Herbal* (London, 1755), 344.

When sow thistle is employed in cookery, it will increase milk in nursing women.

The distilled water of sow thistle is useful for heats and blockages of the liver, and will get rid of jaundice when taken in half-gill doses in the morning before breakfast.

Apuleius wrote that when someone was plagued by fever, and sow thistle was laid unbeknownst to that person under the bedsheets, it would get rid of the person's fever.[221]

Fresh sow thistle can be boiled like other potherbs in milk, meat broth, or water and taken as a potion for all of the above-mentioned illnesses in doses of up to one pint in the morning before breakfast.

Spanish Pellitory

Anthemis pyrethrum, Anacyclus pyrethrum
Sauer: *Bertram* (1769)

> *Spanish pellitory resembles chamomile, but develops a long, cylindrical root that is the part employed in medicine. The plant is native to the Mediterranean, where it is generally perennial. In Germany, a pellitory that originated from North Africa was long cultivated in physic gardens. It is often given as* Anacyclus officinarum *or* Anacyclus pyrethrum. *Its action is hotter and more pungent than the Spanish sort. It is difficult to know which of these was being imported and sold by Sauer, in fact, it is quite possible that both were available and so labeled. This herb should not be confused with masterwort (page 206), which is also called pellitory of Spain. Masterwort has naturalized in the United States Spanish pellitory has not.*

The root of Spanish pellitory operates through a very biting, volatile, oily, aromatic salt. For this reason it is extremely hot, burning, warm, and dry and possesses the faculty to dissolve, to open, and to reduce swelling. It withstands all sourness, and for this reason resists the corruptions arising from it. It forces out crudities through the urine, sweat, and spittle, and dries out fluxes.

Pellitory root ground to a powder and administered in a quint dose in a glass of good strong wine several times for a few hours before the onset of tertian or quartan agues will heal these conditions completely. It will loosen phlegm in the chest very nicely, promote its expectoration, warm and strengthen a cold stomach and matrix, and carry off the thick, cold humors in them. But it is almost too powerful to be used internally.

Valuable toothache pills may be prepared in the following manner from pellitory root: Take one loth of fresh *Theriaca Andromaci* that is somewhat dry, one and a half quints of powdered pellitory root, half a quint of powdered long pepper, twenty grains of ground cloves, half a quint of henbane seeds, and a little double-rectified brandy. Work this together to form a thick paste, then form into pills. One of these

---

221. This little learned tidbit is taken from the *Golden Ass* of Apuleius; it falls under the category of spells and witchcraft. Apuleius was found of such pranks, and one wonders why the herbalist thought it worth mentioning—unless he believed it to be true.

can be placed on the throbbing tooth as often as required.

Pellitory root is quite renowned as a remedy for toothache, and not without reason, for if this root is chewed well and then held in the mouth against the teeth, it will forcefully draw out the thick, sour, salty, cold humors that settle beneath the teeth and cause the pain. If the root is boiled in vinegar and the broth is held in the mouth while warm, it will give the same results. When one loth of pellitory root and a handful of sage are boiled in white wine, and this decoction is then held warm in the mouth, this will also stop toothache.

People in olden times were accustomed to chew pellitory so that it drew down the cold humors and thick phlegm in the head and brain, about which the old poet Serenus had this to say:

Bertham in dem Mund zerbissen
Reinigt das Gehirn von Flüssen.

Pellitory chewed in the mouth
purifies the brain of rheums.

If pellitory is hung around the neck and worn there against the bare skin, it will prove effective against the falling evil when sniffed often, particularly in young people, about which the poet Mancer said:

Bertham an den Hals gehenckt,
ofters dran gerochen,
Hat die Wuth der schweren Roth
Junger Leute offt gebochen.

Pellitory hung about the neck,
and frequently smelled,
has often broken the curse
of falling sickness upon the young.

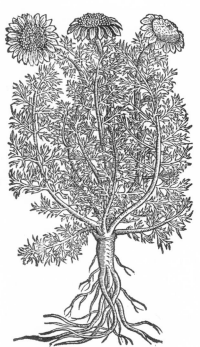

When pellitory is infused in brandy and rubbed over a paralyzed tongue, it will restore lost speech.

If pellitory is hung into fresh beer, it will preserve it from turning sour quickly.

Speedwell (Veronica)
Veronica officinalis
Sauer: *Ehrenpreiss* (1762)

The German name for this aromatic herb is somewhat difficult to render into English, since it consists of two words of similar meaning: honor *and* praise. *But the intent is quite clear: this is a plant of high reputation. Its use in Europe traces to antiquity, and it has continued in use among herbalists to this day. Speedwell is perennial and has naturalized in most parts of the United States. Of all the veronicas, both native and introduced, it is the most distinctive, with its small, spiky pale blue flowers. Because of its medical importance, it was probably planted in kitchen gardens quite early on, especially since the dry herb makes an excellent substitute for tea. It was already well established as an escaped plant within easy access of country people by the time Sauer's herbal was published.*

Speedwell possesses the faculty to withstand all manner of putrification. It dissolves hard phlegm in the chest and elsewhere. It opens obstructions of the chest, liver, spleen, and kidneys, and disperses rheums in the head. It also cleanses and heals wounds, and carries off corruptions through the urine and sweat.

This little herb is highly praised for its virtues in treating numerous internal and external ailments of the body, hence it bears the appropriate name *Ehrenpreiss*. It is particularly efficacious for injuries of the lungs, which it heals and preserves from sluggishness. Shepherds employ this herb to save their distempered sheep, if it is administered with a little salt. For this reason, those who are afflicted by pains in the chest and lungs should use speedwell diligently as follows: Take a handful each of scabious and speedwell leaves, half a loth of grated licorice root, and two or three figs. Chop it all up and boil it in a gallon of water for as long as it takes to hard-cook an egg. Then strain it, add six loths of rock candy, and let the patient drink as wanted.

Speedwell is a choice vulnerary for both internal and external injuries. The foremost surgeons praise this herb for treating fresh as well as old wounds, when it is boiled in water with a little alum and used to flush the wound. It is also useful in treating the itch and scurf, provided they are washed with it diligently.

A good homemade clyster for treating colic, gravel, and kidney stones may be made as follows: Take three handfuls of speedwell, boil it in water, then strain off the liquid. Take half a pound of the decoction and add to it three loths of sweet almond oil, three loths of white sugar, and two loths of goose fat. Mix it all together for the clyster.

The distilled water of speedwell is highly regarded as a cure for jaundice. It also dissolves loin stones, withstands every sort of poison, dispels dizziness, and strengthens the brain. It warms the stomach and encourages digestion, provokes the appetite, and absorbs injurious vapors that arise from the stomach and cause dizziness. Speedwell water also opens obstructions of the liver, spleen, and especially the lungs, for it dissolves hard phlegm in the chest and promotes its expectoration. Other uses include the healing of sores in the lungs and the purification of the blood, provided it is taken in three- or four-loth doses each morning and evening.

If the leaves of speedwell are gathered and dried before the plant flowers, they possess the very same powers as the East Indian plant called tea, and when taken warm like tea for a long continuance, it will dispel rheums from the head and lungs. It is also good for sore eyes, toothache, coughs, and colic. Furthermore, it relieves the salty sharp humors of ardent blood through the urine, cleanses the kidneys, strengthens memory, and is good for treating wounds.

Spikenard
Lavandula spica
Sauer: *Spicanarde* (1775)

Spikenard was widely used in medieval cookery, and was much favored for such recipes as galantines and fish aspics.[222] Indeed, the word aspic *itself is derived from the name of this herb. But we do have a problem of identification, because spikenard meant different things to different people. Old texts, especially herbals, often called it* Nardus italica, *which is now identified as spike lavender* (Lavandula spica). *Yet* Lavandula stoechas *(which grows wild throughout the Mediterranean) was also called spikenard, as indeed was* Andropogon nardus, *a species of beard grass. This latter herb was normally called* Nardus indica *or Indian spikenard, and was imported as a dry powder. It tastes like galingale and was used as a substitute for it in cookery as well as in medicine. This is the "foreign" spikenard to which Sauer refers in the passage below. So which herb is Sauer discussing? Spikenard in the Zwinger herbal is clearly illustrated: it is spike lavender.*

Spikenard and lavender are warm and dry (though spikenard is a little more so), and are not inferior to the foreign nards. They both possess a mild aromatic principle, or an oily volatile salt, from which they derive the capacity to strengthen the head, to prevent fluxes, to protect against apoplexy, and to strengthen the womb and fetus.

Spikenard is one of the most valuable herbs for all cold afflictions of the brain and nerves, as well as for faintness, full and partial apoplexy, the falling evil, lethargy, convulsions, palsy, and paralysis. It warms a cold feeble stomach, dissipates windiness, forces urine and the menses, warms the matrix, opens blockages of the liver and spleen, and takes away jaundice and the commencement of dropsy. For all of the aforementioned maladies, take a handful of spikenard leaves and blossoms and boil them in two quarts of white wine or water. Take this continuously until the condition abates.

The special virtue of spikenard and lavender flower water is well known, and is useful in particular to the elderly for a cold, rheumy head. It fortifies and warms the

---

222. See for example the recipe "Per fare due piattelli di gelatina" in the early 1400s cookery book of Martino de Rossi, *Il libro del maestro Martino de Rossi*, ed. Aldo Bertoluzza (Trento, 1993), 187. In medieval Italian, the herb was called *spiconardo* or *spichenarde*, the latter derived from German.

veins of the nervous system on which the body depends for feeling and motion. It also gets rid of dizziness. A few tablespoons of this water taken in the evening and morning is a valuable remedy for the elderly in preventing convulsion, fits, and paralysis, or for quickly restoring those who have already been so afflicted. If the tongue has become paralyzed due to these troubles, so that the patient cannot speak, or has difficulty speaking, have the patient take the water often and hold it in the mouth for a while. Held accordingly, the water will also get rid of toothache, give the mouth a sweet smell, and strengthen loose teeth. A few spoonfuls taken frequently will warm a cold stomach and other internal organs, such as the liver, spleen, kidneys, reins, and bladder. It will open and cleanse them of cold mucusy matter, and promote urination and the menses. Those who have been overtaken by fainting fits should be rubbed on the temples and nostrils with the water, for it will strengthen their heart and restore their senses, provided the patient is given a tablespoonful to drink as well.

Spinach
Spinacia oleracea
Sauer: *Spinat* (1774)

> *The brevity of Sauer's treatment of spinach is all the more noticeable when weighed against the long discussion of other potherbs in the herbal, especially those like groundsel or sow thistle, which were readily available to country people. Spinach was not. It was a vegetable cultivated in the gardens of the well-off, as its repeated appearance in cookbooks of the period readily attests. As a potherb of choice among persons of quality since the Renaissance, spinach gradually replaced most of the other lesser sorts of greens to such an extent that by the nineteenth century, only the very poor continued to eat them. The herbal's treatment of sow thistle (page 301) provides excellent perspective in this regard.*
>
> *Yet even among the well-off Germans, spinach was never prepared in an elaborate manner, a point also noted in the herbal. A typical recipe of this type, and one which agrees with the presentation of spinach dishes shown in eighteenth-century paintings, appeared in Jacob Melin's* Grätzerisches Kochbuch *of 1791 (7th ed., Graz, 1802). This was not considered a meal, but rather a side dish. Otherwise, it could also serve as a main course for breakfast or supper. The water that is poured off was never thrown out; it was added to the kitchen soup pot, or drunk as the "first broth" for health and medical reasons. "Pick the spinach nicely then put it in water and boil it up. Pour off the water and chop the spinach fine. Then add butter and salt and let it stew gently until the spinach is done. This can be served with chopped hard-cooked eggs as well as with hard-cooked eggs cut in quarters or with strips of bread browned in butter and laid over the top."[223]*

Spinach is of a cold, moist kind and used more in cookery than in medicine. It contains a goodly quantity of watery juice mingled with somewhat nitrous salts. From

223. Jacob Melin, *Grätzerisches Kochbuch* (Graz, 1802), 79. The first edition appeared in 1791; the recipe in this later edition is identical.

this it derives its capacity to emolliate, to moisten, and to keep the body open. It also cools somewhat, which choleric persons and persons suffering from blockages of the gut find quite beneficial as food.

Spinach may be employed usefully as greens for the healthy and sick, for it eases a raw throat and dry coughs, controls the flow of milk in wet nurses, and emolliates the belly.

A water is distilled from spinach that is employed effectively in feverish distempers, and foremost in treating an inflamed gall bladder and in mitigating its choler.

As daily experience has demonstrated, spinach is one of the best and most useful of the kitchen potherbs, for it is very easy to digest, and provides for sick and healthy alike a fitting light dish.

Spleenwort

Asplenium sp.
Sauer: *Miltzkraut* (1778)

> *Spleenworts include some seven hundred species of small ferns that grows on mossy rocks and old walls. The name derives from the leaf shape, which resembles a spleen—the German name means the same thing as well. This is an attribute based on the system of signatures that we have inherited from the Greeks, who valued this fern very highly in treating splenetic afflictions. Owing to the fact that like wall fern it grew from rocks, spleenwort was also thought to possess very powerful forces for countering spells. The spleenwort of Sauer, however, was specifically a European species and is so depicted in Zwinger's herbal. On the other hand, any native American spleenwort resembling this (there are several) was treated as an equivalent.*

Spleenwort operates by a coarse alkaline salt together with numerous earthy elements. From these, it derives its faculty for withstanding all sourness, for sweetening soured blood, for thinning and expelling blockages of the spleen and kidneys, and for stopping diarrhea and hemorrhages.

If a handful of spleenwort is boiled in two quarts of white wine and the decoction drunk, it will prove serviceable against swelling, blockages, tumors, and hardening of the spleen, as well as against black jaundice and quartan fever.

If the distilled water of spleenwort is taken as a drink, it will prove good against stones of the kidneys and bladder.

Squash

Cucurbita sp.
Sauer: *Kürbis* (1773)

> *I have placed this entry under squash even though Sauer specifically used the word* pompkin *in English. Most other colonial Americans called them* pompions, *a term that*

I have retained in the translation because it is safely vague. Today, botanists refer to the common garden cucurbits collectively as squash, regardless of seasonality, size, or species. The question remains, exactly which squash did Sauer have in mind? The seed was the part most used in remedies, and obviously, some squash produce seeds that are better suited to this purpose than others. In fact, in German-speaking Europe a large pear-shaped variety known as Plüzer *or* Pluzer *(Cucurbita pepo) was raised expressly for the oil that could be obtained from its seeds.[224] This oil was used as cooking oil, as well as a base for medical plasters and salves that might normally employ olive oil.*

The squashes most commonly grown in the region inhabited by the German settlers who used the herbal included the neck pumpkin, also called Canada crookneck (Cucurbita moschata); the common field pumpkin (Cucurbita maxima), used primarily for foddering livestock; the cheese pumpkin (Cucurbita moschata); and various vining summer squash, in particular the pattypan (Cucurbita pepo), which came in two sorts: one ripening white, the other ripening yellow. Additionally, there was a small, pear-shaped white summer squash (Cucurbita pepo) that was acculturated directly from the native Lenape peoples. Other squash came under cultivation after the revolution, thus enlarging the list considerably, but it is this core collection that was most common during the period of Sauer's herbal.

Lastly, just as the leaves were used in medicine (see Sauer's comments below), the young, tender shoots of squash plants were employed in salads. Maria Sophia Schellhammer had this to say in her Brandenburg cookbook: "Herr Böckler, in his Feld-und Hauss-Buch, *has written that a fine salad can be prepared with the tenderest, endmost shoots and stems of the pumpkin. Break them where they are softest and tenderest, then poach them in stock. Then let them drain and cool. For serving, prepare them with a dressing of vinegar, olive oil, and pepper."[225]*

Pompions are endowed with numerous watery and somewhat nitrous juices. They cool and moisten considerably, and therefore are poor nourishment. They are only useful to those with strong, hot stomachs, and should at all times be prepared with plenty of pepper or other similar spices.

Pompion seeds belong under the category of the *quatuor semina frigida majora*,[226] and have divers good effects in cooling down and sweetening rushing of the blood. They also operate by urine, and induce a gentle slumber.

A milk can be pressed from shelled pompion seeds and mixed with rosewater, plantain water, or simply with fresh springwater. It is very useful in cases of ardent fever, since it cools and nourishes quickly.

Pompion leaves laid upon a woman's breast will diminish the flow of milk.[227]

224. A small tract was circulated describing the method for creating this oil: *Kurzer Unterricht vom Anbau, und nutzlichen Gebrauche der Kirbse, oder sogenannte Plizer* (Freysing, 1773). The oil from the seeds is still considered equal to olive oil in its culinary merit.

225. Maria Sophia Schellhammer, *Brandenburgisches Koch-Buch* (Berlin, 1734), 509. Böckler is mentioned elsewhere in the present study (see chimney soot, page 97), since Theodor Zwinger also used his books as a source.

226. This was a technical medical term for four large cooling seeds: watermelon, cucumber, squashes, and melons. I have restored the Latin; Sauer actually wrote it out in German.

227. The purpose of this treatment is discussed under chickweed (page 96).

removed, and after cleaning off the skins, infuse the nuts several days in brandy. Eat a few of these nuts for a week every morning before breakfast. This will prove an excellent remedy for restoring blocked menses.

The expressed oil of walnuts is famous for treating the cracked nipples of nursing women, when the oil is swabbed on them, and then finely powdered sugar is sprinkled in the cracks. This oil is also very useful for the itch when rubbed over the affected limbs, for it cools, purifies, eases, and heals the condition thoroughly.

The water distilled from partly washed nuts, taken in a few tablespoon doses every morning, will open blockages of the liver and spleen, awaken the appetite, strengthen the head, and fully dispel tertian and quartan fevers. It protects against miasmas and also expels foul matter, sand, and stones from the kidneys. Some people even use it as a gargle. If a small piece of linen is dipped in it and then laid over a wound, this will prevent all types of inflammation.

Water of walnuts is useful in treating angry open leg wounds that are beginning to develop malignant flesh. It is also good for treating lymphatic humors when these glands are washed with it. For treating buzzing and ringing of the ears, put a few drops into the ears.

A valuable syrup may be prepared in the following manner from green walnut shells, namely: Grind the shells in a mortar and press out the juice. Take one-half pound of this liquid and add one-fourth of a pound of fine honey. Boil this until it become a thick syrup. This is quite useful for treating throat sores, scurvy, and other injuries of the mouth when administered as a gargle with the water or juice of self-heal mixed with a little vinegar and saltpeter.

Unripe, green walnuts can be preserved in the following manner: Pick them before they have hardened inside and stick each one lengthwise with a broom straw. Then set them in fresh water for nine or ten days, shaking them up once or twice a day and refreshing the water until the bitterness is drawn out. Then shell them and gently boil the nuts in a kettle until they become tender but not falling apart. Dry them in a sieve, then prepare a syrup with sugar. Add powdered spices, such as cinnamon, ginger, cloves, nutmeg, galingale, and cubeb, and when the syrup is removed from the fire, add the dry nuts and store away for use. Should there still be too much liquid in the nuts so that the syrup becomes runny, they must be put in the oven during bread baking and allowed to cook until thick. These preserved walnuts will warm a cold stomach, promote digestion, strengthen the vital spirits, and guard against the inclination to indulge in bad, evil pleasures, provided one of these nuts is eaten every morning and evening for a continuance.

Watercress
Nasturtium officinalis
Sauer: *Brunnen-Kresse* (1762)

In 1777, during the revolution, General Peter Muhlenberg and his troops encamped in New Jersey while the British were occupying Philadelphia. The Pennsylvania German general grew concerned about the health of his troops, and advised them to scavenge the countryside for various plants that would help stave off scurvy.[254] One of these was watercress, which by that time was already well established in brooks and streams. It was brought here intentionally from Europe and planted around spring houses. On farms where the old spring houses have not been destroyed, it is still possible to find masses of watercress in late March and April, when it is at its peak.

This herb warms and dries. It possesses quantities of volatile, alkaline salt, but only slightly oily by nature. Thus it has the capacity to cleanse the blood of cold, thick, scorbutic matter. It also opens all internal blockages, drives down sand and pus, and promotes urine. It relieves shortness of breath, opens blockages of the chest arteries, etc., and provides relief for disorders of the spleen.

When watercress is still young and tender, it is eaten as salad. Many people are of the opinion that an overheated stomach can be cooled by it, since watercress is also useful for warming it up. When employed in this manner, it will provoke urine and drive down gravel, and prove useful to persons suffering from afflictions of the spleen, as well as those who have taken cold. But pregnant women should use watercress sparingly.

This herb is among those that can be employed quite advantageously against internal blockages and putrefaction of the liver and spleen. For this reason it is useful not only for dropsical patients but especially for those who are plagued by scurvy. However, if the scurvy is of the ardent type, then watercress is not recommended, unless cooling ingredients are mixed with it. Watercress can also be boiled in water, infused in wine, or a syrup can be made from the juice.

The seeds of watercress, together with the seeds of garden cress, can be taken with one-half or one full quint of chervil water for dissolving clotted blood in persons who have suffered from a hard fall, or who have had a great fright so that their blood has thickened and their pulse begins to falter.

Some people express the juice from freshly pulped watercress; others also add brooklime, scurvy grass, or chervil, and for several days take four to six loths of the juice morning and evening, either with or without sugar. Taking it without sugar is far better, since sugar only turns blood phlegmy and bitter.

Others chop the above-mentioned herbs fresh each morning and evening, then pour over this strong hot bouillon and let it stand well covered until cool enough for drinking. The broth is strained through a fine cloth and drunk warm. Yet another method is to pulp the leaves and press out all the juices, pouring them into a clean, well-glazed pot, which is then placed in warm ashes. This should be allowed to stand several hours until all the cloudy material settles to the bottom. The clear upper part is gently poured off and put in a glass jar. If a little olive oil is poured over it the juice will keep thus for quite a while. Drink half a gill each morning and evening. This liquid or herbal restorative will serve against all the above-named ailments and conditions. Indeed, it is also quite useful in all infirmities of long continuance, as for

254. "Lambs Quarters and Water Cresses for the Soldiers," *Report* 36 (1975): 25.

example the tertian and quartan fevers, which it cures thoroughly. It is likewise good in cases of inveterate coughs and asthmatic conditions, which arise from the retention of phlegm, and for wasting and delirious fevers caused by thickening and stickiness of the vital fluids. It is further useful against dropsy in its initial stages or when already present, since it drives out via the urine the watery humors that have collected in the body. And finally, it kills all kinds of worms, yes, even heartworms, and expels them.[255]

If watercress is wilted a little on a warm hearth, then pulped and heated with rye flour, egg whites, and pigeon manure until it forms a thick mass, it may be spread thickly on a cloth and laid as a plaster over the place pained by pleurisy. This will dissolve immediately the thick humors retained there and thus still the pain. If this plaster is applied over a swollen, hardened spleen several nights in succession, it will not only alleviate the hardness, but also reduce the swelling.

If a person is burned by fire, take watercress, onions, and fresh ivy leaves, chop them up, and foment them in butter or linseed oil. Press the butter or oil though a fine cloth, then smear the burn with it. The burning will thus be drawn out immediately and healed.

If the juice expressed from watercress is mixed with water of marjoram and snuffed frequently into the nose, this will loosen congestion of the nasal passages and thus cause the mucus to come out through the nose and thus clear the head. This will also dispel pains and dullness in the head that have resulted from the above-mentioned congestion.

When a sponge is dipped in the juice of watercress and vinegar, then sprinkled with powdered beaver cod,[256] and held before the nose, it is good for treating that very injurious sleeping disorder known as lethargy.

The expressed juice of watercress is also useful externally not only for washing out and cleansing all manner of putrid, rotting sores and wounds, but also for treating the rank spongy flesh that grows within the nostrils. If the juice is sprayed into the nose frequently, this flesh will gradually loosen and the nose brought back to good order. Long ago, this juice was considered a great secret with which the most fabulous cures could be obtained

Water Germander

Teucrium scordium
Sauer: *Wasserbarthenig, Lachen-Gnoblauch* (1774)

The Old World plant is a creeping vine found in marshes, while the North American Teucrium canadense *is a slender branching perennial some one to two feet tall.*

255. Heartworm is not a real disease, as it is in dogs and cats. My old German dictionary refers to it as a superstition. It was an imaginary condition used to explain various pains and strange sensations in the heart. There were certain individuals who were always "wonderful sick" with a slow-working fatal condition called heartworms (so they explained) or who were excessively paranoid about getting them. These self-diagnosed invalids were the brunt of many jokes among period doctors, as well as the easy victims of patent medicine scams. Today they are called hypochondriacs. The sense of Sauer's passage is that the remedy works so effectively that it will cure even imaginary worms.

256. Beaver's cods are explained on page 62.

Country people during the colonial period employed this American germander (or wood sage, as it was often called) as though it were true water germander, but from a medical standpoint, the two are really quite different. The European plant was sold in colonial apothecary shops as a dried herb, distilled water, or essence. Its German name is rather charming, since it literally means "laughing garlic." This is probably better rendered into English as "fool's garlic." The American plant was also a "fool's" garlic, since it exuded a strong garlic odor when bruised, and if eaten by cattle, would flavor the milk, butter, and cheese of these animals with an overpowering garlic taste.

Water germander possesses a bitter, sharp salt mingled with sundry sulfurous elements. From these derives its capacity to warm gently, to dry, to resist all poison, to kill and expel worms, to operate through sweat, to open, to cleanse, and to dissipate. Only the leaves are used.

The distilled water of water germander and the syrup prepared from the juice will kill worms in children if they are administered a couple of tablespoons from time to time.

Water germander is one of the foremost remedies used against the plague, for which reason it is also taken with *Theriaca Andromaci.*

For cold fevers, water germander is useful when boiled in water with gentian, succory root, and tartar salts. As a potion it works well if after first purging the stomach, the patient drinks a glassful every six hours. The essence of this herb drawn out in brandy is very good for bringing out the purples and red measles when administered in drops. It will also expel poison from the heart during spotted fever, although it must be handled with caution, because great injury can easily occur from its strong expulsive action.

Watermelon
Citrullus lanatus
Sauer: *Wassermelonen* (1776)

Watermelons are recorded in the Delaware Valley as early as the 1640s, and there were many different kinds. The most common sorts were the red- and yellow-fleshed, and both were used extensively by country people as a source of food. Peter Kalm, a Swedish traveler through the region in the late 1750s, remarked that some colonials believed that the overconsumption of watermelon led to malaria, an odd association that does not seem to crop up elsewhere in period observations. It is possible to eat too much watermelon, and the great watermelon fairs held at Marcus Hook during Sauer's era were legendary for the quantities of melons consumed. But debauchery and riotous behavior were also rife, and no doubt some of this was owing to the coveted distillate made from watermelon juice, which in colonial America came out of the still as a form of rum—at least it resembled rum due to its sweetness. It was employed in treating those very fevers that were thought to arise from the melons themselves. Sauer mentions this melon rum in passing.

Melons and pumpkins are all of the same nature, for they are cold and moist and have a close similarity to gourds, only they are more cooling. Weak old people with feeble stomachs should avoid watermelons assiduously, and young persons should not eat them too much. However, healthy people with hot stomachs can enjoy them without ill effect, if only they would control their appetite enough so that they could tell when the stomach has been sufficiently cooled, and be satisfied to stop there. Otherwise, watermelons will cause ardent fevers, diarrhea, and such feebleness of the stomach that many a person has suffered long while others all their lives from them.

People who have recently recovered from an illness should abjure watermelons in particular, because the sickness might easily return and become much worse than before.

Of course, in medicine, nothing of the melon is used but the seeds, although some people distill a water from ripe watermelons that is very famous for getting rid of stone and sand, if it is drunk often and in quantity.

For all manner of feverish illnesses, ardent fevers, and inflammations of the viscera, kidneys, and bladder, the following potion will be of service: Take five loths of shelled almonds and two loths of shelled melon seeds and grind them in a wooden or marble mortar with enough rosewater or plantain water that it yields a drinkable milk. Or instead, use only springwater in which grated hartshorn has been boiled. Sweeten to taste with sugar and then let the patient drink it as thirst demands. As long as the fever lasts, this will cool it quite nicely, and strengthen the stomach and the entire body as well.

Wheat
Triticum x *aestivum* and *Triticum spelta*
Sauer: *Weizen* (1773)

Wheat was the cash crop of the mid-Atlantic colonies prior to the revolution. In particular, the regions settled by the Germans became a rich breadbasket that fed into Philadelphia's huge transatlantic shipping network. Thus for Sauer's readers wheat needed no explanation, but its medical uses were just as valuable as the grain itself.

While several of the remedies call for white bread crumbs or even Mutschelmehl, *the inner crumbs of milk-bread dinner rolls (sourdough rolls prepared with milk instead of water), the herbal makes the revealing remark that spelt bread crumbs can be used in most instances as a substitute. This was noted with full recognition that many German farmers sold their wheat and only kept back spelt for domestic use.*

*Spelt (*Triticum spelta, *or more accurately,* Triticum spelta subsp. spelta) *plays a leitmotif throughout the history of the Pennsylvania Germans, for it was one of the ancient grains that was deeply rooted in their cultural consciousness. There are fourteen known* *varieties. Hildegard of Bingen, the great medieval herbalist, advocated spelt as a health food due to its easy digestibility. Dr. Zwinger likewise recommended it. His recipe for spelt toast soup is typical: "A restorative soup prepared from toasted spelt bread with milk or chicken broth makes a nice dish and a good remedy for fluxes of the stomach."[257]*

Sauer's numerous remedies for livestock are quite in line with the veterinary material the Sauers published in earlier editions of their almanac. The information on foddering geese, however, makes much more sense when it is understood that the geese are being fattened for their livers. Goose liver pie, very similar to the Strasbourg paté, was a great favorite among the German element as a Christmas dish. In fact, a recipe for making it was eventually published in Der Alte Germantown Calender *(Philadelphia, 1863) as a nostalgic set piece for what was then viewed as an "old-time" Christmas treat.*

The only culinary recipe provided by Sauer, albeit sketchy, is the recipe for kalte Schale *or cold soup (there is really no accurate way to translate this). It is a thick, cold, soupy preparation akin to eggnog, which traces its origin to the fermented soups of the Middle Ages. These were originally fasting dishes, but in German culture they evolved into sweet hot-weather health soups to which fruit was often added.*

As one further culinary footnote, it might be worth mentioning that during Sauer's lifetime, bakers in his neighborhood still made the so-called Germantauner Hochzichsweck *(Germantown wedding buns), which were prepared with well-bolted spelt and wheat flours. Essentially they were either one roll molded into the shape of a triangle, or three rolls joined together to form a triangle. These were then brushed with egg and sprinkled with aniseed before baking. The custom of making this type of bun was brought from Westphalia in the 1680s, but died out by the 1850s.*

Wheat operates by a volatile, mild salt together with a sulfurous spirit, and for this reason possesses the virtue and capacity to provide the body with the best nourishment and the blood with the most genuine substance and vigor.

Sextus Pomponius, a Spanish prince who cured himself of gout by using wheat, did so by often sitting in wheat so that it covered him to the knees.[258]

If a pound of wheat flour is well parched in a frying pan, then two quarts of water worked into it and poured down the throat of a cow, it will still its diarrhea.

If a horse becomes sick and no one knows what ails it, stir wheat flour in water and let the horse drink it.

Should a horse become too thin, give him toasted wheat to eat twice a day and three times a day in his drinking water. If the horse is still too thin, mix the wheat with bran, and thereby keep him to his work, but do not go too hard at it.

If one wants to raise young geese quickly, then fodder them on wheat boiled in water as soon as they can be penned up by themselves. In this way, they will become fat very quickly. Furthermore, it is possible to fatten young geese and make them

257. Theodor Zwinger, *Theatrum Botanicum; das ist, Vollkommenes Kräuter-Buch* (Basel, 1744), 371.
258. It should be evident from his name that Sextus Pomponius was a Roman. This anecdote is taken from Pliny.

comely by foddering them until full three times a day with a mixture of two parts wheat bran and one part barley meal combined with warm water. However, they must also be provided with enough to drink.

Should a horse become short-winded and pant often, stir wheat flour into luke-warm water. Do not let the horse drink anything else for several days, but give him enough of this to satisfy his thirst.

When wheat flour is mixed with olive oil to form a plaster, spread on a linen cloth, and then laid over hard tumors on the breasts, it will soften them. Wheat flour can also be boiled with water and olive oil and applied in the same manner. This too will soften the tumors.

If a cow has swollen eyes, take wheat flour and make a plaster of it with honey water and metheglin.[259] Bind this over the eyes, and it will get rid of the swelling.

When a horse has a hard swelling, take wheat flour, bran, vinegar, and honey, together with the white of an egg, and mix it all together to form a plaster. Spread this over the hurt and let it stay there for three days. Then apply a fresh one prepared like the first one. Continue until the swelling has entirely disappeared.

Toast wheat on a hot, glowing baking sheet, then pound it and press out an oil. This is useful for healing ringworm and prickly, gnawing itch.

Grate white bread crumbs into a deep dish and add a little ground cinnamon, wine, and sugar. A *kalte Schale* made thus is very strengthening to the healthy and the sick, provided they do not have a feverish illness.

For tetter of the face, take the crumbs of wheat bread as hot as they come from the oven, and pour white wine and rosewater in equal amounts over them. Let this stand for twenty-four hours in a warm place to soften. Press the bread crumbs, and strain the liquid through a cloth bag. Wash the face with this and let it dry on its own. Repeat this several times, and it will get rid of the tetters and make the complexion beautiful.

If the crumbs of wheat bread are cooked with milk and made into a plaster with a little oil of roses, and a couple of fresh egg yolks and a little powdered saffron also added, then well mixed, this will ease hot swelling of women's breasts, if it is spread on a cloth and laid over them warm. It will also ease the pain of gout. If the flour is only parched and a little camphor and elder flower added, or just the flour alone if these cannot be had, then spread warm over the hurt, it will get rid of Saint Anthony's fire and inflamed swellings, and cool them.

Thin soups made with boiled flour are quite serviceable for divers illnesses. They restrain fluxes and relieve a raw throat and cough, as well as all feverish afflictions of the chest and consumption, inflammation of the lungs, sores of the chest, and all internal sores of the stomach, kidneys, and bladder.

Wheat flour combined with finely powdered gum traganth, and taken thus, will get rid of powerful burning of the urine.

Wheat flour, worked to a dough consistency with rosewater and spread over the

259. Metheglin is a type of mead confected with strong spices. It is a very old medieval drink. The honey water mentioned in the same sentence is not honey mixed with water, but rather distilled honey.

hurt, will heal cracked nipples on women's breasts, if they are smeared with this often. This is also good for milk blisters on the tongues of young children.

Dry wheat flour used as a powder will heal the injury to young children that occurs between the legs and buttocks from the acidity of urine. It can also be applied to raw skin on the neck and behind the ears.[260]

A fine salve for burns may be prepared from wheat flour in the following manner: Take a loth each of wheat flour, silver earth, and white lead, three loths each of rose oil* and St. Johns oil, and one loth of beeswax. Melt the wax and oils over a gentle charcoal heat. When it is cool, add the other ingredients finely ground. Stir well together, and thus you will have a valuable salve.

Spelt flour possesses for many applications similar faculties, although it is somewhat drier.

*Oil of roses is prepared in the following way: Take fresh rose petals, as many as you want, cut off the caps, and then boil them in good-quality olive oil. Strain out the petals, and store away for further use.[261]

White Lily (Madonna Lily)
Lilium candidum
Sauer: *Weisse Lilie* (1763)

> *White lily, sometimes called Madonna lily, was a popular theme in colonial German folk art. It even appeared in some of the Fraktur drawings at Ephrata Cloister while Sauer's mother lived there as a sister. As a source of remedies, it appeared more often in Pennsylvania German handbooks dealing with cosmetics than with medical cures, but all the same, it had specific uses. Jacob Biernauer's 1818 receipt for removing wrinkles from the face was typical: "Take white lily water and wash the face with it. This freshens the color [of the skin] and gets rid of wrinkles."[262]*

In the white lily, the roots as well as the flowers have the capacity to soften, to cool, to open, and to ease. The roots, flowers, and the distilled water and oil are used.

The distilled water takes away all manner of freckles and burns on the face that are caused by the sun. Dip a little piece of cloth in it and lay it over the sunburn sores where they are tender. Also, for the mouth and throat, gargle it in the throat and rinse the mouth with it. It will hinder putrefaction and inflammation.

If someone is burned by scalding water, oil, molten metal, or the like, dip a small piece of cloth into lily water and lay it over the burn. It will draw out heat, and still the pain and burning. Taken internally in a four- to five-loth dose, lily water strength-

---

260. Today we call this diaper rash. In Sauer's era, babies were often wrapped up tightly so that only their faces were exposed, hence the rash on the neck and sides of the head.

261. This appeared as a footnote at the end of the original text, and there I have left it. Sauer realized that nowhere in the herbal did he provide a recipe, yet he referred to the oil often. This recipe was added to correct the omission.

262. Jacob Biernauer, *Das unentbehrliche Haus- und Kunst-Buch* (Reading, Pa., 1818), 26.

ens the head, restores speech, and is good for coughs, congestion of the lungs, and pulmonary consumption.

The root of white lily is used more externally as an emollient for bringing abscesses to a head. To this end, it is customarily used in emollient plasters, to wit: Take marshmallow leaves, wild mallow, chamomile flowers, melilot, and the bulbs of white lily and chop it all very fine. Add winnowed flaxseed and saffron well powdered, and cook it in milk. This makes a choice emollient plaster, which may be smeared thickly over a cloth or white leather and then laid warm over the sore.

The bulb of the white lily is also useful when cooked as emollient clysters for promoting the opening of the bowels. For this, take one loth of the bulb, a handful each of marshmallow and wild mallow, a half handful of chamomile, and boil this in a quart of water or milk. After it is strained, add a tablespoonful each of chamomile and linseed oils, as well as two quints of saltpeter and cream of tartar. Use a pint of this liquid for a clyster, and let it cool only enough so that the patient can bear it where the bladder is inserted.[263]

The oil of white lily is prepared thus: Take a half pound of good-quality olive oil and a quarter pound of the flower petals of the lily. Put this together in a glass vessel, stop it tight, and set it in the sun. If you want the oil to be more concentrated, after fourteen days take out the first batch of petals and add as many fresh ones, and continue as above. Used warm, this oil brings sores quickly to a head, eases swellings, and is very good for oozing scall on the scalp. The petals that sink to the bottom of the oil are of special use for all manner of livid sores, or burns from fire, boiling water and oil, and so forth. They ease the pain promptly, draw out the burn, and heal the injury. These petals are also good for plague blisters. The oil of white lily should not be neglected in clysters, particularly in cases of hard, inflamed constipation, colic of the bowels, and diarrhea.

White Throughwax (Thorowax)
Bupleurum rotundifolium
Sauer: *Durchwachs* (1767)

Sauer's original text referred to this plant in Latin as Perfoliata, *a label given it by Zwinger and used consistently as its genus name. This has thrown a number of historians off, leading them to believe that Sauer was discussing American boneset (*Eupatorium perfoliatum) *when clearly Sauer is discussing a vulnerary, not an herb for agues. Added to this is the problem that* Durchwachs-Bieberkraut *is* Chlora perfoliata, *known in English as yellow wort, not to mention that* Durchwachs *is used in German for a number of very different plants, including honeysuckle and periwinkle. Dr. Woyt appealed to Linnaeus and*

263. This cannot be translated literally since Sauer refers to the anus as an "eye." A bull's or ox bladder was commonly used for administering enemas in this period.

said that the plant was an umbellifer, and indeed that is where it has been until quite recently—it is now placed under Apiaceae. It is even possible to find this herb in some seed catalogs, although it may be passed off as any number of things, even as an ever-lasting. The plant is edible both as a salad and potherb, and it is even used as a spice. Sauer, like Nicholas Culpeper, employed it almost exclusively as a vulnerary. Sauer may have been one of the first to grow it in this country.

Throughwax is warm and rather dry in nature, and operates by its sundry mucilaginous, earthy, coarse, alkaline salt particles. They give it the capacity to glutinate, to draw together gently, to cleanse, and to heal.

The seeds of throughwax ground to a powder and added in pea-size doses to the porridge of young children will heal ruptures. Every morning before breakfast, they should also be given a small draught of distilled throughwax water to drink. If the water is not on hand, then take the dried leaves and prepare a tea from them, and give it to them often. At the same time, keep them well secured with a good, tight-fitting bandage, so that the rupture cannot fall out, and as much as possible, prevent them from screaming until it is completely healed.

Throughwax leaves pounded to a cataplasm are very useful when bound as a poultice over wens.

By using brandy, it is possible to extract a choice essence from throughwax leaves, which is excellent for cleansing and healing all manner of wounds and injuries. Fifteen to twenty drops, taken internally and often, is serviceable for healing ruptures of the navel and groin.

The dried leaves ground to a powder with or without the seeds, as well as the freshly pressed sap, are very useful when applied as vulnerary plasters and salves, and as plasters for hernias.

This herb grows well in Pennsylvania, if only people would take a little trouble to plant it in their gardens.

Wild Carrot
Daucus carota
Sauer: *Wilde Möhre, Wilde Gelbrübe* (1772)

Wild carrot, commonly called Queen Anne's lace or bird's nest, is the bane of every gardener who tries to save seed from carrots and grow them true. Its pollen travels far and wide, but to my knowledge, no one has taken advantage of this and made an industry of wild carrot seeds, which certainly do possess medical value. We are led to believe from Sauer's closing remark that even though this was a cheap and easily obtained medicine, few country people even in his day exerted the effort to collect seed against unforeseen necessities.

Only the seeds are used from wild carrots. They warm and dry, for their salts contain numerous volatile, alkaline, sharp, oily elements. From these the wild carrot derives its special faculties for opening and cleansing blockages of the matrix and kidneys, for driving out phlegmy matter, grit, and sand in the urine, for easing difficult breathing, and for discharging phlegm from the chest.

If a quint of the seeds are taken once a month in strawberry or mallow water, and the body is then gently shaken through riding or travel by carriage, this will cleanse the kidneys vigorously and prevent the growth of stones therein, or the accumulation of sand and gravel.

The seeds can also be boiled in beer for those who are worried about kidney and bladder stones and who are plagued by a continuance of pains in the kidneys. By employing carrot seed beer, they can remain completely free of this condition.

For lumbago, first bleed the patient, then grind half a loth of wild carrot seeds to a powder and administer this twice so that it will relieve the pain quickly.

For upheavals of the matrix, administer thirty grains of the powdered seeds a few times a day in lemon balm tea or mint water.

A few years back it was discovered that these seeds were of uncommon service for treating backache and pain in the kidneys and loins if they were drunk daily as tea. It would be good if people exerted more diligence to gather these seeds during the summer, because no one knows what may occur under their roof during the rest of the year.

Wild Ginger (Wild Nard)

Asarum europaeum
Sauer: *Haselwurtzel* (1763)

The North American wild ginger (Asarum canadense) *is similar to the European species in its medical properties. We may presume that the two were used almost interchangeably. Sauer's original Latin identification of the herb was rather vague, but there is no doubt about the species when he comes to the actual remedies, for they are quite easy to trace to late medieval sources long associated with the Old World plant. Its root, which Sauer mentions, yields a gray powder that smells like pepper, whereas the powdered leaf used as snuff is green. Where he writes that it purges "above and below," Sauer means that the root acts both as an emetic and a strong laxative. The warning to pregnant women is based on this medical action, which will induce abortion and violent discharge from the body. This is what he meant by "great injury." The snuff acts the same way, except on the passages in the head. The powerful sneezing that it induces was known to cause nosebleeds, bleeding from the ears, and even stroke; thus it was generally administered only under the oversight of physicians and rarely given to children.*

Wild ginger is of a warm, dry nature, especially the root, which is the part most employed in medicine. The entire herb possesses the capacity to purge above and below when it is taken in powder form or in wine. When boiled in water, it will not purge, rather, it opens all internal blockages and promotes urination and moderate sweating.

Pregnant women should not use wild ginger, since great injury may readily come to them and to the unborn child.

According to the strength or weakness of the patient, one-half or a full quint of the ground root taken in wine while the use of purging medicines is withheld will open blockages of the liver, spleen, matrix, and hardened tumors. It is also a useful remedy for dropsy and jaundice, sciatica of long continuance, pursy, and coughing. It is especially good for tertian and quartan fevers, for it cleanses the entire body from top to bottom of all putrid humors. But because this is such a strong remedy, it is for the most part only administered to persons of strong constitutions.

The leaves of wild ginger, given to horses in their fodder, will cleanse them and make them more spirited.

Wild ginger can be used effectively along with other herbs in wine bitters that open the liver, spleen, matrix, chest, and kidneys when taken every morning. If one chooses to take it as a powder, measure out twenty to forty grains. This will cleanse the body above and below. The leaves purge too powerfully for human use, but they may be dried in the shade, ground to powder, and then snuffed into the nose along with other herbs. This is a choice remedy for all manner of cold fluxes in the head and purges the same vigorously.

Wild Tansy (Silverweed)
Potentilla anserina
Sauer: *Gänserich* (1774)

This is often found in old herbals under the name "argentina" in reference to its silvery leaves. Otherwise, it is called garden tansy, as opposed to the common (Tanacetum vulgare). *It is this tansy, not the common, that was formerly eaten in the spring. The German name simply means "gander" (male goose), but is actually a shortened form of* ganderwort, *as implied in the species name* anserina. *While the leaves do indeed resemble common tansy in shape, the flowers resemble buttercups, and therefore care should be taken in differentiating the two plants, since buttercup is poisonous.*

This is especially important when gathering the roots, which (like the leaves) were once a common culinary ingredient. Indeed, the German settlers actually planted wild tansy in their kitchen gardens so that they could promote larger and better-shaped roots, which may be likened to branching brown carrots. Tannins in the roots give them a slightly astringent taste, which blends well with sweet-and-sour dishes. For this reason, wild tansy was often cooked with skirrets (page 291), while the leaves were chopped into omelets or Brockle, *or added to soups. The English preferred it for spring puddings. It was generally held among the English and German colonists alike that if wild tansy were eaten in the spring, it would prevent many of the disorders and complaints that appeared during the summer. It was also eaten by women to increase fertility and treated very much like an aphrodisiac by the female sex.*

The plant is native to most parts of North America, where it inhabits salt meadows and brackish wetlands. It will attain a very large size when brought under cultivation.

Wild tansy is cold and dry in nature and operates by its saltpeter-like penetrating salts. They give it great power for forcing urine, for driving down stones and gravel from the kidneys, for opening blockages, and for cleansing and healing. The root is delicious and good to eat.

A handful of wild tansy cooked in equal parts wine and water, and the decoction drunk, will stay all manner of fluxes of the blood and belly. It is good against blood-spitting, and heals ruptures and wounds. If a little vinegar is added to this and the mouth rinsed out with it, it will preserve loose teeth and soft, spongy gums, as well as ease toothaches. If it is gargled, it will raise a fallen glottis.

Wild tansy leaves boiled in half wine and water, then strained through a cloth and used often as a gargle for both the mouth and throat, will heal scurvy of the gums and abscesses in the throat, will firm up loose teeth, and is useful for toothache.

When wild tansy leaves are bound to the soles of the feet, or walked upon when barefoot, they should stop bloody flux and other fluxes of the stomach.

Gather the leaves of wild tansy and corn chamomile in May early in the morning when the dew is fallen.[264] Mash them, press out the juice, mix this with red wine, and then strain it through blotting paper. Drink half a pint of this every morning for a continuance. This is a choice remedy against kidney stones, for it breaks them down and drives them out along with mucusy matter and sand.

A similar result can be achieved with salts extracted from this plant, or with its essence extracted in brandy or May dew.

The salt of wild tansy ground together with table salt and vinegar, and bound to the soles of the feet, will reduce the heat of fevers.

A half gill of the distilled water of wild tansy drunk in the morning and evening is a proven remedy for driving down kidney stones, getting rid of backache, stopping the overflow of the menses, and healing injuries in the intestines. Used externally, it is useful for reddened eyes and getting rid of red spots in them.

Wild Thyme (Creeping Thyme)

Thymus serpyllum
Sauer: *Quendel* (1773)

This perennial plant native to Europe is not to be confused with common garden thyme (Thymus vulgaris). *It was evidently introduced into eastern Canada and New*

---

264. Sauer used the idiosyncratic word *Kornkraut*. He meant *Feldkraut*, which is a name applied to corn chamomile *(Anthemis arvensis)* and sometimes to true German chamomile *(Matricaria chamomilla)*. He intended the former, not the latter.

England during the seventeenth century, because it is now naturalized in those regions. It is also naturalized as far south as Pennsylvania, so we must assume that it was intentionally brought here and at one time cultivated for its medical and culinary uses. The extracted oil, called serpolet, was used to scent soaps. A variety of wild thyme known as lemon thyme was also cultivated. It was sometimes used in the soup mentioned below.

Wild thyme is of a warm, dry nature. It operates by means of an oily, balsamic, volatile, mild salt. From this derives its capacity to strengthen the head, nerves, and matrix. It also dries fluxes, opens obstructions, disperses wind, and stills pain.

Wild thyme has the same virtues as savory, and is used against poison in food and drink. For this reason the ancients put it in the food of weary reapers during harvest, so that while they rested, or if they happened to drink unhealthy water, no harm would come to them and they might remain free of poisonings.

The fresh green wild thyme is also used in cookery for meat and fish dishes, indeed, a delicious and healthy catfish soup can be made with it, so long as you have the fish.[265]

If wild thyme is infused in wine for six or more days, a good vinegar will develop.[266]

Flavor one quart of white wine by boiling thyme in it, then drink from this. It will still colic, promote difficult urination, and drive down gravel and stones, among other things.

Distilled water of wild thyme taken in tablespoon doses will strengthen a weak head, eyes, and stomach. It will dispel dizziness, provide against coughs, force down blocked urine, stone, sand, and so forth, and should also be good for putrid fevers arising from the stomach.

Willow Tree (European White Willow)
Salix alba
Sauer: *Weide* (1778)

Not all willow trees possess medical properties, and this presents us with a problem. The white European willow, the tree discussed in the herbal, is not native to North America, nor is it naturalized in the middle states to any extent. Because of its preference for cooler northern climates, the white willow was grown in New England, and for many years into the nineteenth century the Shakers produced medicines from it. For Sauer's German readers, however, there were few alternatives. The only willow native to their

---

265. Sauer wrote *Cadfisch-Suppe*, which might also be interpreted as cod fish, except that fresh codfish is *Kabeljau* and salt or dried cod is *Stockfisch* in German. Pennsylvania High German employed *Stockfisch* for cod in general and the dialect English adaptations *Cädfisch* or *Cedfisch* for catfish. By inserting this, Sauer was in fact alluding to a well-known summer soup in eighteenth-century Philadelphia, where catfish cookery was developed to a very high degree. The soup in question resembled modern Belgian waterzooi but was treated as a restorative. In rural Germany, wels (a type of catfish) was used for a similar purpose.

266. This is one of the earliest direct references to the preference for thyme-flavored vinegar among the Pennsylvania Germans.

part of the country that was discovered to have medical applications was the glaucus willow (Salix discolor), *commonly known as the pussy willow. Evidently, it was this tree that was understood to serve as a substitute. As for the once-common custom of scattering willow leaves on the floors of rooms to cool them during the summer, any sort of willow leaves will do. Doubtless it was the common black willow that was used for this purpose, since its new shoots or "rods" were also gathered during the summer to make baskets.*

The bark, berries, and leaves of the willow possess an equal amount of numerous, coarse, earthy, mildly sharp, nitrous salty components of a rather watery and slightly sulfurous character. Due to these, the willow dries and cools, is gently astringent, and operates to a small degree by urine.

During the summer, if willow leaves are strewn over the floor of a room in which people afflicted with ardent fevers are lying, they will cause a refreshing coolness in the air.[267]

If the leaves are boiled for a foot bath, and the feet dipped in this, it will cool the feet and induce a gentle slumber.

A bathwater made with willow leaves is very comforting, over all other remedies, for those who are developing a hump on the back, since it reduces the swelling wonderfully.

Branches of young shoots of the white willow distilled, and a half gill drunk every morning and evening, is good for sand and stones. Willow water drives out worms, promotes urine, and will bring down a dead fetus. If the eyes are washed with it, it will take away redness and make them clear. It will also heal scall on the scalp and make beautiful hair. If the water in which the leaves were boiled is drunk, it will allay lewdness. Willow sap has a similar capacity, when it is drained from the slashed shoots in the early spring.

If the bark is burned to ash, acidulated in vinegar, and then applied as a plaster, it will get rid of warts and corns.

Willow catkins bound into wounds will stop the bleeding.[268]

Wine
Vitis vinifera
Sauer: *Wein* (1778)

Theodor Zwinger's Theatrum Botanicum *treats wine in a different manner than Sauer; there is even information on viticulture from Daniel Rhagor's* Pflantz-Garten *(Bern, 1639) as well as advice on the production of wine vinegars. Pertinent to the medical use of wine vinegar, which figures largely in many of the herbal remedies, is*

---

267. This practice was not done solely for the sick; it was also undertaken during hot weather in general both to cool the rooms and to freshen the air. Green rushes and ferns were also used in this manner.

268. The reference here is clearly to pussy willows. The catkins were gathered in the spring before developing pollen, dried, and then used throughout the year as emergency pledgets for deep cuts or wounds.

Zwinger's discussion of using a hot clay roof tile for the purpose of fumigating rooms. The tile is heated until very hot, then scattered with vinegar or with a strongly scented herbal vinegar to create steam. This was thought to purify sickrooms or houses infiltrated by miasmas.

In colonial Pennsylvania, similar roof tiles were also once common in the German settlements, and they were used for this same purpose. However, so-called strewing bricks were employed as well and seem to have replaced the tiles by the early 1800s. The bricks were somewhat oversize and flatter than normal bricks, but used exactly like Zwinger's tile. They were normally heated among hot coals in the fireplace, then carried on a shovel to the room where fumigation was to take place. Thieves Vinegar was often applied to strewing bricks in this manner, especially during outbreaks of yellow fever and cholera. It is discussed on page 81.

Sauer's discussion of wine is focused less on its uses than on moralizing remarks about excess in the same vein as his treatments of chocolate, sugar, and tea. Yet it should be evident from perusing this herbal that wine is used extensively in remedies. It is recommended in small quantities, yet it is perceived as a valid and healthful medium for administering herbs in their most beneficial form. Many of the essential oils and other chemical components of herbs were known to be soluble in wine (due to the alcohol), and thus readily taken into the bloodstream. Modern medicine has now confirmed the healthful benefits of wine, but there is another dimension to this that also needs explanation: the Germans of colonial America were wine drinkers. The use of wine in household medicine was a natural application of a product that was readily on hand. Indeed, for them, wine was food, an integral part of the meal.

Until the outbreak of the revolution, vast quantities of inexpensive Spanish and Portuguese wines entered the ports of Philadelphia and Baltimore for shipment into the interior German settlements. Period accounts often remarked that the Germans preferred wine over all else and that it was readily available in most German-speaking taverns and inns.[269] This situation changed dramatically with the alteration in British trade following the revolution and was one of the reasons the Germans became so interested in establishing commercial viticulture in Pennsylvania and Maryland in the years following 1800. The federal government took the New Englander position that foreign wine was a luxury of suspicious moral value and thus imposed excise taxes on it. This not only made wine expensive, it shifted the consumption of wine to domestic hard liquor, primarily rye and corn whiskey. In short, the sin tax on wine resulted in an even greater excess, thus planting the seeds for many negative social ramifications that are still with us today.

Sauer's point of view was one of moderation, and this atti-

269. For a fuller treatment of this, refer to William Woys Weaver, "Viticulture among the Pennsylvania Germans," *Journal of Gastronomy* 6, no. 3 (winter 1990/1991): 113–29.

tude was prevalent among the Mennonites, Quakers, and other sects who at that period in history had not yet embraced the temperance movement. Imported German wines were expensive due to London intermediaries, but there is considerable evidence in period estate inventories showing that at least the better-off German settlers kept such wines on hand. Indeed, the well-liked Osthofen wines from near Worms were sometimes advertised for sale in German-language newspapers.[270] The most common drink, however, was Portuguese red wine. Where Sauer calls for wine in the herbal without specifying type, he probably means Lisbon red.

Lastly, there is also a good deal of indirect evidence about wine consumption among the Germans. We find this in the form of a large body of recipes intended to correct the taste of off wine. Sauer's herbal even contains such helpful hints under asparagus, where the flowers are used to draw off bad flavors (see page 48). Another remedy employed oranges and cloves, and remained popular with farmers well into the nineteenth century. Daniel Schmidt published it in his Das gemeinnüztige Haus-Artzeneybuch *(Carlisle, Pa., 1826): "Take an orange, stick it full of cloves, and hang it in the barrel so that it does not touch the wine" (150).* Die Englische Goldgrube *(Ulm, 1827) suggested a similar (and less expensive) treatment: "Bake a long bread roll. Hollow it out and fill it with cloves. Hang this in the barrel" (36).*

By nature, wine is varied, for one wine may be hotter, stronger, and healthier than another. Yet all varieties of wine producing grapes possess the noble capacity to warm the stomach, promote digestion, increase and improve the blood, promote circulation, strengthen the constitution, and make men merry. And all of this if kept within bounds and used according to the good advice of Paul to Timothy to take only a little.[271]

However, if wine is used intemperately, it will weaken not only the entire body, the stomach, liver, and heart, but also the brain and nerves, due to its oily, sharp nature and acidic tartaric salts. This results in headache, palsied hands, partial or complete apoplexy, dizziness, the falling evil, lameness, numbness of the limbs, insensibility, fluxes of the head, indigestion, iliac passion, and dropsy. That excessive drinking engenders gout is confirmed by the heathens in their old saying:

Gleich wie das Venus-Spiel, so auch das starke Trinken,
Macht Haupt und Hände schwach, und dass die Füsse hinken.

Like the game of love, so too with heavy drinking,
It muddles head and hands, and trips the feet.

Old weak persons of a cold temperament are much improved by a glass of wine. On the other hand, youthful ardent temperaments have numerous troubles to fear.

270. For example, Johannes Seyl of Lancaster, Pennsylvania, offered Osthofen wine by the demijohn, gallon, or quart in *Der Wöchentliche Philadelphische Staatsbothe*, September 23, 1765.

271. This biblical reference was commonly quoted by antitemperance advocates during the eighteenth and nineteenth centuries. It appears in the letters of Saint Paul: First Timothy 5:23: "Drink no longer water, but use a little wine for thy stomach's sake and thine often infirmities." Sauer makes reference to this same passage in his discussion of tea (page 321).

Needless to say, those who drink a half or one full gill of wine in the morning before breakfast, and nothing more the rest of the day, will feel a very substantial benefit from it, as opposed to those who suck up a quart or more throughout the course of a day. For those in the first case, wine is in company with medicine; in the latter case, it is a corruption of nature.

Wintergreen (Large Wintergreen)
Pyrola rotundifolia
Sauer: *Wintergrün* (1771)

Wintergreen was used rather loosely in the eighteenth century as a name for a number of very different plants. In German, it was a common name for climbing ivy (Hedera arborea) and pipsissewa (Chimaphila umbellata)—found in both the Old and New Worlds—as well as for several species of Pyrola. Of this genus, Woyt listed three species commonly found in Germany: a "greater," a "lesser," and an arbutus-leafed sort. It was the greater, or round-leafed, sort that the Germans preferred for medicine, and it is this species that Sauer brought under discussion below. Furthermore, the Germans appear to be unique in clearly regarding it as a vulnerary, British herbalists applying it more as an internal remedy for quite different ailments.

The essence and distilled water could be imported, but the other remedies require fresh leaves, which brings us to the question of substitutions. Large wintergreen is also native to North America, although restricted more generally to the cooler parts. Evidently, as far as Sauer was concerned, any of the related native wintergreens would do, and this appears to have been the practice in the countryside. The fragrant berries were not used in medicine, but they were used in cookery, especially as a flavoring agent. In the nineteenth century, apple cider and ice cream flavored with wintergreen became popular in the Pennsylvania German region. They can still be found at church suppers and family picnics.

The leaves of wintergreen are gathered in May. They contain a bitter, coarse salt mixed with a few balsamic and many earthy components. From them wintergreen derives its capacity to cool, to dry, and to cleanse and heal wounds and sores.

Wintergreen has a great reputation as a vulnerary for healing open injuries and fistulas, which is well confirmed by experience. Hence it is used for vulnerary potions as prepared in the following manner: Take a handful each of wintergreen, veronica, periwinkle, betony, lady's mantle, and sanicle; and half a handful each of scabious and ribwort plantain. Chop up the herbs, then tie them in a cloth bag. Put this in a vessel with three quarts of good white wine and one quart of water. Cook until reduced by one-third. Give the wounded person one gill of the decoction to drink every morning and evening.

A handful of wintergreen together with one loth of comfrey root cooked in two quarts of white wine will yield a drink that heals sores in the kidneys.

The distilled water of wintergreen taken daily before breakfast in six-tablespoon doses, or half so much of the expressed juice, will heal internal wounds. When used externally to wash old rotten sores, it will cleanse them.

An essence of wintergreen may be extracted in brandy, which is useful in healing wounds and sores, as well as injuries to the lungs and other internal parts. Take twenty to thirty drops a few times a day in water of plantain.

Wood Sorrel
Oxalis acetosella
Sauer: *Sauerklee* (1773)

Few people today would guess that this common weed has so many useful applications, or that it is even beneficial as a food, yet the eighteenth-century Germans in America were great advocates of this unassuming perennial. It is native to both Europe and North America, and is still commonly used in Germany as a salad green and in herbal remedies. It was not used as much by the English, for as John Evelyn pointed out in his Acetaria *(London, 1699), it had already grown "obsolete" by the late seventeenth century (73). However, the salts taken from the sap were sold by colonial druggists under the name Salt of Lemons. The cloverlike leaves and the stems yield the juice used in Sauer's recipes below, and the tiny yellow flowers were gathered to make the conserve or sugar.*

As the herbal emphasizes, the syrup was particularly important to rural people who worked in the fields. Since lemons were expensive, wood sorrel stood in for lemonade. And it was used extensively in Pennsylvania German cookery as a lemon substitute as well as for its inherently refreshing tartness, especially in dishes using kales and collards.

Wood sorrel has an acidic, mildly volatile salt in its sap, from which it derives its pleasantly tart taste. It is cold and dry in nature, and its virtues are similar to sorrel.

A water is distilled from wood sorrel that is serviceable for all internal inflammations. It will quench the thirst, protect against ardent fevers, refresh the heart, and withstand poison, provided a few tablespoons are drunk often. If it is gargled, it will heal sundry scurvies of the gums, and protect against croup.[272]

Conserve of wood sorrel is made like rose sugar, and is used for treating heat exhaustion, thirst, and pestilential ardent fevers. Take a dose the size of a nutmeg each time it is required.

The macerated juice of wood sorrel can be cooked with sugar to make an excellent syrup as follows: Take one pint of wood sorrel juice, strain it through a cloth, then add an equal quantity of white sugar. Let this cook down in a new earthenware pot over gentle coals until it attains the thickness of honey. Once it is cold, then store for later use. During the summer when it is excessively hot, one can prepare an excellent cooling drink with this syrup by stirring one or two tablespoons of it into a pint of fresh water. Take this before going out to work so that the heat will not readily do

272. The gargle was normally made by combining wood sorrel water with water of elecampane in about equal portions. Refer to elecampane on page 132.

harm. Anyone who is afflicted with hot, feverish illnesses can also prepare an excellent thirst- and fever-quenching drink with this syrup.

Wood sorrel can be used very beneficially in salads, soups, and when eaten with cooked greens. It stills rushing of the blood, and protects against its corruption.

Wormwood or Absinthe
Artemisia absinthium
Sauer: *Wermuth* (1762)

> *It was well known in Sauer's time that wormwood would check "immoderate venery." Considering his prudishness, it is surprising that he made no mention of this. When balanced against gentian, which was commonly used as a stomachic, it is apparent that Sauer's hand tilted toward wormwood, at least for afflictions of the stomach. Perhaps wormwood was simply easier to grow and obtain. Whatever the case, his primary concern here is with children's diseases. The dangers of absinthe need no explanation, especially the damage it inflicts upon the brain, but at least Sauer's remedies for children are external. His stomach bitters taken in wine were intended for adults. The taste is similar to Italian Fernet Branca.*

Wormwood warms and strengthens cold and feeble stomachs, purifies the blood from corruptions and gall, resists poison, and checks asthma and violent upheavals of the stomach. Wormwood is especially useful in treating all stomach ailments arising from cold.

Wormwood is equally good for treating cattle and sheep, hence herdsmen feed them wormwood mixed with salt as protection against contagion.

When death is spreading among cattle, fumigate the stables with wormwood every morning and evening.

If young children have worms, foment a mixture of wormwood, rue, centaury, and mint in a skillet with fresh butter. Rub this over the child's stomach during the waning of the moon, two or three times daily, and as warm as the child can bear it.

When children develop a cold stomach and no nourishment will stay in it because they either vomit it up or suffer from copious diarrhea, then smear the pit of their stomach with the above ointment and keep up the treatment for a day or two. Or, take the herbs enumerated above, either fresh or dry, and chop them fine. Put them in a vessel that can be closed tightly, and pour good quality-rum or brandy over them. Place the vessel over coals so that the infusion becomes quite hot but does not boil. When it has cooled enough so that a child can bear it, apply the liquid to the navel. Should this be accomplished prior to the commencement of puking, then put it on the pit of the stomach instead. If chamomile is added, it is quite good for stomachaches in children.

An excellent essence of wormwood can be made in the following manner: Take one loth of wormwood and half a loth each of holy thistle, centaury, galingale, calamus, and orange rind. Put this into a glass jar and pour eight loths of brandy or rum over it. Then strain off the infusion through a fine cloth and store away for future use. Take a dose of twenty to thirty drops or more in the morning in a glass of wine. This is very good for all manner of stomach debilities and for conditions brought on by cold, since it promotes appetite and protects against fevers.

Yarrow
Achillea millefolium
Sauer: *Garbenkraut, Schafribben* (1768)

> *This is not a plant that was normally cultivated in herb gardens. It is a common weed in Europe and is thought to have been naturalized in the eastern United States at a very early period during the colonial era. There is a western yarrow that is native, but Sauer would not have known about it during the mid-eighteenth century. In any event, the herbal is quite clear in pointing out that yarrow is inexpensive, a term used consistently for anything wild and easy to gather. Specifically, this is the white-flowering yarrow commonly found in fields, not the hybridized and richly colored yarrows now raised as ornamentals. Its use in medicine traces back to ancient times, and its reputation as a wound herb appears to have been universal. Yarrow tea is still popular and can be found in most herb shops and health food stores.*

Yarrow is of a middling nature, for it warms and dries softly. It has the capacity to stop all manner of fluxes and bleedings, and to cleanse and heal internal injuries. If the fresh leaves are beaten to a cataplasm and laid upon a wound, they will stop the bleeding. Yarrow is one of the foremost vulnerary herbs, for which it is used as an inexpensive wound potion.

Boil a handful of yarrow in two quarts of water. When drunk, this tea will protect pregnant women from untimely delivery.

Distilled water of yarrow heals all internal injuries. It will dissolve clotted blood, stop excessive flow of the menses and white discharges, and kill tapeworms, provided half a gill is drunk every morning and evening. When the mouth is rinsed with yarrow water, it will heal scurvy of the gums and festers on the gums and in the throat. If a small piece of linen is moistened with yarrow water and laid warm over the privates, it will heal the injury.

The flowers or leaves of yarrow dried in the shade and drunk from time to time as tea will stay pain and bleeding of the hemorrhoids.

The leaves, together with the flowers, are mingled with other herbs used in making brandy bitters. These bitters are of good service when made regular use of in housekeeping.

Zedoary
Curcuma zedoaria
Sauer: *Zitwer* (1772)

Herbalists in Sauer's day differentiated between two kinds of zedoary, the long (Zedoaria longa) and the round (Zedoaria rotunda). These are now recognized as varieties of the same plant, which was historically sometimes further confused with its near relative turmeric (Curcuma longa). Turmeric is the herb used in curries; zedoary is the herb of medicine. Both were imported to colonial America as dry roots from Indo-China and the East Indies.

Medical opinion was divided on zedoary, since its properties were the same as ginger. In fact, ginger was often given as far superior, so there was no need to resort to zedoary. However, its strength as a protection against contagion was undoubted, and this evidently sustained its popularity, especially in German-speaking countries. The idea of holding a piece of the root in the mouth, as similarly directed under angelica (page 52), was a practice held over from the Middle Ages. Unlike ginger root, zedoary will turn the mouth a bright yellow.

Zedoary is of a warm, dry nature and also possesses many oily, volatile, aromatic salts by which it operates in the same manner as ginger.

Zedoary warms all internal organs afflicted by cold, and strengthens the head, heart, and stomach. It is good against dizziness and fainting, takes away stinking breath, promotes digestion, awakens the appetite, prevents consumption, dissipates windiness, quiets choking, colic, and diarrhea, and counters coughing and bellyache such as arise from cold and vapors. It also allays swelling of the matrix, kills worms, opens blockages of the urine, and counteracts poison and contagion.

For all of the conditions and diseases enumerated above, a tincture of zedoary can be purchased from apothecaries. Take it in doses of one-half to a full teaspoon in a glass of wine a few times a day. This bitter tincture can be prepared at home this way: Take half a quint of ground zedoary root with two to three drops of oil of rosemary in warm wine. This is an excellent remedy for painful bloating of the lower belly and gut, and for the gripes in man and woman alike.

When pestilence or other contagious diseases are raging, and one is obliged to go out of the house or to be in the presence of infected persons, hold a small piece of zedoary root in the mouth.

For those who have developed a cough due to a strong cold, eat a little ground zedoary root mixed with a soft-cooked egg, or in wine.

To get rid of freckles on the face quickly, take powdered zedoary root, a little unslaked lime, and mix this with butter or honey. Every night, spread this as an ointment over the freckles and let it remain there. The following morning, wash it off with lukewarm water of solomon's seal or water of celandine. Indeed, if this ointment is smeared thickly over warts on the hands a few times a day, they will shortly dry up and fall off by themselves.

Glossary of Eighteenth-Century Medical Terms with English and German Equivalents

abscess *(Blutgeschwür)*: The German also covers such related conditions as phlegmon, ambury, and furnucle. These are infected areas that remain open and weep blood as well as other bodily fluids.

abortant *(abtreibende Mittel):* Any preparation that causes premature birth or "casting of the fetus."

ague *(kalte Fieber)*: Any cold fever accompanied by chills.

alexipharmic *(gegen Gift dienend)*: Any remedy as a preventive against poison or contagion.

anodyne *(schmertzstillend, schmertzstillende Mittel)*: Any remedy that eases pain.

antilithic water *(harntreibendes Wasser)*: Any herbal water or spirit that dissolves stones, gravel, and sand in the kidneys, loins, and bladder. Also called a diuretic.

apoplexy *(Schlagfluss)*: Equated today with a stroke.

ardent fever *(hitzige Fieber)*: Any hot, burning fever.

bilious *(gallig, gallicht)*: The opposite of phlegmatic; hot or violent. A bilious fever *(Gallenfieber)* is a choleric fever, a disease of Mars, a hot or violent distemper. Biliousness is characterized by hotness and dryness.

blood leech *(Blutegel)*: Any of several species of leeches raised for the purpose of drawing blood.

bloody flux *(rotes Ruhr)*: Dysentery.

capillaries *(Haarpflantze)*: The five capillaries or *quinque herbas capillares*, a group of herbs that included hart's tongue, maidenhair fern, and spleenwort.

carminative *(Wind treibend)*. Any herb employed to expel wind and swelling due to vapors. See **colic**.

cataplasm *(erweichende Unschlag)*: Called *cataplasmata* by Roman and medieval authors. Commonly defined as a poultice, although in its narrowest meaning a cataplasm is a finely pulped herb or herbal mixture.

cephalic *(Hauptstärkend)*: Any remedy that strengthens the brain and head.

chilblains *(Schrunden)*: Large cracks in the skin on the hands and feet.

clyster *(Klystier)*: An enema.

cold evil *(Harnwinden)*: Cold urine, dysury. Referred to in common speech of Sauer's era as cold piss.

colic *(Grimmen)*: A carminative *(Grimmenwasser)* is a remedy for colic, usually administered in liquid form in order to unbind the stomach. Generally associated with gripping, or intense contraction of the stomach and intestines.

constipation *(Verstopfung)*: Blockages of the bowels.

convulsion *(Krampf)*: Includes all conditions resembling convulsion. *Krampf* of the viscera is a stomach cramp.

cordial *(härzstärkend)*: Any medicine designed to lift the spirits.

decoction: An herbal remedy created by boiling or heating an herb in a liquid, which then acquires the properties of the herb and is administered as in internal or external medicine. Sauer normally refers to it simply as *Trank*. It is intended for immediate use.

diarrhea *(Ruhr)*: Remedies intended to mitigate or cure diarrhea were termed diarrhetic. The most common herbal diarrhetic was *Ruhrkraut*, or sandy everlasting *(Gnaphalium arenarium)*.

diet drink *(Arzneitrank, Kräutertrank)*: An herbal beverage taken habitually for a specific health benefit.

discuss *(zertheilen)*: To reduce inflammatory swellings by drawing infected matter away from the region of pain. A discutient remedy *(zertheilendes Mittel)* was any medication that "discussed" or reduced such a swelling. The herbs employed in these remedies were generally astringent in action.

diuretic *(harntreibendes Mittel)*: Medication that promotes urination; see **asparagus**, page 48, for example. Do not confuse with diarrhetic.

dizziness *(Schwindel)*: An herbal spirit used as a remedy for dizziness was called a cephalic water *(Schwindelwasser)*. The German term also includes vertigo.

dropsy *(Wassersucht)*: Watery swellings of the tissues or cavities of the body.

emollientia *(erweichende Kräuter)*: The five emollients *(emollientia)* were blue mallow, French mercury, marshmallow, pellitory-of-the-wall, and violets. All of these herbs share in common a mucilaginous texture and a faculty for softening and loosening gently. They were often employed in enemas.

eructation *(Aufstossen)*: Belching or burping. Caused by a surfeit of vapors.

end gut *(Afterdarm)*: The rectum. The actual opening of the rectum is referred to by Sauer as the "eye" *(Auge)*. In English this was called the arse or fundament.

essence: Chemical properties of an herb that have been drawn out in alcohol and which form the lightest, uppermost part of the infusion.

evil thing *(böses Ding)*: See "felon."

extract: An essence boiled or reduced to the consistency of honey.

falling sickness or **falling evil** *(fallende Sucht)*: Epilepsy.

finger worm *(Fingerwurm)*: See **felon.**

felon *(Fingergeschwüre)*: A whitlow or inflammation of the finger or toe, often involving the quick under the nails.

fetus *(Leibesfrucht)*: Sauer's German implies that the fetus is not a person but rather a product or "fruit" of the female body. The term *Kind*, "child," is not used until after birth takes place. This does not imply that abortion was viewed lightly or in purely clinical terms. The removal of unwanted fetuses was evidently common-place among the German element, but done in secret due to the social and legal stigma attached to it. Many herbs were useful for accomplishing this (see **abortant**).

Another condition treated in Sauer was the *unzeitige Leibesfrucht*, "casting of the fetus," now more generally referred to as miscarriage. This left the woman highly vulnerable to a range of diseases and injuries for which herbal remedies were recommended. Feverfew or *Mutterkraut*, "womb herb," was one of the most important.

fistula *(Fistel)*: An abnormal passage leading from an abscess or hollow organ of the body.

flux *(Fluss)*: Any excessive flow of bodily secretions.

foment *(bähen)*: To boil up to the scalding point, then quickly remove from the heat. Preparations made this way were generally intended for relieving pain. When the verb is used with bread, it means to toast it by the fire. This is found in medieval cookery where sauces are brought to a quick boil for just enough time to soften the ingredients.

gout *(Podagara)*: Extreme pain in the joints, especially in the feet. Flying gout *(läufende Gichtern)* is rheumatic pain in the joints that moves about, as for example, in the wrist one day and perhaps in the shoulder the next.

gravel, the gravel *(Griess)*: *Griesskraut*, known in English as wild mint, bastard mint, or stinking balm, was the most popular herb remedy for this condition. *Lendengriess*, or gravel of the loins, was a painful condition.

gripes, the gripes: See **colic**.

humors *(Feuchtigkeiten des Körpers)*: Fluid components of the body or blood. Also bodily temperaments determined by the condition of the blood. Humors of the blood were specifically referred to as *Säfte* in German. There were several types.

hypochondria *(Miltzweh)* and **hypochondriasis** *(Miltzsucht)*: In the context of the Sauer herbal, any illness or condition arising from the spleen. Splenetic vapors *(Blähung des Miltzes)* were humors thought to originate in the spleen. The neurosis now called hypochondria was known euphemistically as "heart worm" in Sauer's era.

hysterics, hysterical passion, mother fit *(Mutterweh)*: The pain associated with menstruation, commonly known as cramps.

iliac passion *(Darmgicht)*: Volvulus, or twisting of the intestine upon itself.

jaundice *(Gelbsucht)*: A condition characterized by yellowness of the skin, eyes, and urine due to the presence of bile, and generally associated with liver complaints such as hepatitis. Remedies against jaundice are called icteric.

julep *(Julep, Kuhltrank)*: Any drink made from roughly two ounces of syrup in combination with a pint of herbal water (usually distilled), and normally taken to prepare for purging or to open the body of obstructions, or to open the pores. Juleps were generally categorized as camphorated, cordial, expectorating, saline, or vomiting, depending on their purpose.

lumbago or **hip gout** *(Lendenweh)*: Rheumatic pain of the loins and small of the back.

lye *(Lauge)*: Used extensively in scalp and hair remedies. In all cases, the solution is mild rather than the highly caustic grades of lye used for such things as soap making.

matrix *(Mutter)*: The womb or uterus.

may butter *(Maienbutter)*: Butter left in the sun for several days to oxidize and destroy the vitamin A while increasing vitamin D manyfold. Thus enriched with vitamin D, it was employed in medicines, often in anodyne applications.

milk fever *(Milchfieber)*: A condition brought on by clogged milk ducts in the breasts of nursing women.

miscarriage: See **fetus**.

mordant *(scharfe)*: Mordant blood *(schärfes Geblüth)* was thought to contain sharp, cutting, burning constituents that, by modern medical definition, could account for any number of afflictions. Thus it is not so much a malady in and of itself as perhaps a symptom of other, more complex internal dysfunctions.

nervine *(Nervenstärkend)*: A remedy that strengthens the nerves.

oxymel: see **syrup**.

pectoral sores or **empyema** *(Brustgeschwüre)*: An accumulation of pus in the pleura cavity (the region beneath the ribs).

phlegmatic dropsy *(schleimblütige Wassersucht, schleimige Wassersucht)*: Thick, watery swellings of a mucous or viscous character.

phlegmatic humors *(schleimblütige Flüsse)*: Thick, mucusy fluids.

plethoric *(vollblütig)*: A condition of the bodily humors characterized by full-bodiedness, a superabundance of nutritive materials in the bodily organs, an excess of blood, a bloated nature. Often associated with persons of bombastic character.

pleurisy *(Seitenstecken)*: Inflammation of the pleura or ribs accompanied by coughing, difficult breathing, and a buildup of fluids in the region beneath the ribs.

purples *(Friesel)*: Also called rush *(purpurea hemorrhagica)*. It is characterized by bloody spots and bubbles in the skin. There are both red and white strains of the disease, which commonly affects children.

pursiness *(Keuchen)*: Generally defined in Sauer's day as asthmatic panting or shortness of breath. Asthmatic coughing (even tubercular coughing) could also be associated with this condition.

quartan ague *(viertägige Fieber)*: An acute fever of malarial character attended by paroxysms of chills, fever, and sweating at regular intervals every four days. Thought to have been brought on by putrefaction of melancholic humors.

quinsy *(Bräune des Halses)*: An old term for sore throat.

rheums of the head *(Hauptflüsse)*: Watery or catarrhal discharges.

Saint Anthony's fire *(Rothlauf)*: Erysipelas—an acute fever with swelling of the skin, caused by streptococcus—or ergotism, poisoning by a fungus that grows on rye.

scall *(Erbgrind)*: Sores and scabs on the scalp as well as profuse flaking of the skin in the form of dandruff. In severe cases, the sores were runny.

scurvy: Scurvy of the gums *(Mundfäule)* was another common condition brought about by a vitamin C deficiency.

simple *(einfache Heilmittel)*: A drug or medicine composed of one ingredient, usually an herb. The English is derived from Latin *simplicia*.

spleen *(Miltz)* and **splenetic vapors**: See **hypochondria**.

sudorific *(Schweisstreibend)*: A remedy that promotes sweating as a means of driving out bodily poisons and contagions.

syrup *(Syrop, Zuckersaft)*: A decoction made with sugar or honey for longer keeping than a simple decoction. Syrups made with vinegar and honey were called oxymels.

tenesmus *(Stuhlzwang)*: Involuntary sensations of urgent bowel movement or urination.

tertian ague *(dreitägige Fieber)*: An acute fever of malarial character attended by paroxysms of chills, fever, and sweating at regular intervals every three days. Thought to have been brought on by the putrefaction of choleric humors.

tincture *(Tinctur)*: One of the most famous tinctures of Sauer's era was Daffy's Elixir, which was nothing more than a tincture of senna. Refer to **senna** (page 285). It was sold as a laxative.

tunicle *(Häutchen)*: A film or thin covering of fleshy material.

vagina *(Mutterscheide)*: This term is used in many places in the herbal, but never written as a complete word, evidently because it was considered too indelicate to spell out. Instead, Sauer used the abbreviation "M. S." Likewise, he used "M. R." *(monatliche Ruhr)* for menstruation and menstrual blood. See also **hysterics**.

vapors *(Blähungen)*: Gases rising from the stomach, or downward through the body. Also air or gases that were thought to move through the blood and brain, thus causing lightheadedness.

vulnerary *(Wundkraut)*: Any herb used to cleanse or heal open wounds or surgical incisions. A balsam made from such herbs was called a vulnerary balsam *(Wundbalsam)*. A vulnerary potion was a decoction or infusion intended to heal internal wounds and injuries. It could also serve as a dressing to clean and heal external wounds or surgical incisions. A vulnerary water *(Wundwasser)* was a distillate used externally to irrigate and to heal open wounds.

wen *(Kropf)*: Sebaceous cyst.

whites *(Weisseflüsse, or die Weisse)*: White fluids flowing from the uterus, sometimes very thick and milky. Now called leucorrhea, this condition was rather common in eighteenth-century women.

wind or **windiness** *(Winde)*: This is a term that covered a number of conditions from basic flatulence to the **vapors** (burping gas, gurgling of the stomach, and so forth). Also see **eructation**.

Bibliography

Translations of German titles are provided in parentheses after the German. This does not imply that the work cited exists in full English translation. Many of the works cited below are now extremely rare.

Adam's Luxury and Eve's Cookery; or, The Kitchen-Garden Displayed. London, 1744.

Aengeln, P. V. *Der verständige Gärtner/Über die zwölff Monaten des Jahres* (The clever gardener/On the twelve months of the year). Hannover, 1673.

L'Albert moderne (The modern Albert Magnus). Paris, 1769.

Die Amerikanische Goldgrube (The American gold mine). Lebanon, Pa., 1810. The "gold" is nuggets of useful information.

Auer, Johann. *Der Deutsche Weingärtner* (The German vintner). Reading, Pa., 1849. Auer, originally from Switzerland, owned the Schweizerhalle Winery in Bethel, Berks County, Pennsylvania.

Bartram, John. *The Correspondence of John Bartram, 1734–1777.* edited by Edmund and Dorothy Berkeley, Gainesville, Fla.: University Press of Florida, 1992.

Baumann, Helmut. *The Greek Plant World in Myth, Art and Literature.* Portland, Oreg.: Timber Press, 1993.

Baynon, Eliam. *Der Barmherziger Samariter; oder, Freund und Brüderlicher Rath, allerley Krankheiten und Gebrechen des Menschlichen Leibs, innerlich und äusserlich zu heilen* (The Good Samaritan; or, Friendly and brotherly advice for healing divers internal and external maladies and injuries of the human body). Hanover, Pa., 1798.

The Beauties of Creation; or, A New Moral System of Natural History. Philadelphia, 1796.

Becker, Christian. *Unterricht für amerikanische Bauern, Weinberge anzulegen und zu unterhalten* (Instruction to American farmers on the laying out and maintenance of vineyards). Easton, Pa., 1809.

Bernisches Koch-Büchlein (The Bernese handbook of cookery). Bern, 1749. This cookbook is indeed little, as in pocket-size, useful for sticking into an apron pocket.

Biernauer, Jacob. *Das unentbehrliche Haus- und Kunst-Buch* (The indispensable domestic recipe book). Reading, Pa., 1818.

Bock, Hieronymus. *Kreütterbuch* (Herbal). Strasbourg, 1577. First published in 1546.
———. *Teütsche Speizkammer* (The German larder). Strasbourg, 1550.

Böckler, Georg Andreas. *Furnologia; oder, Haushältliche Oefen-Kunst* (Stoveology; or,

The art of building stoves for domestic use). Frankfurt, 1666.

———. *Der nützliche Hauss- und Feld-Schule* (The school of practical management for house and field). Nuremberg, 1678. There was also a 1699 edition.

Bradley, Martha. *The British Housewife.* Blackawton/Totnes, England: Prospect Books, 1996. 6 vols. Facsimile reprint of the 1756 London edition.

Brandt, Harry A. *Christopher Sower and Son.* Elgin, Ill.: Brethren Publishing House, 1938.

Braunschweig, Hieronymus. *Kleines Distillierbuch: Liber de Arte Distillandi de Simplicibus* (Short guide to distilling: The art of distilling pure substances). Strasbourg, 1500.

Briggs, Richard. *The New Art of Cookery, According to the Present Practice.* Philadelphia, 1792.

[Brotherton, Mary]. *Vegetable Cookery.* London, 1833. First published in 1829.

Brown, O. Phelps. *The Complete Herbalist.* Jersey City, N.J., 1875.

Buchan, William. *Domestic Medicine.* Exeter, N.H., 1843.

———. *Every Man His Own Doctor.* New Haven, Conn., 1816.

Byrd, William. *The Secret Diary of William Byrd of Westover, 1709–1712.* 2 vols. Edited by Louis B. Wright and Marion Tinling. Richmond, Va.: Dietz Press, 1941.

Camerarius, Joachim. *Hortus Medicus et Philosophicus.* Frankfurt, 1588.

Cato, Marcus Porcius. *On Farming/De Agricultura.* Trans. Andrew Dalby, Blackawton/Totnes, England: Prospect Books, 1998.

Cavane, Peter. *A Dissertation on the Oleum Palmae Christi, sive Oleum Ricini.* Bath, England: 1764.

Colbatch, Sir John. *The Treatment of Epilepsy by Mistletoe.* London, 1720.

Coler, Johannes. *Calendrium perpetuum; et libri oeconomici* (The perpetual calendar, and books on home and farm management). Wittenberg, 1592 and 1596. Two separate works issued as part I and part II, then later combined as one book.

———. *Economia Ruralis et Domestica darinnen des Gantze Ampt aller Treuer Haus-Vätter und Haus-Mütter* (Rural and domestic economy, in which is found the full employment of all faithful husbands and wives). Frankfurt, 1692.

Le Confiturier françois. Paris, 1667. Sometimes attributed to La Varenne.

Cooper, J. W. *The Experienced Botanist or Indian Physician.* Lancaster, Pa., 1840.

Culpeper, Nicholas. *Culpeper's Complete Herbal and English Physician.* Manchester, 1826. This is essentially a new edition of the title issued in 1673 as *Pharmacopaeia Londonensis.* Hand-colored plates.

Daems, Willem F. *Nomina simplicium medicinarum ex synonymariis medii aevi collecta: Semantische Untersuchungen zum Fachwortschatz Hoch- und Spätmittelalterlicher Drogenkunde* (Semantic research into the body of technical words used in medieval and late medieval pharmacology). Leiden: E. J. Brill, 1993.

D'Andrea, Jeanne. *Ancient Herbs.* Malibu, Calif.: J. Paul Getty Museum, 1989.

Darlington, William. *Flora Cestrica* (Plants of Chester County). West Chester, Pa., 1837.

Davies, John. *The Innkeeper and Butler's Guide.* Leeds, 1806.

[De Benneville, George]. "Hausmittel und Behandlung der Frau vor, während und nach der Entbindung" (Home remedies and treatment of the mother before, during, and following confinement). Manuscript AC.988 Cassel Collection, The Historical Society of Pennsylvannia, Philadelphia. Original manuscript for a handbook never published by the Sauer press.

De Benneville, George. *Der Merkwürdige Lebens-Lauf, die sonderbare Bekehrung und Entzückungen des ohnlängst bey Germantown (in Pennsylvanien) wohnenden und verstobenen Dr. George de Benneville* (The remarkable life, singular conversion and spiritual rapture of the late Dr. George de Benneville, who lived and died at Germantown [in Pennsylvania]). Baltimore, 1798.

de Bonnefons, Nicolas. *Les Delices de la campagne.* Amsterdam, 1661. It may be interesting to note that Jean Blaeu's printing press, used for this book, was sold to Ephrata Cloister in Pennsylvania and used there for publishing books throughout the 1700s.

de Caus, Salomon. *Hortus Palatinus* (The garden of the elector of the Palatinate). Frankfurt, 1620.

de Combles, M. *L'École du potager.* 2 vols. Paris, 1749.

Dembinska, Maria. *Food and Drink in Medieval Poland.* Edited by William Woys Weaver. Philadelphia: University of Pennsylvania Press, 1999.

de Rossi, Martino. *Il libro de maestro Martino de Rossi.* Aldo Bertoluzza, ed. Trento, Italy: Edizzioni U.C.T., 1993. Partial facsimile of a circa 1400 cookbook.

Drey, Rudolf E. *Apothecary Jars.* London: Faber and Faber, 1978.

Dunal, Mich. Felix. *Histoire naturelle, médicale et économique des solanum.* Montpellier, 1813.

Eger, Rudolf, ed. *Rezepte und Hausmittel aus Vier Jahrhunderten* (Four hundred years of receipts and home remedies). Zurich: Fretz und Wasmuth, 1955.

Die Englische Goldgrube für das bürgerliche Leben (The English gold mine for urban living). Ulm, 1827.

Erdmann, Charles. *Das gelbe Fieber in Philadelphia* (Yellow fever in Philadelphia). Philadelphia, 1799.

Evelyn, John. *Acetaria: A Discourse of Sallets.* London, 1699.

Fallopius, Gabriel. *Observationes Anatomicae.* Cologne, 1562
——. *De Simplicibus Medicamentis Purgantibus.* Venice, 1565.

Fiedler, Johann Gottfried. *De Cura Avenacea/Von der Haber-Kur.* Halle, 1714.

Fischer, Christian. *Approbirtes Kunst- und Hausbuch* (The approved domestic receipt book). Reutlingen, 1830. The first edition appeared in 1811.

Flory, John S. *Literary Activity of the German Baptist Brethren in the Eighteenth Century.* Elgin, Ill.: Brethren Publishing House, 1908.

Förster, Johann Christian, and Johann Dietrich Knopf. *Braunschweigisches Kochbuch* (The Braunschweig cookbook). Braunschweig, 1789.

Futhey, J. Smith, and Gilbert Cope. *History of Chester County, Pennsylvania.* Philadelphia, 1881.

Gabriel, Peter. *Kurzer Bericht von der Pest.* Philadelphia, 1793.

Georgiades, Cristos Ch. *Flowers of Cyprus: Plants of Medicine.* Nicosia, Cyprus: Cosmos Press, 1985.

————. *Flowers of Cyprus: Plants of Medicine II.* Nicosia: Loris Stavrinides and Sons, 1987.

Gerard, John. *The General Historie of Plants.* New York: Dover Publications, Inc., 1975. Facsimile reprint of the 1633 edition, revised and enlarged by Thomas Johnson. The herbal originally appeared in 1597.

Germershausen, Christian Friedrich. *Die Hausmutter in allen ihren Geschäfften* (The housewife in all her domestic duties). Leipzig, 1778.

Grabner, Elfriede. "Theodor Zwinger und die Heilkunde" (Theodor Zwinger and the art of healing). In *Festschrift für Robert Wildhaber,* Edited by Walter Escher, Theo Gantner, and Hans Trümpy, 171–84. Basel: Verlag G. Krebs, 1973.

Griggs, Barbara. *Green Pharmacy: A History of Herbal Medicine.* London: Norman and Hobhouse, 1981.

Halle, Johann Samuel. *Magie; oder, Die Zauberkräfte der Natur* (Magic, or the magical powers of nature). 6 vols. Berlin, 1785–86.

Hatch, Peter J. *The Fruits and Fruit Trees of Monticello.* Charlottesville: University Press of Virginia, 1998.

Heinen, Henry. *Gesundheits-Schatzkammer* (Treasury of health). Lancaster, Pa., 1831.

[Heinitsch, Carl Heinrich]. *Anweisung zum Gebrauch der folgenden Gekräuter* (Advice on the use of the following herbs). Lancaster, Pa., ca. 1800. This four-page pamphlet, dealing with such herbs as betony, lemon balm, and wall fern, was distributed by Lancaster druggist Carl Heinrich Heinitsch. The date (suggested by German bibliographer Werner Tannhof) is only tentative; Heinitsch died in 1803.

Hennebo, Dieter, and Alfred Hoffmann. *Geschichte der Deutschen Gartenkunst* (History of German gardening). 3 vols. Hamburg, 1962.

Hildegard of Bingen. *Heilkunde: Das Buch von dem Grund und Wesen und der Heilung der Krankheiten* (The art of healing: The book on its essence and nature and on curing the sick). Edited by Heinrich Schipperges. Salzburg: Otto Müller Verlag, 1957.

Hill, John. *The Useful Family Herbal.* London, 1755.

Hirte, Tobias. *Der Freund in der Noth, oder Zweyter Theil des Neuen Auserlesenen Gemeinnützigen Hand-Büchleins* (Companion to the needy, or part two of the manual of new selections for the common good). Germantown, Pa., 1793.

Hoffmann, Friedrich. *Clavis Pharmaceutica Schroederiana.* Halle, 1675.

Hohman, Johann Georg. *Die Land- und Haus-Apotheke* (The rural and domestic apothecary). Reading, Pa., 1818.

House, E. G. *The Botanic Family Friend.* Boston, 1844.

Hovorka, O. von, and A. Kronfeld. *Vergleichende Volksmedicin* (Comparative folk medicine). 2 vols. Stuttgart: Verlag von Strecker & Schröder, 1909.

Hufeland, Christoph Wilhelm. *Makrobiotik; oder, Die Kunst des menschliche Leben zu Verlängern* (Macrobiotics; or, the art of prolonging human life). 2 vols. Reutlingen, 1817 and 1818. First published in 1796.

Jenner, Thomas. *A Book of Fruits and Flowers*. London, 1653. Reprint, London: Prospect Books, 1984.

Kaiser, Hermann. "Kochen in Dunst und Qualm: Herdfeuer und Herdgerät im Rauchhaus" (Cooking in fumes and smoke: The raised hearth and hearth utensils in the old farmhouse kitchen). *Volkskunst* (Folk art) 10 (November, 1987): 5–10.

Käser, Fredi, et al. *Heilkräutergarten und historische Drogerie* (The medical herb garden and historical pharmacy). Ballenberg, Switzerland: Schweizerisches Freilichtmuseum Ballenberg, 1989.

[Keyser, Johann Gottlieb.] *Die höchst berühmten Wurmverteilgende Zucker-Pflaumen* (The highly renowned worm repellent sugar plums). Philadelphia, ca. 1770. Printed broadside handout distributed by peddlers or by Keyser, the merchant who sold the sugar plums. Roughwood Collection (Devon, Pa.).

Kimball, Marie. *Thomas Jefferson's Cook Book*. 1938. Reprint, Charlottesville, Va.: University Press of Virginia, 1976.

Knörin, R. Christine. *Göppinger Kochbuch; oder, Neue Sammlung vieler Vorschriften* (The Göppinger cookbook; or, New collection of numerous receipts). Stuttgart: 1798.

Körber-Grohne, Udelgard. *Nutzplantzen in Deutschland: Kulturgeschichte und Biologie* (Useful plants in Germany: Cultural history and biology). Stuttgart: Konrad Theiss Verlag, 1988.

Krafft, Michael. *The American Distiller*. Philadelphia, 1804.

Krössler, Heinrich Philipp. *Magia Alba et Nigra*. [Allentown, Pa.], 1847. Illustrated manuscript of ritual and cabalistic magic. Roughwood Collection (Devon, Pa.).

Kurtzer Unterricht vom Anbau, und nutzlichen Gebrauche der Kirbse, oder sogenannte Plizer (Brief instructions on the cultivation and useful applications of the pumpkin, or so-called *Plizer)*. Freysing, 1773.

Kurtzgefasstes Arzney-Büchlein für Menschen und Vieh (Concise manual of remedies for man and beast). Ephrata, Pa., 1798. The printer claimed that this was the seventeenth edition; if so, the earlier ones are not recorded.

Kurtzgefasstes Weiber-Büchlein: Enthält Aristotels und Alberti Magni Hebammen-Kunst, mit den darzu gehörigen Recepten (The midwife's digest: Containing the art of midwifery according to Aristotle and Albertus Magnus, with appropriate remedies). (Harrisburg, Pa.), 1799. The copy studied belonged to Elizabeth Erb, a Lancaster County, Pennsylvania, midwife during the 1830s and 1840s. Interior chapter headings claim that some of the material is taken from Nicholas Culpeper.

Kyger, M. Ellsworth. *An English–Pennsylvania German Dictionary*. 3 vols. Birdsboro, Pa.: Pennsylvania German Society, 1986.

"Lambs Quarters & Water Cresses for the Soldiers." *Report: A Journal of German-American History* (Society for the History of the Germans in Maryland) 36 (1975): 25.

Landsberg, Sylvia. *The Medieval Garden*. New York: Thames & Hudson, 1995.

Le Cuisinier françois. Edited by Philip Hyman and Mary Hyman. Paris: Editions Montalba, 1983. A reprint collection of several French cookery books from the seventeenth century, bound together as one work.

Löffler, Friederike. *Oekonomisches Handbuch für Frauenzimmer* (Economical manual for the domestic arts). Stuttgart, 1795.

Maranta, Venusinus. *Libri duo de theriaca et Mithridatio.* Edited by Joachim Camerarius. Venice, 1576.

Marzell, Heinrich. *Geschichte und Volkskunde der deutschen Heilpflanzen* (History and folklore of German healing plants). Darmstadt: Wissenschaftliche Buchgesellschaft, 1967.

Mawe, Thomas, and John Abercrombie. *Every Man His Own Gardener.* London, 1779.

Mayers, Johann Friedrich. *Neunte Fortsetzung der Beyträge und Abhandlungen zur Aufnahme der Land- und Hauswirtschaft* (The ninth continuation of contributions and treatises on the promotion of agriculture and the domestic arts). Frankfurt, 1780.

Melin, Jacob. *Grätzerisches Kochbuch* (The Gratzer cookbook). 7th ed. Graz, 1802. First published 1791.

McHarry, Samuel. *The Practical Distiller; or, An Introduction to Making, Whisky, Gin, Brandy, Spirits.* Harrisburg, Pa., 1809.

Meier, Louis A. *Early Pennsylvania Medicine.* Boyertown, Pa.: Gilbert Printing, 1976. In spite of the broad title, the book actually focuses on Montgomery County, Pennsylvania.

Meissner, N. N. W. *Vollständiges Englisch-Deutsches und Deutsch-Englisches Wörterbuch* (Complete English-German and German-English dictionary). 2 vols. Leipzig, 1847.

M., W. [authorship unknown]. *The Compleat Cook* and *A Queens Delight.* London: Prospect Books, 1984. Reprint of the 1671 editions, both of which first appeared in 1655.

Meyer, Werner. *Hirsebrei und Hellebarde: Auf den Spuren des mittelalterlichen Lebens in der Schweiz* (Millet mush and halberds: Tracking down the vestiges of medieval life in Switzerland). Olten/Freiburg im Breisgau: Walter Verlag, 1985.

Miller, Joseph. *Der Verborgene Arzt; oder, Nützliche Hausfreund* (The secret physician; or, Useful household companion). New Berlin, Pa., 1830.

Miller, Philip. *The Gardener's Dictionary.* London, 1731.

Millspaugh, Charles. *American Medicinal Plants.* Philadelphia, 1892.

M'Mahon, Bernard. *The American Gardener's Calendar.* Philadelphia, 1806.

Moss, Kay K. *Southern Folk Medicine.* Columbia: University of South Carolina Press, 1999.

Neues Gothaisches Kochbuch (New Gotha cookbook). Gotha, 1804.

Neunteufl, Herta. *Kochkunst im Barock* (Baroque cookery). Graz/Vienna: Leykam Verlag, 1976.

Neuvermehrtes Schlesisches Haus- und Wirtschafts-Buch (New improved Silesian encyclopedia on household economy and agriculture). Breslau, 1746.

Noack, Kurt. *Der Kräutergarten auf Burg Lichtenberg* (The physic garden at Lichtenberg Castle). Kusel: Pfalzmuseum für Naturkunde/Burg Lichtenberg, 1989.

O'Hara-May, June. *Elizabethan Dietary of Health*. Lawrence, Kans.: Coronado Press, 1977.

Padulosi, Stefano, ed. *Oregano: Proceedings of the IPGRI International Workshop on Oregano*. Rome: International Plant Genetic Resources Institute, 1997.

Paulli, Simon. *D. Medici Regii . . . de Simplicium Medicamentorum Facultatibus*. Strasbourg, 1667.

Peuckert, Will-Erich. *Pansophie: Ein Versuch zur Geschichte der weissen und schwarzen Magie* (Pansophia: An investigation into the history of white and black magic). Berlin: Erich Schmidt Verlag, 1956.

Pfisterer, M. Daniel. *Barockes Welttheater: Ein Buch von Menschen, Tieren, Blumen, Gewächsen und Allerley Einfällen* (The Baroque world-theater: A book of people, animals, flowers, garden plants, and sundry impressions). 2 vols. Stuttgart: Quell Verlag, 1996. Facsimile reprint of an illustrated manuscript begun in 1716.

Pomet, Pierre. *A Complete History of Drugs*. 2 vols. London, 1712.

Prince, William Robert. *The Pomological Manual*. New York, 1832.

Querner, Emil. *Der Selbstarzt; oder, Doctor und Apotheker* (Your own physician; or, Doctor and apothecary). Allentown, Pa., 1886.

Reichman, Felix. *Christopher Sauer, Sr., Printer in Germantown, 1694–1758: An Annotated Bibliography*. Philadelphia: Carl Schurz Foundation, 1943.

Rhagor, Daniel. *Pflantz-Garten*. Bern, 1639.

Roberts, Job. *The Pennsylvania Farmer*. Philadelphia, 1804.

Rohr, Julius Bernhard von. *Compendieuse Haushaltungs-Biblotheck* (The compendious household library). Leipzig, 1716.

Roze, Ernest. *Charles de l'Escluse d'Arras: Le Propagateur de la pomme de terre*. Paris, 1899.

Rozier, Abbé Françoise. *Cours complet d'agriculture* (Complete course on agriculture). 10 vols. plus 2 supplements. Paris, 1781-1805.

Ruata, C. *Farmacopea nazionale e generale: Materia medica e terapia*. Padova, 1883.

Rupp, I. Daniel. *The Farmer's Complete Farrier*. Lancaster, Pa., 1842.

Ruthven, Lord. *The Ladies Cabinet Enlarged and Opened*. London, 1654.

Schellhammer, Maria Sophia. *Das Brandenburgische Koch-Buch* (The Brandenburg cookbook). Berlin, 1732. This is the sixth edition of two separate works that first appeared in 1697 and 1699.

———. *Der Wohl-unterweisenen Köchin zufälliger Confect-Taffel* (A suprise platter of sweets for the well-instructed cook). Berlin, 1732. Published separately from the Brandenburg cookbook, but often bound with it.

Schmidt, Daniel. *Das gemeinnützige Haus-Artzeneybuch* (Book of domestic medicine for the common good). Carlisle, Pa., 1826.

Schmidt, Johann Jakob. *Biblischer Medicus; oder, Betrachtung des Menschen, nach der Physiologie, Pathologie und Gesundheitslehre* (The biblical physician; or, the consideration of man according to the teachings of physiology, pathology, and health). Züllichau, 1743.

Schoepf, Johann David. *Travels in the Confederation, 1783–1784*. Translated by Alfred

J. Morrison. New York: Burt Franklin, 1968. Reprint of the Philadelphia edition of 1911.

———. *Materia Medica Americana Potissimum Regni Vegetabilis.* Cincinnati: Bulletin of the Lloyd Library of Botany, 1903. Reprint of the Erlangen edition of 1787.

Schroeder, Johann. *Pharmacopoeia Medico-Chymica, sive Thesaurus Pharmacologicus.* Leiden, 1672.

Schwinn, Karl. *Speis und Trank im Odenwald* (Food and drink in the Odenwald). Mörlenbach: Verlag Marga Hosemann, 1984.

Seidensticker, Peter. *Corpus Herbariorum: Frühe Deutsche Kräuterbücher* (Corpus Herbariorum: Early German herbals). Lahr: Moritz Schauenburg Verlag, 1990. Vol. 1 (1990) begins with the *Promptuarium Medicinae* (Magdeburg, 1483); other works in this series are planned.

de Serres, Olivier. *Théatre d'agriculture et mesnage des champs.* Rouen, 1623.

Spencer, Darrell. *The Gardens of Salem: The Landscape History of a Moravian Town in North Carolina.* Winston-Salem, N.C.: Old Salem, 1997.

Spolverini, Gian Battista. *La coltivazione del riso* (The cultivation of rice). Verona, 1758.

Sprague, T. A. "The Herbal of Otto Brunfels." *Journal of the Linnean Society of London* 48 (1928): 79–124.

Stepan, Eduard. *Das Ybbstal* (The Ybbs Valley). Vienna: Verlag Dr. Eduard Stepan, 1948. See specifically "Pflanzenwelt," 51–89, for folk terminologies and plant uses.

Stoeffler, F. Ernst. *Continental Pietism and Early American Christianity.* Grand Rapids, Mich.: William B. Erdmans, 1976.

Stoffler, Hans-Dieter. *Der Hortulus des Wahlafrid Strabo* (The herb garden of Wahlafrid Strabo). Sigmaringen: Jan Thorbecke Verlag, 1978.

Tennent, John. *Ein Jeder sein eigner Doctor* (Every man his own doctor). Philadelphia, 1749.

Thieme, Johann Christoph. *Haus-, Feld-, Arzney-, Koch-, Kunst-, und Wunder-Buch* (Household encyclopedia of domestic, field, medical, cookery, craft, and natural sciences). Nuremberg, 1700.

Thomson, Samuel. *Neue Anweisung zu Gesundheit* (A new method for health). Lancaster, Ohio, 1828.

Tobyn, Graeme. *Culpeper's Medicine: A Practice of Western Holistic Medicine.* Shaftesbury, Dorset, England: Element Books, 1997.

Vollständiges Nürnbergisches Koch-Buch (The complete Nuremberg cookbook). Nuremberg, 1691.

von Sazenhofen, Carl J. *Gerätfibel: Bauernküche* (A utensil primer: The farmhouse kitchen). Munich: L. Staackmann Verlag, 1979.

Die wahre Brantwein-Brennerey; oder, Brantwein-, Gin-, und Cordialmacher-Kunst (True brandy distillery; or, The art of making brandy, gin, and cordials). York, Pa., 1797. This is an adaptation of a popular English manual.

Walde, Kurt. *Der Innsbrucker Hofgarten und andere Gartenanlagen in Tirol* (The palace garden at Innsbruck and other landscaped gardens in Tyrol). Innsbruck: Universitätsverlag Wagner, 1964.

Weaver, William Woys. *Heirloom Vegetable Gardening.* 2nd ed. New York: Henry Holt, 1999.

Weber, L. W. *Der kluge Land-Medicus und Haus-Apotheke* (The handy rural doctor and domestic apothecary). Chambersburg, Pa., 1846. Weber's index of herbs in German and English is based on the Sauer herbal.

Weiler, Sophie Juliane. *Augsburgisches Kochbuch* (The Augsburg cookbook). Augsburg, 1790.

Wheaton, Barbara. *Savoring the Past.* Philadelphia: University of Pennsylvania Press, 1983.

Wilkinson, Alix. *The Garden in Ancient Egypt.* London: Rubicon Press, 1998.

Willich, A. M. F. *The Domestic Encyclopedia.* 3 vols. Edited by Thomas Cooper. Philadelphia, 1821.

Wilmann, Christa M.. "A Small Herbal of Little Cost, 1762–1778: A Case Study of a Colonial Herbal as a Social and Cultural Document." Ph.D. diss., University of Pennsylvania, Philadelphia, 1980.

Wilson, C. Anne. *Food and Drink in Britain.* New York: Barnes and Noble, 1974.

———. *The Book of Marmalade.* New York: St. Martins/Marek, 1985.

Wolf, Johann Christian. *Neues Leipziger Koch-Buch* (The new Leipzig cookbook). Frankfurt/Leipzig, 1779.

Wollenweber, Ludwig. *Die Berg-Maria* (Mountain Mary). Philadelphia, 1882.

Woyt, Johann Jacob. *Gazophylacium Medico-Physicum; oder, Schatz-Kammer medicinisch- und natürlicher Dinge* (Medico-physical phylacian riches; or, Treasury of medicinal and natural things). Leipzig, 1784.

Zückert, Johann Friedrich. *Materia Alimentaria* (Food substances). Berlin, 1769. This Latin work appeared in German in 1775.

———. *Medicinisches Tischbuch; oder, Cur und Präservation der Krankeiten durch diätetische Mittel* (The medicinal table-manual; or, Cure and protection from diseases through dietary remedies). Berlin, 1785. Zückert was an advocate of cures and the control of diseases through diet as well as the use of diet for improving one's well-being and longevity.

Zwinger, Theodor. *Theatrum Botanicum; das ist, Vollkommenes Kräuter-Buch* (The botanical theater; or, Complete herbal). Basel, 1696. The 1744 edition was printed at Basel by Hans Jacob Bischoff.

———. *Sicherer und Geschwinder Artzt* (A sure and ready doctor). Basel, 1725.

Index of Persons, Physicians, and Herbalists

331

Galen, Claudius (Greek physician, 130–200 A.D.): garlic 150

Gesner, Konrad (Swiss physician, 1516–1565): 11, flax 142

Glasse, Hannah (English cookbook author): senna 285

Heinitsch, Carl Heinrich (Pennsylvania druggist, d. 1803): wall fern 338

Helvetius, Adrian (French physician, 1661–1727): ipecacuanha 177

Hieronymus of Braunschweig (German surgeon, d. 1534): 11, valerian 331

Hildegard of Bingen (medieval herbalist): lovage 199

Hill, John (English botanist and physician, 1716–1775): asparagus 48, basil 54, birthwort 60, butterbur 76, fenugreek 1380, rosemary 262, sanicle 273, senna 285, sow thistle 301, tea 321

Hippocrates (Greek physician, ca. 460–ca. 377 B.C.): barley 52

Hoffmann, Friedrich (German physician and chemist, 1660–1742): germander 153, marigold 203, nettle 224, pilewort 245, walnut 339

Iserloh, Maria (Pennsylvania German herb doctor): introduction 24

Jackson, Benjamin (Philadelphia mustard manufacturer): mustard 220

Job (Biblical prophet): nettle 224

Knörin, R. Christine (German cookbook author, 1745–1809): scorzonera 278

Krafft, Michael (Pennsylvania distiller): bryony 72, peony 244

Lemery, Louis (French physician, 1677–1743): ipecacuanha 177

Löffler, Friederike (Swabian cookbook author, 1744–1805): basil 54, burnet 75

Masawayk al-Maridini. See Mesue the Younger.

Mattioli, Pier' Andrea (Italian commentator on Dioscorides, 1500–1577): bracken 69, peony 244

Mesue the Younger or Masawayk al-Maridini (Jacobite physician in Cairo, d.

1015): apricot 46, senna 285

Miller, Philip (English horticulturist, 1691–1771): parsley 236

Mithradates VI Eupator of Pontis (Pontic king, 123–63 B.C.): 43, mustard 220, rue 264

M'Mahon, Bernard (Philadelphia seedsman, 1775–1816): fenugreek 138

Mynsicht, Adrian von (German Rosicrucian, 1603–1638): sassafras 274

Paracelsus: Philippus Theophrastus Bombastus von Hohenheim (Swabian nobleman and physician, 1493–1541): 6

Paulli, Simon (German physician, 1603–1680): figs 141

Penn, William (founder and governor of Pennsylvania, 1644–1718): 103 (citron), mustard 220

Pfisterer, M. Daniel (German preacher and folk artist, 1651–1728): clove gillyflower 107

Pomet, Pierre (French druggist to Louis XIV, 1658–1699): camphor 81

Pomponius, Sextus (Roman nobleman in Spain): wheat 345

Rembert, also known as Rembert Dodoens (Dutch botanist, 1517–1585): figs 141

Riverius, Lazarus or Lazare Riviere (French physician, 1589–1655): valerian 331

Rolsinci, Dr.: 310

Rozier, Abbé (French agricultural author): radish 254

Sarnigshausen, Dr. (German-American physician): centaury 90

Schellhammer, Maria Sophia (German cookbook author): 11, Indian cress 176, mulberry 219, purslane 251, rampion 256, sorrel 297, squash 307

Schmidt, Johann Jakob (German Pietist physician): 25, locust pod 198, nettle 224, saffron 269

Schmucker, John George (Lutheran minister, 1771–1854): 26

Schroeder, Johann (German physician and druggist, 1600–1664): 11

Socrates (Greek philosopher, 469–399 B.C.): hemlock 165

Stephanus, Carolus. See Charles Estienne.

General Index

Abortants: birthwort 60, bracken 69, calamint 212, camphor 81, coffee 108, dittany 128, gentian 153, mugwort 218, peach tree 240, pennyroyal 243, peony 244, sowbread 300, tarragon 320, thyme 323, wild ginger 155, willow tree 354

acorns. See oak 226.

agaric 35

agate (in remedies): turpentine 330

agrimony 35

agriot (griotte) cherries. See cherries 92.

Aldi Fraa (goose mother). See mugwort 218.

alembic (distilling vessel): lily-of-the-valley 195

alexipharmic (poison and contagion preventive): butterbur 76, calamus 79, camphor 81, carline thistle 86, cinquefoil 102, citron 103, clove gillyflower 107, devil's bit 124, dittany128, elderberry 129, elecampane 132, fumitory 146, galingale 147, garlic 150, gentian 153, goldenrod 156, goldilocks 157, hazelnut 163, juniper 181, lesser scabious 192, marigold 203, masterwort 206, myrrh 222, onion 232, rue 264, sage 271, self-heal 284, snakeweed 296, southernwood 299, speedwell 304, swallow wort 315, tormentil 325, valerian 331, water germander 153, wild thyme 323, wormwood 360, zedoary 362

algaroba. See locust pods.

almond 37

aloe 39

Alsatian clover. See trefoil 326.

Althea Salve. See marshmallow 205

amber (in remedies): juniper 181, lavender 185,

ambergris (in remedies): ragwort 256

American arum (wake robin). See wake robin.

American blue flag (rush root). See iris.

American elder. See elderberry.

American elm. See elm 133.

American dittany. See dittany 128.

American masterwort (purple angelica). See masterwort 206.

American mountain ash (rowan tree) 47 (under servis)

American red currant. See red currant 257.

Angelica 40

Animus hepates (Heart of Liver). See rhubarb 260.

Anise 42

anthills (in remedies): lily-of-the-valley 195

anti-lithic powder: savifrage 277

anti-lithic water: horseradish 171, strawberry 309.

antimony (poison): borage 67, lignum vitae 194, myrrh 222

antioxidants: blackberry 62, blueberry 65, chocolate 99, mulberry 219, plums and prunes 248, tea 321

apéritifs: mustard 220

aphrodisiacs. See Venereous substances.

apoplectic water: goldilocks 157

apostemes (remedies for): lesser scabious 192

apple 44

apple wine (to taste like muscatel) (basil) 54

apricot 46

ash tree 47

asparagus 48

asphodel. See king's spear.

attic food storage (Speicher): southernwood 299

Assyrian plum (in remedies): figs 141, hys-

low 66, borage water (basil) 54, borage
water 67, broad bean flower water 69,
brooklime water 71, bryony water 72,
buckshorn plantain 73, burnet water 75,
butterbur water 76, calendula water (borage) 67, cardamom aquavitae 85, carline
thistle 86, celandine water 88, 362 (under
zedoary); centaury 90, chervil 94, (under
watercress) 341; chickweed 96, chimney
soot 97, cinnamon water (borage) 67, citron water 103, clove water 106, columbine
water 112, comfrey root water 114, (under
hemlock) 165, coriander water 116, corn
poppy 117, cranesbill 118, daisy 120,
dame's rocket 122, devil's bit 124, dill 126,
dwarf elder 129, elderberry blossom 129,
elecampane water (under wood sorrel)
359, endive water 134, eyebright 135, fennel water 136, (camphor 81) (clary sage
104); flixweed 143, fumitory 146, garden
cress 148, goldenrod 156, groundsel 161,
hart's tongue 162, water of holy thistle
(with angelica) 40, water of hops 169,
horehound water 170, water of horsetail
172, house leek 173, hyssop water 175,
juniper 181, Kümmelwasser 84, larkspur
184, lavender 185, water of lemon balm
189, lesser scabious 192, lily-of-the-valley
195, linden 196, lindenblossom water
(camphor 81), linden blossom (under
columbine) 112, liverwort 198, lungwort
201, marigold 203, marjoram 204, marjoram water (with beets) 56, (with watercress) 341, masterwort 206, melilot 210,
milk thistle 210, millet 211, mint 212,
mouse ear 216, mugwort water (under
birthwort) 60, oak 226, oregano 235, parsley water 236, parsley water (under cherries) 92, peach blossoms 240, pennyroyal
water 243, pennyroyal water (under dittany) 128, plantain 246, plantain water
(camphor 81), plantain water (columbine)
112, plantain water (scurvy grass) 280,
plantain water (squash) 307, plantain
water (wintergreen 358), poppy water 117,
primrose water 250, purslane water 251,
(camphor 81); rosemary 262, rue 264, rye
268, sage 271, sanicle 273, scorzonera
278, scurvy grass 280, self heal (scurvy
grass) 280, self-heal 284, skirret 291, sloes
292, smallage 294, spleenwort 307, succory 310, rosewater (camphor) 81, rosewater

(ginger) 155, rosewater (squash) 307, rosewater (watermelon) 344, savine 276, savifrage 277, scabious water (camphor 81),
sea holly water 282, sharp-pointed dock
287, snakeweed water 296, speedwell
water 304, solomon's seal 362 (under
zedoary), sorrel water (camphor 81), sow
thistle 301, spikenard water 305, spinach
306, strawberry 309, succory water
(columbine) 112, sweet woodruff 317, tarragon 320, trefoil 326, spirit of turpentine
330, valerian 331, veronica water (under
birthwort) 60, vervain water 333, wake-
robin water 337, wall fern water 338, wall-
flower 339, walnut 339, water germander
153, water lily water (camphor 81), watermelon 344, white lily 348, wild tansy 319,
wild thyme 323, willow water 354, wintergreen water 358, wood sorrel 297, yarrow
361

dittander 127
dittany (white dittany) 128
dog manure (in remedies): figs 141
douche (for women): clary sage 104, skirret
291
drunkenness (cures): cabbage 78, coffee 108,
ivy 180, peach kernels 240, sauerkraut 78,
wine 355
dwarf elder 129
dyes: ragwort 256

ear remedies: fennel 136, ground ivy 160,
marjoram 204, mustard 220, oregano 235,
peach tree 240, rye 268, sea onion 232,
sowbread 300
earthworms (in remedies): groundsel 161,
olive 229
Easter foods: snakeweed 296,
eau d'orme (elm gall water). See elm.
eggs (in remedies): flax 142, mouse ear 216,
oak 226, oregano 235, parsley 236, plantain 246, rye 268, sorrel 297, toad flax 142,
tormentil 325
egg oil (in remedies): onion 232
egg shells (for dosing): turpentine 330
elderberry 129
elecampane 132
electuaries: blueberry butter 65, bryony 72,
cherry butter 93, cinquefoil butterscotch
102, Cure of Mithradates 43, (under nutmeg) 225, (under rue) 264; dwarf elder
129, elderberry 129, elecampane 132,